MW01128785

MORE PRAISE FOR *HADITH*

'It is impossible to understand the Islamic tradition without getting some knowledge of *the sciences of hadith*. In this fascinating introduction, Jonathan A. C. Brown provides the reader with the necessary means to navigate between the traditional framework and contemporary issues. A brilliant essay written by a widely-acknowledged scholar in the field.'

Tariq Ramadan, Professor of Contemporary Islamic Studies, University of Oxford

'A must read and a great read. The combination of impeccable, critical scholarship with a storyteller's style has produced an introductory volume that is both substantive and remarkably engaging.'

John L. Esposito, Founding Director of the Center for Muslim-Christian Understanding, Georgetown University

'A comprehensive study of the scholarship throughout Islamic history dealing with the traditions of the Prophet. A combination of critical analysis and informed understanding that presents a significant new perspective on a much-debated subject.'

John O. Voll, Professor Emeritus of Islamic History, Georgetown University

FOUNDATIONS *of* ISLAM

Series Editor: Omid Safi

Other Titles in this Series

Pilgrimage in Islam: Traditional and Modern Practices by Sophia Rose Arjana

The Qur'an: An Introduction by Anna M. Gade

Shar'iah Law: An Introduction by Mohammad Hashim Kamali

ABOUT THE AUTHOR

Jonathan A. C. Brown is Associate Professor and Alwaleed bin Talal Chair of Islamic Civilization at Georgetown University. He is the author of *Misquoting Muhammad*, which is also published by Oneworld. He lives in Washington, DC.

Hadith

Muhammad's Legacy in the Medieval and Modern World

JONATHAN A. C. BROWN

ONEWORLD
ACADEMIC

Oneworld Academic

An imprint of Oneworld Publications

First published by Oneworld Publications 2009

This revised edition published by Oneworld Academic 2018

A CIP record for this title is available
from the British Library

ISBN 978–1–78607–307–5
eISBN 978–1–78607–308–2

Typeset by Jayvee, Trivandrum, India
Printed and bound in Great Britain by Clays Ltd., St Ives plc

Oneworld Publications
10 Bloomsbury Street
London WC1B 3SR
England

'Whoever has preserved one life, it is as if he has saved all of humanity.'
Quran 5:32

To Julia Taft
My godmother and the noblest woman I have known ...

CONTENTS

Illustrations viii

Preface to the Revised Edition ix

Preface xi

Acknowledgments xii

Conventions, Abbreviations, and Transliteration xiv

1. The Prophet's Words Then and Now: Hadith and Its Terminology 1
2. The Transmission and Collection of Prophetic Traditions 16
3. The Methods and History of Hadith Criticism 69
4. Prophetic Traditions in Shiite Islam 135
5. The Function of Prophetic Traditions in Islamic Law and Legal Theory 162
6. The Function of Prophetic Traditions in Theology 185
7. The Function of Prophetic Traditions in Sufism 196
8. The Function of Prophetic Traditions in Politics 210
9. The Authenticity Question: Western Debates over the Historical Reliability of Prophetic Traditions 226
10. Debates over Prophetic Traditions in the Modern Muslim World 277
11. Conclusion 308

Glossary 316

Bibliography 322

Index 338

ILLUSTRATIONS

2.0	Leading Hadith Transmitters from the Companions	20
2.1	Transmission and Criticism of Hadiths from the Companions of the Prophet and Successors	25
2.2	Subchapter from 'Abd al-Razzāq's *Musannaf* Concerning Ablutions	27
2.3	*Musnad* Organization	30
3.0	Types of Errors and Forgery in Hadiths	78
3.1	Generations of Sunni Hadith Critics	81
3.2	Corroboration	95
3.3	Rating of Hadiths and Their Uses among the Early and Later Hadith Critics	106
3.4	Hadith Prohibiting Putting on one's Shoes while Standing: the Transmission of Abū Hurayra	117
3.5	Hadith Prohibiting Putting on one's Shoes while Standing: the Transmission of Anas b. Mālik	118
3.6	Hadith Prohibiting Putting on one's Shoes while Standing: the Transmission of Jābir b. 'Abdallāh	119
3.7	Hadith Prohibiting Putting on one's Shoes while Standing: the Transmission of Ibn 'Umar	120
3.8a	Hadith 1 on the Qadarite Heresy: 'Two types...' – the Narration of Ibn 'Abbās	125
3.8b	Hadith 1 on the Qadarite Heresy: Sundry Narrations	126
3.9	Hadith 2 on the Qadarite Heresy: 'The Zoroastrians of my nation ...'	128
4.0	The Twelve Imams	136
4.1	Forms of Imami Shiite Hadiths	137
9.0	Schacht's Common Link	246
9.1	Juynboll's Common Link Theory	250
9.2	Cook's Theory of *Tadlīs* and Spread of *Isnād*s	257
9.3	*Isnād*/*Matn* Analysis	264

PREFACE TO THE REVISED EDITION

It has been almost ten years since I wrote the preface to the first edition of this book, sitting in an upper-floor room in a house in Sana, the red and orange light bathing the battered furniture through colored glass. How much the world has changed, how much people have suffered, and how many of the pillars of my own world have fallen. Sana is bombed and besieged. Its already impoverished people starve. Syria lies in ruins beyond tragedy. Egypt, the place I felt most at home, has mutated from the warm and open world of deep knowledge that drew me in, to a kitschy-dark caricature of mid-twentieth-century fascism. Those Egyptian scholars from whom I had benefited and learned so much have either died or become loyal servants of a dictatorship that only fools and the myopically vicious could embrace.

So then either my teachers were fools, in which case, does the knowledge they imparted to so many have any value? Or they were vicious, in which case, can such a vessel truly carry 'this knowledge, which is religion,' without sullying it? How does one make sense of things when one's exemplars make choices that seem so profoundly wrong? I've long pondered this, and the answer I'm led to again and again is both comforting and supremely disturbing.

The political sphere appears of supreme import. Men triumph or are humiliated or killed; innocent women and children suffer unspeakable abuse; war is fought, peace is made, prosperity nurtured or squandered. But in the vaulted chamber of ideas, of knowledge, this sphere occupies just a portion of one of many shelves. Some who have brought great misery in human history have aimed only at satisfying themselves, but far more have been pursuing the same abstract goods as their righteous, often martyred, opponents. Bond villains are often very well intentioned. Political trauma, as total as it is, is created less by ideas than by their interpretation and implementation. Like all those who have reflected on human polity, my teachers valued both justice and order. But order had priority for them. Others would put justice first. This is a question of priority, and it has consequences. But, phrased like this in the abstract, reasonable people can disagree. And in that small space of disagreement the dimensions of our world are warped in inversion, and endless wrongs and suffering are inflicted. All on part of one shelf in the great library of our human heritage and its divine inspiration.

As impossible as it seems, as impossible as it is for me, we must keep our political disagreements in perspective. A report in *Sahih al-Bukhārī* describes how, as Islam's first, bloody civil war erupted, there was a diplomatic meeting. On one side was 'Ammār bin Yāsir, who would soon die in the war, and on the other Abū Mūsā and Abū Mas'ūd. The two men say to 'Ammār, 'In all the time since you've been Muslim, we haven't seen you undertake anything more distasteful to us than your haste in this matter.' 'Ammār replies, 'And I haven't seen from you two, since the time you became Muslims, anything more distasteful to me than your hesitation on this matter.' Then Abū Mas'ūd dresses each of the other two in robes, and they all head off to the mosque for prayer.[1]

Enough serious talk! What does this new edition have that the old one doesn't? First, I've fixed as many of the errors or oversights as possible. Second, it includes an entirely new chapter on the role of hadith in politics. Third, I've significantly expanded the section on the development of the Western Historical Critical Method in Chapter 9. I've also added a new case study on hadith authentication at the end of Chapter 3. Finally, I've replaced some of the examples and case studies throughout the book with new ones that are either more varied or more interesting.

Jonathan A. C. Brown
Khādim al-hadīth al-sharīf
Istanbul, 2017

ENDNOTE

1 *Sahīh al-Bukhārī*: *kitāb al-fitan*, *bāb* 19.

PREFACE

The science of hadith is a noble one, and generations of scholars far, far more capable and devoted than I have dedicated their lives to transmitting, analyzing, and sorting through the legacy attributed to Muhammad. One could spend a lifetime reading the works of scholars like al-Bukhārī, al-Dhahabī, and Ibn Hajar, and two lifetimes trying to keep up with them. Matching their accomplishments is inconceivable to me. I can only hope that this book provides an adequate introduction to their work and the influence it has had on Islamic civilization.

Students and colleagues always ask me whether the Sunni hadith tradition provides an accurate representation of Muhammad's teachings. In truth, I can only say that projects such as this book are part of my search for the answer to that question. As the Chinese art collector Lu Shih-hua (d. 1779 CE) once wrote, such matters 'came to us from the ancients. The ancients are gone, and we cannot raise them from the Nether World to question them. So how can we arrive at the truth without being vain and false in our wrangling noisily about it?'[1]

Jonathan A. C. Brown
Khādim al-hadīth al-sharīf
Sana, Yemen, 2007

ENDNOTE

1 Wen Fong, 'The Problem of Forgery in Chinese Painting: Part One,' p. 99.

ACKNOWLEDGMENTS

First of all, I must thank the editor of Oneworld's Foundations of Islam series, Omid Safi, whose generosity and good manners have improved my life immensely. I extend my gratitude to all the friends and colleagues whom I bothered with this book. I sincerely thank Omar Anchassi, Ovamir Anjum, Christopher Anzalone, Andrew Booso, Sarah Eltantawi, Alyssa Gabbay, Andreas Görke, Najam Haider, Majid Khan, Suheil Laher, Mohammed Rustom, Saleem Seedat, Justin Sterns, and Devin Stewart for reading the manuscript and providing me with invaluable feedback. I am very grateful to my friends Garrett Davidson, Mohamed El-Sharawi, Matthew Ingalls, and Scott Lucas, without whose insightful (and lengthy) discussions I could not have covered much of the material in this book. Garrett Davidson deserves special thanks for expanding my understanding of the *isnād* in later Islamic history. I am grateful to Drs. Mark Goodacre of Duke University and Martin Jaffe for discussing biblical parallels of hadith with me. I must also thank my students at the University of Washington and the esteemed UW Historians Reading Group, who helped me work out the contents of this book. Generous financial support for writing this book came from the Center for Arabic Study Abroad (CASA II), the American Institute for Yemeni Studies, and the University of Washington.

As for my own contributions, I am entirely indebted to my teachers, particularly Fred Donner, John Esposito, Maysam al-Faruqi, Musa Furber, ʻAlī Zayn al-ʻĀbidīn al-Jifrī, ʻAlī Jumʻa, Wadad al-Kadi, Haifaa Khalafallah, ʻImād ʻAbbās Saʻīd, Sayyid Shaltūt, Barbara Stowasser, Tareq al-Suwaidan, and John Voll. The bulk of the credit goes to an exceptional scholar, Osama al-Syed Mahmoud, who opened my eyes to the study of hadith. Although I know them only through their books and recorded lectures, I must admit my inestimable debt to Muhammad Abū Zahra, ʻAbdallāh al-Saʻd, Muhammad Nāsir al-Dīn al-Albānī, ʻAbd al-Fattāh Abū Ghudda and the two hadith masters of our age, Ahmad and ʻAbdallāh, the sons of al-Siddīq al-Ghumārī, *rahimahum Allāh*. Of course, any failings in this book are my own responsibility and no fault of those who instructed me.

I must also thank my wonderful family, especially my mother, Dr. Ellen Brown, who remains a scholarly inspiration to me. My sisters Kate, Lucinda, and Senem, my aunt Kate and my friends Asad Naqvi and Brenden Kerr require special thanks for keeping me sane and making sure I dress decently.

CONVENTIONS, ABBREVIATIONS, AND TRANSLITERATION

Dates in this book will follow the Hijrī/Common Era format, where the first date (the Hijrī date) is that of the Islamic lunar calendar, which begins with Muhammad's emigration to Medina in 1/622. Obviously, pre-Islamic dates will follow the standard Before Common Era (BCE) and Common Era (CE) dating system. After the 1700s CE we no longer include Hijrī dates as they serve little use after that point.

Abbreviations used in this book include '**b.**' for the Arabic '*ibn*,' or 'son of...', and **(s)** for the honorific Arabic phrase 'May the peace and blessings of God be upon him (*sallā Allāh 'alayhi wa sallam*),' which is commonly said and written after Muhammad's name.

The transliteration characters in this book represent the long vowels in Arabic and Persian: **ā**, **ī**, and **ū**. The **'** character represents a simple glottal stop, like the initial sounds of both syllables in 'uh oh.' The **'** symbol indicates the Arabic letter *'ayn*, a sound that resembles the 'Aaah' noise a person makes when getting their throat checked by the doctor. In Arabic and Persian words, '**q**' represents a voiceless uvular sound produced at the back of the throat and is non-existent in English. One could most closely approximate this sound with the 'c' sound at the beginning of the crow noise 'caw! caw!' '**Gh**' indicates a sound similar to the French 'r', and '**kh**' represents a velar fricative like the sound of clearing one's throat. '**Dh**' indicates the 'th' sound in words like 'that' or 'bother.' '**Th**' represents the 'th' sound in words like 'bath.'

1

THE PROPHET'S WORDS THEN AND NOW: HADITH AND ITS TERMINOLOGY

'We have a question,' the man said, his rural accent betraying the long trip he must have made from his provincial hamlet to the metropolis of Cairo. 'We have built a school for boys and girls,' the man continued, sitting cross-legged on the carpet with his eyes angled reverently upward at the scholar seated in the sturdy wooden chair before him. 'But some members of our community say that we cannot allow the girls to attend because they will mix with the boys in the hallways. Are we allowed to open the school?' The man waited anxiously, as did the students seated deferentially around the scholar, I among them. The fall of 2003 was unusually hot, and the hesitant breezes that penetrated the wooden lattice walls were welcomed by all.

The scholar, a middle-aged man who would soon be elevated to one of the most influential religious positions in the Sunni Muslim world, the chief jurisconsult (*muftī*) of Egypt, leaned down towards the tape recorder that the man had dragged with him on his long journey. 'Do you have the Nile down where you are?' the scholar asked. 'Yes,' the man replied. 'Listen, then, whoever you are who objects to opening this school to girls,' the scholar said into the recorder, 'go throw yourself in the Nile! For did the Messenger of God, may the peace and blessings of God be upon him, not say **"Do not prevent the female servants of God from the mosques of God"**?'[1]

For over a thousand years Muslim peasants, merchants, and princes have flocked to the vaulted rooms that line the great courtyard of Cairo's al-Azhar Mosque to seek the counsel of the ulema, those scholars who define Islamic faith and religious law. Seated in this courtyard on a fall day in 2003, the future 'Grand Mufti of the Egyptian Lands' could look back on over fourteen hundred years of the Islamic religious tradition, that corpus of scholarship that elucidated the message brought by Muhammad and is one of the world's most elaborate and rich intellectual edifices. In responding to the question of this simple man, the mufti could draw from the capacious tradition of Islamic legal discourse: the bodies of law of the four major Sunni legal schools, the obscure opinions of medieval scholars long eclipsed by time, or the general principles that governed Islamic law and its derivation.

Although his mind was no doubt scanning this abundant legal heritage as he pondered the man's question, the scholar did not reply with any high legal language or dry legal ruling. Instead, he answered the man with the words of a figure whom Muslims are taught from childhood to love and venerate as a moral exemplar and object of devotion, a person 'dearer to them than their own child or parents.'[i] The scholar reached back through the centuries to the words of the Prophet Muhammad, words that he knew would resonate in this simple man's heart as clearly as the day they were first spoken and would lay all the concerns of his rural community to rest. Even amid the confusion of the modern world, today as before, 'the Prophet of God is most worthy of being followed.'[2]

Muhammad's precedent has been invoked in places and times far distant from the Nile Valley. His words speak with compelling power throughout the Muslim world, among Sunnis and Shiites alike. A year after I had heard the future 'Grand Mufti of the Egyptian Lands' issue his opinion, I sat in the lush courtyard of the Khan Madrasa in the ancient Persian city of Shiraz, discussing issues of Islamic thought with an Imami Shiite cleric. As the morning sun shone on the intricate floral tiles of the mosque's vaulted enclosure, we were debating whether or not 'Alī, the Prophet's son-in-law and well-spring of the Shiite tradition, possessed revealed knowledge of future events. 'The Commander of the Faithful, 'Alī, may God's blessings be upon him, knew that oil would be found in these lands and that "steel birds would fly",' the Shiite cleric expounded energetically. 'This knowledge he got from the Messenger of God, his teacher, for did the Messenger not say, **"I am the city of knowledge and 'Alī is its gate. So whoever seeks knowledge let him approach it by its gate"?**'[3]

[i] See the hadith 'None of you truly believes until I am dearer to him than his child, his parent and the people altogether': Ahmad b. Shu'ayb al-Nasā'ī, *Sunan al-Nasā'ī: kitāb al-īmān, bāb 'alāmat al-īmān.*

Among Western readership, the question 'What does Islam say about' some issue is usually followed by reference to the Quran. A Western journalist writing about the dress habits of Egyptian women informs us that wearing the headscarf is not an injunction from the Quran,[4] while pundits discussing jihad note that the Quran says 'slay the unbelievers wherever you find them' (Quran 9:5). Certainly, to Muslims the Quran is the literal word of God. It is a text revered to such an extent that many Muslims memorize it in its entirety as children, and many Muslims believe that a state of ritual purity is required to touch its pages.

Yet the Quran is not the source to which a curious reader should refer in order to answer the question 'What does Islam say about' a particular issue. The Quran is not a book of law, and many tenets of Islamic theology are never mentioned in the holy book. To consult the Quran is only to get part of the picture. Large portions of the Islamic legal, theological, and popular religious traditions come not from the book that Muslims hold to be God's revelation, but rather from the legacy of Muhammad, whom they believe God chose to explain and elucidate His message through word and deed. It is in his teachings that we find Muslim dress codes as well as the rules and restrictions for holy war.

The normative legacy of the Prophet is known as the **Sunna**, and, although it stands second to the Quran in terms of reverence, it is the lens through which the holy book is interpreted and understood. In this sense, in Islamic civilization the Sunna has ruled over the Quran, shaping, specifying, and adding to the revealed book. Understanding how the message of Islam spread outward from Arabia in the seventh century and how it nurtured the various legal, theological, mystical, and cultural dimensions of Islamic civilization must begin with the study of the heritage left by Muhammad.

For much of Islamic history, the unit through which the Sunna was preserved, transmitted, and understood has been the ***hadīth*** (Arabic plural, *ahādīth*), or a report describing the words, actions, or habits of the Prophet. Unlike the Quran, the hadiths were not quickly and concisely compiled during and immediately after Muhammad's life. Because hadiths were recorded and transmitted over a period of decades and even centuries, they are not in and of themselves contemporary historical documentation of what Muhammad said and did. In the century after the Prophet's mission, the Muslim community passed through no less than three civil wars and numerous sectarian schisms. As a result, hadiths were forged by different parties trying to manipulate the authority of the Sunna. The question of the authenticity of hadiths and how one can distinguish true ones from forgeries has been a perennial concern to both the Muslim scholars who turned to the Sunna to elaborate the Islamic tradition and Western scholars who have studied it.

The tool that Muslim scholars developed to help ensure the authenticity of hadiths was the ***isnād*** (Arabic, 'support'), or the chain of transmitters through which a scholar traced the ***matn***, or text, of a hadith back to the Prophet. The *isnād* was an effort to document that a hadith had actually come from Muhammad, and Muslim scholars from the eighth century until today have never ceased repeating the mantra 'The *isnād* is part of the religion – if not for the *isnād*, whoever wanted could say whatever they wanted.'

The Prophet's words, however, have always been more than just a type of proof used in discussions of Islamic law and dogma. The *isnād* and the hadith it transmits have been more than fodder for debates over authenticity and means of establishing it. For the Muslim scholarly class, the ulema, tracing the *isnād* of a hadith back to Muhammad is to follow one's genealogy of sacred knowledge back to its source. It is a medium of connection to the Prophet, 'the beloved of God,' and a link to the scholarly titans of the past. Even today, reciting one's *isnād* is to walk back in memory through the pantheon corridor of great scholars whose labors had built up Islamic tradition. The students who sat gathered around the future Mufti of Egypt on that hot fall day in Cairo had each folded gingerly a piece of paper listing the scholar's *isnād* back to the earliest hadith collection, the *Muwatta'* of Mālik b. Anas (d. 179/796), and from that eighth-century author through his *isnād*s back to the Prophet. Each paper stated that the Mufti had given these students permission to transmit the hadiths in the collection via his *isnād*. By hearing this book of hadiths through the Mufti's chain of transmission, these students had become part of the timeless tradition of passing knowledge from one generation to the next.

For over a thousand years, Muslim students, 'the seekers of knowledge,' have traveled from city to city in the Muslim world to hear hadiths recited by master scholars, receive their permission to transmit them, and be incorporated into the living *isnād* tradition. In the summer of 2007 I traveled from Egypt across the Red Sea to the sweltering, sandy coastal plain of Tihama in Yemen. There I made my way inland to the ancient trading city of Zabid, its whitewashed brick walls and dust-blown winding alleys seemingly immune to the passage of time. Over the centuries, this city had more than any other place in the Muslim world preserved the tradition of narrating hadiths by full *isnād*s back to Muhammad. In an old madrasa I found the mufti of the city seated on one of the high wicker beds so common to the region, surrounded by his students. The mufti set down the book he was explaining, and the students stared inquisitively as he asked who I was and why I had come. 'To hear a hadith through your *isnād*, the *isnād* of the people of Zabid, O virtuous teacher,' I replied. After hearing my request, the mufti agreed to recite the hadith that a scholar must always give his students first. 'Write this down,' the mufti instructed, 'and do not forget us in your most sincere prayers':

> I, Muhammad 'Alī al-Battāh of the Ahdal clan, heard from my teacher Ahmad son of Dāwūd al-Battāh, who heard from his teacher the Mufti Sulaymān son of Muhammad al-Ahdal, from Muhammad son of 'Abd al-Bāqī al-Ahdal, from Muhammad son of 'Abd al-Rahmān al-Ahdal, from the Mufti 'Abd al-Rahmān son of Sulaymān al-Ahdal, from his father Sulaymān son of Yahyā al-Ahdal, from Abū Bakr al-Ahdal, from Ahmad al-Ahdal, from the Pillar of Islam, Yahyā son of Umar al-Ahdal, from Abū Bakr al-Battāh, from Yūsuf son of Muhammad al-Battāh, from Tāhir son of Husayn al-Ahdal, from the hadith master Ibn Dayba', from the sheik Zayn al-Dīn al-Sharijī of Zabid, from Nafīs al-Dīn Sulaymān al-'Alawī, from 'Alī son of Shaddād, from the imam Ahmad the Candlemaker, from his father Sharaf al-Dīn the Candlemaker, from Zāhir son of Rustum of Esfahan, from 'Abd al-Malik of Karūkh, from Abū Nasr son of Muhammad of Herat, from Abū Muhammad 'Abd al-Jabbār al-Jarrāh of Merv, from Abū al-'Abbās Muhammad son of Ahmad of Merv, from the definitive hadith master Muhammad son of 'Īsā of Tirmiz, from Ibn Abī 'Umar, from Ibn 'Uyayna, from 'Amr son of Dīnār, from Abū Qābūs, from 'Abdallāh son of 'Amr, from the Messenger of God, who said, **'The merciful, indeed the Most Merciful God has mercy upon them. Have mercy in this earthly world, and He that is in the heavens will have mercy on you.'**[5]

THE CONTENTS OF THIS BOOK

This book is an introduction to the hadith tradition, its collection, its criticism, its functions in Islamic civilization and the controversies surrounding it to this day. This present chapter will introduce you to some crucial terminology for the study of hadiths. In Chapter 2, we will discuss the collection and transmission of hadiths in Sunni Islam, as well as the various genres of hadith literature that developed from the early Islamic period until modern times. Chapter 3 will explain the science of hadith criticism developed by Sunni scholars and the various debates and developments that affected it throughout Islamic history. Chapter 4 looks at the hadith traditions of Imami and Zaydi Shiism as well as their interaction with that of Sunni Islam. Chapter 5 explores the functions of hadiths in Islamic law and legal theory, and Chapter 6 investigates the role of hadiths in elaborating Islamic theology. Chapter 7 tackles the important functions of hadiths in the Islamic mystical tradition, commonly known as Sufism. Chapter 8 looks at the role of hadiths in Islamic political thought and contemporary controversies. Chapter 9 turns away from Muslim discourse on hadiths to trace the Western academic study of hadiths and Western debates over their historical reliability. Finally, Chapter 10 explores debates among modern Muslims over the reliability of hadiths and their proper role in understanding Islam today.

WHAT IS A HADITH? CRUCIAL TERMINOLOGY AND EXAMPLES OF HADITHS

The Prophet Muhammad's mission lasted twenty-three years, from 610 CE when he announced to his wife that he had received a revelation from God through the Angel Gabriel in a cave outside Mecca, to his death in 632 CE as the head of the powerful Islamic state in Medina. During his career as a prophet and leader, there was no courtroom stenographer assiduously recording his every word and furnishing an official transcript of his orders, religious edicts, or everyday speech. Instead, the generation of Muslims who lived with the Prophet, known as the **Companions** (Arabic: *Sahāba*), sought to preserve Muhammad's words and deeds either in their memories or through some means of writing, passing these recollections on to others. These reports were passed on from generation to generation, in oral and/or written form, until scholars compiled them in permanent collections.

Each hadith, or report about the Prophet, consists of a text (*matn*) describing his words or actions, and a chain of transmission (*isnād*) by which this report was communicated. Clearly, more than one Companion could report the Prophet saying or doing something, or a Companion could recount this report to more than one person. This would result in more than one chain of transmission for the report. We must thus distinguish between an instance of the Prophet speaking or acting, which we will refer to either by its Arabic term 'hadith' or by the term '**tradition**,' and the various chains of transmission of this tradition.

As in a game of 'Telephone,' a report could mutate as it was passed from person to person. As we know from our own daily lives, reports could also be repeated in expanded or contracted form depending on context. Each of these varying transmissions of the tradition we will call a **narration** of the hadith. For example, it is transmitted from the Companion ʿAbdallāh b. al-Zubayr that the Prophet said, **'Whoever misrepresents me, let him prepare for himself a seat in Hellfire.'**[6] But the mainstream narrations of this tradition, from many Companions such as Anas b. Mālik, Ibn Masʿūd and Abū Hurayra, quote the Prophet as saying **'Whoever misrepresents me *intentionally*, let him prepare for himself a seat in Hellfire.'** Here we see how two narrations of one Prophetic tradition differ in an important way.

The following are some examples of hadiths addressing a range of legal, ritual, theological, and ethical topics from the major sects of Islam. From the most revered Sunni hadith collection, the *Sahīh* of al-Bukhārī (d. 256/870), we find a hadith that served as evidence in Islamic theological debates over whether believers will meet God on the Day of Judgment:

> Al-Bukhārī writes: it was narrated to us by Yūsuf b. Mūsā: it was narrated to us by Abū Usāma: it was narrated to me by al-Aʿmash, from Khaythama, from the Companion ʿAdī b. Hātim, who said that:
>
> The Messenger of God, may God's peace and blessings be upon him, said, **'There is not one among you except that he will be spoken to directly by his Lord with no translator or any barrier separating them.'**[7]

From the *Sunan* of the Sunni scholar Abū Dāwūd al-Sijistānī (d. 275/889), this hadith was used to help derive Islamic laws on taxation:

> Abū Dāwūd writes: it was narrated to us by Muhammad b. Dāwūd b. Sufyān: it was narrated to us by Yahyā b. Hassān: it was narrated to

us by Sulaymān b. Mūsā: it was narrated to us by Ja'far b. Sa'd: it was narrated to me by Khubayb b. Sulaymān, from his father, from the Companion Samura b. Jundub, who said [in a speech]:

> **Indeed the Messenger of God, may the peace and blessings of God be upon him, would order us to pay the charity tax on things that we were preparing for sale.**[8]

From the *Muʿjam al-saghīr* of the Sunni scholar al-Tabarānī (d. 360/971) we find a hadith that indicates both Muhammad's character and the permissibility of lending items:

> Al-Tabarānī writes: it was narrated to us by Ahmad b. Mansūr al-Jundīsābūrī: it was narrated to us by 'Alī b. Harb: it was reported to us by Ash'ath b. 'Attāf, from 'Abdallāh b. Habīb, from al-Sha'bī, from the Companion Jābir b. 'Abdallāh, that:
>
> **The Messenger of God bought a camel from me and then let me ride it back to the city.**[9]

From the *Amālī* of the famous Imami Shiite scholar Ibn Bābawayh (d. 381/991) we find a hadith that emphasizes two important themes in Islamic legal and theological discourse: first, religion is not the purview of personal opinion, and, second, God is not to be compared to created beings:

> Ibn Bābawayh writes: it was narrated to us by Muhammad b. Mūsā b. al-Mutawakkil: it was narrated to us by 'Alī b. Ibrāhīm b. Hāshim: it was narrated by his father, from al-Rayyān b. al-Salt, from the Imam 'Alī b. Mūsā al-Ridā, from his father, from his forefathers, from the Commander of the Faithful 'Alī b. Abī Tālib, that:
>
> The Messenger of God, may God's peace and blessings be upon him, said, **'God said, "He does not believe in Me who interprets My speech [in the Quran] with merely his own opinion. He has not known Me who compares Me with My creation, and he is not in My religion who uses analogical reasoning [in questions of law] in My religion."'**[10]

Finally, in the *Amālī al-sughrā* of the Zaydi Shiite scholar Ahmad b. al-Husayn al-Hārūnī (d. 421/1030) we find a hadith describing the way in which a pious Muslim should view death:

> Al-Hārūnī writes: It was reported to us by Abū al-Husayn al-Burūjirdī: it was narrated to us by Abū al-Qāsim al-Baghawī: it was

narrated to us by Hudba: it was narrated to us by Hammām, from Qatāda, from the Companion Anas, from the Companion ʿUbāda b. al-Sāmit, that:

> The Messenger of God, may the peace and blessings of God be upon him, said: **'He who would love to encounter God, God loves encountering him. And he who would dislike encountering God, God dislikes encountering him.' So Aisha, or another one of the Prophet's wives, asked, 'O Messenger of God, but indeed we dislike death.' The Prophet replied, 'It is not like that, but rather the believer, when death comes to him, he receives the glad tidings of God's pleasure and His munificence. So that there is nothing dearer to the believer than what lies ahead of him. Thus he wants to encounter God, and God wants to encounter him. But the unbeliever, when death comes to him, he receives tidings of God's displeasure and His impending punishment. So there is nothing more hated to him than what lies ahead. Thus he despises meeting God, and God despises meeting him.'** [11]

THE NATURE OF MUHAMMAD'S AUTHORITY IN ISLAM

The role of the Prophet Muhammad as a teacher, role model, and living example of the revelation he delivered is discussed in the Quran.[ii] The holy book repeatedly instructs Muslims to 'Obey God and His prophet' (Quran 8:1), adding that he was for the Muslims 'a most goodly example' (Quran 33:21). Although the Quran reiterates that Muhammad is nothing but a mortal who has merely been favored with direct communication from God, Muslims consider him above any ethical shortcomings. There has been disagreement among Shiite and Sunni Muslims as well as within the two sects as to the degree to which prophets in general are immune from sin, but Muslims agree that after the beginning of his prophetic mission Muhammad was incapable of any serious sin or moral failing. In fact, reports of rare errors or instances of forgetfulness on his part are treated as part of the Prophet's teachings. The Quran, for example, reprimands Muhammad for turning away in frustration from a blind Muslim who distracted

[ii] We shall see that in both the classical Islamic and modern periods, this role has been debated; see Chapter 10.

him with a question when he was busy negotiating with his Meccan opponents. The Quran uses this as an opportunity to remind the Muslims that one should not prefer influential infidels over sincere, if tactless, believers (Quran 80:1–7). There is even a hadith in which the Prophet states, **'Indeed I forget or am made to forget so that I may furnish the Sunna.'**[12] Hadiths about mistakes that Muhammad made in prayers, for example, Muslims treat as instructions on how to act when they themselves make those errors.[iii]

No traditional Muslim scholar would ever consider it possible that the Prophet had made a statement or acted out of anger or weakness. When opponents of the Muslims mocked the Companion 'Abdallāh b. 'Amr for recording everything the Prophet said, Muhammad comforted him by saying **'Write it down, for by Him whose hand holds my soul, nothing comes out of my mouth but the truth.'**[13] As the Quran states, Muhammad 'does not speak out of his own desires, it is but revelation revealed' (Quran 53:3–4).

As a mere mortal, Muslims believe that Muhammad had no independent ability to prophesy. He was simply a medium for God's revelation. Hence, he is made to say in the Quran, 'I do not know what will be done with me or with you. I do but follow what is revealed to me' (Quran 46:9). But Muslims believe that Muhammad did have access to direct knowledge of the future from God in both the formal revelation of the Quran, which predicts events like Muslim victories over their Meccan opponents, and in private inspirations made known to him alone. Many hadiths therefore describe future events such as the moral decline of humanity or the events that will precede the Day of Judgment. In one famous hadith, the Prophet states that '**there will not come upon you a time except that the eras coming after it will be worse than it.**'[14]

Hadiths could describe the Prophet's authoritative legacy in three possible ways: they could communicate Muhammad's words, or his actions, or describe things done in his presence to which he did not object. The above hadith examples describe Muhammad's edicts and normative behavior. But Muslim scholars also assumed that anything done during the Prophet's time that he did not forbid must have been acceptable. The Companion Jābir b. 'Abdallāh thus reported, 'We used to practice *coitus interruptus* during the time of the

[iii] Some Muslim scholars even hold that the Prophet intentionally made these 'mistakes' to teach his followers; Qāḍī 'Iyāḍ, *Kitāb al-shifā*, p. 342.

Prophet when the Quran was being revealed.'[15] Muslim scholars thus interpreted this as a major proof for the permissibility of birth control in Islam.

Although a hadith could refer to any aspect of the Prophet's life and legacy, not everything the Prophet did was authoritative. The Prophet was forty years old when he received his first revelation. Although Muhammad was admired for his upstanding character and integrity even before his mission, Muslims do not consider his teachings authoritative before he received God's sanction. In addition, revelation had not made the Prophet a master of all trades. In one famous hadith, the Prophet came across some farmers trying to graft small date palms. When he suggested that the farmers take a different course of action and that advice proved wrong, he replied, **'I am but a man, if I give you a command regarding religion then take it. But if I make a statement out of my own judgment, then I am but a man ... you are more knowledgeable about the matters of your world.'**[16]

The scope of what concerns 'religion' in the Islamic tradition, however, is much wider than in the modern Western world. Although the Prophet consulted his Companions on affairs of state, governance, and military tactics (in fact, on several occasions the Quran validated his Companions' opinions rather than his own), his decisions as a statesman and military leader have been considered authoritative by Muslim jurists. Were his decisions, after all, not ultimately guided by God?

Certainly, not all aspects of the Prophet's behavior required imitation or obedience. Since the Prophet did not state, for example, that wearing the long robes of an Arab was required dress for a Muslim, this has been viewed as a matter of choice. Injunctions by the Prophet encouraging Muslim men to grow beards, however, have led Muslim jurists to view this as either a requirement or laudable behavior. And while such factors limited the extent to which the Prophet's personal tastes and habits were legally compelling, there has been no limit to *optional* imitation of the Prophet done out of supererogatory piety. Some Muslims thus replicate even the mundane aspects of the Prophet's behavior, such as the position in which he slept and the food he ate. The famous jurist and hadith scholar of Baghdad, Ibn Hanbal (d. 241/855), once claimed that he had acted on every hadith he had heard about the Prophet at least once.[17]

THE NATURE OF PROPHETIC SPEECH: PREACHER VS. LAWYER

In a 2012 study, a computer-run stylistic analysis of the Quran and a selection of hadiths demonstrated that the Quran and the hadiths come from two different speakers.[18] That is not surprising. What is interesting is that the study shows a stylistic consistency in the language of the hadith corpus. There has always been disagreement over whether the orthodox collections of hadiths in Islam represent an intact record of the Prophet Muhammad's words. But whether they actually came from the Prophet's mouth or not, there is certainly a Prophetic *style* of Arabic expression, one that anyone who reads even a small selection of hadiths quickly notices.

One of the most striking features of the Prophetic style in hadiths is the frequency of hyperbole. In one hadith the Prophet states, **'Cursing a Muslim is iniquity and fighting one is unbelief (*kufr*).'** In another he says, **'No one will enter Heaven who has even a grain's weight of pride in his heart,'** and in another hadith he declares, **'One who cheats is not from among us.'** These are all dramatic statements, but the way in which Muslim scholars have understood them has differed dramatically from their evident meaning.

By the time hadiths were being collected systematically in the eighth century, Muslim scholars had already developed filters for translating such hyperbole into legal or theological statements. These filters were needed because the Quran, other reliable hadiths, and overall Muslim practice made it clear that interpreting such hadiths literally was a grave error. 'Fighting a Muslim' was not unbelief (*kufr*) in the same way that renouncing Islam or atheism were. Rather, as early Muslims explained, it was a 'lesser form of unbelief (*kufr dūn kufr*)' or the type of act that an unbeliever would do. This was clear from explanations of the hadith by Companions and also from other hadiths in which the Prophet implied that a murderer remained Muslim. The ban on those 'with a grain's weight of pride in their hearts' from entering Heaven was only temporary, since sound hadiths explained that anyone 'with even a grain's weight of faith in their heart' will eventually be allowed to exit Hellfire and enter Paradise. Early Muslim scholars realized that the Prophet's phrase 'not from among us' did not mean that someone was not Muslim. Rather, it meant that a certain action or characteristic was 'not part of our Sunna' or not the conduct of a good Muslim.[19]

The sheer range and detail of material included in the hadith corpus makes it clear that it was meant to provide guidance for the details of daily life. But it also seems clear from how widespread hyperbole was in the corpus of Prophetic speech that its original function was also exhortation, preaching, and delivering unambiguous moral messages. As much as Muslim scholars have had to apply filters to the hadith corpus in order to mine it for clear rules of law or dogma, they also appreciated its exhortative dimension. Hadiths were and remain teaching tools. So, while many early Muslim scholars were careful to filter out the hyperbole when explaining hadiths to people, others, like the Meccan scholar Ibn 'Uyayna (d. 196/811), delivered them unfiltered to audiences so that the morals embedded in them would sink in.

THE SCOPE OF THE BOOK: WHAT DEFINES HADITH LITERATURE?

Stories and reports about the Prophet Muhammad permeate all genres of scholarship and expression in Islamic civilization. Hadiths appear in books of law, theology, Quranic commentary, mysticism, politics, Arabic grammar, history, and etiquette. If we are to be introduced to the hadith tradition, how do we define its scope?

Early Islamic writing combined both pre-Islamic Arab sensitivities and new Islamic concerns. Muslim authors of the eighth and ninth centuries expressed the tribal nature of Arab and early Islamic society by writing books of genealogy (*ansāb*), such as the *Kitāb al-ansāb* of Ibn al-Kalbī (d. 204/819). Other early Muslims gathered and recorded religious folklore from Arab, Jewish, Persian, and Christian sources. The Yemeni Wahb b. Munabbih (d. 114/732) was one of the most famous authors in this genre, which became known as 'stories of the prophets (*qasas al-anbiyā'*).' Other early authors collected information about the military campaigns of the early Muslim community and traced its historical course. This genre was known as 'campaigns (*maghāzī*)' and 'historical reports (*tārīkh* or *akhbār*),' including such works as the *Maghāzī* of Mūsā b. 'Uqba (d. 141/758). Another important genre combined these fields: the study of the Prophet's biography, or *sīra*. The most famous biography of Muhammad is the *Sīra* of Ibn Ishāq (d. 150/767). Some early Muslim scholars concentrated on collecting reports about the meaning and contexts of Quranic verses, compiling exegetical books called '*tafsīr*.' Finally, some scholars turned their attention to reports of the Prophet's legal, ritual, and theological statements. These were known as 'rulings (*ahkām*)' and formed the core of the hadith tradition.

The defining characteristic of hadith literature as it emerged in the mid eighth century was that it consisted of reports attributed to Muhammad and transmitted by full *isnād*s from him. Books of Quranic exegesis, history, genealogy, and folklore often included reports from Muhammad or describing his actions. But these represented the minority of their contents. Quranic exegesis most often relied on the opinions of Companions or later Muslims for the meaning of Quranic words. History works frequently described events that occurred decades after Muhammad's death, such as the Muslim conquests of Syria and Iran. Stories of the prophets involved subjects as distant as Adam and Eve. These genres were distinct from *ahkām* and the nascent hadith tradition because they were not focused on the persona of Muhammad.

But what about *sīra*, the biography of the Prophet? By definition, this was focused on Muhammad. Here, the second defining characteristic of hadith literature proves key: the *isnād*. The *Sīra* of Ibn Ishāq rarely includes full *isnād*s for the stories it tells about the Prophet or its quotations of his words. The *isnād*s that it does include are often incomplete, meaning that the sources that transmitted the report are often omitted or left unnamed.

It was the presence of full *isnād*s leading back to the Prophet and transmitting his legacy that defined the core of hadith literature, what early hadith scholars called the genre of 'supported reports (*al-musnadāt*).' Of course, if we open up famous hadith collections such as the *Sahīh* of al-Bukhārī, we find chapters on Quranic exegesis (*tafsīr*) and the Prophet's campaigns (*maghāzī*). What distinguishes these chapters from separate books of *tafsīr* or *maghāzī*, however, is that the chapters of hadith books focus on reports with full *isnād*s that quote the Prophet instead of later Muslims.

Regardless of their precise subject, any books in Islamic civilization that include hadiths with full *isnād*s back to the Prophet are subsumed under the genre of hadith literature. Of course, later books of hadiths written after the use of *isnād*s became obsolete or books specifically discussing or analyzing aspects of hadiths may not provide full *isnād*s, but their subject matter clearly places them in this genre as well.

ENDNOTES

1 J. Brown, field notes, Sept. 2003.
2 This quote is attributed to the famous ninth-century scholar al-Shāfiʿī.
3 J. Brown, field notes, July 2004.
4 See Max Rodenbeck's excellent book, *Cairo: the City Victorious*, p. 111.
5 J. Brown, field notes July 2007. This hadith can be found in Muhammad b. ʿĪsā al-Tirmidhī, *Jāmiʿ al-Tirmidhī*: *kitāb al-birr wa al-sila, bāb mā jā'a fī rahmat al-muslimīn*.
6 Muhammad b. Ismāʿīl al-Bukhārī, *Sahīh al-Bukhārī*: *kitāb al-ʿilm, bāb man kadhaba ʿalā al-Nabī*.
7 *Sahīh al-Bukhārī*: *kitāb al-tawhīd, bāb qawl Allāh ʿwujūhuhum yawma'idhin nādira.'*
8 Abū Dāwūd al-Sijistānī, *Sunan Abī Dāwūd*: *kitāb al-zakāt, bāb al-ʿurūd idhā kānat li'l-tijāra hal fīhā min zakāt*.
9 Abū al-Qāsim al-Tabarānī, *al-Muʿjam al-saghīr*, vol. 1, p. 76.
10 Ibn Bābawayh, *Amālī al-Sadūq*, p. 6.
11 Ahmad b. al-Husayn al-Hārūnī, *al-Amālī al-sughrā*, p. 8; *Sahīh al-Bukhārī: kitāb al-riqāq, bāb man ahabba liqā' Allāh* ....
12 *Muwatta'*: *kitāb al-sahw*.
13 ʿAbdallāh b. Abd al-Rahmān al-Dārimī, *Sunan al-Dārimī*: introductory chapters, *bāb man rakhkhasa fī kitābat al-ʿilm*.
14 *Sahīh al-Bukhārī*: *kitāb al-fitan, bāb lā ya'tī zamān illā alladhī baʿdahu sharr minhu*.
15 *Sahīh al-Bukhārī*: *kitāb al-nikāh, bāb al-ʿazl*.
16 Muslim b. al-Hajjāj, *Sahīh Muslim*: *kitāb al-fadā'il, bāb wujūb imtithāl mā qālahu sharʿan*. See also *Sunan Abī Dāwūd: kitāb al-qadā', bāb fī qadā' al-qādī idhā akhta'a*.
17 For the issue of beards, see *Sahīh al-Bukhārī: kitāb al-libās, bāb taqlīm al-azfār*. Al-Khatīb, *al-Jāmiʿ*, vol. 1, p. 225.
18 Halim Sayoud, 'Author discrimination between the Holy Quran and the Prophet's statements,' pp. 427–444.
19 *Jāmiʿ al-Tirmidhī*: *kitāb al-īmān, bāb mā jā'a fī sibāb al-muslim*; *kitāb al-birr wa'l-sila, bāb mā jā'a fī al-kibr, bāb mā jā'a fī rahmat al-sibyān*; *Sunan* of Abū Dāwūd: *kitāb al-ijāra, bāb al-nahy ʿan al-ghishsh*; Ibn Hajar, *Fath al-Bārī*, vol. 13, pp. 30, 33.

2

THE TRANSMISSION AND COLLECTION OF PROPHETIC TRADITIONS

INTRODUCTION

Despite its seemingly arcane nature, the hadith tradition emerged in the early days of Islam as a practical solution to the needs of the Muslim community. In the wake of the Prophet's death, his teachings served as an obvious source of guidance for the nascent Islamic community as it struggled to determine how to live according to God's will now that he was gone. The study of hadiths began as a practical attempt to gather, organize, and sift through the authoritative statements and behavior attributed to the Prophet. In the subsequent centuries, the hadith tradition developed to meet new needs as they evolved. By the close of the tenth century, the transmission and collection of hadiths had acquired a new dimension – quite apart from the contents of any hadith, the report and its *isnād* became a medium of connection to the Prophet that created authority and precedence within the Muslim community. The development of hadith literature is thus best understood in light of the two general functions that hadiths fulfilled, that of an authoritative maxim used to elaborate Islamic law and dogma, and that of a form of connection to the Prophet's charismatic legacy.

This chapter traces the origins and development of Sunni hadith transmission and collection from the beginning of Islam until the modern period. Any mention of the notion of 'authenticity' or 'authentic (*sahīh*)' hadiths in this chapter refers to the Sunni Muslim criteria for reliability and its system of hadith criticism, the mechanics of which will be discussed fully in the next chapter. 'Authentic' or 'forged' here thus has no necessary correlation to whether or not the Prophet Muhammad *really* said that statement or not. Debates over 'what really happened' in the history of hadith will occupy us in Chapter 9.

INHERITING THE PROPHET'S AUTHORITY

In Islam, religious authority emanates from God through His Prophet. Whether by referring to the Prophet's teachings directly or through the methods of religious problem-solving inherited from him, only through a connection to God and His Prophet does a Muslim acquire the right to speak authoritatively about Islamic law and belief. In the formative period of Islam, Muslims thus turned back again and again to the authoritative legacy of the Prophet's teachings as it radiated outwards through the transmission and interpretation of pious members of the community. It was the form through which this authoritative legacy was transmitted – whether via Prophetic reports or methods of legal reasoning – that created different schools of thought in the early Islamic period and led to the emergence of the hadith tradition.

In the Prophet's adopted home, the city of Medina, al-Qāsim b. Muhammad b. Abī Bakr (d. 108/726–7), the grandson of the first caliph of Islam, and Sa'īd b. al-Musayyab (d. 94/713), the son-in-law of the most prolific student of the Prophet's hadiths, Abū Hurayra, became two of the leading interpreters of the new faith after the death of the formative first generation of Muslims. Their interpretations of the Quran and the Prophet's legacy, as well as those of founding fathers such as the second caliph 'Umar b. al-Khattāb, were collected and synthesized by the famous Medinan jurist Mālik b. Anas (d. 179/796). In Kufa, the Prophet's friend and pillar of the early Muslim community, 'Abdallāh b. Mas'ūd (d. 32/652–3), instructed his newly established community on the tenets and practice of Islam as it adapted to the surroundings of Christian, Jewish, and Zoroastrian Iraq. His disciple 'Alqama b. Qays (d. 62/681) transmitted these teachings to a promising junior, Ibrāhīm al-Nakha'ī (d. 95/714), who in turn passed on his approaches and methods of legal reasoning to Hammād b. Abī Sulaymān (d. 120/738). His student of eighteen years, Abū Hanīfa (d. 150/767), would become a cornerstone of legal study in Iraq and the eponym of the Hanafī school of law. Unlike Medina, the cradle of the Muslim community where Muhammad's legacy thrived as living communal practice, the diverse environment of Kufa teemed with ancient doctrines and practices foreign to the early Muslim community. Many such ideas found legitimation in the form of spurious hadiths falsely attributed to the Prophet. Abū Hanīfa thus preferred relying cautiously on the Quran, well-established hadiths and the methods of legal reasoning learned from his teachers rather than risk acting on these fraudulent hadiths.

By the mid eighth century, two general trends in interpreting and applying Islam had emerged in its newly conquered lands. For both these trends, the Quran and the Prophet's implementation of that message were the only constitutive sources of authority for Muslims. The practice and rulings of the early community, which participated in establishing the faith and inherited the Prophet's authority, were the lenses through which scholars like Abū Hanīfa and Mālik understood these two sources. Another early scholar, ʿAbd al-Rahmān al-Awzāʿī of Beirut (d. 157/773–4), thus stated that 'religious knowledge (*ʿilm*) is what has come to us from the Companions of the Prophet; what has not is not knowledge.'[1] In Sunni Islam, a Companion is anyone who saw the Prophet while a Muslim and died as a Muslim. When presented with a situation for which the Quran and the well-known teachings of the Prophet and his Companions provided no clear answer, scholars like Abū Hanīfa relied on their own interpretations of these sources to respond. Such scholars were known as the *ahl al-ra'y*, or the Partisans of Legal Reasoning.

Other pious members of the community preferred to limit themselves to the opinions of the earliest generations of Muslims and more dubious reports from the Prophet rather than speculate in a realm they felt was the exclusive purview of God and His Prophet. The great scholar of Baghdad, Ahmad b. Hanbal (d. 241/855), epitomized this transmission-based approach to understanding law and faith in his famous statement: 'You hardly see anyone applying reason (*ra'y*) [to some issue of religion or law] except that there lies, in his heart, some deep-seated resentment. An unreliable narration [from the Prophet] is thus dearer to me than the use of reason.'[2] Such transmission-based scholars, referred to as 'the Partisans of Hadith (*ahl al-hadīth*),' preferred the interpretations of members of the early Islamic community to their own. For them the Muslim confrontation with the cosmopolitan atmosphere of the Near East threatened the unadulterated purity of Islam. A narcissistic indulgence of human reason would encourage heresy and the temptation to stray from God's revealed path. Only by clinging stubbornly to the ways of the Prophet and his righteous successors could they preserve the authenticity of their religion.

For the *ahl al-hadīth*, reports traced back to the Prophet, bearing his name and conveying his authority, were *prima facie* compelling. Even if a scholar were not sure that a hadith was reliable, the powerful phrase 'the Messenger of God said…' possessed great authority. Many unreliable hadiths were used in efforts to understand the meaning of Quranic words, to reconstruct the campaigns of the Prophet, to document the virtues of the Companions or simply in preaching that exhorted Muslims towards piety. Even in legal issues, where as we shall see scholars like Ibn Hanbal were more rigorous about authenticating hadiths, *ahl al-hadīth* scholars sometimes depended on unreliable hadiths. It was amid this vying between the *ahl al-hadīth* and *ahl al-ra'y* schools that the Sunni hadith tradition emerged.

EARLY HADITH COLLECTION AND WRITING

From the beginning of Islam, Muhammad's words and deeds were of the utmost interest to his followers. He was the unquestioned exemplar of faith and piety in Islam and the bridge between God and the temporal world. Although, as we shall see, there was controversy over setting down the Prophet's daily teachings in writing, it is not surprising that those Companions who knew how to write tried to record the memorable statements or actions of their Prophet. As paper was unknown in the Middle East at the time (it was introduced from China in the late 700s), the small notebooks they compiled, called ***sahīfa***s, would have consisted of papyrus, parchment (scraped, limed and stretched animal skins), both very expensive, or cruder substances such as palm fronds. Although there is some evidence that the Prophet ordered the collection of his rulings on taxation, these *sahīfa*s were not public documents; they were the private notes of individual Companions.[3] Some of the Companions recorded as having *sahīfa*s were Jābir b. 'Abdallāh, 'Alī b. Abī Tālib, Abū Hurayra and 'Abdallāh b. 'Amr b. al-'Ās.

Certain Companions were more active in amassing, memorizing, and writing down hadiths than others. Like grandchildren eager to collect stories and recollections about a grandparent they barely knew, we find that it is often the most junior Companions of the Prophet who

1. Abū Hurayra: 5,300 hadiths
2. Ibn ‘Umar: 2,600 hadiths
3. Anas b. Mālik: 2,300 hadiths
4. Aisha: 2,200 hadiths
5. Ibn ‘Abbās: 1,700 hadiths

Figure 2.0 Leading Hadith Transmitters from the Companions

became the most prolific collectors and transmitters of hadiths. Abū Hurayra (d. 58/678), who knew the Prophet for only three years, is the largest single source for hadiths, with approximately 5,300 narrations in later hadith collections.[4] Although he did not write hadiths down in his early career, by his death Abū Hurayra had boxes full of the *sahīfa*s he had compiled.[5] ‘Abdallāh b. ‘Umar, the son of ‘Umar b. al-Khattāb, was twenty-three years old when the Prophet died and is the second largest source for hadiths, with approximately 2,600 narrations recorded in later collections. Ibn ‘Abbās (d. 68/686–8), who was only fourteen years old (or nine according to some sources) when the Prophet died, is the fifth largest source, with around 1,700 hadiths.[6]

Since Companions like Ibn ‘Abbās and Abū Hurayra only knew the Prophet for a short time, they apparently amassed their vast numbers of hadiths by seeking them out from more senior Companions. Abū Hurayra is thus rarely recorded as saying ‘I heard the Prophet of God say…’ – more often he simply states indirectly that ‘the Prophet said …’ Just as today we regularly quote people whom we did not hear directly, this would have been normal for the Companions. The obsession with specifying direct oral transmission with no intermediary, which characterized later hadith scholarship (see Chapter 3), did not exist during the first generations of Islam. Ibn ‘Abbās probably heard only forty hadiths directly from the Prophet. The rest he frequently narrates by saying ‘the Prophet of God said…’ or through a chain of transmission of one, two, or even three older Companions.[7]

Not surprisingly, those who spent a great deal of intimate time with the Prophet were also major sources of hadiths. Anas b. Mālik, who entered the Prophet's house as a servant at the age of ten, and the Prophet's favorite wife, Aisha, count as the third and fourth most prolific hadith sources, with approximately 2,300 and 2,200 narrations in later books respectively.[8] Interestingly, those Companions who spent the most time with the Prophet during his public life rank among the least prolific hadith transmitters. The Prophet's close friend and successor, Abū Bakr, his cousin/son-in-law 'Alī b. Abī Tālib, and close advisor 'Umar are the sources for only 142, 536 and 537 hadiths respectively. These prominent early Muslims, who were looked to as leaders responsible for decisions and religious rulings after the Prophet's death, seem to have preserved the spirit of Muhammad's teachings in their actions and methods of reasoning rather than by citing his hadiths directly.

When reading books of hadiths, at first it appears arbitrary which Companion narrates a hadith from the Prophet. Certain Companions, however, demonstrated particular interests and expertise in certain subjects. The Prophet's wives, especially Aisha, not surprisingly serve as the sources for hadiths about the Prophet's personal hygiene, domestic habits, and sexual life. Most of the hadiths in which the Prophet instructs his followers about the protocol for using dogs – animals whose saliva is considered ritually impure by most Muslims – for hunting come from the Companion 'Adī b. Hātim, who clearly was very curious about this topic.

So dominant is the presence of Muhammad in the formative period of Islam that we forget that after his death it was his Companions who assumed both complete religious and political leadership in the community. It was Companions like Ibn 'Abbās in Mecca, Ibn Mas'ūd in Kufa and Salmān al-Fārisī in Isfahan who had the responsibility of teaching new generations of Muslims and new converts about the religion of a prophet they had never known. The generation who learned Islam from the Companions and in turn inherited from them the mantle of the Prophet's authority became known as the **Successors** (*al-tābi'ūn*). Like the Companions, they too recorded those recollections that their teachers recounted to them about the Prophet's words, deeds, and rulings. In addition to compiling their own *sahīfa*s from the lessons of the Companions, these Successors also passed on the Companions' own *sahīfa*s.

Some of the early *isnād*s that appear most regularly in hadith collections seem to be a record of *sahīfa*s being handed down from teacher to student or from father to son. We thus often find the *sahīfa-isnād* of Abū Hurayra to 'Abd al-Rahmān, to his son al-'Alā'. The Successor Abū al-Zubayr al-Makkī received the *sahīfa* of the Companion Jābir b. 'Abdallāh, and one of the most famous Successors, al-Hasan al-Basrī (d. 110/728), received the *sahīfa* of the Companion Samura b. Jundub. The *sahīfa* of ʿAmr b. al-ʿĀs, passed down to his grandson, to his son Shuʿayb, became an essential resource for the Prophet's rulings on liability for injuries and compensation for homicide. An example of a *sahīfa* that has survived intact today, the *sahīfa* of the Successor Hammām b. Munabbih (d. *circa* 130/747), contains 138 hadiths from the Prophet via Abū Hurayra.[9]

The vast preponderance of the hadiths that the Successors heard from the Companions, however, were not in written form. Arabian society of the seventh and eighth centuries had a highly developed tradition of oral poetry, and the Companions more often recounted their memories of the Prophet in oral form only. Even to modern readers accustomed to writing everything down, this is understandable to an extent; to them the Prophet was a contemporary figure whose words and deeds lived on in their memories as freshly as we remember our own teachers or parents. Only rarely do we put down these memories on paper.

Of course, the Prophet was no average person, and many of his Companions did seek to record his legacy even during his own lifetime. There are several hadiths, however, in which the Prophet warns his followers not to record his words out of fear that they might be confused with God's words as revealed in the Quran. As the Quran was still being set down in writing during the Prophet's lifetime by numerous scribes and in many private notebooks, collections of the Prophet's teachings might easily be conflated with the holy book. We thus find a famous hadith in which the Companion Abū Saʿīd al-Khudrī states, 'We used not to write down anything but the testimony of faith said in prayer (*al-tashahhud*) and the Quran.' In another hadith, the Companion Zayd b. Thābit states that the Prophet had forbidden his followers to write down any of his words.[10]

It was unrealistic, however, that a lawmaker and political leader like the Prophet could allow *no* written record keeping. It would simply have been impossible for Muslims to preserve accurately the teachings they heard from the Prophet without some recourse to writing. Alongside hadiths banning writing, we thus also find reports encouraging it. The Companion Anas b. Mālik is even quoted as saying, 'We did not consider the knowledge of those who did not write it down to be [real] knowledge.'[11] We thus also find hadiths in which the Prophet allows new Muslims visiting from outside Medina to record lessons he gave in a sermon.[12]

This contradictory evidence concerning the writing down of hadiths has proven very problematic for both Muslim and Western scholars. Some Muslim scholars, such as the Damascene prodigy al-Nawawī (d. 676/1277), have reconciled the material by assuming that the reports condemning the writing of hadiths came from the earlier years of the Prophet's career, when he was concerned about his words being mistaken for the Quran. Permission to write down his teachings would have come later, when the Quran had become more established in the minds of Muslims, and the Prophet's role as the leader of a functioning state required some written records.[13]

Western scholars, on the other hand, have often understood the tension between the writing of hadiths and its prohibition to reflect competing values within the Islamic hadith tradition itself. In Islam, religious knowledge is primarily oral in nature – a written book only serves as a guide for the oral recitation of its contents. On a conceptual level, it is almost as if written pages are dead matter that only comes alive when read aloud. It is interesting that the importance of oral knowledge kept the debate over whether or not one should write down hadiths alive into the 1000s CE, over two hundred years after it had been rendered moot by the popularization of written hadith collections!

In the early Islamic period, however, this focus on orality was very practical. The Arabic alphabet was still primitive, and many letters were written identically and could only be distinguished from one another by context. Even today, the Arabic script does not indicate short vowels. We can imagine an English sentence written with only consonants and a few vowels, such as 'I wnt t ht the bll.' Is it 'I want to hit the ball,' 'I want to hit the bell, ' 'I went to hit the ball,' *et cetera*? We could only know the correct reading of the sentence if we knew its context. With the Arabic script, then, knowing the context and even the intended meaning of a written text is essential for properly understanding it. The *sahīfa*s of the Companions and Successors thus only served as memory-aids, written skeletons of hadiths that would jog the author's memory when he or she read them.

These *sahīfa*s could not thus simply be picked up and read. One had to hear the book read by its transmitter in order to avoid grave misunderstandings of the Prophet's words. If hadith transmitters had reason to believe that a certain narrator had transmitted hadiths without hearing them read by a teacher, in fact, they considered this a serious flaw in the authenticity of that material. Abū al-Zubayr al-Makkī had heard only part of the Companion Jābir b. ʿAbdallāh's *sahīfa* read aloud by Jābir, and this undermined his reliability in transmission for some Muslim hadith critics. Some early hadith transmitters, like ʿAtā' b. Muslim al-Khaffāf, were so concerned about their books of hadiths being read and misunderstood after their deaths that they burned or buried them.[14]

Of course, this practical and cultural emphasis on direct oral transmission did not mean that Muslims ignored the reliability of written records. Even when transmitting a hadith orally, it was best for a scholar to be reading it from his book. The famous hadith scholar Ibn Maʿīn (d. 233/848) thus announced that he preferred a transmitter with an accurate book to one with an accurate memory.[15] By the early 700s CE, setting down hadiths in writing had become regular practice. The seminal hadith transmitter and Successor Muhammad b. Shihāb al-Zuhrī (d. 124/742) considered writing down hadiths to be absolutely necessary for accurate transmission.

Collectors like al-Zuhrī were encouraged to collect and record hadiths by the Umayyad dynasty, which assumed control of the Islamic empire in 661 CE. The Umayyad governor ʿAbd al-ʿAzīz b. Marwān requested that the Successor Kathīr b. Murra send him records of all the hadiths he had heard from the Companions.[16] ʿAbd al-ʿAzīz's son, the Umayyad caliph ʿUmar b. ʿAbd al-ʿAzīz, ordered the governor of Medina to record all the hadiths concerning administrative and taxation matters.[17]

Another important question that arose during the early transmission and collection of hadiths was whether or not one had to repeat a hadith word for word or if one could just communicate its general meaning. Most early Muslim scholars understood that keeping track of the exact wording of hadiths was not feasible and that 'narration by the general meaning (*al-riwāya bi'l-maʿnā*)' was an inescapable reality. The Companion Wāthila b. Asqaʿ had admitted that sometimes the early Muslims even confused the exact wording of the Quran, which was universally well-known and well-preserved. So how, he asked, could one expect any less in the case of a report that the Prophet had said just once? Al-Hasan al-Basrī is reported to have said, 'If we only narrated to you what we could repeat word for word, we would only narrate two hadiths. But if what we narrate generally communicates what the hadith prohibits or allows then there is no problem.' Some early Muslim scholars insisted on repeating hadiths exactly as they had heard them. Ibn Sīrīn (d. 110/728) even repeated grammatical errors in

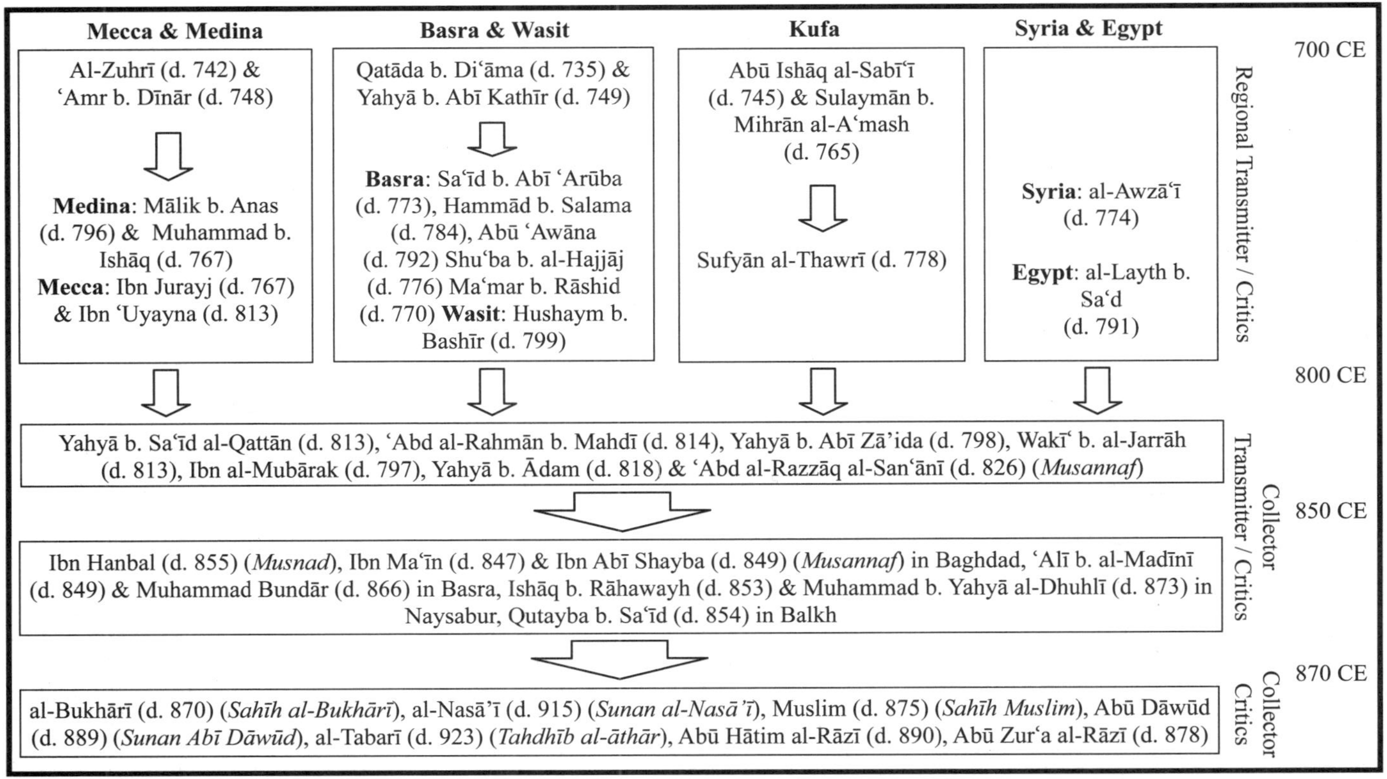

Figure 2.1 Transmission and Criticism of Hadiths from the Companions of the Prophet and Successors

hadiths that he had heard.[18] Eventually, Muslim scholars arrived at the compromise that one could paraphrase a hadith provided that one was learned enough to understand its meaning properly.[19]

TRANSCRIPTS OF LEGAL DEBATES: THE EMERGENCE OF *MUSANNAF* COLLECTIONS

If we imagine the world of Islam in the early and mid eighth century CE, the next stage of hadith literature appears as a direct reflection of Muslim scholarly discourse of the time. We can picture the prominent Successor al-Hasan al-Basrī, who had studied with Companions like Anas b. Mālik and who had been brought up in the house of one of the Prophet's wives, as a pillar of piety in Basra and recourse for the questions of the city's inhabitants. Seated under a reed awning, al-Hasan would answer questions concerning how to pray, how to divide inheritance and how to understand God's attributes by drawing on all the religious knowledge he had gained. He might reply by quoting the Quran or something that his mother had heard from the Prophet. On other occasions he might tell his audience how 'Alī b. Abī Tālib, whom he had met as a young man, had ruled on a particular case. Sometimes al-Hasan might use his own understanding of the principles put forth in the Quran or the Prophet's teachings to provide a new answer to a question. A few decades later in Medina, we can picture Mālik b. Anas seated against one of the pillars of the Prophet's mosque and answering questions in a similar way.

The first organized works of Islamic scholarship, called ***musannafs***, or 'books organized topically,' were basically transcripts of this discourse as it had developed during the first two centuries of Islam. Arranged into chapters dealing with different legal or ritual questions, they were topical records of pious Muslims' efforts to respond to questions about faith and practice. The earliest surviving *musannaf*, Mālik's *Muwatta'*, is thus a mixture of Prophetic hadiths, the rulings of his Companions, the practice of the scholars of Medina, and the opinions of Mālik himself. The version of the *Muwatta'* that became famous in North Africa and Andalusia contains 1,720 reports. Of these, however, only 527 are Prophetic hadiths; 613 are statements of the Companions, 285 are from Successors, and the rest are Mālik's own opinions.[20] Likewise, the earliest known *musannaf*, that of Ibn

Jurayj (d. 150/767), was a collection of reports from the Prophet, Companions, and Successors such as 'Atā' b. Abī Rabāh (d. 114/732). Another famous scholar from this period who compiled a *musannaf* was the revered scholar of Kufa, Sufyān al-Thawrī (d. 161/778).

A very large *musannaf* surviving from this earlier period was written by a student of Mālik and Ibn Jurayj, 'Abd al-Razzāq al-San'ānī (d. 211/827), but is much larger than the one-volume *Muwatta'*. The *Musannaf* of 'Abd al-Razzāq, an inhabitant of Yemen, is eleven

Chapter on Whether or not One Should Wipe One's Head with the Water Remaining from One's Hands

From 'Abd al-Razzāq, from Ma'mar, who said that he was informed by someone who heard al-Hasan [al-Basrī] say, 'It suffices you to wipe your head with what water is left over in your hands from ablution.'
(Note: this is a Successor opinion with an incomplete *isnād*)

From 'Abd al-Razzāq, from Isrā'īl [b. Yūnus], from Mūsā b. Abī 'Ā'isha, who said that he heard Mus'ab b. Sa'd, when a man asked him, say, 'I perform my ablutions and wash my face and arms, and what water is in my hands suffices me for my head, or I get new water for my head. Nay, rather, get new water for your head.'
(Note: this is a Successor opinion with a complete *isnād*)

'Abd al-Razzāq said that Ma'mar informed him, from Nāfi' that Ibn 'Umar used to get new water for wiping his head.
(Note: this is a Companion opinion with a complete *isnād*)

From 'Abd al-Razzāq, from Ibn Jurayj, who said that he was informed by 'Ajlān that the Prophet used to wipe his ears along with his face one time and wipe his face. Then he would put his palms in the water and wipe his head from front to back to the back of his neck, then his temples. Then he would wipe his ears once – all of this with what water he had in his hand from that one wipe.
(Note: this is a Prophetic hadith with an incomplete *isnād*)

From 'Abd al-Razzāq, from Ibn Jurayj, who said, 'I said to 'Atā', "Is it with the water left over from your face that you wipe your head?" and he said, "No, I put my hands in the water and wipe with them, and I do not shake the water off them or wait for them to dry. In fact I try to keep the hairs [on my hands and arms] wet."'
(Note: this is a Successor opinion with a complete *isnād*)

Figure 2.2 Subchapter from 'Abd al-Razzāq's *Musannaf* Concerning Ablutions

printed volumes. As Figure 2.2 demonstrates, ʻAbd al-Razzāq drew mostly from his teachers Maʻmar b. Rāshid and Ibn Jurayj.[21] Another famous *musannaf*, written by a scholar from the generation of ʻAbd al-Razzāq's students, comes from the hadith scholar of Baghdad, Abū Bakr b. Abī Shayba (d. 235/849). Figure 2.2 provides an example of the type of material and sources that a *musannaf* would draw upon.

In many ways, the *musannaf* genre predates the emergence of classical hadith literature rather than being part of it. If hadith collections are characterized by a predominant focus on reports from the Prophet that include *isnād*s as a means for critics to verify their authenticity, then books like the *Muwatta'* and the *Musannaf* of ʻAbd al-Razzāq are not technically hadith collections. Both Mālik and ʻAbd al-Razzāq cite rulings of Companions and Successors more frequently than they cite Prophetic hadiths. But even when quoting the Prophet directly, the obsession with complete, unbroken chains of transmission that would characterize the classical period of hadith collection is absent. Even when Mālik does cite Prophetic hadiths, on sixty-one occasions he completely omits the *isnād* and simply states, 'The Prophet said…' Rather, we should think of *musannaf*s as early works of Islamic law that represent the diversity of sources from which legal and doctrinal answers could be sought during the first two centuries of Islam. In a *musannaf*, a scholar like Mālik was trying to answer questions with the resources he felt were reliable and was not concerned with proving their authenticity according to a rigid system of *isnād* authentication.

Of course, *musannaf*s would serve a very important function in law, hadith literature, and hadith criticism. Later scholars would turn to *musannaf*s to know the legal opinions of Companions and Successors, and hadith critics would use them as evidence when investigating whether a hadith was really something said by the Prophet or a statement actually made by a Companion or Successor.

But if Muhammad was the ultimate interpreter of God's will, why would a scholar like Mālik so infrequently rely on his words in a *musannaf* collection? This question has cast a shadow of doubt over the authenticity of the hadith corpus, a question addressed in Chapter 9. Here, however, we can provide a few possible explanations. As Figure 2.1 demonstrates, during the time of Mālik and Ibn Jurayj hadith transmission was localized. When Mālik was asked by a student whether or not one should wash in between one's toes when performing ritual ablutions, he said that it was not required. Another student, 'Abdallāh b. Wahb, objected, saying that in his native Egypt they had a hadith through the Companion Mustawrid b. Shaddād telling how the Prophet did wash between his toes. Hearing the *isnād*, Mālik said, 'That hadith is good, and I had not heard it until this moment.' He acted on it from that point on.[22] It is not surprising that Mālik had not heard the hadith, since he only left his home in Medina to perform pilgrimage to the nearby city Mecca. Many of the hadiths that were widespread in Syria, Egypt, or among the students of Abū Hanīfa in Iraq were unknown to him. It is thus very likely that Mālik did not cite a Prophetic hadith on an issue because he knew of none. As Figure 2.1 indicates, it was only among the generation of Mālik's students, and even more so among their students, that hadith scholars traveled widely in order to unify the corpus of hadiths.

In addition, *musannaf*s drew on such a wide variety of authoritative figures because they were all legitimate inheritors of the Prophet's authority. The Companions, who had lived with the Prophet for years and understood the principles upon which he acted, and the Successors, who learned from them, were seen as the carriers of the Prophet's message and were heeded accordingly. Even a scholar like Mālik, living in the generation after the Successors, was so esteemed as a pious interpreter of the Prophet's message that he could give his opinion without citing any sources at all.

THE *MUSNAD* ERA AND THE EMERGENCE OF HADITH LITERATURE PROPER

The shift from the variety of the *musannaf* to the focus on Prophetic hadiths that characterizes hadith literature occurred with the emergence of the ***musnad*** collections in the late eighth and early ninth centuries CE. While *sahīfa*s had been mere *ad hoc* collections, and *musannaf*s were arranged as topical references, *musnad* collections were organized according to *isnād*. All the hadiths narrated from a certain Companion would fall into one chapter, then all those transmitted from another into the next, *et cetera*. The appearance of *musnad* collections occurred due to impetuses from both the broader study of Islamic law and within the more narrow community of Muslim hadith critics.

During the late eighth and early ninth centuries, the regional schools of Islamic law, each based on the teachings and interpretation of learned figures like Mālik and Abū Hanīfa, faced a new challenge. A young scholar named Muhammad b. Idrīs al-Shāfiʿī (d. 204/820), who had studied with Mālik in Medina and the students of Abū Hanīfa in Iraq, and had traveled widely in Egypt and Yemen, asserted that it should be the direct hadiths of the Prophet, and not his precedent as understood by local scholars, that supplemented the Quran as the second major source of law. In the face of a contrasting hadith that they had not previously known, al-Shāfiʿī argued, the followers of Mālik and Abū Hanīfa should take the Prophet's words over the stances of their local schools. Through his students and especially the study of his major legal work, the *Umm* (The Motherbook), al-Shāfiʿī had an immediate and powerful influence on *ahl al-hadīth* jurists. From this point on in the hadith tradition, the testimony of Muhammad would trump all other figures of authority and become the predominant focus of hadith collections. *Musnad*s reflected this interest, as they focused almost entirely on Prophetic hadiths and included Companion or Successor opinions only as occasional commentaries.

Quite apart from broader questions of legal theory, the burgeoning class of Muslim hadith critics that emerged in the mid and late eighth century had good reason to start organizing their personal hadith collections along *isnād* lines. First, the growing number of reports erroneously attributed to the Prophet had made the *isnād* an indispensable tool. Limiting hadith collections to material that had an *isnād* was a solid first line of defense against hadith forgery – if you claimed that the Prophet had said something but could provide no *isnād*, your hadith had no place in a *musnad*. Second, as we will see in the next chapter, the single most important factor in judging the reliability of

Prophet → Companion A → Successor A → Transmitter A
→ Transmitter B
→ Transmitter C
→ Successor B → Transmitter A
→ Transmitter B
→ Transmitter C
→ Companion B → Successor A → Transmitter A
→ Transmitter B
→ Transmitter C
..., etc.

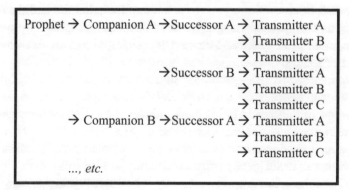

Figure 2.3 *Musnad* Organization

a hadith transmitter was determining if he or she was corroborated in the material he or she reported. In order to know if a hadith transmitter is corroborated in his transmissions, critics compared the hadiths he reported to those of others who studied with his teachers. Thus we find that many *musnad*s, such as that of al-Rūyānī (d. 307/919–20), are organized into chapters as shown in Figure 2.3 above.

In order to determine whether or not Transmitter A is generally corroborated in the material he or she transmits, we need only flip through the chapters of the *musnad* comparing the hadiths that Transmitter A related from each Successor with those of Transmitters B and C.

The earliest known *musnad*, which has also survived intact, is that of Abū Dāwūd al-Tayālisī (d. 204/818). The most famous *musnad* is that of Ibn Hanbal, which consists of about 27,700 hadiths (anywhere from one fourth to one third of which are repetitions of hadiths via different narrations) and was actually assembled into final form by the scholar's son. Ibn Hanbal claimed he had sifted the contents of his *Musnad* from over 750,000 hadiths and intended it to be a reference for students of Islamic law. Although he acknowledged that the book contained unreliable hadiths, he supposedly claimed that all its hadiths were admissible in discussions about the Prophet's Sunna – if it was not in his *Musnad*, he claimed, it could not be a proof in law.[23]

Other well-known and widely read *musnad*s from the ninth century include those of al-Humaydī (d. 219/834), of al-Hārith b. Abī Usāma (d. 282/896), of al-Musaddad (d. 228/843), of Abū Bakr al-Bazzār (d. 292/904–5), and of the Hanafī scholar Abū Ya'lā al-Mawsilī (d. 307/919). The largest *musnad* ever produced, which has tragically not survived, was that of Baqī b. Makhlad (d. 276/889).

Instead of compiling large *musnad*s that included the hadiths of numerous Companions, some scholars devoted books to only one Companion: Abū Bakr al-Marwazī (d. 292/904–5), for example, compiled a small *musnad* with all the hadiths he had come across transmitted from the Companion Abū Bakr.

Although some *musnad*s, like that of al-Bazzār, contained some discussion of the flaws (*'ilal*) found in the *isnād*s of a hadith, in general *musnad*s were not limited to hadiths their compilers believed were authentic. Instead, they functioned as storehouses for **all** the reports that a certain hadith scholar had heard. As Figure 2.1 shows, by the time of Ibn Hanbal, hadith collectors were no longer constrained by regional boundaries. Hadith collectors like Muhammad b. Yahyā al-Dhuhlī or Qutayba b. Saʿīd were originally from Nishapur in Iran and Balkh in Afghanistan, but they traveled throughout the Muslim world on what was known as 'the voyage in the quest for knowledge (*al-rihla fī talab al-ʿilm*)' to collect hadiths from transmitters like ʿAbd al-Razzāq in Yemen or Layth b. Saʿd in Egypt. Throughout their travels they recorded the hadiths they heard in their *musnad*s regardless of their authenticity or their legal and doctrinal implications. The staunch Sunni Ibn Hanbal's *Musnad* thus contains a hadith – shocking to the sensibility of Sunni Muslims – that describes how an early copy of the Quran had been stored under Aisha's bed only to be found and partially eaten by a small animal leaving the record of God's revelation permanently truncated![24]

THE *SAHĪH* AND *SUNAN* MOVEMENT

*Musannaf*s and *musnad*s both had their advantages: *musannaf*s were conveniently arranged by subject, and *musnad*s focused on Prophetic hadiths with full *isnād*s. From the early ninth to the early tenth century, a large number of respected *ahl al-hadīth* jurists combined the two genres in the form of ***sunan / sahīh*** books. A *sunan* was organized topically, and thus easily used as a legal reference, but also focused on Prophetic reports with full *isnād*s. More importantly, the *ahl al-hadīth* jurists who compiled these *sunan*s devoted great efforts to assuring or discussing the authenticity of the books' contents. In general, the authors of *sunan* books sought only to include hadiths that had been relied upon by Muslim scholars and were known to be authentic either because they had strong *isnād*s or because the community of scholars had agreed that they truly reflected the Prophet's teachings. This new focus on producing collections of hadiths with an emphasis on authenticity led many of the collections produced in the *sunan* movement to be dubbed *sahīh* (authentic) books by either their authors or later Muslim readers. Two of the earliest known *sunan*s are those of Saʿīd b. Mansūr al-Khurāsānī (d. 227/842) and ʿAbdallāh al-Dārimī (d. 255/869).

Two participants in the *sunan* movement in particular, Muhammad b. Ismāʿīl al-Bukhārī (d. 256/870) and his student Muslim b. al-Hajjāj al-Naysābūrī (d. 261/875), broke with the *ahl al-hadīth*'s traditional willingness to use weak hadiths in law. Unlike their teacher Ibn

Hanbal, al-Bukhārī and Muslim felt that there were enough authentic hadiths in circulation that the *ahl al-hadīth* jurists could dispense with less worthy narrations. Al-Bukhārī and Muslim were thus the first to produce hadith collections devoted **only** to hadiths whose *isnāds* they felt met the requirements of authenticity. Their books were the first wave of what some have termed 'the *sahīh* movement.'[25] Known as the *Sahīhayn* (literally 'the two *Sahīhs*'), the collections of al-Bukhārī and Muslim would become the most famous books of hadith in Sunni Islam. It is therefore worth examining their contents and structure.

It is reported that al-Bukhārī devoted sixteen years to sifting the hadiths he included in his *Sahīh* from a pool of six hundred thousand narrations.[26] The finished work was not a mere hadith collection – it was a massive expression of al-Bukhārī's vision of Islamic law and dogma backed up with hadiths the author felt met the most rigorous standards of authenticity. The book covers the full range of legal and ritual topics, but also includes treatments of many other issues such as the implication of technical terms in hadith transmission. The book consists of ninety-eight chapters, each divided into subchapters (according to the standard printings; see endnote 27). The subchapter titles indicate the legal implication or ruling the reader should derive from the subsequent hadiths, and often include a short comment from the author or a report from a Companion or Successor elucidating the hadith. Al-Bukhārī often repeats a Prophetic tradition, but through different narrations and in separate chapters. Opinions have varied about the exact number of hadiths in the *Sahīh*, depending on whether one defines a 'hadith' as a Prophetic tradition or a narration of that tradition. Generally, experts have placed the number of full-*isnād* narrations at 7,397. Of these many are repetitions or different versions of the same report, with the number of Prophetic traditions at approximately 2,602.[27]

Muslim's *Sahīh* is much more a raw hadith collection than al-Bukhārī's work. It contains far fewer chapters (only fifty-four in the accepted Amīriyya edition) and lacks al-Bukhārī's legal commentary, but it contains a similar number of narrations (7,748). Unlike al-Bukhārī, Muslim keeps all the narrations of a certain hadith in the same section. Muslim also diverges significantly from al-Bukhārī in his near exclusion of commentary reports from Companions and later figures.

There is considerable overlap between the *Sahīhayn*. Muslim scholars generally put the number of traditions found in both books at 2,326. Al-Bukhārī and Muslim drew on essentially the same pool of transmitters, sharing approximately 2,400 narrators. Al-Bukhārī narrated from only about 430 that Muslim did not, while Muslim used about 620 transmitters al-Bukhārī excluded.

Al-Bukhārī's and Muslim's works had a great deal of influence on their students and contemporaries. Ibn Khuzayma (d. 311/923), a central figure in the Shāfiʿī school who studied with al-Bukhārī and Muslim, compiled a *sahīh* work that came to be known as *Sahīh Ibn Khuzayma*. Abū Hafs ʿUmar al-Bujayrī of Samarqand (d. 311/924) produced a collection called *al-Jāmiʿ al-sahīh,* and even the famous historian and exegete Muhammad b. Jarīr al-Tabarī (d. 310/923) attempted a gigantic *sahīh* work but died before he finished it. Saʿīd b. al-Sakan (d. 353/964) of Egypt also collected a small *sahīh* book consisting of hadiths necessary for legal rulings and whose authenticity he claimed was agreed on by all. Ibn Khuzayma's student Ibn al-Jārūd (d. 307/919–20) compiled a similar work called *al-Muntaqā* (The Select). Ibn Hibbān al-Bustī's (d. 354/965) massive *Sahīh* is usually considered the last installment in the *sahīh* movement.

Other participants in the *sahīh* movement also focused on hadiths with strong and reliable *isnād*s, but they nonetheless featured some reports that they acknowledged as being unreliable but included either because they were widely used among jurists or because the authors, like Ibn Hanbal, could find no reliable hadith addressing that topic. Four of these books in particular attained great renown. The *Sunan* of Abū Dāwūd al-Sijistānī (d. 275/889), a close student of Ibn Hanbal, contains about 5,276 hadiths and focuses on reports used in deriving law. The author alerts the reader to any narrations which have serious flaws in their *isnād*s. The *Jāmiʿ* of Muhammad b. ʿĪsā al-Tirmidhī (d. 279/892), one of al-Bukhārī's disciples, contains about 4,330 narrations and also focuses on hadiths that different schools of law had used as legal proofs. It also includes detailed discussions of their authenticity. Although al-Tirmidhī's *sunan* does include numerous unreliable hadiths, the author notes their status. As such, later scholars often called the work *Sahīh al-Tirmidhī*. Ahmad b. Shuʿayb al-Nasāʾī (d. 303/916), another student of al-Bukhārī, compiled two *sunan*s: the larger one contained many hadiths that the author acknowledged as unreliable. The smaller one, known as the *Mujtabā* (The Chosen), contains 5,770 narrations and focused on reliable hadiths. It has thus been known as *Sahīh al-Nasāʾī*. Finally, Muhammad b. Yazīd b. Mājah's (d. 273/887) *Sunan* is an interesting case. Although the author seems to have tried to include only reliable hadiths, some later Muslim scholars noted that as much as one fourth of the book's 4,485 narrations are actually unreliable.[28]

With the *sahīh/sunan* movement, the hadith tradition had reached a watershed. The works of scholars like al-Bukhārī, Muslim and al-Tirmidhī were possessed of a definitiveness that seemed both to reject many aspects of the culture of hadith transmission and to offer themselves as the ultimate hadith references for legal scholars. Muslim wrote his *Sahīh* as a response to what he saw as the laxity and misplaced priorities of hadith scholars and transmitters. He believed that those scholars who strove to collect as many hadiths as possible regardless of their quality were doing so only to impress others.[29] Muslim expressed serious concern over would-be hadith scholars who transmitted material of dubious nature to the exclusion of well-known and well-authenticated hadiths. They provided this material to the common people when in fact it is hadith scholars' duty to leave the common folk with trustworthy reports only. Muslim composed his *Sahīh* to fulfill this function. Abū Dāwūd expressed a similar purpose for his *Sunan*. He states confidently that he knows of 'nothing after the Quran more essential for people to learn than this book [his *Sunan*], and a person would suffer no loss if he did not take in any more knowledge after it.'[30]

TOPICAL HADITH WORKS

During the ninth and tenth centuries, Sunni hadith scholars were not merely writing comprehensive *sunan* works. They also compiled collections of hadiths dealing with individual topics. In fact, these specific treatises were often bound together to form a *sunan* or added on to the standard legal chapters of a *sunan* to add a new component to the work.

The earliest genre of topical works was that of ***zuhd***, or asceticism and pious excellence. These books included hadiths describing the Prophet's supreme piety and abstention from any religiously ambiguous behavior, as well as the superlative practice of early Muslim saints and even pre-Islamic prophets. The earliest known book of *zuhd* is that of Ibn al-Mubārak (d. 181/797). The great hadith transmitters and collectors Wakīʿ b. al-Jarrāh (d. 197/812) and Ibn Hanbal also compiled books of *zuhd*. Even as late as the eleventh century the Shāfiʿī scholar Abū Bakr al-Bayhaqī (d. 458/1066) wrote a hadith collection devoted to the *zuhd* theme.

Other scholars wrote books similarly addressing the question of perfecting Muslim manners. Al-Bukhārī wrote his 'Book Devoted to Manners (*al-Adab al-mufrad*)', and a scholar named Ibn Abī al-Dunyā (d. 281/894) of Baghdad wrote dozens of such hadith works on topics such as the importance of giving thanks, understanding dreams, and coping with sadness and grief. The hadith scholar Humayd b. Zanjawayh (d. 251/855–6) composed a book of hadiths that warned Muslims about the punishments that awaited them in Hellfire for certain deeds as well as the heavenly rewards they could expect in Paradise for goodly acts. Known as the *Kitāb al-targhīb wa al-tarhīb* (The Book of Enjoining and Warning), Ibn Zanjawayh's book was very popular and was transmitted widely. In the 1200s CE, ʿAbd al-ʿAzīm al-Mundhirī (d. 656/1258) wrote another famous book in this genre with the same title. Al-Nasāʾī and his student Ibn al-Sunnī (d. 364/975) both wrote hadith books entitled 'Deeds of the Day and Night (*ʿAmal al-yawm wa al-layla*)' on the pious invocations that the Prophet would say in various daily situations. The famous young scholar of Damascus, al-Nawawī (d. 676/1277), also wrote two very popular hadith books on manners and perfecting Muslim practice. His small *Adhkār* (Prayers) contains hadiths on the prayers one says before activities such as eating, drinking, and traveling with no *isnād*s but with the author's comments on their reliability. Al-Nawawī's *Riyād al-sālihīn min kalām sayyid al-mursalīn* (The Gardens of the Righteous from the Speech of the Master of Prophets) is a larger book of ethical, piety, and etiquette-related hadiths which has become extremely popular, serving as a main hadith text for the Tablīgh-i Jamāʿat, one of the largest missionary institutions in the modern Muslim world.

Similarly designed to frighten readers about the impending apocalypse and coming of 'the Days of God' was an early topical hadith book written by al-Bukhārī's teacher Nuʿaym b. Hammād (d. 228/842) entitled *Kitāb al-fitan* (The Book of Tribulations). *Sunan* and *sahīh* books regularly contained chapters on these apocalyptical 'tribulations' as well.

The most popular subject for topical hadith collections among Sunni scholars in the ninth and tenth centuries was the importance of adhering to the Sunna of the Prophet and the ways of the early

Muslim community on issues of belief and practice. These books of '*sunna*' contained Prophetic hadiths and reports from respected early Muslims that exhorted readers to derive their understanding of religion solely from the revealed texts of the Quran and Sunna while avoiding the heretical pitfalls of speculative reasoning about God, His attributes and the nature of the afterlife. *Sunna* books emphasized all the components of the Sunni Muslim identity as it was emerging in the eighth and ninth centuries: a reliance on transmitted knowledge instead of speculative reasoning, a rejection of the *ahl al-ra'y* legal school, an affirmation that all the Companions of the Prophet were upright (but that the best were Abū Bakr, 'Umar, 'Uthmān then 'Alī), and political quietism. The most famous books of *sunna* are those of Ibn Hanbal's son 'Abdallāh (d. 290/903), Ibn Abī 'Āsim (d. 287/900), Muhammad b. Nasr al-Marwazī (d. 294/906), and al-Barbahārī (d. 329/941).

Some later *sunna* hadith collections went into more detail on issues of proper Sunni belief. The staunch Hanbali Sufi Khwāje 'Abdallāh al-Ansārī of Herat (d. 481/1089) wrote a multi-volume hadith work condemning speculative theology and theologians (*Dhamm al-kalām wa ahlihi*). Ibn al-Waddāh (d. 286/899) wrote a small book on heretical innovation (*Kitāb al-bida'*), while al-Dāraqutnī (d. 385/995) wrote one treatise collecting all the hadiths affirming that Muslims would actually see God on the Day of Judgment (*Kitāb al-ru'ya*) and another one bringing together all the hadiths telling that God descends during the night to answer the prayers of the believers.

The collective affirmation that all the Companions of the Prophet were righteous and reliable transmitters of the Prophet's teachings, as opposed to the Shiite denigration of all the Companions who did not support 'Alī's claim to leadership, prompted another important topical genre in the ninth century. Books on the 'Virtues of the Companions (*fadā'il al-sahāba*)' became an important statement of Sunni belief. Ibn Hanbal thus collected all the hadiths he could find in which the Prophet described the excellence or special characteristics of each Companion in his *Fadā'il al-sahāba*. Al-Nasā'ī also wrote a shorter *Fadā'il al-sahāba* work as well as a hadith collection specifically devoted to 'Alī's virtues (*Khasā'is 'Alī*).

Although only a few books were written in the genre, books of ***shamā'il***, or the virtues and characteristics of the Prophet, were extremely popular in Islamic civilization. Such books discussed all aspects of the Prophet's personality, appearance, conduct, and miracles, and were often the only books through which the less educated segments of Muslim society from Mali to India would have had contact with high religious tradition. Al-Tirmidhī's *Shamā'il* was extremely widely read, as was al-Qādī 'Iyād's (d. 544/1149) *Kitāb al-shifā*. The Egyptian Jalāl al-Dīn al-Suyūtī (d. 911/1505) also wrote a later *shamā'il* work entitled *al-Khasā'is al-kubrā*. As al-Qādī 'Iyād explained, these books were not designed to convince non-Muslims of Muhammad's prophethood, but rather to reinforce Muslims' faith in the unique and unparalleled virtues of 'the last of God's messengers.'[31]

Another genre of topical collections focused on stories about Muhammad that proved or illustrated his standing as a prophet. The most famous works of *Dalā'il al-nubuwwa* (proofs of prophethood) come from the eleventh-century scholars al-Hākim al-Naysābūrī (d. 405/1014) and his students Abū Nu'aym al-Isbahānī (d. 430/1038) and Abū Bakr al-Bayhaqī.

Like *musnad*s, these various monographs were unconcerned with assuring the authenticity of the hadiths they contained. In fact, books on the virtues of Companions and *sunna* often contained reports that later Sunni scholars and sometimes the authors themselves found baseless or reprehensible. The *Kitāb al-sunna* of Ibn Abī 'Āsim, that of Ibn Hanbal's son 'Abdallāh and the *Kitāb al-tawhīd* (Book of God's Unity) of Ibn Khuzayma all included a hadith describing how when God sits on His throne it squeaks like a saddle mounted by its rider. But even Ibn Hanbal's son notes the hadith's *isnād* is weak, and later Sunni scholars were so shocked by this blatant anthropomorphism that some of them called Ibn Khuzayma's book 'The Book of Heresy.'[32] In his *Fadā'il al-sahāba*, Ibn Hanbal includes a report stating that 'Alī's name is written on the doorway to Paradise, a hadith rejected by Sunni scholars as forged.[33]

The question of why hadith scholars would knowingly include unreliable or obviously forged reports in any of their books is a perpetual quandary in the study of the hadith tradition and will be discussed in depth in the next chapter. In the context of books exhorting Sunnis to the proper beliefs and worldview, however, it makes sense from the authors' standpoint. These books were often polemics aimed at other sects, such as Muslim rationalists (known as **Mu'tazilites**) or Shiites. Sunni compilers of these books were not trying to prove anything to other Sunnis, who shared their system of hadith evaluation. They 'knew' they were upholding the correct set of beliefs, so they packed their books with whatever evidence they could find to support them regardless of its reliability. Authors of books of *sunna* were arguing that, instead of relying on reason, Muslims should believe in material transmitted from the Prophet *no matter what it said*. A hadith about God's throne squeaking was as useful in this cause as more reliable hadiths.

THE HADITH CANON

It would be some time before the landmark contribution of the *sahīh* and *sunan* books was recognized. By the dawn of the eleventh century, however, a selection of these books had been recognized as authoritative. This canon of books would fulfill two important functions in Islamic civilization: providing a common language for discussing the Prophet's Sunna and providing a manageable representation of the vast hadith corpus.

Surprisingly, al-Bukhārī's and Muslim's decision to compile books limited only to hadiths they deemed authentic was initially rejected by many *ahl al-hadīth* scholars. This seems counterintuitive from a modern standpoint; why would a tradition that prided itself on following the authentic legacy of the Prophet object to books of only authentic hadiths? In order to understand this we must remember that, for the *ahl al-hadīth*, authentic hadiths only represented the most reliable end of the hadith spectrum. Hadiths with less stellar *isnād*s were also used in law, and weak hadiths were used very commonly in preaching, Quranic exegesis, and books of *zuhd* and good manners.

Many *ahl al-hadīth* scholars during al-Bukhārī's and Muslim's time therefore criticized the compilation of the *Sahīhayn*. A famous hadith scholar from Rayy in Iran, Abū Zur'a al-Rāzī (d. 264/878), said of the two authors, 'These are people who wanted prominence before their time, so they did something of which they could boast; they wrote books the likes of which none had written before to gain for themselves precedence.' The *ahl al-hadīth* also worried that if hadith scholars wrote books limited to authentic hadiths, their opponents from the *ahl al-ra'y* would use that as a weapon against them. Abū Zur'a described Muslim as 'making a path for the people of heresy against us, for they see that they can respond to a hadith that we use as proof against them by saying "That is not in the *Sahīh*!" ' Under fire from such critics, al-Bukhārī and Muslim defended themselves by saying that their books did not include *all* the *sahīh* hadiths in circulation. Al-Bukhārī had only selected *sahīh* hadiths useful for his legal discussions, and Muslim had limited his book to hadiths whose authenticity he believed was agreed on by all.[34]

By the mid tenth century, however, the contribution of the *sahīh*/*sunan* movement was beginning to be realized. Previously, it was the collectors of the great *musnad*s, al-Bukhārī's and Muslim's teachers like Ibn Hanbal and al-Humaydī, who had been viewed as the pillars of hadith scholarship. In the late 900s, however, Ibn Manda of Isfahan (d. 395/1004–5) announced that the four masters of hadith were those who had produced the *sahīh* books: al-Bukhārī, Muslim, Abū Dāwūd, and al-Nasā'ī. Ibn Manda described these four as well as others of their generation as the group of hadith masters 'accepted by all by consensus, and their knowledge trumps all others.'[35]

The need for a selection of hadith collections acknowledged as superior by all the *ahl al-hadīth* was essential at that point in time. In light of all the *musannaf*s, *musnad*s, and *sunan*s in circulation between the various cities that hadith scholars visited on their 'travels in search of knowledge,' which books should students focus on as the foundation for understanding the Prophet's legacy? When a group of intimidated hadith students asked the Egyptian scholar Ibn al-Sakan (d. 353/964) this question, he entered his house and reemerged with four books in his hands. 'These are the foundations of Islam,' he said, 'the books of Muslim, al-Bukhārī, Abū Dāwūd, and al-Nasā'ī.'[36]

Different scholars had different visions of which books best represented the Prophet's Sunna. These shifting canons are usually referred to as 'The Five Books,' 'The Six Books,' or 'the Authentic Books (*al-Sihāh*).' The foundation of the canon, however, is unchanging: the four works of al-Bukhārī, Muslim, Abū Dāwūd, and al-Nasā'ī. The Shāfi'ī scholar Abū Bakr al-Bayhaqī (d. 458/1066) adds that, together with these four, al-Tirmidhī's and Ibn Khuzayma's books had identified a substantial amount of the authentic hadiths in circulation. Muhammad b. Tāhir al-Maqdisī (d. 507/1113) described the Six Books as those of al-Bukhārī, Muslim, al-Tirmidhī, al-Nasā'ī, Abū Dāwūd, and Ibn Mājah. 'Abd al-Karīm al-Rāfi'ī of Qazvīn (d. 623/1226) also enumerates this six-book series, as does the Indian Hanafī scholar al-Saghānī (d. 650/1252), adding the *Sunan* of al-Dāraqutnī as well. The Andalusian hadith scholar, al-Saraqustī (d. 524/1129), on the other hand, counts the Six Books as those of al-Bukhārī, Muslim, al-Tirmidhī, Abū Dāwūd, al-Nasā'ī, and Mālik. Al-Silafī of Alexandria (d. 576/1180), Abū Bakr al-Hāzimī (d. 584/1188-9), and al-Nawawī mention only Five Books: the works of al-Bukhārī, Muslim, al-Tirmidhī, Abū Dāwūd, and al-Nasā'ī.[37] Together, the Six Books contain approximately 19,600 hadiths (around 35,000 with repetitions).

The flexible boundaries of the hadith canon make sense when we consider one of its two primary functions. Even as early as 800 CE, al-Shāfi'ī had said that it was impossible for one person to know all the hadiths in circulation.[38] If the Prophet's Sunna was essentially boundless, the Muslim community needed a tangible and manageable selection of hadith books to represent its core. Whether the canon was five or six books, or exactly which books these were, did not affect this function.

In the 1200s and 1300s the hadith canon's ability to represent the Prophet's blessings endowed the *Sahīhayn* in particular with a special ritual relevance. In cities from Damascus to Timbuktu the *Sahīhayn* would be read in mosques as part of celebrations culminating in the month of Ramadan. Al-Bukhārī's *Sahīh* in particular was read as a cure for illness from Egypt to India, and the great Moroccan conqueror Mawlā Ismā'īl (d. 1727) had a copy of the *Sahīh* carried in front of his army 'like the Ark of the Children of Israel.'[39]

The second, more important function of the hadith canon was limited to the *Sahīhayn* – the only two books of the canon which included exclusively authentic hadiths. These two books served as a common reference for determining hadith authenticity. In the early 1000s the two schools of law that had emerged from the *ahl al-hadīth*, the Hanbalī and the Shāfi'ī, agreed that the contents of the *Sahīhayn* were totally authentic and had been agreed upon as such by the whole Muslim community. Scholars of the Mālikī school soon agreed, and by the 1300s even the hadith-wary Hanafī school had found acknowledging this convention unavoidable. For all the Sunni schools of law and theology, the *Sahīhayn* would be the common language for evaluating the authenticity of hadith in interschool debates.

The *Sahīhayn* canon was an ideal polemical weapon to use against one's opponents. But that did not mean that scholars felt they had to obey all the hadiths found in the two collections in their own work. If a scholar of the Shāfi'ī or Hanafī school of law found a hadith in al-Bukhārī's or Muslim's collections that he disagreed with, he had no compunction about criticizing its authenticity.[40]

The *Sahīhayn* were thus not immune to criticism. Only in the early modern and modern periods has it become controversial to criticize the *Sahīhayn*, but this is primarily due to Muslim scholars' eagerness to protect the status of two books that they see as symbols of an Islamic tradition under attack from modernity. It is important to note here, as will be discussed further below, that Muslim scholars recognized that other *sahīh* hadiths existed *outside* the hadith canon.

THE PINNACLE OF HADITH COLLECTION AND THE END OF HADITH TRANSMISSION

As al-Bukhārī's and Muslim's critics had insisted, the *sahīh* movement did not mean the end of hadith transmission and collection. Nor did it mean that Muslims believed that all the *sahīh* hadiths in circulation had been recorded. In fact, from the standpoint of volume, the peak of hadith collection occurred in the tenth century – over one hundred years after the Six Books had been written.

Indeed, the compilation of titanic personal *musnad*s continued after and even despite the *sahīh* movement, with scholars in Iran continuing the tradition of collecting *musnad*s with many weak and even forged hadiths. Abū al-Qāsim al-Tabarānī (d. 360/971) of Isfahan compiled a huge collection, his *Mu'jam al-kabīr*, which is today printed in twenty-eight volumes. 'Alī b. Hamshādh of Nishapur (d. 338/950) produced a personal *musnad* twice as large as al-Tabarānī's, and al-Hasan al-Māsarjisī of Nishapur (d. 365/976) compiled a *musnad* that if published today would occupy an astounding 182 volumes.[41] Even as late as the mid 1100s Shahrudār b. Shīrawayh al-Daylamī (d. 558/1163) compiled a famous hadith collection entitled *Musnad al-Firdaws* (The *Musnad* of Paradise).

Into the 1000s scholars with strong affiliations to certain schools of law produced massive *sunan*s and *musnad*s to bolster their schools' bodies of substantive law. The vast *Sunan al-kubrā* of the Shāfi'ī Abū Bakr al-Bayhaqī (d. 458/1066) is a landmark in the Shāfi'ī legal school, supporting every detail of its law code with a myriad of reports from the Prophet and his Companions. Abū al-'Abbās al-Asamm of Nishapur (d. 346/957) collected all the hadiths that al-Shāfi'ī had transmitted with full *isnād*s in his *magnum opus*, the *Umm*, and organized them into the *Musnad al-Shāfiʿī*.[42] Even a non-Hanafī like Abū Nuʿaym al-Isbahānī (d. 430/1038) participated in efforts to find chains going back to the Prophet for Abū Hanīfa's reports and composed a *musnad* collection of them.[43] A much larger *musnad* of the famous jurist's narrations was compiled by al-Khwārazmī (d. 655/1257). The Mālikī scholar Ibn al-Jabbāb (d. 322/934) created a *musnad* of Mālik's hadiths.[44]

All these scholars continued to transmit hadiths in the great mosques of Iraq and Iran before audiences of hundreds and even thousands of students. These 'dictation sessions' were recorded by students in collections called ***amālī*** (dictations). The chief judge of Kufa, al-Husayn b. Ismāʿīl al-Mahāmilī (d. 330/942), was described as the most knowledgeable person in hadith of his time and was famous for his *amālī*.[45] Abū al-ʿAbbās al-Asamm was equally well known for his dictation sessions.

Not only did hadith transmission and collection continue unabated after the *sahīh* movement, scholars continued to identify hadiths that they felt merited the title of *sahīh* and that al-Bukhārī and Muslim should have included in their works. The great hadith scholar of Baghdad, Abū al-Hasan al-Dāraqutnī (d. 385/995) and the Mālikī hadith master of the Hejaz, Abū Dharr al-Harawī (d. 430/1038), both wrote one-volume collections called *ilzāmāt* (addendums) of hadiths that they considered up to the standards of the *Sahīhayn*. Al-Dāraqutnī's student, al-Hākim al-Naysābūrī (d. 405/1014), compiled a voluminous *ilzāmāt* work entitled *al-Mustadrak* (with approximately 8,800 hadiths) in which he sought, once and for all, to demonstrate to those opponents of the *ahl al-hadīth* the multitude of authentic hadiths that remained outside the *Sahīhayn*.[46]

By the mid 1000s, however, it was clear that the process of recording the hadiths in circulation – regardless of whether they were authentic or forgeries – was coming to an end. In the mid eleventh century, al-Hākim's student al-Bayhaqī declared that all the hadiths that could reliably be attributed to the Prophet had been documented, and thus any previously unrecorded attributions to Muhammad should be considered *de facto* forgeries.[47] In practice, in the 1100s we see that fewer and fewer hadith scholars were able to record hadiths with full *isnād*s (even highly unreliable hadiths) back to the Prophet that had not already been written down in some earlier collection. Ibn al-Jawzī of Baghdad (d. 597/1201), for example, is the only person to have transmitted the admittedly unreliable hadith **'Sweeping the**

mosque is the dowry for heavenly beauties (*kans al-masājid muhūr al-hūr al-ʿīn*).' The last hadiths that I have seen recorded with full *isnāds* are found in the *Tadwīn fī akhbār Qazwīn* (Recording the History of the City of Qazvin) of ʿAbd al-Karīm al-Rāfiʿī (d. 623/1226): **'Civil strife (*fitna*) is sleeping, and God curses whomever wakes it,'** and **'Sanjar will be the last of the Persian kings; he will live eighty years and then die of hunger.'** (Sanjar was the Seljuq sultan of Persia; he died in 1157 CE at around seventy-five).[48] Even this second report is undoubtedly forged. By the 1300s, not even the greatest hadith scholars of their day such as Shams al-Dīn al-Dhahabī (d. 748/1348) or Jamāl al-Dīn al-Mizzī (d. 742/1341) would dare to claim that they were in possession of a hadith reliably said by the Prophet that had gone unnoticed until their time.

THE PRACTICE OF HADITH TRANSMISSION AND CONNECTION TO THE PROPHET AFTER THE HADITH CANON

In the early period of the hadith tradition the importance of oral transmission, or **'audition (*samāʿ*)'**, where the student either read the hadith to his teacher or vice versa, had been very practical. One had to hear hadiths through a chain of teachers (*isnād*) because the Arabic script was too ambiguous to assure the correct understanding of any written document. The practical emphasis on oral transmission – only accepting material if it came through a living *isnād* of transmitters – was equally applicable to whole books of hadiths. The transmission of a book required the same care and concern as the transmission of an individual hadith, and collections like *Sahīh al-Bukhārī* or Mālik's *Muwatta'* were transmitted from teacher to student in the same manner as hadiths.

For hadith scholars, any referral to a hadith collection was contingent on hearing it from a chain of transmitters back to the author. A book could not simply be taken off the shelf and used. Like a single report, only a student copying a text in the presence of his teacher could protect against the vagaries and errors of transmission. Abū Bakr al-Qatīʿī (d. 368/979), who was the principal transmitter of Ibn Hanbal's *Musnad*, was severely criticized for transmitting one of Ibn Hanbal's books from a copy which he had not heard directly from his teacher, Ibn Hanbal's son. Although al-Qatīʿī had in fact heard this book from his teacher previously, the copy he had used was destroyed in a flood, leaving him with only the other non-*samāʿ* copy. This case demonstrates the sensitivity of hadith scholars to the question of oral transmission. Even a respected scholar who had actually heard a book from his teacher could be criticized for relying on another copy if he had not read *that* copy in the presence of his teacher (since he would not have been able to make any corrections to it). The scholar who transmitted the *Musnad* from al-Qatīʿī, Ibn al-Mudhhib (d. 444/1052–3), was also accused of lax transmission practices. Specifically, he did not have *samāʿ* for certain sections of the *Musnad*. Later scholars thus explained that, because of this, 'material with unreliable texts (*matn*) and *isnād*s entered into the *Musnad*.'[49] In the ninth, tenth, and eleventh centuries the *isnād to* the book was thus as important as the *isnād*s contained *within* the book for authenticating its hadiths. Oral transmission was the key to maintaining these *isnād*s.

In the 1000s, however, the fact that hadith collections such as the Six Books had become so well known and widely transmitted meant that scholars could relax the practical strictures of oral transmission. *Sahīh al-Bukhārī* was sufficiently widespread that if alterations were made to any one copy of the book there existed enough other transmissions of the book to identify this error. Although devout hadith scholars would maintain into the thirteenth century that one could not simply pick up a book of hadith and read it without having heard it from a transmitter via an *isnād*, Sunni scholars not specializing in hadith found this unnecessarily cumbersome. By the mid 1000s revered Sunni theologians and jurists like Abū Hāmid al-Ghazālī (d. 505/1111) and his teacher al-Juwaynī (d. 478/1085) had declared that if one found a well-copied text of al-Bukhārī's *Sahīh* one could read and use it without an *isnād* to the book.[50]

Even among scholars focused narrowly on the study of hadith, in the 1000s the practice of ***ijāza* (permission for transmission)** began to supersede *samāʿ* as the medium of the *isnād*. *Ijāza* for transmission meant that instead of reading an entire hadith collection in the presence of an authorized transmitter, a student might only read part of it and receive 'permission' from the teacher to transmit the rest. Although it was a less rigorous form of authentication, *ijāza* still provided scholars with *isnād*s for books. Although this practice had existed in some forms even in the ninth century, by the mid 1000s it had become very common. Al-Hākim al-Naysābūrī, author of the massive *Mustadrak*, thus gave a group of students an *ijāza* to transmit his works provided they could secure well-written copies of them.[51]

Of course, if you could get an *ijāza* for a book you had not actually read in the presence of a teacher, you could get *ijāza*s for any number of books that the teacher was able to transmit. This led to the practice of acquiring a 'general *ijāza* (*ijāza 'āmma*)' for all the books a teacher had. In the 1000s many scholars also accepted the practice of getting *ijāza*s from teachers one had not actually met at all through writing letters. This '*ijāza* for the non-present person (*ijāzat al-ma'dūm*)' meant that scholars could acquire *ijāza*s for their infant children or even for children not yet born!

This *ijāza* for transmission (*ijāzat al-riwāya*) should not be mistaken for another, much less easily attained form of *ijāza* in Islamic civilization, 'the *ijāza* of knowledge (*ijāzat al-dirāya*).' The *ijāza* of transmission served only to preserve the tradition of the *isnād*, while the *ijāza* of knowledge showed that a teacher acknowledged that a student had mastered a text and was able to teach its contents to others.

It is evident from these developments that by the late eleventh century the transmission of hadiths and books *via* a living *isnād* possessed little practical value. Why then did it continue? Simply put, the foundational principle of the Islamic tradition, that authority comes through a connection to God and His Prophet, still dominated Muslim scholarly culture. The *isnād* was that chain that connected a scholar to the Prophet and allowed him to act as an authoritative interpreter of Islam. Hearing a hadith or a book of hadiths by an *isnād*, even if by *ijāza*, breathed a soul into otherwise lifeless pages and rendered the book legally compelling. One Arabic poem describes someone reading a book without receiving it from a teacher as 'someone trying to light a lamp with no oil.'[52] The Andalusian scholar Ibn Khayr al-Ishbīlī (d. 575/1179) thus stated that no one could introduce a statement with the formula 'the Prophet said…' without possessing some personal chain of transmission, even if by *ijāza*, back to the Prophet for that report.[53]

The *isnād* conveyed authority in Muslim scholarly culture, and it is no coincidence that acquiring and possessing *isnād*s was one of the means by which the Muslim scholarly elite could distinguish themselves from the laity. One of the reasons that Ibn Khayr al-Ishbīlī gave for requiring some form of *isnād* for quoting the Prophet was the phenomenon of uneducated simpletons preaching in mosques instead of qualified scholars. Receiving *isnād*s for books and hadiths was the equivalent of being ordained into the priesthood, and it is no surprise that even today at the Islamic Institute in Kerala, India, the graduation ceremony for Muslim scholars involves the rector of the school reading them his *isnād* for a hadith that involves the transmitters, all the way back to the Prophet, investing the student to whom they recited the hadith with the turban of a scholar.

Perhaps the last large hadith book to include full *isnād*s for every hadith it included was the *Aḥādīth al-mukhtāra* (Selected Hadiths) of Diyā' al-Dīn al-Maqdisī (d. 643/1245). But even this book did not include previously unrecorded hadiths. The author's *isnād*s for his hadiths consist of his *isnād*s to earlier hadith collections, which then continue from the author of those collections back to the Prophet. After the 1200s, hadith scholars would cultivate their own full-length *isnād*s back to the Prophet in small booklets produced only for the pietistic purpose of linking themselves to his blessings and imitating the great hadith scholars of yore. As Muhyī al-Dīn al-Nawawī described it, collecting *isnād*s back to the Prophet is an act of 'preserving the *isnād*, which is one of the unique features of the Muslim community.'[54] The famous hadith scholar of Cairo, Zayn al-Dīn al-'Irāqī (d. 806/1404), thus conducted occasional *amālī* sessions in an effort to imitate the practice of earlier hadith scholars. In the twentieth century, the Moroccan hadith scholar Ahmad al-Ghumārī (d. 1960) recited hadiths with full *isnād*s back to the Prophet in dictation sessions in Cairo's al-Husayn Mosque. Today, the practice of transmitting hadiths is carried out by hearing hadiths known as ***musalsalāt***, or hadiths always transmitted in a certain context. The first hadith a student hears from his teacher is known as the *hadīth al-musalsal bi'l-awwaliyya*, 'the hadith always transmitted first': **'God the Most Merciful is merciful towards those who act with mercy – be merciful on the earth and He that is in the heavens will be merciful with you'** (see Chapter 1).

Historically, transmitting hadiths via full *isnād*s back to the Prophet carried another advantage as well. Not only did the chain connect one to Muhammad himself, it also linked one to all the great scholars of the past through whom the *isnād* passed. The staunchly orthodox thirteenth-century Sufi 'Umar al-Suhrawardī (d. 632/1234) began most of the chapters of his popular manual on Sufism, *'Awārif al-ma'ārif*, with hadiths that reached all the way back to the Prophet through major figures in the Sufi tradition, such as Abū al-Qāsim al-Qushayrī (d. 465/1072) and Abū Nu'aym al-Isbahānī.[55] These scholars had recorded their hadiths in book-form, but the religious capital gained by providing living *isnād*s for hadiths transmitted through them proved more compelling to al-Suhrawardī than simply citing their books.

*Isnād*s thus linked scholars to the great figures who had preceded them in Islamic civilization and allowed one to speak with their voices as well as that of the Prophet. As the great Sufi of the sixteenth century, al-Shaʿrānī (d. 1565 CE) said, someone with an *isnād* 'is like a link in the chain, whenever he moves on any matter the whole chain, up to our master the Messenger of God, moves with him.'[56]

ELEVATION IN *ISNĀD*S, AUTHORITY, AND PRECEDENCE IN POST-CANONICAL HADITH TRANSMISSION

After the late tenth and eleventh centuries CE the primary purpose of the *isnād* was to provide a connection to the Prophet's authority and establish a person as part of the Muslim scholarly class. As a result, one's proximity to the Prophet in the *isnād* and access to hadiths that other scholars lacked served as marks of precedence in the scholarly community. Like the importance of oral transmission (*samāʿ*), the notion of a short or **'elevated (*ʿālī*)'** *isnād* began as a very practical concern for hadith authenticity: the fewer the links in the *isnād* to the Prophet, the fewer opportunities for error in transmission to occur. Hence we find even an early collector like Ibn Abī Shayba (d. 235/849) exhorting scholars that 'seeking elevated *isnād*s is part of religion.'[57]

By the mid 900s CE, however, seeking elevated *isnād*s had become a goal in its own right. In a society where connection to the Prophet was the source of both authority and blessing, the proximity of that connection was very valuable. As one early hadith scholar phrased it, 'A close *isnād* is closeness to God.'[58] As in any society, Muslim religious scholars and pious individuals established a system of honors and valuable items that individuals could earn or attain; like educational degrees, Muslim scholars sought out shorter and shorter *isnād*s, rarer and rarer hadiths, as a way to gain precedence, fame, and respect in their religious culture. Like coin collectors fretting over acquiring rarities, Muslims flocked to those scholars lucky enough to hear old hadith transmitters as young children, or who had heard a rare hadith from a certain transmitter from a far-away land. Such people could offer young Muslim scholars, eager to earn their place among the scholarly elite or merely to feel especially connected to their Prophet, a chance at excellence.

Of course, in none of these cases did the authenticity of the hadith in question actually matter – hadith scholars could distinguish themselves by their short *isnād*s and their rare hadiths regardless of whether or not these *isnād*s were reliable or the rare hadiths were baseless. To return to the analogy of coin collecting, it is the rarity of the coin and its condition (analogous to the elevation of an *isnād*) not the original value of the coin (or the authenticity of the hadith) which matter to the collector.

Perhaps the most prominent example of a hadith scholar who prioritized elevated *isnād*s and rare hadiths far above authenticity was al-Tabarānī (d. 360/971), who began hearing hadiths from teachers at the age of thirteen and died at the age of one hundred. Of his many hadith collections, his three *mu'jam*s (see below), one large, one medium, and one small, are testimonies to his priorities in hadith study. In the small and medium collections, al-Tabarānī follows most narrations with a brief discussion of how rare that narration is.

Al-Tabarānī's *isnād*s border on the impossibly short. While ninth-century scholars like al-Bukhārī generally narrated by *isnād*s of four, five, six, or seven transmitters to the Prophet (and in al-Bukhārī's case, twenty-eight instances where he narrated by only three), one hundred years later al-Tabarānī still regularly narrated hadiths with four-person *isnād*s. In one case we find him narrating a hadith *via* only three people: Ja'far b. Hamīd al-Ansārī ← his grandfather 'Umar b. Abān ← the Companion Anas b. Mālik, who showed him how to perform ablutions like the Prophet.

Of course, later Muslim critics cast aside this *isnād* as inauthentic since Ja'far b. Hamīd was unknown to anyone but al-Tabarānī.[59] But in a scholarly culture where proximity to the Prophet granted precedence regardless of authenticity, al-Tabarānī was the most sought after hadith transmitter of his time. The last of his students to die was one Ibn Rīdha (d. 440/1049), and the most long-lived person to hear al-Tabarānī's collections from him was a woman named Fātima al-Jūzdāniyya (d. 514/1120). If you were lucky enough to receive *ijāza* from Fātima as a child for al-Tabarānī's hadiths, you could be living in the late 1100s, some 550 years after the Prophet had died, with only six degrees of separation between you and him!

Two other famous hadith collections that embody the desire for connection to the Prophet, whatever the authenticity, in this period are the *Musnad al-Shihāb* (The Meteor Musnad) of the Egyptian al-Qudāʿī (d. 454/1062) and the *Musnad al-Firdaws* of al-Daylamī (d. 558/1163). These books represent some of the last large hadith collections to feature full-length *isnād*s, but their contents are on the whole so unreliable that later scholars devoted whole books to the forged hadiths they contained and assumed any hadith cited from the books to be weak.[60]

Today, the shortest realistic *isnād*s include twenty intermediaries to the Prophet. As al-Tabarānī's impossibly short *isnād* suggests, however, a chain of transmission can be as short as one is willing to believe. A great cultivator of *isnād*s in the early modern period, Murtadā al-Zabīdī (d. 1791), claimed to have heard a hadith via an *isnād* of two *jinn* (supernatural beings living alongside humans, the origin of our word 'genie') from the Prophet.[61] A modern hadith scholar from Morocco, ʿAbdallāh al-Ghumārī (d. 1993), noted that while teaching in Fez he had met a man who claimed to have heard hadiths from his grandfather, who had heard hadiths from al-Zabīdī.[62] If we combine this with the *jinn*'s *isnād*, this would mean that in the 1990s al-Ghumārī had a hadith from the Prophet narrated by only five intermediaries! Of course, neither al-Zabīdī nor al-Ghumārī *believed* that such transmissions were reliable enough to be the basis for law or dogma (as we'll see, *jinn* could not be pinned down to be evaluated as transmitters). They believed that *jinn* existed, however, so these *isnād*s were worth collecting for the blessing (*baraka*) of having a close, albeit tenuous, connection to the Prophet.

Women and hadith transmission

The transmission of hadith collections and even the compilation of new ones with very elevated *isnād*s in the post-canonical era was an area in which women could excel. Because they often lived longer than men, women could become the most sought after transmitters of books. Major hadith scholars like al-Khatīb al-Baghdādī traveled to Mecca to read *Sahīh al-Bukhārī* in the presence of Karīma al-Marwaziyya (d. 463/1071), who had an especially elevated *isnād* to the book, and Fātima al-Jūzdāniyya was the main transmitter of al-Tabarānī's works. Until her death in 2008, Muslim students flocked to a small village in Yemen's Hadramawt Valley to receive a hadith *ijāza* from the 105-year-old woman Safiyya al-ʿAmdiyya.

Independent collections of hadiths by women were very rare; in the early period of hadith they were non-existent. But we know of at least two selections of hadiths from the post-canonical period compiled by women. A twelfth-century woman named Shuhda al-Kātiba (d. 574/1178–9) put together a list of 115 hadiths that she picked from books she had been authorized to transmit, often with shorter *isnād*s than the hadiths in the actual books themselves.[63] The *Musnad* of Amat Allāh Miryam al-Hanbaliyya of Nablus (d. 758/1357) has also survived until today.

MUʿJAMS, THABATS, AND THE CVs OF HADITH SCHOLARS

With the transformation of hadith transmission and collection into a means of connection to the Prophet and status in the scholarly community, hadith collections emerged that were structured to display the breadth of a hadith scholar's learning. ***Muʿjam*s** were books of hadiths in which the author chose a certain theme and then provided as many hadiths as possible to demonstrate the breadth of his hadith corpus within that theme. In a sense, the *muʿjam* functioned as *curriculum vitae* of the hadith scholar, displaying the range of teachers with whom he had studied, the rarity of his hadiths, and the elevation of his *isnād*s. *Muʿjam*s had emerged in the ninth century, with Abū al-Qāsim al-Baghawī's (d. 317/929–30) *Muʿjam al-sahāba*, where the author provided one hadith from him all the way back to each Companion. The *muʿjam* came into its own as a genre, however, in the tenth to the twelfth centuries.

A common theme for a *muʿjam* was a ***muʿjam al-shuyūkh*** (*muʿjam* of teachers), or a collection where the author provided one hadith with a full *isnād* through each of his teachers. An early example of this is the *Muʿjam al-shuyūkh* of Abū Bakr al-Ismāʿīlī (d. 371/981–2) and the *Muʿjam al-saghīr* (small *muʿjam*) of al-Tabarānī. A *muʿjam al-shuyūkh* could be massive and contain far more than merely hadiths: the *muʿjam* composed by Abū Saʿd al-Samʿānī (d. 562/1166) is published in four volumes and contains hadiths, information about his teachers' lives, and the books they studied and wrote, as well as about his own studies.

Other *muʿjam*s were designed to display the breadth of a scholar's travels in the search of hadiths. One scholar of the 1100s who was particularly well known for his elevated *isnād*s and wide travel (born in Iran, he eventually settled in Alexandria), Abū Ṭāhir al-Silafī (d. 576/1180) wrote three *mu'jam*s, one for his teachers in his native Isfahan, one for those in Baghdad, and one for the teachers he had heard from on his travels (the *Mu'jam al-safar*).

With the end of the general practice of writing hadith collections with full *isnād*s in the late twelfth and early thirteenth centuries, the hadith scholar's CV shifted away from using the *isnād*s of hadiths to demonstrate wide learning to using the *isnād*s of books. In the mid 1100s we thus see the emergence of *thabat*s, or collections in which a scholar listed all his *isnād*s to the books he had received permission to transmit from his teachers, in the place of *mu'jam*s. Early *thabat*s include that of the famous Andalusian hadith scholars al-Qāḍī 'Iyāḍ b. Mūsā (d. 544/1149) and Ibn Khayr al-Ishbīlī (d. 575/1179). *Thabat*s would remain until modern times the premier medium through which scholars could demonstrate their connection to the great scholars of yesteryear, and through those books to the Prophet himself. In the twentieth century the Moroccan hadith scholar Muhammad 'Abd al-Hayy al-Kattānī (d. 1963) compiled the *Fahris al-fahāris*, a *thabat* collection with *isnād*s to over one thousand earlier *thabat* collections.

CHANNELING THE CONNECTION TO THE PROPHET: *MUSTAKHRAJS*, COMMENTARIES, LOCAL HISTORIES, AND FORTY HADITH BOOKS

The capacity of hadith to function as a connection to the Prophet has allowed Muslim scholars to channel and mold this charismatic medium to serve a variety of scholarly and non-scholarly purposes. Hadiths have provided the material through which other discourses are constructed. From the 900s to the present day, scholars have therefore used hadiths as a medium for discussing any number of legal, doctrinal, or spiritual issues.

Mustakhrajs

The genre of *mustakhraj* books flourished from the late 800s until the early 1000s, during the period in which the focus on elevated *isnād*s became pronounced. A *mustakhraj* involved a hadith scholar taking an existing hadith collection and using it as a template for his own hadith book; so for every hadith found in the template collection, the author of the *mustakhraj* would provide his own narration of that hadith.

This seems counterintuitive – why would a scholar who had collected a large body of hadiths not write his own collection in order to express his own legal or doctrinal worldview? The reason for composing a *mustakhraj* becomes obvious when we consider the nature and objectives of the genre. First, *mustakhraj*s appeared during the period when the hadith canon was forming. As a result, collections such as the *Sahīhayn* and the *Sunan* of Abū Dāwūd were greatly sought after, and scholars would travel far and wide to hear the books from their authorized transmitters. If a scholar was unable to hear the books from a transmitter with an elevated *isnād* to its author, however, he would have to suffice with an unattractively long *isnād* to the book.

*Mustakhraj*s provided a solution. By reconstituting the template collection with his own, often elevated *isnād*s, a scholar could effectively possess the book without compromising the quality of his *isnād* to it. Abū Nuʿaym al-Isbahānī states that he composed his *mustakhraj* of Muslim's *Sahīh* for the benefit of those who had 'missed' hearing that book from authorized transmitters. A twelfth-century scholar who had heard al-Isbahānī's *mustakhraj* bragged to friends that some of the *isnād*s for hadiths in the book were so short that he was just as close to the Prophet as Muslim had been.[64]

Second, authors of *mustakhraj*s used the template collection to display the authenticity and elevation of their own *isnād*s. We thus find that the books used as template collections for *mustakhraj*s were all products of the *sahīh* movement; dozens of *mustakhraj*s were produced based on the *Sahīhayn* of al-Bukhārī and Muslim, with three on the *Sunan* of Abū Dāwūd, one on al-Tirmidhī's *Jāmiʿ* and one on the *Sahīh* of Ibn Khuzayma. The majority of *mustakhraj*s based on the *Sahīhayn* thus attempted to replicate the criteria used for authenticity by al-Bukhārī and Muslim. Finally, by selecting narrations of hadiths that varied slightly from the template collections or adjusting the chapter titles, the authors of *mustakhraj*s could introduce their own legal or doctrinal ideas into the text. In this sense, *mustakhraj*s were the first generation of commentaries on hadith collections. In the *mustakhraj* genre, the template collection served as a forum for the author to display the quality and elevation of his *isnād*s as well as to express his own doctrinal and legal vision.

Commentaries

A commentary on a hadith collection, or ***sharh***, served two general functions. First, scholars composed such a work to assist students in the basic task of reading and understanding the difficult phrases, names, and obscure meanings embedded in the *isnād*s and *matn*s of a hadith work. Second, commentaries provided scholars with an opportunity to elaborate in detail on any legal, dogmatic, ritual, or historical issue that they found relevant to the hadiths in the book they were discussing. The book commented on thus acted as a medium for a much more expanded discussion in which the author could express his own vision of the Islamic worldview.

The majority of hadith commentaries were devoted to books in the hadith canon. The earliest known commentary was devoted to Mālik's *Muwatta'* by the Mālikī Abū Tāhir al-Umawī (d. 250/864). Two other very early examples are the Shāfi'ī scholar Hamd al-Khattābī's (d. 388/998) commentaries on the *Sunan* of Abū Dāwūd and on *Sahīh al-Bukhārī*. The first known commentary on Muslim's *Sahīh* was written by the North African scholar Muhammad b. 'Alī al-Māzarī (d. 536/1141), with one devoted to the *Jāmi' al-Tirmidhī* by another North African, Abū Bakr b. al-'Arabī (d. 543/1148). The first known commentary on *Sunan Ibn Mājah* came from the Cairene Hanafī scholar Mughaltāy (d. 762/1361). *Sunan al-Nasā'ī* would have to wait until al-Suyūtī (d. 911/1505) devoted a commentary to it.

The most famous hadith commentaries overall are undoubtedly Ibn Hajar al-'Asqalānī's (d. 852/1449) *Fath al-bārī*, a huge commentary on *Sahīh al-Bukhārī*, and al-Nawawī's commentary on *Sahīh Muslim*. Both are so encyclopedic in their discussion of the hadith-science issues and broader questions raised in the *Sahīhayn* that Muslim scholars regularly cite them instead of specialized books of law or theology.

Because commentaries provided such an excellent forum for legal discussion, the hadith collections tied to specific schools of law also attracted them. Early commentaries on Mālik's *Muwatta'* came from the Mālikī scholars Ibn 'Abd al-Barr (d. 463/1060) of Lisbon and Abū al-Walīd al-Bājī (d. 474/1081), both of whom wrote several commentaries of various sizes on the work. Ibn 'Abd al-Barr's

Kitāb al-tamhīd and the later work of al-Zurqānī (d. 1122/1710) are the two best known commentaries on the *Muwatta'*. There have been occasional commentaries on the *Musnad* of Abū Hanīfa, such as that of the Meccan Mullā 'Alī Qārī (d. 1014/1606). Al-Suyūtī wrote a small commentary on the *Musnad* of al-Shāfi'ī, and even the massive *Musnad* of Ibn Hanbal has attracted occasional commentaries, such as that of the Medinan scholar Muhammad b. 'Abd al-Hādī (d. 1726) or the Yemeni Abū al-Hasan al-Sindī (d. 1728).

Commentaries attained an important station in the late 1300s, when writing one on al-Bukhārī's or Muslim's *Sahīh* became the principal means for scholars throughout the Sunni Muslim world to interact with the hadith tradition. At the peak of intellectual activity in Mamluk Cairo in the fourteenth and fifteenth centuries, almost every hadith scholar of note wrote a commentary on *Sahīh al-Bukhārī*, and in India from the 1600s onward writing a commentary on one of the *Sahīhayn* was *de rigueur* for accomplished Muslim scholars.[65]

Hadith commentaries have continued to be written until modern times. The most famous commentary on al-Tirmidhī's *Jāmi'*, the *Tuhfat al-ahwadhī* (The Gem of the Competant) of the Indian Muhammad 'Abd al-Rahmān al-Mubārakpūrī (d. 1935), is a regularly cited encyclopedic source for Sunni Muslim scholars worldwide. The twenty-nine-volume *Awjaz al-masālik ilā Muwatta' Mālik* (ironically titled, The Shortest of Paths to Mālik's *Muwatta'*), written by the Indian Muhammad Zakariyyā Kāndahlawī (d. 1982) is the largest commentary devoted to the one volume *Muwatta'* of Mālik.

Sometimes scholars devoted commentaries to selections of hadiths they made themselves and not to any existing books. The leading Hanafī hadith scholar of his time, the Egyptian Abū Ja'far al-Tahāwī (d. 321/933), wrote one commentary on hadiths of legal consequence to the Hanafī school, the *Sharh ma'ānī al-āthār*, and one on hadiths he found legally or doctrinally problematic, the *Sharh mushkil al-āthār*. The Sufi Abū Bakr al-Kalābādhī (d. 384/994) wrote a commentary on a selection of hadiths he found morally and spiritually important, the *Bahr al-fawā'id* (Ocean of Benefits).

Local histories

From the late ninth century, scholars also began using hadiths as a medium for a less scholastic topic: narrating the history of their native city, its virtues, and the accomplishments of its inhabitants. These local histories formed part of the larger genre of biographical dictionaries that featured so prominently in Islamic civilization. In such works history is told through collective biography.

Local histories generally set forth the history of a city, the people associated with it and its role in the Islamic world. The introductory chapters on the virtues of the city usually included outrageously patriotic forged hadiths. In the eleventh century, al-Hākim al-Naysābūrī and Abū Nu'aym al-Isbahānī wrote local histories on their respective cities of Nishapur and Isfahan, both in Iran and both featuring this hadith: **'The people with the greatest destiny in Islam are the people of Persia** (*a'zam al-nās nasīban fī al-islām ahl fāris*).'[66] Local histories then generally list the famous inhabitants or visitors to the city in either chronological or alphabetical order, providing biographies for each entry.

Many local histories fit squarely within the genre of hadith literature because they focused on the lives and accomplishments of hadith scholars, describing the teachers from whom they heard hadiths and the students to whom they transmitted, and rating their reliability. Local histories also included vast arrays of hadiths. The earliest known local history is the history of Wāsit in southern Iraq (*Tārīkh Wāsit*) written by Aslam b. Sahl Bahshal (d. 292/905). The work includes many hadiths, including the only known narration of the hadith through Ibn Abbas in which the Prophet condemns speaking during the Friday prayer sermon.[67]

The most famous local histories rank among the largest books written in Islamic civilization. The *History of Baghdad* (literally, *The History of the City of Peace*, *Tārīkh madīnat al-salām*) of al-Khatīb al-Baghdādī (d. 463/1071) is fourteen printed volumes, while the mammoth *History of Damascus* (*Tārīkh madīnat Dimashq*) of Ibn 'Asākir (d. 571/1176) fills eighty! Since the authors of these two books include at least one hadith for each entry, with a full *isnād* from the author through the subject in question back to the Prophet, the *History of Baghdad* and the *History of Damascus* are actually two of the largest and most important hadith collections. As with *musnad*s and *mu'jam*s, their authors were unconcerned with the authenticity of hadiths in the books, and the works are thus indispensable sources for some of the rarest and most bizarre hadiths in circulation.

Forty hadith collections

One the most common and enduring forms of using hadiths as a medium for scholarly or pious expression has been books of *Arbaʿūn hadīth*, or 'Forty Hadith' books. Supposedly the first Forty Hadith book was composed by the early scholar Ibn al-Mubārak (d. 181/797) on the basis of a hadith that, although attributed to the Prophet through many narrations and permutations, Muslims have agreed is unreliable: **'Whoever memorizes for my community forty hadiths from my Sunna, I will be his intercessor on the Day of Judgment** (*man hafiza ʿalā ummatī arbaʿīn hadīthan min al-sunna kuntu lahu shafīʿan yawm al-qiyāma*).' Despite its unreliability, this hadith has served consistently as a catalyst in Islamic scholarly culture, and even Muslim scholars not known for any special interest in hadith have composed forty hadith collections on its basis. Among the non-hadith specialists who did so are the famous Shāfiʿī legal theorist al-Juwaynī (d. 478/1085) and the seminal Sufi theosopher Ibn Arabi (d. 638/1240). Some of the earliest known forty books are those of Ahmad b. Harb al-Naysābūrī (d. 234/848) and Ibrāhīm b. ʿAlī al-Dhuhlī (d. 294/905).[68]

Like *muʿjam*s, forty hadith collections could be tailored to display the elevation or rarity of a scholar's hadiths or be devoted to specific topics. Ibn ʿAsākir and al-Silafī had forty hadith collections with one hadith for each of the forty lands they had visited. Abū Nuʿaym al-Isbahānī composed one with forty hadiths important to Sufis and one with forty hadiths about the Messiah (*Mahdī*). Muhammad b. Abd al-Rahman al-Tujīnī of Morocco (d. 610/1213) wrote several forty hadith collections, including one on the topic of praying for the Prophet.

The most exorbitant displays of the breadth of a scholar's hadith corpus are certainly the forty hadith collections of Ibn al-Abbār (d. 658/1259) and Muhammad b. ʿAbd al-Wāhid al-Ghāfiqī (d. 619/1222), which were entitled 'Forty hadiths from forty different teachers from forty different books by forty different scholars via forty different *isnād*s to forty different Successors, from forty different Companions with forty different names from forty different tribes on forty different issues.'[69] Convinced that all possible forty-hadith-book themes had been exhausted, al-Hasan b. Muhammad al-Naysābūrī (d. 656/1258) replicated this same topic but also drew his forty hadiths from forty different forty-hadith collections![70]

One forty hadith book in particular, al-Nawawī's 'Forty Hadiths about the Principles of the Religion (*Arbaʿūn hadīth fī usūl al-dīn*)' is one of the most widely read books after the Quran among Sunni Muslims. It has served as an important tool for scholars to instruct the masses and has been the subject of numerous commentaries, such as the frequently studied *Jāmiʿ al-ʿulūm wa al-hikam* (Compendium of the Sciences and Wisdoms) of Ibn Rajab (d. 795/1392) and Ibn Hajar al-Haytamī's (d. 974/1566) *Fath al-mubin bi-sharh al-arbaʿīn*.

CONSOLIDATION AND ANALYSIS IN THE LATE SUNNI TRADITION

In the wake of the emergence of the hadith canon at the dawn of the eleventh century, a process of consolidation and analysis began in parallel with the continued transmission of hadith as a medium of connection to the Prophet. This consolidation and analysis entered a period of exceptional activity with the solidification of what we can refer to as the Late Sunni Tradition, or the version of Sunni orthodoxy that emerged in the 1300s and has characterized Islamic civilization in the Middle East and South Asia until the modern period. It consists of an institutional combination of the four Sunni schools of law, the Ashʿarī or Māturīdī schools of speculative theology, and Sufi brotherhoods. A Muslim scholar in the Late Sunni Tradition would loyally follow one of the established schools of law, one of the established schools of speculative theology, and participate in one or more Sufi brotherhoods.

Digest collections

The emergence of the hadith canon resulted naturally in the composition of digest collections that combined and consolidated the canon's contents into a more manageable form. The first digests addressed the core of the hadith canon: the two *Sahīh*s of al-Bukhārī and Muslim. An Andalusian who moved to Baghdad, Muhammad b. Futūh al-Humaydī (d. 488/1095) combined the *Sahīhayn* into one book, noting any material that one of the two books featured apart from the other. Zayn al-Dīn al-Zabīdī (d. 893/1488) later wrote a small one-volume digest of all the hadiths of *Sahīh al-Bukhārī*, called *Tajrīd al-Sahīh* (Stripping Down the *Sahīh*), that removed *isnād*s and any repetitions.

Ibn Razīn al-Saraqustī (d. 524/1129) of Saragossa produced a more thorough digest of what he perceived as the hadith canon: the *Sahīhayn* and the books of Abū Dāwūd, al-Nasā'ī, al-Tirmidhī and Mālik. The Syrian Ibn al-Athīr (d. 606/1210) replicated this work in his large and very popular *Jāmi' al-usūl min ahādīth al-rasūl*, a copy of which the great Mongol grand vizier Rashīd al-Dīn (d. 718/1318) ordered to be placed in the mosque he endowed as a counterpart to the Quran. The famous scholar of Baghdad, Ibn al-Jawzī (d. 597/1201), compiled a digest collection reflecting his loyalty to the Hanbali school; his *Jāmi' al-masānīd* combined the hadiths of the *Sahīhayn*, the *Sunan* of al-Tirmidhī, and the *Musnad* of Ibn Hanbal.[71]

Ibn Athīr's *Jāmi' al-usūl* was a huge, multivolume work. Other digests were meant to be portable, easily thumbed-through personal handbooks. Al-Husayn al-Baghawī (d. 516/1122), known as 'the Reviver of the Sunna,' wrote his one-volume *Masābīh al-sunna* (Lamps of the Sunna) for this purpose. He digested the canon into 4,434 hadiths, half of them from the *Sahīhayn*.[72] Organized topically, each chapter is divided into *sahīh* and the *hasan* (see next chapter for discussion of these terms) hadiths. The work is so small because the author omitted the *isnād*s, relying on the reputation of the books he drew on to vouch for the reliability of the hadiths.[73] Muhammad al-Khatīb al-Tabrīzī (d. *c.* 737/1337) added 1,511 hadiths to al-Baghawī's work in his expanded digest, the *Mishkāt al-masābīh* (Niche of the Lamps). The *Mishkāt* became a standard hadith textbook for Muslim religious students, especially in India, and was the subject of several commentaries, including the famous *Mirqāt al-mafātīh sharh Mishkāt al-masābīh* of Mullā 'Alī Qārī.

Supplemental collections

The Six Books contained approximately 19,600 traditions altogether (around 35,000 with repetitions), but vast numbers remained in other works. While digest works sought to consolidate the material within the canon, supplemental collections (*kutub al-zawā'id*) brought material outside the canon within easy reach of scholars. In his *Majma' al-zawā'id*, the Cairene scholar Nūr al-Dīn al-Haythamī

(d. 807/1405) listed all hadiths from the *Musnads* of Ibn Hanbal, Abū Ya'lā al-Mawsilī, and al-Bazzār as well as the *Mu'jams* of al-Tabarānī that are not found in the Six Books, organized topically and without *isnāds*. Al-Haythamī also evaluated the transmitters in the *isnād* of each supplemental hadith (but, note, not necessarily the *authenticity* of the hadith itself!).[74] In his *Ithāf al- khayyira al-mahara bi-zawā'id al-masānīd al-'ashara,* Ahmad al-Būsīrī (d. 840/1436) performed the same service for the hadiths in the *Muwatta'*, the *Musnad* of al-Shāfi'ī, *Sunan al-Dārimī, Sunan al-Dāraqutnī, Sahīh Ibn Khuzayma, Sahīh Ibn Hibbān*, the *Muntaqā* of Ibn al-Jārūd, Abū 'Awāna's *Mustakhraj* of *Sahīh Muslim*, the *Mustadrak* of al-Hākim, and the *Sharh ma'ānī al-āthār* of al-Tahāwī. In his *Matālib al-'āliya bi-zawā'id al-masānīd al-thamāniya*, the great Ibn Hajar al-'Asqalānī (d. 852/1449) added the hadiths from a wide selection of less well-known early *musnads*: those of al-Tayālisī, al-Humaydī, Ibn Abī 'Umar, al-Musaddad, Ahmad b. Manī', Ibn Abī Shayba, 'Abd b. Humayd, al-Hārith b. Abī Usāma, Ishāq b. Rāhawayh, and al-Rūyānī.[75]

With these supplemental collections at their disposal, Muslim scholars could easily reference hadiths outside the canonical collections as well as the rulings of major late hadith masters on their *isnāds*. Ibn Hajar attempted a comparable feat for *sahīh* hadiths. He compiled a work called *Zawā'id al-sunan al-arba'a mimmā huwa sahīh* (Supplements [to the *Sahīhayn*] from what is *Sahīh* from the Four *Sunan*), but it seems not to have survived (sadly).[76] The modern Yemeni scholar Muqbil b. Hādī al-Wādi'ī (d. 2001) performed a similar service in the modern period; in his *al-Jāmi' al-sahīh mimmā laysa fī al-Sahīhayn* he collected all the hadiths he deemed authentic but that are not found in al-Bukhārī's and Muslim's collections.

Mega-collections

Rather than collecting extra-canonical hadiths in manageable form, several late Sunni scholars attempted the more ambitious task of encompassing the whole hadith corpus in one book. The encyclopedic Shāfi'ī scholar of Egypt, Jalāl al-Dīn al-Suyūtī (d. 911/1505), sought to accomplish this after he had a dream in which the Prophet appeared to him and ordered him to 'Bring forth the Sunna! Bring forth the hadiths!'[77] Al-Suyūtī attempted this in his *Jam' al-jawāmi'* (Consolidation of Compendia), also known as his *Jāmi' al-kabīr*.

Tragically, al-Suyūṭī died before he completed this work, having collected some 100,000 hadiths in his draft. What survived has been published in thirty volumes. In this work, the author synthesized the contents of all the hadith collections available to him alphabetically according to the beginning of the hadith (*taraf*) along with its *isnād*. The book stops about nine tenths of the way through the alphabet, never reaching hadiths describing the Prophet's actions. While still working on this massive compendium, al-Suyūṭī took all the hadiths (10,031 in total) documenting Prophetic sayings (as opposed to actions), rated their authenticity (or most of them), and combined them in a one-volume work called *al-Jāmiʿ al-saghīr*. This work has become one of the most relied upon references for Muslim scholars not specializing in hadiths. Realizing he had omitted some material, al-Suyūṭī penned an addendum entitled *al-Ziyāda ʿalā al-Jāmiʿ al-saghīr*.

The Indian scholar ʿAlī b. ʿAbd al-Malik Muttaqī (d. 975/1567) took the *Jāmiʿ al-saghīr*, added hadiths that al-Suyūṭī had missed as well as hadiths describing the Prophet's actions and rearranged them all topically in his massive *Kanz al-ʿummāl fī sunan al-aqwāl wa al-afʿāl* (The Laborers' Treasure from the Spoken and Acted Sunna). The Egyptian ʿAbd al-Raʾūf al-Munāwī (d. 1031/1622) estimated that al-Suyūṭī had only succeeded in exhausting two thirds of the extant Prophetic sayings and objected to the widespread belief that if a hadith was not in the *Jāmiʿ al-kabīr* it did not exist. In his *al-Jāmiʿ al-azhar min hadīth al-nabī al-anwar*, al-Munāwī therefore added in Prophetic sayings that al-Suyūṭī had missed and also completed the work from where al-Suyūṭī had left off (at *man taraka* ...).[78] Other late scholars also complained about al-Suyūṭī's omissions; the Moroccan Abū ʿAlāʾ al-Fāsī (d. 1770–1) wrote in the margins of his copy of the *Jāmiʿ al-kabīr* over five thousand hadiths that al-Suyūṭī had missed.

*Indices/*Atrāf *collections*

One of the most practical genres of books produced in the consolidation movement was that of *atrāf*. The *taraf* (pl. *atrāf*) of a hadith was the first section of the *matn* or its most prominent section. If a scholar knew the text of the hadith and had no other information about it, an index of hadiths arranged according to *atrāf* would be the easiest way to find it. An *atrāf* work listed the *matn* of the hadith and then provided all its various chains of transmission and the books in which they appear.

As with other genres, *atrāf* collections took the *Sahīhayn* as the first subject. Abū Mas'ūd al-Dimashqī (d. 401/1010–11) and Khalaf al-Wāsitī (d. 400/1010) of Baghdad each wrote an *atrāf* work for the hadiths included in al-Bukhārī's and Muslim's collections, although their books were clearly not meant for people to use as accessible indices, since the works are organized along *musnad* lines and not alphabetically. The Mālikī scholar of Andalusia, 'Uthmān b. Sa'īd al-Dānī (d. 444/1053) also wrote an early *atrāf* of the hadiths in the *Muwatta'*.[79]

Ibn 'Asākir composed a more useful and ultimately widely copied *atrāf* work of the Five Book canon. Abū al-Fadl al-Maqdisī (d. 507/1113) wrote an *atrāf* book of the Six Books, but it was not widely used. Jamāl al-Dīn al-Mizzī (d. 742/1341) wrote a much more comprehensive *atrāf* of the Six Books (and several smaller, minor works) entitled *Tuhfat al-ashrāf bi-ma'rifat al-atrāf* (The Gem of the Noble for Knowing the *Atrāf*), which quickly became a mainstay for scholars. It contains 19,626 hadiths. Al-Mizzī's son-in-law, the famous Ibn Kathīr (d. 774/1373) (no doubt attempting to impress his in-laws), compiled his *Jāmi' al-masānīd wa al-sunan al-hādī li-aqwam al-sunan*, which added the *atrāf* of hadiths from the *musnad*s of Ibn Hanbal, al-Mawsilī, al-Bazzār, the *Mu'jam al-kabīr* of al-Tabarānī, and the *Ma'rifat al-sahāba* of Abū Nu'aym al-Isbahānī. Ibn Hajar al-'Asqalānī's *Ithāf al-mahara bi-atrāf al-'ashara* listed all the *atrāf* of the hadiths that al-Būsīrī had included in his *Ithāf al-khayyira* (see above section on Supplemental Collections).

Ahkām al-hadīth *works*

This genre included many fewer and less voluminous works than those composed in other genres discussed here but has exercised a significant influence on Islamic scholarship. *Ahkām al-hadīth*, or 'the laws derived from hadith' collections, were books that listed hadiths regularly used in deriving Islamic law along with their ratings and the collections in which they are found. *Ahkām al-hadīth* works also often included discussions of the hadiths' legal implications. This genre seems to have arisen in imitation of *ahkām al-Qur'ān* works, which addressed the legal implications of Quranic verses. The first *ahkām al-hadīth* books are *Ahkām* of the Andalusian scholar Ibn al-Tallā'

(d. 497/1104) and the *Ahkām al-sughrā* (Small *Ahkām*), *al-Ahkām al-wustā* (Medium *Ahkām*) and *al-Ahkām al-kubrā* (Large *Ahkām*) of the Andalusian jurist and hadith scholar Ibn al-Kharrāt al-Ishbīlī (d. 581/1185). The famously conservative Hanbali scholar of Jerusalem, 'Abd al-Ghanī al-Maqdisī (d. 600/1203), wrote the very influential *'Umdat al-ahkām* (The Foundation of Rulings), which was expanded and commented on by the Egyptian Ibn Daqīq al-'Īd (d. 702/1302) in his *Ihkām al-ahkām* (Bolstering the Rulings), which consisted of five hundred legal hadiths taken from the *Sahīhayn*. The leading Hanbali scholar Majd al-Dīn b. Taymiyya (d. 653/1255, the grandfather of the controversial reformer Taqī al-Dīn b. Taymiyya) wrote the three-volume *Muntaqā al-akhbār* (Choice Reports), but the most influential *ahkām al-hadīth* book has been the *Bulūgh al-marām min adillat al-ahkām* (Reaching the Aspiration for the Proofs of Legal Rulings) of Ibn Hajar al-'Asqalānī.

Ahkām al-hadīth books were written as references and teaching tools for Muslim scholars of religious law, but they became highly influential with the rise of the Salafī movements of revival and reform in the eighteenth century until today (see Chapter 10). These movements encourage a return to the original sources of Islam and highlight the importance of hadiths in Islamic law and dogma. As a result, in many cities of the Muslim world cheap pocket-copies of *Bulūgh al-marām* can be found in book stores as popular references for Muslims' daily lives. Two influential Yemeni scholars of the early modern period, Muhammad b. al-Amīr al-San'ānī (d. 1768) and Muhammad b. 'Alī al-Shawkānī (d. 1834) devoted their commentaries, *Subul al-salām sharh Bulūgh al-marām* and *Nayl al-awtār sharh Muntaqā al-akhbār*, to the *Bulūgh al-marām* and *al-Muntaqā* respectively. These commentaries have become frequently used references and textbooks for the study of Islamic law today.

QUOTING GOD: *HADĪTH QUDSĪ*

Hadiths in which the Prophet quotes God's speech constitute a species of hadiths known as 'holy hadiths (***hadīth qudsī***).' Famous ones include God saying 'Spend [in charity], O son of Adam, and I will spend on you ... (*anfiq yā ibn Ādam unfiq 'alayk. ...*).' Qudsī hadiths are distinguished from the Quran in that they are not considered to be the *literal* word of God. Only their meaning issues from God, while their wording comes from Muhammad. Muslims believe that they were not revealed via the intermediacy of the angel Gabriel, as the Quran was. Instead, the Prophet may have heard them during his Ascension to heaven (*Miʿrāj*), in a dream or through inspiration (*ilhām*).

Several scholars authored collections of *hadīth qudsī*: Ibn ʿArabī's (d. 638/1240) expanded Forty Hadith collection, the *Mishkāt al-anwār*, consisted of 101 *hadīth qudsī*, and the Yemeni Ibn al-Daybaʿ (d. 944/1537) also devoted a book to this type of report.[80] ʿAbd al-Ra'ūf al-Munāwī wrote a collection entitled *al-Ithāfāt al-saniyya bi'l-ahādīth al-qudsiyya* with 272 *qudsī* hadiths in it. Muhammad al-Madanī (d. 1786) added to that book, compiling a work with the same title that included some 863 hadiths.

SUGGESTIONS FOR FURTHER READING

The best Arabic editions of major Sunni hadith collections come from Tradigital's *Encyclopaedia of Hadith*, which includes the Six Books, the *Muwatta'*, and the *Musnad* of Ibn Hanbal (in particular, Tradigital has produced critical editions of the *Musnad* and the *Sunan* of Ibn Mājah), and from the Dār al-Ta'sīl publisher in Cairo. For *Sahīh Muslim*, however, the most critical edition has been published by Muhammad Zuhayr al-Nāsir through Dār al-Minhāj. There are several translations of major Sunni hadith collections. These include Mālik b. Anas's *Al-Muwatta of Imam Malik ibn Anas*, trans. Aisha Bewley (London: Kegan Paul Intl., 1989); an excellent translation of the first chapters of *Sahīh al-Bukhārī* entitled *Sahih al-Bukhari*, trans. Muhammad Asad (Lahore: Arafat Publications, 1938); a full translation can bc found in *The Translation of the Meanings of Sahīh Bukhārī*, trans. Muhammad Muhsin Khan (Riyadh: Darussalam, 1997); an abridgement of Muslim's *Sahīh* entitled *Sahih Muslim*, trans. Aftab Shahryar (New Delhi: Islamic Book Service, 2004); Abū Dāwūd's *Sunan*, trans. Ahmad Hasan (Lahore: Sh. Muhammad Ashraf, 1984); and the *Sunan* of al-Nasā'ī, *Sunan Nasā'ī*, trans. Muhammad Iqbal Siddiqi (Lahore: Kazi Publications, 1994); a selection of hadiths from al-Bukhārī's *al-Adab al-mufrad* entitled *Moral Teachings of Islam:*

Prophetic Traditions from al-Adab al-Mufrad (Walnut Creek, CA: Altamira Press, 2003); al-Nawawī's famous *Forty Hadiths*, trans. Ezzeddin Ibrahim and Denys Johnson-Davies (Cambridge, UK: Islamic Texts Society, 1997); al-Tabrīzī's *Mishkāt al-masābīh* in five volumes, trans. James Robson (Lahore: Sh. Muhammad Ashraf, 1963). A selection of *shamā'il* have been translated into English by Muhammad Zaynū as *al-Shamā'il al-muhammadiyya* (Fairfax, VA: Institute of Islamic and Arabic Studies, 1995). The Riyadh publisher Dar al-Salam has published passable translations of the entire Six Book Sunni hadith canon. Dar al-Salam has also translated Ibn Hajar's famous *ahkām al-hadīth* collection, *Bulūgh al-marām* (Riyadh, 1996). Al-Nawawī's *Riyād al-sālihīn* is translated as *The Gardens of the Righteous*, trans. Muhammad Zafrulla Khan (London: Curzon Press, 1975).

An Indian hadith scholar, Shāh 'Abd al-'Azīz (d. 1824), wrote a history of hadith literature from a Muslim perspective; it is published as *The Gardens of Hadith Scholars*, trans. Aisha Bewley (Santa Barbara, CA: Turath Publishing, 2007). Although it is part of the *sīra* genre and not hadith proper, the famous biography of the Prophet edited by Ibn Hishām has been translated: *The Life of Mohammad*, trans. A. Guillaume (New York: Oxford University Press, 1978).

For discussions of the debates over writing hadiths and the importance of orality in early Islamic history, see Michael Cook's, 'The Opponents of the Writing of Tradition in Early Islam,' *Arabica* 44 (1997): 437–530; and Gregor Schoeler's *The Oral and the Written in Early Islam*, trans. Uwe Vagelpohl (New York: Routledge, 2006). For an excellent discussion about the importance of the *isnād* in Islam as a paradigm of connection, see William Graham's 'Traditionalism in Islam: An Essay in Interpretation,' *Journal of Interdisciplinary History* 23, 3 (1993): 495–522 and Garrett Davidson's *Carrying on the Tradition: An Intellectual and Social History of Post-Canonical Hadith Transmission* (Brill, 2018). For a study of hadith *qudsī*, see William Graham, *Divine Word and Prophetic Word in Early Islam* (The Hague: Mouton, 1977). For a study of the early transmission of hadiths, see Scott Lucas, *Constructive Critics: Ḥadīth Literature and the Articulation of Sunnī Islam* (Leiden: Brill, 2004). For a new study on hadith commentary, see Joel Blecher's *Said the Prophet of God* (University of California Press, 2018).

ENDNOTES

1 Ibn 'Abd al-Barr, *Jāmi' bayān al-'ilm wa fadlihi*, vol. 2, p.36.
2 Muhammad Abū Zahra, *Ibn Hanbal*, p. 239. For the original quote, see 'Abdallāh b. Ahmad, *Masā'il al-imām Ahmad Ibn Hanbal riwāyat ibnihi*, p. 438; al-Makkī, *Qūt al-qulūb*, vol. 1, p. 177.
3 'Abdallāh al-Ghumārī, *Tawjīh al-'ināya li-ta'rīf 'ilm al-hadīth riwāya wa dirāya*, p. 7.
4 Shams al-Dīn al-Sakhāwī, *Fath al-mughīth*, vol. 4, p. 103.
5 Yahyā Ibn Ma'īn, *Kitāb al-'ilal wa ma'rifat al-rijāl*, p. 19.
6 Al-Sakhāwī, *Fath al-mughīth*, vol. 4, p. 103.
7 Ibn Hajar al-'Asqalānī, *Fath al-bārī sharh Sahīh al-Bukhārī*, vol. 11, p. 466. The Egyptian scholar 'Abd al-Ghanī b. Sa'īd (d. 409/1019) found four hadiths with four Companions narrating from one another in the *isnād*; ibid., vol. 13, p. 15.
8 Al-Sakhāwī, *Fath al-mughīth*, vol. 4, p. 103.
9 Hammām b. Munabbih, *Sahīfat Hammām b. Munabbih*. Scholars like Juynboll have questioned the historicity of Hammām b. Munabbih, since he would have had to have lived eighty or ninety years to play his supposed part in transmitting this *sahīfa*. But that is not an outrageously long lifespan, considering that St. Antony of Egypt (d. 365) lived to ninety-four.
10 *Sunan Abī Dāwūd*: *kitāb al-'ilm, bāb fī kitāb al-'ilm.*
11 Al-Khatīb al-Baghdādī, *Taqyīd al-'ilm*, p. 96.
12 *Sunan Abī Dāwūd*: *kitāb al-'ilm, bāb fī kitāb al-'ilm.*
13 Muhyī al-Dīn al-Nawawī, *Sharh Sahīh Muslim*, vol. 1, p. 357, al-Dhahabī, *Siyar*, vol. 3, p. 81.
14 Ibn Abī Hātim al-Rāzī, *al-Jarh wa al-ta'dīl*, vol. 6, p. 336.
15 Al-Khatīb, *al-Jāmi'*, vol. 2, p. 85.
16 Ibn Sa'd, *al-Tabaqāt al-kubrā*, vol. 7, p. 448.
17 *Sahīh al-Bukhārī*: *kitāb al-'ilm, bāb kayfa yuqbad al-'ilm*; Nabia Abbott, *Studies in Arabic Literary Papyri II: Qur'ānic Commentary and Tradition*, vol. 2, p. 26.
18 Abū Khaythama Zuhayr b. Harb, *Kitāb al-'ilm*, p. 32; al-Khatīb, *al-Jāmi'*, vol. 2, pp. 71, 78–79.
19 Ibid., vol. 2. p. 81.
20 Muhammad Abd al-Rauf, '*Ḥadīth* Literature – I: The Development of the Science of *Ḥadīth*,' p. 273; Abū al-Hasan 'Alī al-Qābisī, *Muwatta' al-imām Mālik*.
21 Harald Motzki, 'The *Muṣannaf* of 'Abd al-Razzāq al-Ṣan'ānī as a Source of Authentic *Aḥādīth* of the First Century A.H,' pp. 3–4.
22 Ibn Abī Hātim al-Rāzī, *al-Taqdima*, pp. 31–32.
23 Ibn Nuqta, *Kitab al-Taqyīd li-ma'rifat ruwāt al-sunan wa al-masānīd*, p. 161. For details on the numbers of hadiths in the *Musnad*, see Christopher Melchert, 'The *Musnad* of Aḥmad Ibn Ḥanbal,' pp. 32–51.
24 *Musnad Ibn Hanbal*, vol. 6, p. 269.
25 See Muhammad Abd al-Rauf, '*Ḥadīth* Literature – I: The Development of the Science of *Ḥadīth*.'
26 Tāj al-Dīn al-Subkī, *Tabaqāt al-shāfi'iyya al-kubrā*, vol. 2, p. 221.
27 Ibn Hajar al-'Asqalānī, *Huda al-sārī*, p. 661. The number of chapters (*kitāb*) in al-Bukhārī's *Sahīh* varies depending on recension (*riwāyāt*) of the book, though the content remains the same. The recension of Abū Dharr al-Harawī,

for example, has numerous chapters that only appear as subchapters (*bāb*) in others. The valuable copy made by al-Buqāʿī in the fifteenth century has seventy-three chapters, while the authoritative Sultāniyya-Amīriyya edition, printed by the Ottoman sultan in 1895, has only forty three. Editions today are based on the Dutch scholar AJ Wensinck's formatting of ninety-eight chapters.

28 Shams al-Dīn al-Dhahabī, *Siyar aʿlām al-nubalā'*, vol. 13, p. 279.
29 *Sahīh Muslim*: *muqaddima*, introduction.
30 Abū Dāwūd al-Sijistānī, 'Risālat al-imām Abī Dāwūd al-Sijistānī ilā ahl Makka fī wasf Sunanihi,' p. 46.
31 Qādī 'Iyād, *Kitāb al-shifā*, p. 153.
32 'Abdallāh b. Ahmad b. Hanbal, *Kitāb al-sunna*, p. 301; Muhammad Zāhid al-Kawtharī, *Maqālāt al-Kawtharī*, p. 404.
33 Ibn Hanbal, *Kitāb fadā'il al-sahāba*, vol. 2, p. 665.
34 Abū Zurʿa al-Rāzī, *Abū Zurʿa al-Rāzī wa juhūduhu fī al-sunna al-nabawiyya*, p. 2:674–676; Jonathan A. C. Brown, *The Canonization of al-Bukhārī and Muslim*, pp. 92–94.
35 Ibn Manda, *Shurūt al-a'imma*, pp. 67–68.
36 Ibn 'Asākir, *Tārīkh madīnat Dimashq*, vol. 58, p. 93.
37 Brown, *The Canonization of al-Bukhārī and Muslim*, p. 9. See also Brown, 'The Canonization of Ibn Majah: Authenticity vs. Utility in the Formation of the Sunni Hadith Canon,' *Revue des mondes musulmans et de la Méditerranée* 129, July (2011): 169–81.
38 Muhammad b. Idrīs al-Shāfiʿī, *al-Risāla*, pp. 42–43.
39 Brown, *The Canonization of al-Bukhārī and Muslim*, pp. 340–345.
40 Ibid., pp. 255–260.
41 Al-Dhahabī, *Tadhkirat al-huffāz*, vol. 3, pp. 50, 111.
42 Ibn Nuqta, *al-Taqyīd li-maʿrifat ruwāt al-sunan wa al-masānīd*, p. 123.
43 See Fuat Sezgin, *Geschichte des arabischen Schrifttums*, vol. 1, pp. 414–416.
44 Al-Dhahabī, *Tadhkirat al-huffāz*, vol. 3, p. 25.
45 Ibn al-Nadīm, *The Fihrist*, p. 560.
46 I thank my colleague Scott Lucas for this number.
47 Ibn al-Salāh, *Muqaddimat Ibn al-Salāh*, p. 307.
48 Muhammad b. 'Abd al-Karīm al-Rāfiʿī, *al-Tadwīn fī akhbār Qazwīn*, vol. 1, pp. 291, 452.
49 Al-Khatīb, *Tārīkh Baghdād*, vol. 4, pp. 293–294; al-Dhahabī, *Mīzān al-iʿtidāl fī naqd al-rijāl*, vol. 1, pp. 511–512.
50 Brown, *The Canonization of al-Bukhārī and Muslim*, pp. 63–64.
51 Al-Rāfiʿī, *al-Tadwīn fī akhbār Qazwīn*, vol. 3, p. 131.
52 'Abd al-Rahmān b. Sulaymān al-Ahdal, *al-Nafas al-yamānī*, p. 63.
53 Muhammad b. Khayr al-Ishbīlī, *Fahrasat mā rawāhu ʿan shuyūkhihi*, pp. 17 ff. See also Zayn al-Dīn al-ʿIrāqī, *Al-Bāʿith ʿalā al-khalās min hawādith al-qussās*, p. 97.
54 Al-Nawawī, *Sharh Sahīh Muslim*, vol. 1, p. 119. Abū Tālib al-Makkī, *Qūt al-qulūb*, vol. 1, p. 137.
55 Al-Suhrawardī, *ʿAwārif al-maʿārif*, vol. 1, pp. 49, 60.
56 Ahmad al-Ghumārī, *Al-Burhān al-jalī fī tahqīq intisāb al-sūfiyya ilā ʿAlī*, p. 3.
57 Al-Khalīlī, *Al-Irshād fī maʿrifat ʿulamā' al-hadīth*, p. 6.
58 Al-Khatīb, *Jāmiʿ akhlāq al-rāwī wa ādāb al-sāmiʿ*, vol. 1, p. 205.
59 Al-Tabaranī, *Al-Muʿjam al-saghīr*, p. 116.

60 Al-Suyūtī, *Jam' al-jawāmi'*, vol. 1, pp. 3–4.
61 Stefan Reichmuth, 'Murtaḍā al-Zabīdī (d. 1791) in Biographical and Autobiographical Accounts,' p. 75. The famous Sufi of Cairo, Shams al-Dīn al-Hanafī (d. 847/1443–4), also claimed to have had an *isnād* of two beings, one person and one *jinn*, to the Prophet; al-Sha'rānī, *al-Tabaqāt al-kubrā*, p. 438.
62 'Abdallāh al-Ghumārī, *Tawjīh al-'ināya*, p. 42.
63 Asma Sayeed, 'Shifting Fortunes: Women and Ḥadīth Transmission in Islamic History,' p. 277.
64 Brown, *The Canonization of al-Bukhārī and Muslim*, pp. 107–108.
65 See Ishaq, *India's Contribution to Hadith Literature*.
66 Abū Nu'aym al-Isbahānī, *Dhikr akhbār Isbahān*, vol. 1, p. 23.
67 Al-Wāsitī, *Tārīkh Wāsit*, p. 125.
68 Al-'Awd, *Al-Mu'īn 'alā ma'rifat kutub al-arba'īn*, p. 29.
69 Ibid., pp. 63, 153.
70 Ibid., p. 151.
71 Ibn al-Jawzī, *Kitāb al-qussās wa al-mudhakkirīn*, p. 146.
72 J. Robson, trans., *Miskhat al-Masabih*, vol. 1, p. xiii.
73 Al-Baghawī, *Masābīh al-sunna*, vol. 1, p. 2.
74 Ahmad al-Ghumārī, *Al-Mudāwī li-'ilal al-Jāmi' al-saghīr*, vol. 1, p.95.
75 Ibn Hajar al-'Asqalānī, *Al-Matālib al-'āliya fī zawā'id al-masānīd al-thamāniya*, vol. 1, p. 4.
76 Al-Suyūtī, *Nazm al-'iqyān*, p. 50.
77 Muhammad Nāsir al-Dīn al-Albānī, *Sahīh al-Jāmi' al-saghīr*, vol. 1, pp. 42–43; Najm al-Dīn al-Ghazzī, *al-Kawākib al-sā'ira*, vol. 1, pp. 228–9.
78 Al-Munāwī, *Al-Jāmi' al-azhar min hadīth al-nabī al-anwar*, vol. 1, p. 3.
79 Al-Kawtharī, *Maqālāt*, p. 173.
80 'Abd al-Rahmān b. Sulaymān al-Ahdal, *Al-Nafas al-yamānī*, p. 43.

3

THE METHODS AND HISTORY OF HADITH CRITICISM

INTRODUCTION: REPORTERS THEN AND NOW

Arabic and English textbooks introducing Islamic methods of hadith criticism begin with presenting the complex technical vocabulary (*mustalahāt*) of hadith critics as it was formalized after the thirteenth century. These books assume that by learning this set of terms students will understand how hadith criticism operated in the early Islamic period when scholars like al-Bukhārī and Muslim were compiling their *Sahīh*s. In reality, however, the critical methods of early Muslim hadith scholars were diametrically opposed to this later, rigid description. Theirs was an intuitive and commonsense way of trying to determine whether a report could be reliably attributed to a source or not – a method not unlike those employed by modern investigative reporters. To set the stage for our study of how Muslims tried to sift reliable from unreliable 'reports' from the Prophet, let us imagine a journalist working for a newspaper today.

If our reporter tells her editor that she has a major story about a senior political figure, the editor will ask her two questions: who is your source, and is your source corroborated? How could our reporter reply? She knows that certain sources are reliable for certain information. If the president's spokesperson announces that the president will make a visit to England, there is no need to double-check this information. Imagine, however, that the reporter has found a source who gives her rare and valuable information about an important issue but whom she as yet has no reason to trust. Our reporter is not going to stake her journalistic reputation on this one tip, but how does she determine the accuracy of her source's information?

Imagine that this source tells her that there has just been an earthquake in China. Our reporter would call her contacts in China to confirm. If these contacts tell her that indeed a quake had occurred, the source has been proven correct. If no one she spoke to had noticed anything, the source's story would be uncorroborated and our reporter would conclude that the source was unreliable. Suppose that next the source tells our reporter valuable information about the condition of the country's economy. Again, our reporter proceeds cautiously, so she conducts thorough research and finds that the source's information was correct. The source provides tips on a few more stories, and after checking out the information, our reporter finds that these stories are true as well. Eventually our reporter concludes that this source is reliable, and if the source provides a tip on a hot story in the future, the reporter will feel comfortable writing her story based on the source's testimony alone.

Reporters understand that the reliability of a source is based upon the accuracy of the information they provide. The best way to confirm the accuracy of a source is to check with other sources that have access to the same information and see if they agree. Corroboration 'is what turns a tip into a story.'[1]

These two pillars of modern journalism, the reliability of a source and determining the reliability of a source or story through corroboration, are familiar to us all in our daily lives. We all know people who pass on information reliably and others who tend to forget, lie, or exaggerate. We all instinctively seek out corroboration and know when it matters and when it does not. If a student is absent for a day of class in university and hears from a classmate that the professor has changed the date of the final exam, he or she will not be content to take the word of just one classmate; the student will ask other students who were also in that class. If no other students heard the professor make that announcement, he or she will have serious doubts about the information.

Another fact is equally evident to us in our daily lives: the contents of reports we hear have a strong influence on our view of their reliability and our confidence in their transmitters. If our reporter met a source who swore that he had seen a herd of flying elephants downtown, she would probably both disbelieve him and consider him unreliable from that point on. There are generally accepted standards of what is possible and impossible. Furthermore, we all have a sense of what is important information and what is not, and we treat this information accordingly. If our reporter hears a rumor that the president is about to announce a major change in the government's economic policy, she will want to verify this information before writing her story. If she hears that the president has changed his favorite dessert from ice cream to angel-food cake, she will probably be content to cite this information as is.

We must remember, however, that such notions of what is possible or impossible, important or unimportant, are culturally determined, and as such they may differ with time and place. If, in 1990, a student had come to class holding a small device they claimed contained any piece of music, information or published material one could think of, the professor would have called them delusional. Today professors compete daily for attention with such devices. If a professor in the US claimed to have eaten a great dog meat dinner at a specialized dog meat restaurant, students would think this was a disgusting joke. But if the professor had just flown in from China, where dog meat has long been 'a minor but regular part of the diet' and where an annual dog meat festival is held, he might be telling the truth.[2]

While modern reporters are charged with determining the veracity of stories about what is happening in the world today on the basis of contemporary sources, the architects of the Islamic hadith tradition were faced with a more daunting task: they had to establish a system of distinguishing between true and false stories about a man who had lived over a century earlier and whose revered status cast a commanding shadow over the entire Islamic tradition.

In this chapter we will discuss the origins, mechanics, and development of Sunni hadith criticism. We will divide its history into two periods: early hadith criticism, roughly 720–1000 CE, and later hadith criticism, from roughly 1000 CE to today. As in the previous chapter, notions of 'authenticity' and 'forgery' mentioned here refer to the judgment of Muslim scholars of hadith and not necessarily to that of modern Western historians.

THE PROBLEM OF HADITH FORGERY

The Prophet Muhammad is the single most dominant figure in the Islamic religious and legal tradition. From the time of his emigration to Medina to debates over Islam today, to disobey directly his established teachings has been to place oneself outside the Muslim community. Because the Prophet possessed such eminent authority, early Muslims looked to his legacy to support or legitimize their different schools of thought, beliefs, or political agendas. It seems that even during the Prophet's own lifetime he understood that people could misrepresent him. In one report, a man claiming to be the Prophet's representative established himself as the mayor of a small town in Arabia until the Prophet uncovered his hoax and punished him.[3]

The first crisis to afflict the Muslim community after the Prophet's death – the question of who would succeed him as religious and political leader – revolved around competing claims about the Prophet's words. The supporters of ʿAlī b. Abī Ṭālib argued that the Prophet had announced him as his successor, while those who affirmed the successive caliphates of Abū Bakr, ʿUmar, and ʿUthmān did not. In this and many other Islamic sectarian and political disagreements, all sides agreed on what the Prophet had said but disagreed on its implications. Both Sunnis and Shiites, for example, agreed that the Prophet had said that ʿAlī was to him what Aaron was to Moses, but they disagreed on whether that meant that ʿAlī should succeed the Prophet politically.

Actually forging reports about the Prophet also quickly became a problem. When civil war broke out openly between ʿAlī, then the fourth caliph to succeed the Prophet, and the then governor of Syria and future founder of the Umayyad dynasty, Muʿāwiya b. Abī Sufyān, both sides waged a propaganda war using the Prophet's words as ammunition. ʿAlī's supporters falsely claimed that Muhammad had said, **'If you see Muʿāwiya ascend my pulpit, then kill him,'** while Muʿāwiya's side countered by forging hadiths such as **'It is as if Muʿāwiya were sent as a prophet because of his forbearance and his having been entrusted with God's word'** (Muʿāwiya had served as one of the Prophet's scribes).[4] There are even reports from the early historian al-Madā'inī (d. 228/843) that Muʿāwiya encouraged the systematic forging and circulation of hadiths affirming the virtues of the other caliphs and Companions at ʿAlī's expense.[5]

In light of how quickly the Prophet's legacy became a tool to be manipulated by vying parties among Muslims, we should not be surprised at the veritable slogan of Muslim hadith criticism. It is the most widely transmitted hadith in all of Islam, with Muslim scholars counting between sixty and a hundred Companions transmitting it from the

Prophet: **'Whoever mispresents me intentionally, let him prepare for himself a seat in Hellfire.'**

During the lifetime of leading Companions like 'Umar b. al-Khattāb, 'Abdallāh b. Mas'ūd, or Anas b. Mālik, many of whom had been with the Prophet since his early days in Mecca, it was difficult to attribute something untrue to the Prophet without a senior Companion noticing. In fact, there are many reports documenting the Companions' vigilance against misrepresentations of the Prophet's legacy. 'Alī is quoted as requiring an oath from any Companion who told him a hadith from the Prophet that he himself had not heard.[6] When the Companion Abū Mūsā al-Ash'arī told 'Umar that the Prophet had said that if you knocked on someone's door three times and they did not answer you should depart, 'Umar demanded that he find another Companion to corroborate the report.[7]

On a number of occasions after the Prophet's death, his wife Aisha objected to hadiths that other Companions related. She rejected 'Abdallāh b. 'Umar's statement that the Prophet warned mourners that a dead relative would be punished for his family's excessive mourning over him because she believed that it violated the Quranic principle that 'No bearer of burdens bears the burdens of another' (Quran 53:38).[8] Sometimes she corrected Companions who had misunderstood what the Prophet had said. Abū Hurayra quoted the Prophet as saying that women, beasts and houses could be bad omens. When Aisha heard this she 'split in half in anger,' exclaiming that the Prophet had mentioned this, but only to explain that it was a pre-Islamic superstition condemned by the Quran.[9] Abū Hurayra's extensive efforts at hadith collection in particular drew the ire and concern of some leading Companions. There is one report that 'Umar b. al-Khattāb told him, 'Indeed, I say let the Prophet's words alone or indeed I'll send you back to the lands of [your tribe] Daws!'[10]*

Hadith forgery emerged as a blatant problem when the generation of Muslims who had known the Prophet well died off. With the death of the last major Companion, Anas b. Mālik, in Basra in 93/711 (the last Companion to die was Abū al-Tufayl 'Āmir b. Wāthila, who died between 100/718 and 110/728) lies about the Prophet quickly

* The early scholar al-Dārimī (d. 255/869) interpreted 'Umar's command 'Be frugal in narrating from the Prophet' to apply only to reports about his battles, not to hadiths about law and belief; *Sunan al-Dārimī*: intro chapters, *bāb man hāba al-futyā*.

multiplied. It is especially in the generation of the Successors that we begin seeing notebooks (*sahīfa*s) of hadiths, many supposedly narrated from Anas b. Mālik, filled with forged hadiths of a highly partisan or controversial nature.[11]

From that point onward the forgery of hadiths would be a consistent problem in Islamic civilization. The heyday of hadith forgery was the first four hundred years of Islamic history, when major hadith collections were still being compiled. As we discussed in the last chapter, by the late 1100s any hadith that entered circulation that had not already been recorded in some existing book was automatically deemed a forgery. In the great urban centers of Mamluk Cairo or Ottoman Istanbul in the fourteenth and fifteenth centuries, the masses might mistakenly think that a popular saying such as 'The Muslim community is sinful but its Lord is most forgiving (*umma mudhniba wa rabb ghafūr*)' was said by the Prophet, but in general hadith forgery had run its course.[12]

Political and sectarian conflicts were a major engine for hadith forgery. All the major political conflicts in classical Islamic history were accompanied by hadiths forged for propagandistic purposes. The Prophet's access to knowledge of the future provided endless possibilities in this realm. In one hadith, the Prophet supposedly tells his uncle 'Abbās, progenitor of the Abbasid dynasty, to look at the stars. The Prophet foretells, **'From your descendents a number like the number of the Pleiades will rule the Muslim community.'**[13] In one forged pro-Shiite hadith, the Prophet predicts that **'al-Husayn will be killed sixty years after my emigration to Medina,'** referring to the Umayyad caliph's massacre of the Prophet's grandson at Karbala in 61/680.[14] We have seen already that even in the twelfth century, an opponent of the Seljuq Turkish sultan Sanjar forged a hadith in which the Prophet predicted that, **'Sanjar will be the last of the non-Arab kings; he will live eighty years and then die of hunger.'**[15] In fact, in the early 1990s one Arab scholar claimed that he had found an old manuscript with a hadith predicting that 'A leader whose name is derived from the word "tree" (Bush, perhaps?) will invade and liberate a small hill fort (in Arabic, 'Kuwait').'[16]

Many hadiths were also forged in legal and theological debates. Here the Sunni/Shiite schism once again has certainly produced the largest numbers of propagandistic hadiths. Less well-known conflicts have also yielded countless forgeries. In the first half of the ninth century, when the Abbasid caliphate was trying to impose its rationalist beliefs on Sunni scholars like Ibn Hanbal by torturing or imprisoning anyone who would not uphold the belief that the Quran was God's created word and not an eternal part of His essence, pro-Sunni hadiths conveniently appeared in which the Prophet said, **'Whoever dies believing the Quran is created will meet God on Judgment Day with his head up his ass.'** In eighth-century debates over whether Muslims could wear pants as opposed to robes, a hadith appeared in which the Prophet said, **'O people, take pants as clothing, for indeed they are the most modest of clothes, especially for your women when they leave the house.'**[17] As legal schools solidified and competed with one another, forged hadiths appeared with statements such as **'There will be in my community a man named Abū Hanīfa, and he will be its lamp ... and there will be in my community a man named Muhammad b. Idrīs [al-Shāfi'ī] whose strife is more harmful than that of Satan.'** [18]

Hadiths were forged to give voice to all sorts of chauvinisms. Some were virulently racist, such as a forged hadith saying **'The black African, when he eats his fill he fornicates, and when he gets hungry he steals** (*al-zanjī idha shabi'a zanā wa idhā jā'a saraqa*).'[19] Others voiced civic pride, such as the hadith '**[The city of] Askalon [near modern-day Gaza] is one of the two Brides, from there God will resurrect people on the Day of Judgment** (*'Asqalān ihdā al-'arūsayn ...*)' or a whole Forty Hadith collection that one Ahmad b. Muhammad al-Marwazī (d. 323/934–5) forged about the virtues of the Iranian city of Qazvin.[20]

Another major source of forged hadiths was the popular storytellers (*qāss*, pl. *qussās*) who entertained crowds on the streets of metropolises like Baghdad. These storytellers would attribute Jewish, Christian, or ancient Persian lore to the Prophet. In one fantastic story, someone named Ishāq b. Bishr al-Kāhilī from Kufa told of the Prophet meeting an old man in the desert. The man claimed to be named Hāma, the great-grandson of Satan, and to have been alive since the days of Cain and Abel. In an account resembling a Rolling Stones song, he proceeds to tell Muhammad how he had met all the great prophets, from Noah to Jacob and Joseph. Moses had taught him the Torah, and Jesus had told him to convey his greetings to Muhammad, the messenger to come.[21]

A surprisingly large number of hadiths were forged and circulated by pious Muslims in an effort to motivate those around them both religiously and morally. One Abū 'Isma was asked by his contemporaries to explain how the hadiths he narrated from ʿIkrima, the disciple of the Companion Ibn ʿAbbās, about the virtues of reading different chapters of the Quran, were not narrated by any of ʿIkrima's other students. He replied that he had seen the people becoming obsessed with the legal scholarship of Abū Ḥanīfa and the *Sīra* of Ibn Isḥāq. He had forged these hadiths to try and steer people once again towards the Quran.[22]

Many of those who forged hadiths for these pious purposes were themselves revered saintly figures. The famous hadith critic Yaḥyā b. Saʿīd al-Qaṭṭān (d. 198/813) once said, 'I have not witnessed lying [about the Prophet] in anyone more than I have seen it in those known for asceticism and piety.'[23] A venerated saint of Baghdad, Ghulām Khalīl, was so beloved that on the day he died in 275/888–9 the markets of the city shut down. Yet when he was questioned about some dubious hadiths he narrated concerning righteous behavior, Ghulām Khalīl replied, 'We forged these so that we could soften and improve the hearts of the populace.'[24]

Certainly pious figures such as Ghulām Khalīl or the scholars of religious law understood the enormity of the sin of lying about their Prophet. How could they have contradicted their own mission of preserving his authentic teachings by doing so? Pious figures sometimes replied that the Prophet had forbidden the Muslims to lie *about* him, whereas they were lying *for* him. In the case of those early jurists who forged legal hadiths to support their school of law, it seems that they saw no contradiction between their actions and their commitment to preserving the Prophet's teachings. After all, as one famous hadith put it, '**The scholars are the inheritors of the prophets** (*al-ʿulamāʾ warathat al-anbiyāʾ*).' It was the scholars who interpreted the message of Islam as it faced new challenges and circumstances. Phrasing their conclusions about proper acts or beliefs in the formula of 'the Prophet said ...' was simply neatly packaging their authority as Muhammad's representatives. As one early jurist explained, 'When we arrived at an opinion through reasoning we made it into a hadith.'[25] Hadith critics, of course, found such excuses reprehensible.[26]

Not all forgery of hadiths was a malicious act. Early transmitters sometimes confused the opinions or statements of Companions with Prophetic hadiths, such as a rule expounded by numerous Companions: 'Ward off capital punishment from the Muslims as much as possible, and if there is some way out of it then let the person go, for it is better for the judge to err in mercy than in severity,' which some casual transmitters attributed to the Prophet. Sometimes the comments of one of the hadith's transmitters could be accidentally written as part of the hadith, a phenomenon that Muslim critics called *idrāj* (interpolation).

Often the words of scholars or saintly figures or simply popular sayings could be accidentally elevated to the status of Prophetic hadiths. The saying 'The love of the earthly life is the start of every sin (*hubb al-dunyā ra's kull khatī'a*)' was generally attributed to Jesus until it became confused with a Prophetic hadith.[27] A legal principle used by Muslim jurists, 'Necessities render the forbidden permissible (*al-darūriyyāt tubīhu al-mahzūrāt*)' was also accidentally attributed to Muhammad.[28] In the ninth century a hadith appeared saying **'Beware of flowers growing in manure, namely a beautiful woman from a bad family** (*iyyākum wa khadrā' al-diman* ...).' In this period another supposed hadith surfaced that **'Whoever says something then sneezes, what he says is true** (*man haddatha hadīthan fa-'atasa 'indahu fa-huwa haqq*).' Neither report had any basis in Prophetic hadiths.[29]

Forgery of Isnāds

Hadith forgery was not limited to inventing Prophetic sayings or attributing existing maxims to Muhammad. In light of the importance of the *isnād* to accessing authority in the Islamic tradition, *isnād* forgery was arguably more common than *matn* forgery. Equipping existing hadiths with one's own *isnād*s or constructing entirely new chains of transmission was known as 'stealing hadiths (*sariqat al-hadīth*)' or 'rigging *isnād*s (*tarkīb al-asānīd*).'

Today no one would look askance at someone who cited a hadith without mentioning its *isnād*. In the early Islamic period, however, *ahl al-hadīth* scholars or those who debated them could not cite a hadith without providing their own *isnād* for the report. A scholar who had heard about a hadith without a firm *isnād* or from a transmitter considered unreliable by the *ahl al-hadīth* critics could thus not credibly present his hadith in any discussion. Forging a new *isnād* offered a solution. 'Amr b. 'Ubayd (d. 144/761), who belonged to the Muslim rationalist camp known as the Mu'tazilites, whom the *ahl al-hadīth* considered their mortal enemies, was thus attacked for lying in his narration of the hadith **'He who carries weapons against us [Muslims] is not one of us** (*man hamala 'alaynā al-silāh fa-laysa*

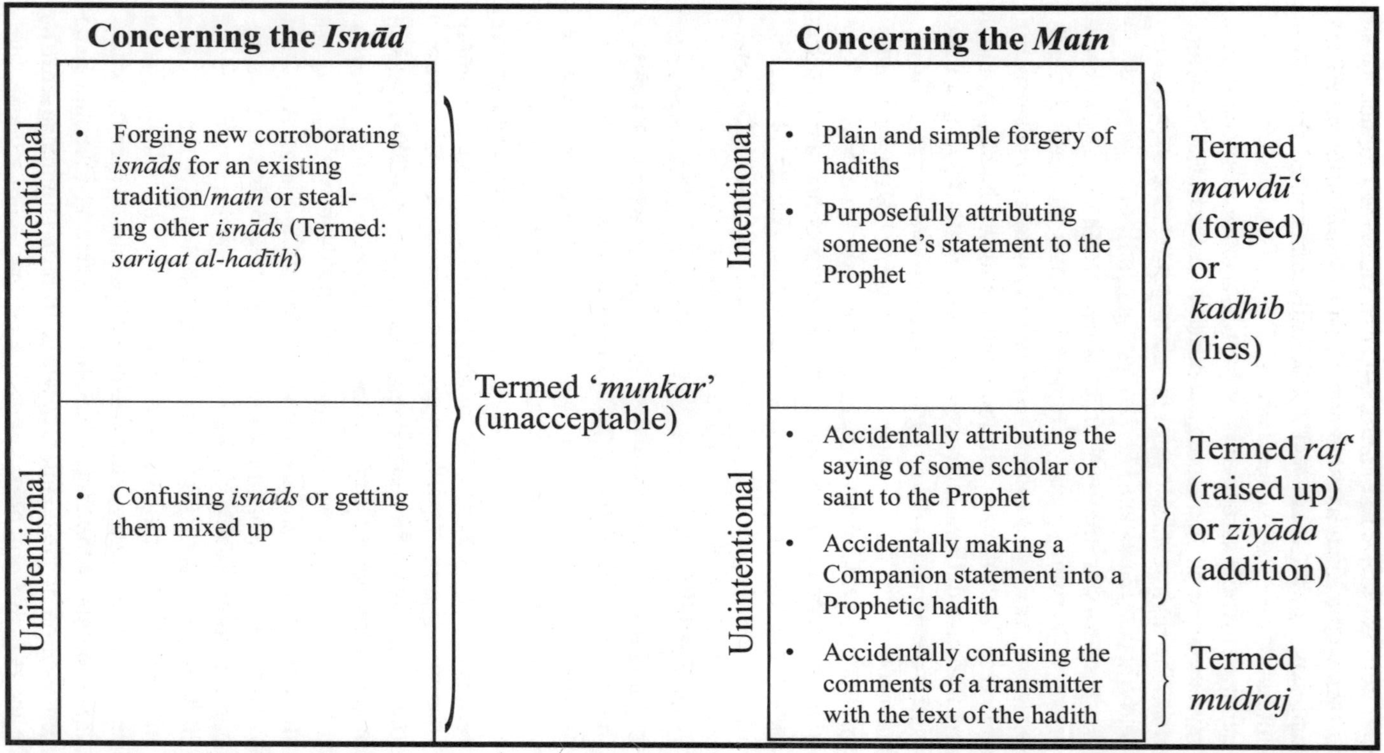
Concerning the *Isnād*
Intentional
Forging new corroborating *isnāds* for an existing tradition/*matn* or stealing other *isnāds* (Termed: *sariqat al-hadīth*)
Unintentional
Confusing *isnāds* or getting them mixed up
Termed '*munkar*' (unacceptable)
Concerning the *Matn*
Intentional
Plain and simple forgery of hadiths
Purposefully attributing someone's statement to the Prophet
Termed *mawdū'* (forged) or *kadhib* (lies)
Unintentional
Accidentally attributing the saying of some scholar or saint to the Prophet
Accidentally making a Companion statement into a Prophetic hadith
Termed *raf'* (raised up) or *ziyāda* (addition)
Accidentally confusing the comments of a transmitter with the text of the hadith
Termed *mudraj*

Figure 3.0 Types of Errors and Forgery in Hadiths

minnā)' from his teacher al-Hasan al-Basrī, from the Prophet. This hadith was well known as authentic among the *ahl al-hadīth*. The problem was that al-Hasan had not actually transmitted this from the Prophet. 'Amr b. 'Ubayd had heard of the report somewhere else and then tried to use it to support the Mu'tazilite position that committing grave sins assured Muslims a place in hell. But he did not have his own *isnād* for it. So he manufactured one from his teacher al-Hasan so that he could use it in debates.[30]

The second major motivation to forge an *isnād* for an existing hadith was to bolster its reliability by increasing evidence of its transmission. According to the great hadith critic of Baghdad, al-Dāraqutnī (d. 385/995), a whole notebook of hadiths praising human reason (*'aql*) was forged by Maysara b. 'Abd Rabbihi. This book was then taken by Dāwūd al-Muhabbir, who equipped the reports with his own new *isnād*s. One 'Abd al-'Azīz b. Abī Rajā' then stole these hadiths and provided them a new set of *isnād*s. Sulaymān b. 'Īsā al-Sinjarī then did the same. A person who came across the hadiths in this book therefore could find four different sets of *isnād*s leading to four different scholars for hadiths that were in fact total forgeries.[31]

Especially in the tenth century and afterwards, when rare and elevated *isnād*s assumed a particular value among hadith collectors, disingenuous scholars could forge *isnād*s with these characteristics. We already saw the hadith that al-Tabarānī (d. 360/971) narrated via the impossibly short *isnād* of three people to the Prophet: Ja'far b. Hamīd al-Ansārī ← 'Umar b. Abān ← Anas b. Mālik ← the Prophet. The fact that al-Tabarānī was the only hadith scholar to narrate from the transmitter Ja'far b. Hamīd strongly suggests that this Ja'far might have been a purveyor of forged elevated *isnāds*, which a collector like al-Tabarānī would have found irresistible.

THE DEVELOPMENT OF EARLY SUNNI HADITH CRITICISM – THE THREE-TIERED METHOD

As false attributions to the Prophet multiplied in the late seventh century, how were those Muslims who sought to preserve Muhammad's authentic legacy to distinguish between true and forged hadiths? While the *ahl al-ra'y* scholars in Iraqi cities like Kufa attempted to rise above the flood of forged hadiths by depending on the Quran, well-established hadiths, and their own legal reasoning, the school that would give birth to the Sunni tradition, the *ahl al-hadīth*, evolved the three-tiered approach to determining the authenticity of a hadith. The first tier was demanding a source (*isnād*) for the report, the second evaluating the reliability of that source, and the third seeking corroboration for the hadith.

The processes of this three-tiered critical method did not emerge fully until the mid eighth century with critics like Mālik b. Anas and Shu'ba b. al-Hajjāj. Certainly, Successors like al-Zuhrī and even Companions had examined critically material they heard attributed to the Prophet. Moreover, the critical opinions of Successors would inform later hadith critics. A formalized system of requiring *isnād*s and investigating them according to agreed conventions and through a set of technical terms, however, did not appear until the time of Mālik.

STEP ONE: THE *ISNĀD*

The *isnād*, or 'support,' was the essential building-block of the hadith critical method. So essential would the *isnād* be to the Sunni science of hadith criticism that it became the veritable symbol of the 'cult of authenticity' that is Sunni Islam. One of the most oft-repeated slogans among hadith critics comes from the famous scholar Ibn al-Mubārak (d. 181/797), who said, 'The *isnād* is part of religion, if not for the *isnād*, whoever wanted could say whatever they wanted. But if you ask them, "Who told you this?" they cannot reply.' The great jurist al-Shāfi'ī provided a similarly famous declaration, 'The person who seeks knowledge without an *isnād*, not asking "where is this from?" indeed, he is like a person gathering wood at night. He carries on his back a bundle of wood when there may be a viper in it that could bite him.' Sunnis thus understood the *isnād* as the prime means of defending the true teachings of the Prophet against heretics as well as protection from subtle deviations that might slip into Muslims' beliefs and practice.[32]

The origins of the *isnād* were as commonsense as its function, beginning with the rise of hadith forgery. As the Successor Muhammad b. Sīrīn (d. 110/729), a leading student of the Companion Anas b. Mālik, explained:

Period 1 100–200 AH / 720–820 CE
First Generation:
- Early Critics: al-Zuhrī, al-Aʿmash

Second Generation:
- Primary Critics: Shuʿba, al-Thawrī, al-Awzāʿī, Mālik, Ibn ʿUyayna
- Lesser Critics: Ibn Jurayj, Hammād b. Salama, al-Layth b. Saʿd, Hammād b. Zayd, Hushaym b. Bashīr

Third Generation:
- Primary Critics: Ibn al-Mubārak, Wakīʿ b. al-Jarrāh, Yahyā al-Qattān, ʿAbd al-Rahmān b. Mahdī
- Lesser Critics: al-Shāfiʿī, Abū Mushir ʿAbd al-Aʿlā b. Mushir

Period 2 200–300 AH / 820–910 CE
Fourth Generation:
- Primary Critics: Ibn Maʿīn, ʿAlī b. al-Madīnī, Ibn Hanbal
- Lesser Critics: Ibn Numayr, Abū Khaythama, Ibn Abī Shayba, Ibn Rāhawayh, Abū Hafs al-Fallās

Fifth Generation:
- Primary Critics: al-Bukhārī, Abū Zurʿa al-Rāzī, Abū Hātim al-Rāzī
- Lesser Critics: al-Jūzajānī, Muslim b. al-Hajjāj, al-Nasāʾī

Period 3 300–400 AH / 910–1010 CE
Sixth Generation
- Primary Critics: Ibn Abī Hātim al-Rāzī, Ibn ʿAdī
- Lesser Critics: al-ʿUqaylī, Ibn Hibbān

Seventh Generation
- Primary Critics: Abū al-Fath al-Azdī, al-Dāraqutnī, al-Hākim al-Naysābūrī

See Lucas, *Constructive Critics*, p. 125

Figure 3.1 Generations of Sunni Hadith Critics

> In the early period no one would ask about the *isnād*. But when the Strife [most probably the Second Civil War, 680–692CE] began they would say 'Name for us your sources' so that the People of the Sunna (*ahl al-sunna*) could be looked at and their hadiths accepted, and the People of Heresy (*ahl al-bidʿa*) could be looked at and their hadiths ignored.[33]

In the milieu of the early Islamic period, simply demanding an *isnād* for reports attributed to the Prophet was an excellent first line of defense against inauthentic material entering Muslim discourse. We can imagine the newly Muslim inhabitants of Kufa, still clinging to Christian or Zoroastrian lore, or even Bedouins eager to insinuate tribal Arab values into Islam, ascribing a saying to the Prophet as evidence for their ideas. If they provided no *isnād* at all, the reports would not enter the *musnad* collections of scholars like Abū Dāwūd al-Tayālisī. The formative critic Shuʿba b. al-Hajjāj (d. 160/776) is quoted as saying, 'All religious knowledge (*'ilm*) which does not feature "he narrated to me" or "he reported to me"[the components of the *isnād*] is vinegar and sprouts.'[34]

STEP TWO: RATING TRANSMITTERS AND ESTABLISHING CONTIGUOUS TRANSMISSION

On their own, however, *isnād*s could not deter a determined forger. As we saw with the hadiths on human reason, an *isnād* could be made up or inauthentic material simply equipped with one and then circulated. Moreover, merely requiring someone to provide a source for a hadith they cited did not tell you if that source was reliable. The second tier of criticism thus involved identifying the individuals who constituted *isnād*s, evaluating their reliability, and then determining if there were any risks that someone unreliable might also have played some part in transmitting the report.

1) Transmitter Evaluation

A hadith transmitter was evaluated according to two criteria. First, his or her character, correct belief, and level of piety were scrutinized in order to determine if he or she was 'upright (*ʿadl*).' Second, and much more importantly, the transmitter's corpus of reports and narration practices were evaluated to decide if he or she was 'accurate (*dābit*).'

Hadith transmitter criticism (known as *al-jarh wa al-taʿdīl*, 'impugning and approving') and *isnād* evaluation began in full with the first generation of renowned hadith critics, that of Shuʿba b. al-Hajjāj, Mālik b. Anas, Sufyān al-Thawrī, al-Layth b. Saʿd, and Sufyān b. ʿUyayna, who flourished in the mid to late eighth century in the cities of Basra, Kufa, Fustat (modern-day Cairo), Mecca, and Medina (see Figure 3.1). These scholars began the process of collecting people's hadith narrations and examining both their bodies of material and their characters to determine if the material they purveyed could be trusted. Mālik is the first scholar known to have used technical terms such as '*thiqa* (reliable)' to describe these narrators, while Shu'ba's evaluations did not utilize any specialized vocabulary.[35]

The evaluations of this first great generation were studied and added to by their students, especially the two great Basran critics 'Abd al-Rahmān b. Mahdī (d. 198/814) and Yahyā b. Sa'īd al-Qattān (d. 198/813). The later analyst Shams al-Dīn al-Dhahabī notes that 'whoever they both criticize, by God, rarely do you find that criticism refuted [by others], and whoever they both agree on as trustworthy, he is accepted as proof.'[36] The critical methods and opinions of Ibn Mahdī and al-Qattān passed on to their three most respected students, who can be seen as the beginning of the heyday of Sunni hadith criticism: Ibn Hanbal (d. 241/855) and his friend Yahyā b. Ma'īn (d. 233/848) in Baghdad and 'Alī b. al-Madīnī in Basra (d. 234/849). Their students refined hadith criticism into its most exact and lasting form: the 'Two Shaykhs' al-Bukhārī and Muslim, the two senior critics of Rayy (modern Tehran), Abū Zur'a al-Rāzī (d. 264/878) and his friend Abū Hātim al-Rāzī (d. 277/890), as well as influential younger critics of that generation such as al-Nasā'ī (d. 303/916).

The 900s saw several generations of critics who reviewed and reassessed the judgments of these earlier scholars and also continued to evaluate those involved in the ongoing transmission of hadiths: Ibn Abī Hātim al-Rāzī (d. 327/938), Ibn 'Adī (d. 365/975–6), Ibn Hibbān al-Bustī (d. 354/965), Abū al-Hasan al-Dāraqutnī (d. 385/995), and al-Hākim al-Naysābūrī (d. 405/1014).

Although the apex and most active period of hadith transmitter criticism is usually considered to be the eighth to tenth centuries, subsequent generations of critics contributed to this science as well. Hadiths were still transmitted with full *isnād*s into the early 1200s, so it was possible until that time for previously unrated hadiths to be in circulation among transmitters. Master hadith scholars like al-Khatīb al-Baghdādī (d. 463/1071) and Ibn 'Asākir (d. 571/1176) therefore continued to rate transmitters living in their times. Furthermore, they synthesized, reconciled, and reexamined existing opinions on earlier transmitters.

This reconsideration of earlier transmitters' standing has, in fact, never really ended. If we look at al-Dhahabī's list of the expert critics whose opinions should be heeded, we find that it continues until al-Dhahabī's own time in the 1300s. One of the most commanding critics in the Sunni hadith tradition, 'the Hadith Master (*al-ḥāfiẓ*)' Ibn Hajar al-'Asqalānī, died in 852/1449. Hadith transmitter criticism has continued until the modern day. This is possible because, as we shall see, determining if someone was reliable or not had little to do with any personal experience with their character, its flaws, or fine qualities. Ultimately, it was the analysis of the body of their transmissions for corroboration that determined their accuracy (*dabt*) and thus their station.

How would a hadith critic such as Shu'ba, al-Bukhārī, or Ibn 'Adī actually evaluate a transmitter? First, it was essential to know who this transmitter was. If one was presented with a hadith transmitted from 'someone,' 'Ahmad,' or 'a group of people in Medina,' how could one evaluate the strength of its *isnād*? By the mid 800s it had become accepted convention among hadith critics that a person needed two well-known transmitters to identify him sufficiently, prove that he existed and narrate hadiths from him in order to qualify for rating. Otherwise, the transmitter would be dismissed as 'unknown (*majhūl*)' and the report automatically considered unreliable.

Second, the critic would collect all the reports that the transmitter had narrated from various teachers and then analyze them for corroboration, a process known as 'consideration (*i'tibār*).' As mentioned last chapter, *musnad*s would be very useful for this task, but ultimately a critic would have to rely on a robust memory in order to recall all the different *isnād*s in which the transmitter in question played some part. For every hadith that the transmitter narrated from a certain teacher, the critic asks 'Did this teacher's other students narrate this report too?' If the critic finds that, for all the teachers that the transmitter narrates from, his fellow students corroborated him for a very high percentage of his hadiths, then he is considered to be reliable in his transmissions. When asked what kind of transmitters should be abandoned as unreliable, Shu'ba explained:

> Someone who narrates excessively from well-known transmitters what these well-known transmitters do not recognize, his hadiths are cast aside. And if he makes a lot of mistakes, his hadiths are cast aside. And if he is accused of forgery (*kadhib*), his hadiths are cast aside. And if he narrates a hadith that is agreed upon as an error, and he does not hold himself accountable for that and reject the report, his hadiths are cast aside.[37]

Muslim b. al-Hajjāj describes the telltale signs of a weak hadith transmitter as someone who, 'when his narrations are compared with those of people known for preservation [of hadith] and uprightness of character, his narrations do not concur with their narrations, or do so only rarely. If the majority of his hadiths are like that then he is rejected and not used in hadith.'[38]

Early hadith critics understood very well that no one transmitter was immune from error. Below the level of master transmitters, Ibn Mahdī described a lesser type of narrator 'who makes errors but most of his hadiths are *sahīh*. This kind of person's hadiths should not be abandoned, for if they were, all the people's hadiths would disappear.'[39]

Finally, the critic would examine the transmitter's character, religious beliefs, and piety in order to determine his 'uprightness (*'adāla*).' Although later legal theorists would establish very formal requirements for someone to be declared 'upright,' such as the requirement widely accepted by Sunnis after the 1200s that the transmitter be 'Muslim, of age, of sound mind, free of sinful behavior and defects in honor,' early hadith critics were actually very flexible with determining uprightness.

This is most evident in the issue of transmitters who espoused beliefs that Sunnis considered heretical, such as Shiism, belonging to the Kharijite sect, or a belief in free will (*qadar*). Although al-Shāfi'ī had declared that one could accept hadiths from transmitters regardless of their sectarian affiliations as long as they did not belong to certain Shiite sects that allowed lying, by the mid 900s scholars like Ibn Hibbān had declared a consensus among Sunni hadith critics that one could accept hadiths from any heretical transmitter provided he was not an extremist and did not actively try to convert others to his beliefs. In theory, this meant that one could accept hadiths from Shiite transmitters as long as they did not engage in virulently anti-Sunni practices such as cursing Abū Bakr or 'Umar or transmit hadiths that seemed to preach the Shiite message.

In truth, however, early hadith critics did not follow these strictures. As the eighteenth-century Yemeni hadith analyst Ibn al-Amīr al-San'ānī (d. 1768) observed, later theorists had set up principles that did not apply to the realities of early hadith criticism. Al-Bukhārī, the most revered of all hadith critics, narrated two hadiths in his famous *Sahīh* through the Kharijite 'Imrān b. Hittān, who was so extreme in his beliefs that he wrote a poem praising the Kharijite who murdered the fourth caliph ʿAlī. In his *Sahīh*, Muslim narrated the hadith that **'Only a believer loves 'Alī, and only a hypocrite hates him'** through the known Shiite transmitter ʿAdī b. Thābit. As we can see, the two uncontested masters of Sunni hadith criticism could narrate hadiths that they considered authentic through extremists and heretics who proselytized for their cause!

The explanation for this lies in the priorities of the early hadith critics. Simply put, if a transmitter consistently and accurately passed on hadiths he had heard from the previous generation, hadith critics had little interest in his beliefs or practice. Ibn Maʿīn described the Shiite transmitter ʿAbd al-Rahmān b. Sālih as 'trustworthy, sincere, and Shiite, but who would rather fall from the sky than misrepresent half a word.'[40] One major early hadith transmitter, Ismāʿīl b. ʿUlayya (d. 193/809), became so shamefully intoxicated on one occasion that he had to be carried home on a donkey. Yet he was a reliable transmitter, so his hadiths were accepted.[41] Although later theorists of the hadith tradition would talk of the two pillars of reliability as 'uprightness (*ʿadāla*) and accuracy (*dabt*),' al-Sanʿānī rightly pointed out that one should reorder them 'accuracy and uprightness,' since the former greatly outweighed the latter.[42]

Ultimately, Sunnis could not escape their dependency on the role of 'non-Sunnis' in hadith transmission. The early critic Ibn Saʿd (d. 230/845) notes how one Khālid al-Qatwānī was a staunch Shiite but that hadith scholars 'wrote down his hadiths out of necessity.'[43] Without such 'heretics,' critics knew that few hadiths would ever have been transmitted.

Guaranteeing the transmitter's 'uprightness (*ʿadāla*),' however, did have an important function. Regardless of a transmitter's accuracy, if they were known to have intentionally misrepresented the Prophet or forged a hadith then they could not be trusted. Sulaymān b. Dāwūd al-Shādhakūnī (d. 234/848–9), for example, was considered to have the most prodigious memory of hadiths in his time and one of the biggest hadith corpora. Yet he was known to have lied about hadiths and altered them to fit certain situations, so he was excluded from transmission. Al-Shādhakūnī was so untrustworthy that when he awed a gathering by claiming that he knew a hadith from Rayy that Abū Zurʿa al-Rāzī did not know, people believed that he had just made it up on the spot to impress them.[44]

Although in the eighth and ninth centuries each hadith critic used slightly different and sometimes shifting terms to describe a transmitter's level of reliability, by the early tenth century a conventional jargon had emerged. Ibn Abī Hātim al-Rāzī (d. 327/938) lists the levels as:

1. 'Reliable' (*Thiqa, mutqin, thabt*) → transmitter's hadiths can be used as proof in legal scholarship with no hesitation
2. 'Sincere' (*sadūq, lā ba's bihi*) → transmitter's hadiths are recorded and can be taken as proof if bolstered or corroborated
3. 'Venerable' (*shaykh*)
4. 'Righteous' (*sālih*)
5. 'Lenient on hadith' (*layyin al-hadīth*)
6. 'Not strong' (*laysa bi-qawī*)
7. 'Weak' (*da'īf*)

   } transmitter's hadiths are used for identifying corroboration depending on strength
8. 'Liar, abandoned' (*matrūk al-hadīth, dhāhib al-hadīth, kadhdhāb*) → the transmitter's hadiths are not used at all.[45]

Books of transmitter criticism

Hadith transmitter criticism often took place in discussion sessions among critics or with their students, but its results were set down by master critics in dictionaries of transmitter evaluation (*kutub al-rijāl*). Early works include the *Tabaqāt al-kubrā* (The Great Book of Generations) of Ibn Sa'd (d. 230/845), the *Ahwāl al-rijāl* (Conditions of the Transmitters) of al-Jūzajānī (d. 259/873), the massive 'Great History (*al-Tārīkh al-kabīr*)' of al-Bukhārī, and the *Jarh wa al-ta'dīl* of Ibn Abī Hātim al-Rāzī. Some books focused specifically on discussing transmitters whom the author felt were reliable; these included al-'Ijlī's (d. 261/875) *Tārīkh al-thiqāt* and Ibn Hibbān's *Kitāb al-thiqāt*. Voluminous books were devoted to listing and discussing weak transmitters as well. The most important are the *Kitāb al-du'afā' al-kabīr* of al-Bukhārī (now lost), the *Kāmil fī du'afā' al-rijāl* of Ibn 'Adī and Ibn Hibbān's *Kitāb al-majrūhīn*. Such works presented critics' opinions of a transmitter along with a selection of the unacceptable narrations that they transmitted. Because they consistently evaluated the reliability of personalities they mention, local histories like al-Khatīb's *History of Baghdad* are also works of transmitter criticism.

In the period of consolidation and analysis from the 1300s to the 1600s, later critics amalgamated and digested these earlier works of hadith criticism. 'Abd al-Ghanī al-Maqdisī (d. 600/1203) wrote his *al-Kamāl fī ma'rifat asmā' al-rijāl* (The Perfection in Knowing the

Names of Transmitters), presenting earlier descriptions and evaluations of all the transmitters in the Six Books. Jamāl al-Dīn al-Mizzī (d. 742/1341) added to this work and further analyzed the ratings of the transmitters within the Six Books in his *Tahdhīb al-kamāl* (The Refinement of Perfection), published today in thirty-five volumes. Ibn Hajar al-ʿAsqalānī produced an abridgement of this work with his own comments entitled *Tahdhīb al-tahdhīb* (The Refinement of the Refinement). Scholars like the Egyptian Ibn al-Mulaqqin (d. 804/1401) added the transmitters found in other hadith collections such as the *Musnad*s of Ibn Hanbal and al-Shāfiʿī as well as the *Sahīh* of Ibn Khuzayma and the *Mustadrak* of al-Hākim to expanded versions of al-Mizzī's book. The Hanafī scholar of Cairo, Badr al-Dīn al-ʿAynī (d. 855/1451), devoted a *rijāl* work to the transmitters in al-Tahāwī's collections.

Other later analysts focused on the subject of weak transmitters. Shams al-Dīn al-Dhahabī wrote his masterful *Mīzān al-iʿtidāl fī naqd al-rijāl* (The Fair Scale for Criticizing Transmitters), collecting all the information on any transmitter impugned by earlier figures. Ibn Hajar added his own comments in a revision of this work, *Lisān al-mīzān* (The Pointer of the Scale).

As we saw in the last chapter, the *isnād*s *to* hadith books could affect the reliability of hadiths in them, especially during the ninth and tenth centuries. Scholars like Ibn Nuqta of Baghdad (d. 629/1231) therefore wrote books of transmitter criticism addressing the people who conveyed books from their authors. Ibn Nuqta's *al-Taqyīd fī maʿrifat ruwāt al-sunan wa al-masānīd* and Abū ʿAlāʾ al-Fāsī's (d. 1770) addendum to that book are examples of this genre.

Reconciling disagreements among critics

With the plethora of transmitter critics from the eighth century on, how was a later critic or analyst supposed to know whose opinion to take on the reliability of a narrator or a hadith? Ibn Ishāq (d. 150/767), for example, the author of the famous biography of the Prophet, was a very controversial figure. Mālik, Ibn al-Qattān, Ibn Hanbal, and others considered him highly unreliable because he accepted hadiths from questionable narrators as well as Christians and Jews. But Shuʿba felt he was impeccably reliable, ʿAlī b. al-Madīnī named him one of the pivots of hadith transmission in his age, and all the Six Books except *Sahīh al-Bukhārī* relied on him as a narrator. Certainly, this created a great potential for disagreement over the reliability of transmitters and, hence, of hadiths themselves.

To a certain extent, such disagreement was the inevitable result of the complicated careers of transmitters and the contrasting critical thresholds of the many individual analysts examining them and their reports. One critic could change his mind about a transmitter, as al-Bukhārī did when he reduced Muhammad b. Humayd al-Rāzī's rating from 'good' to 'weak.' As the hadith scholar al-Ismā'īlī (d. 371/981) noted, critics often rated transmitters in relation to certain of their teachers. So a critic might describe a transmitter positively in one place and negatively in another.[46]

In general, however, later analysts erred on the side of caution and operated on the principle that 'criticism supersedes approval provided that the reason for the criticism is provided.' There were limits to this, however. Scholars who had personal vendettas against one another – Mālik's criticism of Ibn Ishāq was the result of a well-documented personal feud between them – were not accepted as fair critics of one another.

Later analysts were often aware of such issues and took earlier critics' idiosyncrasies and personal leanings into consideration. Al-Jūzajānī was known to have a vehement dislike for Shiism, so any rejection by him of a transmitter as 'a heretical Shiite' was probably an overstatement. If he approved of a transmitter, however, it meant that he was certainly free of any Shiite tendencies. Abū Hātim al-Rāzī was well known as a very stringent critic – even the seminal legal and hadith scholar al-Shāfi'ī had only merited a 'sincere (*sadūq*)' rating with him. Ibn Ma'īn was very harsh – once calling a narrator who criticized a Companion a 'sucker of his mother's clitoris' – so his approval carried great weight.[47] Ibn 'Adī was generally very objective. He would limit his evaluations to strict examinations of transmitters' hadiths for corroboration or its absence. As a result, he would often overturn the disapproval of an earlier critic with a comment such as 'I have not found uncorroborated reports among his hadiths.'

The standing of the Companions

The Companions of the Prophet achieved a unique place in the worldview of Sunni hadith critics. Although some early historians and transmitters like al-Wāqidī (d. 207/822–3) only considered those who reached adulthood during the lifetime of the Prophet to be Companions, the definition that became accepted by Sunnis was much less strict.[48] As al-Bukhārī notes in his *Sahīh*, a Companion is anyone who saw the Prophet, even for a moment, while a believer and who then died as a Muslim.[49]

This had tremendous consequences for hadith transmission, for by 900 CE Sunnis considered that all the Companions of the Prophet were automatically 'upright (*'adl*).' This belief was based on Quranic verses such as 'You are the best community brought out for humanity (*kuntum khayr umma ukhrijat li'l-nās*)' (Quran 3:110) and Prophetic hadiths such as **'The best of generations is the one in which I was sent, then that which follows, then that which follows.'** In effect, then, the first generation of hadith transmitters was beyond criticism. In fact, the famous ninth-century hadith critic Abū Zur'a al-Rāzī stated that anyone who criticized a Companion was a heretic.[50]

Later analysts would refine this understanding of the Companions' uprightness. As Ibn Taymiyya (d. 728/1328) explained, the Companions were not perfect – Mughīra b. Shu'ba had lied, and Walīd b. 'Uqba was a known drunkard. But none had ever lied about the Prophet.[51] Many Sunni scholars have thus understood uprightness as meaning that the Companions' exposure to the tremendous spiritual charisma of Muhammad prohibited them from lying about the Prophet but not other sins.[52]

It is no surprise, then, that Sunni hadith scholars strove to identify who was a Companion. 'Alī b. al-Madīnī (d. 234/838) wrote an early work (now lost) listing them, to be followed by Ibn Qāni' (d. 351/962), Abū Nu'aym al-Isbahānī, and others. Ibn Hajar al-'Asqalānī's *Isāba fī ma'rifat al-sahāba* is the most widely cited biographical dictionary of the Companions. There was great disagreement over the actual number of Companions: al-Shāfi'ī estimated their number at sixty thousand, Abū Zur'a al-Rāzī at over a hundred thousand. In his biographical dictionary of Companions, Ibn Hajar listed approximately twelve thousand three hundred. On a practical level, the Companions who actually played a noticeable role in hadith transmission were many fewer: the Six Books include hadiths from only 962 Companions.[53]

The Sunni critics' view of the Companions was both ideologically driven and practical. Sunni Islam was built on the idea that the Companions of the Prophet had inherited his authority and passed on his teachings reliably. In that sense, as a group they were above reproach. In terms of hadith criticism, however, the critics' reach did not extend far enough back to apply the rules of transmitter criticism to the Companions. The earliest critic, al-Zuhrī, had met only the youngest of the Companions, and his hadith criticism mostly addressed the reports he heard from other Successors. Al-Zuhrī, Mālik, and Shu'ba had direct experience with the Successors, but they had no real way to evaluate the uprightness or accuracy of Companions. In a sense, reports such as Aisha's aforementioned rejection of hadiths for content reasons represent vestiges of hadith criticism from the Companion generation. That the collective impunity of the Companions was a later construct of the Sunni worldview is evident when one finds occasional minor Companions listed in early books of weak hadith transmitters.[54]

The chicken and the egg – Who made the early experts experts?

As you might have noticed, the names of the early generations of master hadith critics (Figure 3.1) overlap to a large extent with Figure 2.1 on major hadith transmitters. So did just transmitting a vast number of hadiths make a person a reliable hadith transmitter or an expert critic? The answer seems to be no – just because one was a major transmitter did not mean that one was reliable. Ibn Ishāq was an essential pivot of hadith transmission in Medina, but it became clear to many critics even in his own lifetime that he was not at all discriminating in what he transmitted. Mālik, on the other hand, only transmitted from two people ('Abd al-Karīm b. Abī al-Mukhāriq and 'Atā' al-Khurāsānī) that he (and later critics) did not feel were reliable (*thiqa*). Later critics also distinguished between an early critic/transmitter's own transmissions and his evaluations of others. Al-Zuhrī's opinions carried great influence, but later critics all agreed that his *mursal* hadiths (see below for a discussion of this term) were too unreliable to use. The great critic Sufyān al-Thawrī regularly narrated hadiths that others considered unreliable, whereas when Shu'ba transmitted a hadith it was understood that he believed it was authentic.

In a similar vein, in the formative period of Sunni Islam in the ninth century, did hadith scholars such as Ibn Hanbal decide which early transmitters to accept based on their Sunni beliefs? Was Sunni hadith criticism just a tool for excluding non-Sunnis? The answers to these questions are certainly 'no,' since, as we have seen, Sunni critics regularly accepted the hadiths of people whose beliefs they considered anathema. Beyond merely accepting non-Sunnis as transmitters of hadiths, Sunnis even accepted one as a hadith *critic*. Despite his fervent Shiism, Ibn ʿUqda (d. 332/944) was listed by staunch Sunnis like al-Dhahabī as 'the oceanic hadith scholar,' whose criticisms of transmitters and narrations carried great weight.[55]

2) Contiguity of transmission (al-ittisāl)

Evaluating the sources of a hadith was of little use, however, if a critic could not be sure who these sources were. If one transmitter had never actually met the person from whom they quoted the hadith or if it was known that he had not heard *that* hadith from his teacher, then who was the intermediary? With no way to guarantee that intermediary's reliability, there were endless possibilities for what sort of deviation or forgery could have occurred. Establishing that a hadith had been transmitted by a contiguous, unbroken *isnād* from the Prophet was thus as crucial as transmitter reliability for determining the authenticity of a hadith. If it could not be established that the people in the *isnād* had heard from one another, then hadith critics considered the chain of transmission broken (*munqatiʿ*) and thus unreliable.

In order to determine if an *isnād* was 'contiguous (*muttasil*),' hadith critics attempted to identify all the people from whom a narrator had heard hadiths. If a transmitter was not a known liar, then one could infer this from his saying 'So-and-so narrated to me (*haddathanī*),' 'so-and-so reported to us (*akhbaranā*),' or 'I heard from so-and-so (*samiʿtu min* ...).' Other phrases for transmission did not necessarily indicate direct transmission. 'According to (*ʿan*)' could mean that someone had heard a hadith directly from the person in question or not. In addition to looking at this terminology, a critic would compare the death date of the teacher with the age of the student and investigate the possibility that they were in the same place at the same time.

Because establishing contiguous transmission was so important, by the mid 700s transmitters had become very serious about specifying exactly how hadith transmission occurred. The most accurate forms of direct transmission were either reading a teacher's hadiths back to him (often indicated by the phrase 'he reported to us, *akhbaranā*') or listening to the teacher read his hadiths (often indicated by 'he narrated to us, *haddathanā*'). If a teacher gave a student his books of hadiths to copy, this was termed 'handing over (*munāwala*).' We have already discussed 'permission to transmit (*ijāza*)' in the last chapter. Although there was debate over whether reading hadiths to a teacher or hearing them read was more accurate, all scholars acknowledged that 'handing over' and 'permission to transmit' were the most tenuous forms of transmission. Reading a book with no transmission from the teacher at all ('finding, *wijāda*') inspired no confidence at all.

Transmitters fretted over these forms of narration and often debated the proper terminology. The Hanafī al-Tahāwī (d. 321/933) wrote a short treatise on how the technical terms '*akhbaranā*' and '*haddathanā*' actually meant the same thing (also the opinion of the majority of scholars). When al-Awzā'ī gave a book of hadiths to a student in an act of 'handing over,' the student asked, 'About this book, do I say "*haddathanī*"?' Al-Awzā'ī replied, 'If I narrated it directly to you, then say that.' The student inquired, 'So do I say "*akhbaranī*"?' Al-Awzā'ī replied that no, he should say 'al-Awzā'ī said' or 'according to al-Awzā'ī.'[56]

Not all critics agreed on the requirements for a contiguous *isnād*. There was disagreement over whether the phrase 'according to ('*an*)' should be interpreted as an indication of direct transmission or not. Muslim b. al-Hajjāj claimed that the great hadith critics had all accepted '*an* as indicating direct transmission provided that the two people involved were contemporaries and that it was likely that they had met one another. Others, like Ibn 'Abd al-Barr (d. 463/1070) and al-Khatīb al-Baghdādī, claimed that hadith critics had agreed that one needed proof that the two transmitters had actually met at least once.

*Obfuscation in Transmission (*Tadlīs*)*

Critics of the eighth, ninth, and early tenth centuries often attempted to be more exact than just establishing if two transmitters had met. They sought to determine exactly which hadiths certain transmitters had heard from their teachers. Shu'ba thus studied the hadiths of his teacher Qatāda until he found that he had only heard three from his teacher Abū al-'Āliya.[57] This was especially important in the case of ***tadlīs***, or obfuscation in transmission. *Tadlīs* occurred when a transmitter cited an *isnād* in an ambiguous manner, such as saying 'so-and-so said,' implying that he had heard the hadith directly from the person when in fact he was omitting his immediate source for the hadith. Transmitters might hide their immediate source because he or she was considered unreliable or espoused beliefs unacceptable in Sunni Islam. *Tadlīs* did not always occur for insidious reasons. If a student had to leave a dictation session to answer nature's call, for example, he would hear the hadiths that he had missed from a classmate. When narrating those hadiths, however, he might leave out the classmate's name and simply say 'Teacher so-and-so said.' Because *tadlīs* was often innocuous, very few transmitters were totally innocent of it. Only Shuʿba b. al-Hajjāj was known to never lapse into it.

Identifying *tadlīs* was a primary concern of critics in the eighth century and beyond. By interrogating a transmitter a critic could determine whom he omitted from *isnād*s in instances of *tadlīs*. Transmitters like Sufyān b. ʿUyayna, who only omitted the names of reliable figures, could be trusted even when doing *tadlīs*. Others who often omitted the names of weak narrators, like Ibn Ishāq, could not be relied upon unless they specified direct transmission.[58] Al-Khatīb al-Baghdādī and Ibn Hajar both wrote books discussing *tadlīs* and those accused of it.

Mursal *Hadiths*

Similar to *tadlīs* was the phenomenon of *mursal* hadiths, or instances in which someone quoted the Prophet without ever having met him. If a Successor or an early scholar like Mālik said 'the Prophet said,' this was clearly an incomplete *isnād* since Mālik never met the Prophet. *Mursal* hadiths occurred because, especially in the first few generations of Muslims, scholars were not obsessive about providing detailed *isnād*s for every report all the time. Al-Zuhrī, Mālik, or Abū Hanīfa might quote the Prophet while discussing a legal issue informally without bothering to provide an *isnād*.

When such *mursal* hadiths were recorded in *musannaf* works like the *Muwatta'* or the legal responses of Abū Hanīfa, however, they presented a problem for later hadith critics. How should they be treated? Because *mursal* hadiths had incomplete *isnād*s and one could not be sure from whom a Successor was narrating, *mursal*s were almost always considered unreliable by hadith critics. After extensive research on the *mursal* reports of certain early transmitters, however, and attempts to find counterparts to them with full *isnād*s, critics approved of certain transmitters' *mursal* hadiths. Al-Shāfiʿī concluded that the *mursal*s of the Successor Saʿīd b. al-Musayyab (d. 94/713) were reliable because the source he omitted, his father-in-law Abū Hurayra, was the most knowledgeable Companion about hadiths. Critics debated the reliability of al-Hasan al-Basrī's *mursal* hadiths – his contemporary Ibn Sīrīn said that al-Hasan was totally uncritical about his hadith sources, so his *mursal*s were useless. Yahyā al-Qattān said that he had studied all of al-Hasan's *mursal*s and found versions with full *isnād*s for all but two of them.[59] Ibn Abī Hātim al-Rāzī composed a whole book entitled *Kitāb al-marāsīl* (The Book of Mursals) in an attempt to determine which Successors had heard hadiths from which Companions.

STEP THREE: FINDING CORROBORATION FOR THE HADITH

Corroboration had played a central role in determining the reliability of a transmitter – if he narrated hadiths that other students of his source did not, then his reliability was questioned. But a forger could still simply take an *isnād* of a respected transmitter and attach it to a freshly concocted hadith. The third and final step in hadith criticism thus involved looking for corroboration for the hadith itself.

Corroboration took two general forms. Since a '*hadīth*' was generally associated with the Companion who narrated it, another version of the same Prophetic tradition transmitted by a second Companion or an instance of the Prophet saying something similar on another occasion were both considered corroboration for a hadith. Such a report was termed a 'witness (*shāhid*).' When one transmitter corroborated

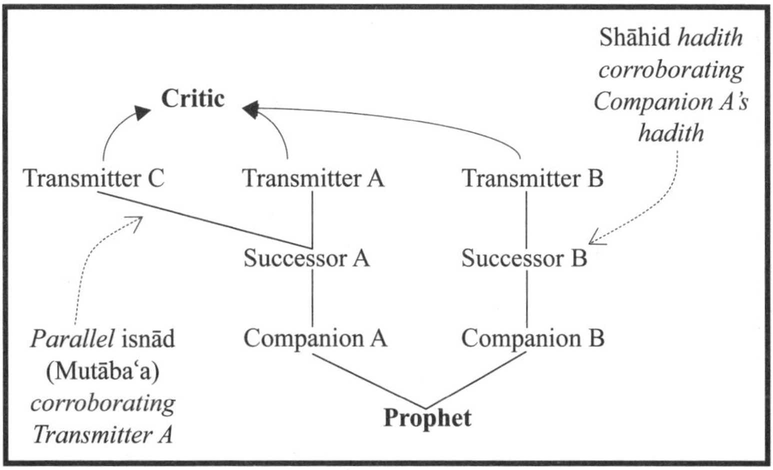

Figure 3.2 Corroboration

the report related by another transmitter that they had both heard from a common source, this was termed a 'parallelism (*mutāba'a*).' Hadith scholars described these two forms of corroboration with the aphorism 'parallelism bolsters the narration, a witness bolsters the tradition.' A witness report need not be exactly the same tradition as the hadith it supports. Even a report with a different wording but the same meaning corroborated the fact that the Prophet had expressed a certain idea or sentiment. Parallelisms solidified the reliability of a particular narration of a hadith.

A famous tenth-century hadith critic, Ibn Hibbān, describes the process of searching for corroboration (called *i'tibār*, 'consideration') thus:

> Let us say we come across [the transmitter] Hammād b. Salama, and we see that he has narrated a report from Ayyūb [al-Sakhtiyānī] ← Ibn Sīrīn ← Abū Hurayra ← the Prophet (s), but we do not find that report from anyone else from the students of Ayyūb. What is required of us now is to refrain momentarily from criticizing Hammād, and to consider what his contemporaries narrated. So we must start by looking at this report: Did Hammād's students in general narrate it from him, or just one of them? If it is the case that his students narrated it from him, then it has been established that Hammād really did narrate that report, even if that comes through a weak narrator from him, because that narration is added to the first narration from Hammād. So if it has been established correctly that Hammād narrated a report from Ayyūb that is not corroborated by others, again we must pause. For it does not follow automatically that there is some weakness here, but rather we must ask: Did any of the reliable transmitters (*thiqāt*) narrate this report from Ibn Sīrīn other than Ayyūb? If we find one, then it has been established that the report has some basis (*asl yarji'u ilayhi*). If not, then we must ask: Did anyone from among the reliable transmitters narrate this report from Abū Hurayra other than Ibn Sīrīn? If such a narration is found, then it has been established that the report has a basis (*asl*). If not, we ask: Did anyone narrate this report from the Prophet (s) other than Abū Hurayra? If so, then it has been established correctly that the report has some basis. But when that is not the case, and the report contradicts the compilations of these three [people at three levels in the *isnād*], then it is established without a doubt that the report is forged, and that the lone person who narrated it forged it.[60]

As Ibn Hibbān describes, if a report is not corroborated at any one level of the *isnād*, then the reliability of that transmitter's narration from his source is dubious. If the report is uncorroborated at all levels of the *isnād*, then it is almost certainly totally baseless. If a report was not corroborated either at some level of the *isnād* or from the Prophet in general, early hadith critics deemed it 'unacceptable (***munkar***).'

Here we see that Muslim critics worked backwards in time when authenticating hadiths. What probably first occurs to readers today (as is clear in the hadith charts in this book), is that an *isnād* 'starts' with the Prophet and 'ends' when the hadith is recorded in a book. But this assumes that the hadith actually existed in the time of the Prophet and that we are merely tracing how it came to us. For a Muslim hadith critic, a hadith was at first just an unverified claim; its *isnād* began with the person who told him the hadith. It only extended backward in time when the critic verified each link in the *isnād*, step by step, until it 'reached (*wasl*)' the Prophet.

Of course, this process of demanding corroboration took context into consideration. As Muslim b. al-Hajjāj informs us, 'If it has been established that your hadith corpus agrees with those of the other reliable narrators, then narrating some uncorroborated material is acceptable.'[61] If a transmitter studied with a certain teacher for ten years, then it is not surprising that he might narrate a selection of hadiths from his teacher that students who only studied with him for six months did not recount. The great critic Abū Hātim al-Rāzī was asked to criticize 'Abdallāh b. Sālih, the secretary of Layth b. Sa'd, for having narrated uncorroborated hadiths from Layth. Abū Hātim replied sarcastically, 'You ask me this about the closest person to Layth, who was with him on voyages and at home and spent much time alone with him?'[62] But, Muslim continues, if some lesser known transmitter narrated a hadith from a prolific hadith scholar like al-Zuhrī whose numerous and respected students did not recognize that hadith, then that report would be automatically declared 'unacceptable (*munkar*).'[63]

Like our modern investigative reporter's source, however, a transmitter could earn such a level of confidence in the eyes of critics that he could narrate uncorroborated reports without arousing concern. Critics like al-Bukhārī and Ibn 'Adī had examined the hadiths of master transmitters like al-Zuhrī, Mālik, Ibn al-Mubārak or Qutayba b. Sa'īd and found that they were corroborated to such a great extent that they could be relied upon for a number of uncorroborated hadiths as well. These figures were so central to hadith transmission in general that if anyone were to have heard a rare hadith, it would be them. An uncorroborated hadith narrated by an *isnād* of such pillars was known as 'an authentic rare (*sahīh gharīb*)' hadith. The hadith of Mālik ← al-Zuhrī ← Anas that **the Prophet entered Mecca upon its conquest with a mail helmet on his head and ordered the killing of Ibn Khatal**, an infamous enemy of Islam, was known only by this *isnād*. Because this hadith was narrated by transmitters whose collections of hadiths were vaster than almost any other people of their time, this hadith was considered authentic even though it was uncorroborated.[64]

Conversely, less stellar figures inspired no such confidence. As al-Tirmidhī explained, 'Anyone from whom a hadith is narrated who is accused [of poor performance in hadith] or is criticized as weak in hadiths for his lack of carefulness and numerous mistakes, if that hadith is only known through that narration, it cannot be used as proof.' So the hadith narrated by the lone *isnād* of Nāsih al-'Ajamī ← Simāk b. Harb ← Jābir b. Samura ← the Prophet: **'For a man to teach his child proper manners is better than to give a whole bushel in charity** (*li'an yu'addiba al-rajul waladahu khayr min an yatasaddaqa bi-sa'*)' was considered unacceptable (*munkar*) because neither Nāsih nor Simāk were consistently reliable transmitters.[65]

Books of 'Ilal al-Hadīth

Even when an *isnād* looked perfect, early hadith critics did not completely ignore the need for comparing it with other narrations of the report. As the eleventh-century critic al-Khalīlī (d. 446/1054) warned, 'Even if a hadith is provided to you with an *isnād* from al-Zuhrī or another one of the masters, do not declare it authentic merely because of that *isnād*, for even a reliable transmitter (*thiqa*) can err.'[66] By comparing different versions of the same hadith, critics could uncover flaws, known as ***'ilal***, which might have evaded the best transmitter. Such flaws included one narration of a hadith adding additional words into the text of the report that are not found in more reliable versions. A very common flaw was that one narrator would confuse a Companion's or Successor's statement with a Prophetic hadith. The great *'ilal* critic of Baghdad, al-Dāraqutnī, found such an error in Muslim's famous *Sahīh*. By examining all the narrations of a report describing how God will grant the believers a vision of Himself on the Day of Judgment, al-Dāraqutnī concluded that these were actually the words of the Successor 'Abd al-Rahmān Ibn Abī Laylā (d. 82/701–2) and not of the Prophet.[67]

To uncover these *'ilal*, a critic would gather all the narrations of a hadith and attempt to determine which ones were the most reliable. If the majority of respected transmitters, for example, reported that a certain saying was the statement of a Companion, even one strong *isnād* tracing that report back to the Prophet would be considered a mistake.

This advanced level of seeking out corroboration and comparing narrations was set down in books of *'ilal*, a genre that flourished in the ninth and tenth centuries. The *'ilal* works of 'Alī b. al-Madīnī, Ibn Hanbal, and Ibn Abī Hātim al-Rāzī were very famous, but the massive *'ilal* book of al-Dāraqutnī, published in eleven volumes, dwarfs them all. After the 1000s, *'ilal* books became rare, and only unusually competent later critics like the Moroccan Ibn al-Qattān al-Fāsī (d. 628/1231) or Ibn al-Jawzī (d. 597/1201) produced them. *'Ilal* criticism was only possible for critics in the early period when hadiths were still narrated by full *isnād*s and critics had access to versions of reports that may not have survived into later times.[68] As al-Suyūtī admitted, by the 1400s hadith critics did not have the vast array of *musannaf*s, hadith notebooks, and dictation sessions available to a scholar like al-Dāraqutnī. Such later scholars could only judge hadiths based on material they received from earlier critics.[69]

CONTENT CRITICISM: THE HIDDEN COMPONENT OF EARLY HADITH CRITICISM

When we think of how one should evaluate the reliability of things we hear, we focus on their content as much as their source. Even the most trustworthy source would arouse suspicion if he announced that aliens had landed in his backyard. Yet when we thumb through books of transmitter criticism or *'ilal*, one of the most obvious characteristics of early hadith criticism is that early scholars *almost never* discussed the contents of hadith, let alone explicitly rejected a hadith because its meaning was unacceptable. Why is this?

Certainly, the esteem in which Muslims held Muhammad and their belief that God spoke to him of the distant past and events to come affected their approach to criticizing hadiths. Unlike a modern person skeptically dismissing the sayings of a television psychic, a Muslim critic would not declare a report attributed to Muhammad to be a forgery simply because it described something that average men could not know.

Nonetheless, we know that early critics like al-Bukhārī and Muslim were willing and able to reject a hadith because they found its contents inherently flawed. In his entry on the transmitter ‘Awn b. ‘Umāra al-Qaysī in his ‘Great Book of Weak Transmitters,’ al-Bukhārī noted that one of the unacceptable hadiths he narrated was **‘The signs of the Day of Judgment are after the year 200/815.’** Al-Bukhārī rejects the hadith because ‘these two hundred years have passed, and none of these signs have appeared.’[70] In another work on transmitters, al-Bukhārī criticizes Muhammad b. Fadā’ because he narrated the hadith **‘The Prophet forbade breaking apart Muslim coins in circulation.’** Al-Bukhārī notes that Muslims did not mint coins until early Umayyad times, ‘they did not exist at the time of the Prophet.’[71] Muslim b. al-Hajjāj rejects a hadith saying that there are five chapters of the Quran that are the equivalent of one-fourth of the holy book – a total of five-fourths. He calls this logical contradiction ‘reprehensible, and it is not conceivable that its meaning is correct.’[72] But why were such instances of content criticism so rare?

To answer this question, we have to remember that Sunni hadith criticism emerged in the context of intense ideological struggle between the *ahl al-hadīth* and the school of early Muslim rationalists, known as the Mu‘tazila. For the Mu‘tazila, the only sources on which one could rely to interpret properly Islamic law and dogma were the Quran, reports from the Prophet that were so well-known they could not possibly be forged, and human reason (*‘aql*). In order to know if any hadith was authentically from the Prophet, Mu‘tazilite scholars like Abū al-Qāsim al-Balkhī (d. 319/931) believed that it had to agree with the Quran and reason.

For Mu‘tazilites, the idea that one could examine the *isnād* of the hadith to know if it was reliable or not was preposterous. The Mu‘tazilite master Abū ‘Alī al-Jubbā’ī (d. 303/915–16) was once asked to evaluate two hadiths narrated through the same *isnād*. He declared the first hadith authentic but rejected the second as false. When a surprised student asked al-Jubbā‘ī, ‘Two hadiths with the same *isnād*, you authenticate one and reject the other?’, al-Jubbā’ī replied that the second one could not be the words of the Prophet because ‘the Quran demonstrates its falsity, as does the consensus of the Muslims and the evidence of reason.’[73]

The *ahl al-hadīth*'s understanding of man's relationship to religion was the converse. Only by submitting oneself completely to the uncorrupted ways of the Prophet and early Muslim community as transmitted through the *isnād* could one truly obey God and His Messenger. Unlike the Mu'tazila, whom they saw as arrogantly glorifying human reason, or the *ahl al-ra'y*, whom they viewed as rejecting or accepting hadiths arbitrarily when it suited their legal opinion, the *ahl al-hadīth* perceived themselves as 'cultivating the ways of the Messenger, fending off heretical innovation and lies from revealed knowledge.'[74] It was not man's right to question the revealed religion that the Prophet brought and that was preserved from him through the *isnād*. We thus find the Companion 'Imrān b. Husayn (d. 52/672) instructing new Muslims that the Prophet had said, **'Whoever is grieved for [by his family] will be punished [for that mourning] (*man yunāhu 'alayhi yu'adhdhab*).'** When a person questioned the reasonableness of this notion, 'Imrān replied, 'The Messenger of God has spoken the truth, and you have disbelieved!'[75] A defender of the *ahl al-hadīth* against the Mu'tazila, Ibn Qutayba (d. 276/889) states:

> We do not resort except to that to which the Messenger of God resorted. And we do not reject what has been *transmitted authentically* from him because it does not accord with our conjectures or seem correct to reason ... we hope that in this lies the path to salvation and escape from the baseless whims of heresy.[76]

But we know from the examples above that early Sunni hadith critics did note problems in the meanings of certain hadiths. In their context, however, it is clear why they could not do so *openly*. The whole purpose of the *isnād* was to guarantee that the Prophet said something without relying on man's flawed reason. If hadith critics admitted that a hadith could have an authentic *isnād* but still be a forgery because its meaning was unacceptable, then they would be admitting that their rationalist opponents were correct! If you could not have a strong *isnād* with a forged report, then any problem in the meaning of a hadith *must* mean that there was a problem in the *isnād*. When *ahl al-hadīth* critics like al-Bukhārī came across a hadith whose meaning they found unacceptable, they examined the *isnād* to find how the error occurred and listed the hadith in the biography of that transmitter as evidence of his weakness. Ibn 'Adī often states that the questionable hadiths that a certain transmitter narrates 'demonstrate that he is unreliable.'

The Emergence of Mawdū'āt *Books and Open Content Criticism after 1100 CE*

Because early hadith criticism was so openly focused on the *isnād* as the primary means of authentication, it was very often difficult to tell when a critic was rejecting a whole Prophetic tradition or just one narration of that hadith. The term 'unacceptable (*munkar*)' for a hadith could mean that this version of the hadith narrated through a certain *isnād* was unreliable but other authentic versions existed, or that the tradition was entirely forged. Another phrase used to reject a hadith, 'it has no basis (*laysa lahu asl*),' could mean that the hadith had no basis from that transmitter (but was well established from others) or that the Prophetic tradition was baseless in general. But even concluding that the terms *munkar* or *lā asl lahu* denoted 'forged' does not necessarily mean that the critic found the meaning of the hadith in question unacceptable. As Ibn 'Abd al-Barr (d. 463/1070) explained, 'How many hadiths are there with a weak *isnād* but a correct meaning?'[77] Al-Tirmidhī notes that Yahyā al-Qattān had declared the following hadith narrated by Anas b. Mālik to be *munkar*: 'A man said, "O Messenger of God, should I tie up [the camel] and trust in God or leave it free and trust in God." The Prophet said, **"Tie it up and trust in God."** ' Al-Tirmidhī adds that this report was totally baseless from Anas, 'but its likes have been narrated from another Companion 'Amr b. Umayya al-Damrī, from the Prophet.'[78]

Starting in the late 1000s, however, as the Mu'tazilite rationalist threat faded from view and Sunni Islam emerged triumphant, hadith critics began writing books that rejected whole Prophetic traditions, often because their meanings were unacceptable. These books were known as works of ***mawdū'āt***, which listed '*mawdū'*,' or 'forged' hadiths. The earliest known *mawdū'āt* book, unfortunately lost to us, was that of Abū Sa'īd al-Naqqāsh al-Isbahānī (d. 414/1023).[79] The earliest surviving one is the *Tadhkirat al-mawdū'āt* of Muhammad b. Tāhir al-Maqdisī (d. 507/1113). Perhaps the most famous *mawdū'āt* work is the huge *Kitāb al-mawdū'āt* of Ibn al-Jawzī (d. 597/1201). *Mawdū'āt* books flourished in later Islamic times, with well-known works including the *Ahādīth al-da'īfa* of Ibn Taymiyya (d. 728/1328), the *al-La'ālī al-masnū'a* of al-Suyūtī, the *Asrār al-marfū'a* of Mullā 'Alī Qārī, the *Fawā'id al-majmū'a* of the Yemeni Muhammad al-Shawkānī (d. 1834), and the *Kitāb al-āthār al-marfū'a* of the Indian 'Abd al-Hayy al-Laknawī (d. 1886-7). Some of these scholars wrote books on forged hadiths designed to be useful references for non-experts. ʿUmar b. Badr al-Mawsilī (d. 622/1225), for example, wrote the book *Sufficing One from Memorization and Books on Issues on which there are No Reliable Hadīths* (*al-Mughnī ʿan al-hifz wa al-kitāb fīmā lam yasihha shay' fī al-bāb*).

Early *mawdūʿāt* books listed hadiths along with the *isnād* flaws that showed they were forged, relying on the criticisms of specific narrations made by the likes of al-Bukhārī and Ibn ʿAdī. This was highly problematic, since these books implied that any hadith with that wording was forged, while there might be other, sound narrations. In the mid twelfth century the genre began shifting to openly rejecting hadiths because of their meaning. The *mawdūʿāt* book of al-Jawzaqānī (d. 543/1148–9), for example, states 'Every hadith that contradicts the Sunna is cast away and the person who says it is rejected as a transmitter.'[80] This process reached a plateau with the *al-Manār al-munīf fī al-sahīh wa al-daʿīf* (The Lofty Lighthouse for Authentic and Weak Hadiths), the *mawdūʿāt* book of Ibn Qayyim al-Jawziyya (d. 751/1350), who devoted a large section of the work to listing all the features of a hadith's contents that demonstrated it was forged.

Of course, freely engaging in content criticism was opening a Pandora's box. A critic might fall into exactly that trap that the early *ahl al-hadīth* claimed they were avoiding: making man's flawed reason the arbiter of religious truth. Although later critics would maintain, as Ibn al-Jawzī states, 'any hadith that you see contradicting reason or fundamental principles [of Islam], know that it is forged,' they would also insist that one should not be too hasty in such judgments. After all, the critic might not have grasped the proper way of reconciling such contradictions.[81] A few Sunni hadith critics in the later period, such as al-Dhahabī and ʿAbdallāh al-Ghumārī, seemed at ease openly rejecting hadiths based on their contents, sometimes even when their *isnāds* seemed sound. But the mainstream Sunni tradition is much better exemplified by scholars like al-Suyūtī and Mullā ʿAlī al-Qārī. The former warned that a hadith could be rejected due to its contents only after all efforts to reconcile its meaning with the Quran and established Sunna had failed. And 'the door of possible interpretation is definitely wide,' added al-Qārī. Prominent scholars declared a hadith in which the Prophet dreamt he saw God as a beardless youth to be a blatant forgery due to its anthropomorphism. Al-Qārī replied that dreams are merely symbolic, not reality. Thus, he argued, the hadith's meaning was sound.[82] This tension between submitting one's reason to a transmitted text and using one's reason to evaluate the text's authenticity has furnished fertile ground for debate among Muslim scholars until today.

LEVELS OF HADITH, THEIR USES AND THE PRIORITIES OF THE HADITH TRADITION

From the time of Mālik (d. 179/796) to the late ninth century, hadith critics conceived of hadiths as falling between two poles in terms of the strength of their *isnād*s: *sahīh* ('sound,' 'authentic') and *da'īf*/ *saqīm* ('weak' or 'unsound,' literally 'sick'). In terms of their level of corroboration, critics described hadiths as being 'well-known (*mashhūr*)' or 'unacceptable, unknown (*munkar*)' ones. A hadith that was declared *sahīh* or *mashhūr* represented the authenticated words of the Prophet, while weak or *munkar* hadiths were those not fully established as emanating from him.

It is difficult to know exactly how early hadith critics defined *sahīh* hadiths, since they were very laconic in their works. Ibn Khuzayma defined the hadiths that he selected for his *sahīh* collection as those 'that an upright (*'adl*) transmitter narrates from another upstanding transmitter continuously to [the Prophet] without any break in the *isnād* or any impugning of the transmitters.'[83] Later analysts such as Ibn al-Salāh (d. 643/1245) and Ibn Hajar al-'Asqalānī (d. 852/1449) examined the methodologies of the early masters and defined a *sahīh* hadith as one narrated by an unbroken *isnād* of reliable (*thiqa*) transmitters, namely those who combined upstandingness and accuracy, all the way back to Prophet without any concealed flaws (*'ilal*) or contradicting a more reliable source.[84]

For hadith scholars of the eighth and ninth centuries, any hadith that did not reach the standard of *sahīh* was declared 'weak.' The category of 'weak' hadiths was thus very broad, ranging from hadiths whose *isnād*s suggested they were forged to those with relatively minor flaws (see Figure 3.0). This helps explain why *ahl al-hadīth* jurists like Ibn Hanbal were willing to employ hadiths they themselves described as 'weak' for deriving laws when no other evidence was available. The later scholar of Ibn Hanbal's school of law, Ibn Taymiyya (d. 728/1328), explains that weak hadiths fell into two categories: 1) those that did not have a *sahīh isnād* but were still reliable enough that one could use them in law, 2) hadiths that were so unreliable that they had to be set aside.[85]

Beginning with the work of al-Bukhārī's student Abū ʿĪsā al-Tirmidhī (d. 279/892), hadith scholars developed a new name to describe the hadiths that were not *sahīh* but still strong enough to use as proof in Islamic law: ***hasan***, or 'fair.' Al-Tirmidhī describes a *hasan* hadith as one that 'does not have in its *isnād* someone who is accused of lying or forgery, is not anomalous (*shādhdh*), and is narrated via more than one chain of transmission.'[86] For al-Tirmidhī, a *hasan* hadith was thus a report whose *isnād* was not *seriously* flawed and enjoyed corroboration through other narrations, which mitigated the chances of a serious error creeping into the text of the report. The later jurist and hadith scholar al-Khattābī (d. 388/998) described *hasan* hadiths as those 'with an established basis and whose transmitters were well-known.'[87]

All Sunni scholars have accepted both *sahīh* and *hasan* hadiths as compelling proof in matters of law. As we will discuss in Chapter 6 on the role of hadith in theology, there was prolonged debate over whether hadiths narrated through a handful of *isnād*s were reliable enough to inform Islamic dogma.

Just as we do today, Muslim critics felt that certain topics required more strenuous efforts at authentication than others. From the times of early critics and *ahl al-hadīth* jurists like Ibn al-Mubārak and Ibn Hanbal, it was accepted that hadiths that were not reliable enough to be admitted in discussions of law could still be used for other purposes. When Ibn al-Mubārak was asked what to do with the hadiths of one weak narrator, he replied that they should not be used as proof in legal discussions. 'It is still,' however, 'possible to narrate from him what he has on issues like good manners (*adab*), goodly preaching (*mawʿiza*), pious abstemiousness (*zuhd*) and such things.'[88] Ibn Hanbal stated:

> If we are told hadiths from the Messenger of God concerning what is permissible and forbidden, the *sunan* and laws, then we are strict with their *isnād*s. But if we are told hadiths from the Prophet about the virtues of certain acts (*fadāʾil al-aʿmāl*), or what does not create a rule or remove one, then we are lax with the *isnād*s.[89]

In addition to moralizing or exhortatory preaching, the standards for hadith authenticity also dropped for genres outside what was considered the purview of *musnad* hadiths, or hadiths with full *isnād*s originating with the Prophet and generally addressing legal issues. These

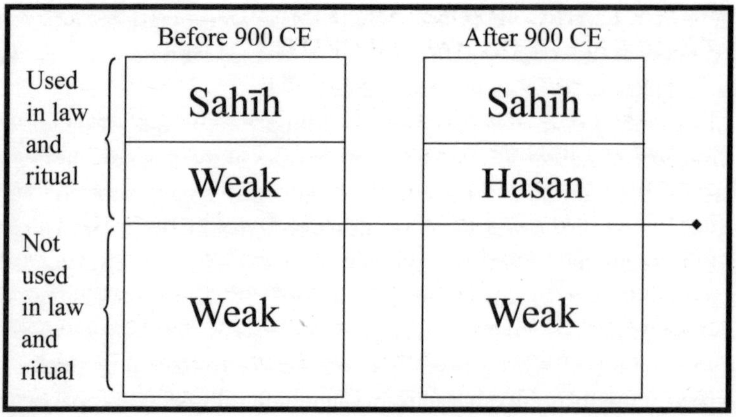

Figure 3.3 Rating of Hadiths and Their Uses among the Early and Later Hadith Critics

included stories about the Prophet's campaigns and the subsequent Islamic conquests (*maghāzī*), reports from Companions and Successors about the meanings of Quranic words or the contexts in which Quranic verses were revealed (*tafsīr*) and stories foretelling the end of days (*malāhim*). As Ibn Hanbal stated, these three genres 'had no basis (*asl*)' – namely, they often consisted of statements made by Companions or Successors. In other words, they were not Prophetic hadiths at all.[90]

Even when such reports were attributed to the Prophet, the critics' standards were lax. *Maghāzī*, along with what emerged as the genre of 'history (*tārīkh*),' demanded less rigor because scholars did not feel that they impacted the core of the Islamic tradition: law, dogma, and ritual. *Malāhim* hadiths, like hadiths dealing with good manners or urging Muslims to do good deeds, were admitted for use in teaching even if their contents were not reliable, because they encouraged Muslims to fear God.

Here we can note a remarkable feature of the way in which Sunni Muslims understood the boundaries of religion and prioritized the functions of scripture. Today we consider the stories that religious traditions tell about the apocalypse and the means by which they propagate a moral vision of the world to be essential dimensions of a faith. For Muslims in the classical period, however, they were merely tools by which scholars could purvey the true substance of Islam, which the hadith tradition was designed to preserve: law, ritual, and essential beliefs about God.

ENTER LEGAL THEORY: MUSLIM LEGAL THEORISTS AND THEIR EFFECT ON HADITH CRITICISM

Ahl al-hadīth jurists like al-Shāfiʿī, his student Ibn Hanbal and *his* student al-Bukhārī understood well that one could not simply take every hadith that one heard from the Prophet as the law. Even if a legal hadith was authentic, the Prophet could have said it in a specific circumstance, intended it for a specific person, or changed the ruling mentioned in the hadith later on. Senior scholars were thus venerated not only for their knowledge of hadiths, but also for their ability to understand how those hadiths related to one another, fit under, added to or modified Quranic rulings. Early expressions of the *ahl al-hadīth* legal theory appear in the chapter of al-Bukhārī's *Sahīh* on holding fast to the Quran and Sunna, and most eminently in al-Shāfiʿī's works the *Umm* and the *Risāla*.

Another tradition of legal theory developed parallel to that of the *ahl al-hadīth*. Hanafī jurists of the ninth century, many of whom subscribed to the Muʿtazilite rationalist outlook, derived this system partially from the Hellenistic tradition of philosophy prevalent in the Near East before Islam. In addition to the *ahl al-hadīth* division of hadiths into *sahīh/hasan/daʿīf* or *mashhūr/munkar*, the Hanafī/Muʿtazilite school of legal theory elaborated a gradated system based on the level of certainty that various forms of reports conveyed. Reports about the past, whether hadiths or simply historical accounts, that were so widespread that they could not have been forged by any one group were called ***mutawātir*** (massively transmitted) and yielded epistemologically certain knowledge (*ʿilm yaqīn*). One might not have ever actually gone to China, but the number of reports that one has heard about it convey utter certainty that the place actually exists. There was a wide range of opinions among Muʿtazilite scholars about how many transmissions of a report were required to make it *mutawātir*, with scholars asserting anywhere from four (the number of witnesses required in Islamic law to prove a case of adultery) to seventy (the number of people believed to have accompanied Moses up Mount Sinai to receive the Ten Commandments). This number was required at every stage of transmission. Any hadith that did not fulfill the requirements for a *mutawātir* hadith was known as ***āhād***, or a hadith of individual narrators. Unlike *mutawātir* hadiths, *āhād* hadiths only yielded strong probability (*zann*) of what the report described.

As we have seen, Muʿtazilites had no compunction about making content criticism the centerpiece of their method of hadith evaluation. The Hanafī judge ʿĪsā b. Abān (d. 221/836) thus argued that the early Muslim community rejected *āhād* reports that contradicted the Quran or established Sunna, or described an event that would have been more widely reported had it really occurred. He also makes the verdict of reason the ultimate arbiter for judging the veracity of a report, not the *isnād*.[91]

Although Sunnis considered Muʿtazilism to be a heresy, Muʿtazilite legal theory and its perspective on hadiths had a major impact on Sunni legal theory. A seminal figure in Sunni legal theory and theology, Abū al-Hasan al-Ashʿarī (d. 324/935–6), was a former Muʿtazilite who had embraced the Sunni theological worldview and then used Muʿtazilite rationalism to defend it. The major architects of what is known as the *Jumhūr* (Majority) school of Sunni legal theory followed in his footsteps, essentially tailoring Muʿtazilite thought to the contours of Sunni belief. In the early 1000s, two of the most influential Shāfiʿī legal theorists, al-Qādī ʿAbd al-Jabbār (d. 415/1025) and his student Abū al-Husayn al-Basrī (d. 436/1044), were actually Muʿtazilites in their conception of knowledge and theology. Their works in this field greatly informed the scholars who defined Sunni legal theory after them, such as al-Juwaynī (d. 478/1085) and his student Abū Hāmid al-Ghazālī (d. 505/1111).

With the work of the hadith master al-Khatīb al-Baghdādī (d. 463/1071), the Muʿtazilite-inspired thinking of Sunni legal theorists entered Sunni hadith criticism. Specifically, al-Khatīb and all the theorists of hadith criticism who followed him adopted the division of hadiths into *mutawātir* and *āhād* (which we will discuss in more depth in Chapter 6) along with the levels of certainty they yielded. *Mutawātir* hadiths yielded total certainty that the Prophet had in fact said the report, while *āhād* hadiths yielded only strong probability. This was, however, strong enough for them to be used in deriving law.

Sunni legal theorists introduced a middle tier between *āhād* and *mutawātir* dubbed ʻwide-spread (*mashhūr* or *mustafīd*).ʼ These hadiths were reports that started out as *āhād*, being transmitted by only a few people in the first few generations, before spreading out and becoming *mutawātir*. But because these hadiths had been accepted as reliable by the community of scholars, they were known to be authentic. This was based on the Sunni belief, phrased in the Prophet's words, that **ʻGod will not let my community agree on an**

error' (see Chapter 5). Hadith criticism also absorbed the principles of content criticism described by Ibn Abān.

The result of this merging was a composite tradition that joined two perspectives on hadith criticism that were originally in opposition, if not antithetical, to one another. Since the eleventh century, Sunni hadith criticism has therefore produced many internal contradictions. The most prominent display of this schizophrenia has been theories of hadith criticism that do not correspond to the work of hadith critics. We have already seen how the Sunni legal theorist's definition of upstanding character (*'adāla*) did not apply at all to the criteria that early hadith critics like al-Bukhārī used to determine the reliability of a narrator. In terms of content criticism, al-Khatīb al-Baghdādī affirms the principles derived from Ibn Abān. Not once, however, in the course of his criticism of the thousands of hadiths in his vast *History of Baghdad*, does al-Khatīb openly reject a hadith because its contents were unacceptable! As mentioned earlier, it was not until the *mawdū'āt* work of al-Jawzaqānī (d. 543/1148–9) and those who followed him that Sunni hadith critics actually overtly applied rules of content criticism in the course of their hadith evaluations. Even then their use of content criticism was fraught with tension. Essentially every Sunni hadith scholar since al-Khatīb has upheld Ibn Abān's rules of content criticism. But few have ever applied them.[92]

The categories of *mutawātir* and *āhād* were similarly unsuitable for the hadith tradition, for essentially all hadiths were *āhād*. As Ibn al-Salāh (d. 643/1245), the most famous scholar of hadith criticism in the later period, explained, *at most* one hadith (**'Whoever lies about me intentionally, let him prepare for himself a seat in Hellfire'**) would meet the requirements for *mutawātir*.[93] No hadiths could actually be described as being narrated by a large number of narrators at every stage of their transmission. In fact, when Mu'tazilites had insisted that hadiths be transmitted by a mere two people at every stage, the Sunni Ibn Hibbān had accused them of trying to destroy the Sunna of the Prophet in its entirety.[94]

THE 'BIG TENT' OF THE LATE SUNNI TRADITION: INCREASED ACCEPTANCE AND USE OF WEAK HADITHS

The absorption of Mu'tazilite legal theory into the Sunni hadith tradition in the 1000s is indicative of the major changes that occurred in the later period of hadith criticism. From the eleventh century onward, hadith criticism would be characterized by an increasing distance from the methods of early critics. Especially with the solidification of the Late Sunni Tradition in the 1300s, we can see a tendency towards authenticating more and more hadiths that had previously been considered outside the pale of usage. Partially explained by the broader perspective enjoyed by later critics and partially justified by manipulations of the methods of hadith critics, hadith criticism became an increasingly 'Big Tent' of inclusivity.

We note the beginning of the critical laxity of the later period in the *Mustadrak* collection of al-Hākim al-Naysābūrī (d. 405/1014), in which the author claimed he had collected thousands of hadiths that met the authenticity requirements of al-Bukhārī and Muslim. In reality, however, al-Hākim's methods of authentication fell far short of his two predecessors. He declared a hadith authentic if its *isnād* consisted of transmitters used in the *Sahīhayn* or transmitters similar to them. The later analyst Jamāl al-Dīn al-Zayla'ī (d. 762/1361), however, uncovered the weakness at the heart of al-Hākim's strategy: he had relied on the same transmitters as al-Bukhārī and Muslim, but he did not examine the hadiths for corroboration or ensure contiguous transmission.[95] According to al-Dhahabī, only half of the *Mustadrak*'s contents were actually authentic. The other half was of dubious reliability.[96]

Neglecting the need for corroboration has been a hallmark of later hadith criticism. Whereas a critic like al-Bukhārī would accept a hadith narrated by only one chain of transmission as long as it consisted of master scholars like al-Zuhrī and Mālik, later critics often authenticated hadiths based on only one chain regardless of the inferior standing of some transmitters. Ibn Abī Hātim, Ibn 'Adī, and other early critics had declared the hadith saying that **'The most truthful speech is that said after sneezing'** was weak or forged. In the thirteenth century, however, al-Nawawī (d. 676/1277) argued for its reliability based on a solitary narration from the *Musnad* of Abū Ya'lā al-Mawsilī (d. 307/919) even though one of its transmitters had been severely impugned.[97]

Later critics did have one tangible advantage over earlier critics. A later scholar like Ibn Hajar or al-Suyūtī had access to works that consolidated and synthesized the vast and diverse expanse of the hadith corpus as well as collections that might not have been within reach of an early critic. As the case studies at the end of this chapter demonstrate, where early critics like al-Bukhārī or al-Tirmidhī had access to only some narrations of a Prophetic tradition when they declared it weak, in the 1400s Ibn Hajar could take into consideration additional narrations that might raise that hadith to *hasan* or *sahīh* status. Ibn al-Salāh used the term '*hasan* due to other narrations (*hasan li-ghayrihi*)' and 'authentic due to other narrations (*sahīh li-ghayrihi*)' to describe this procedure. The twentieth-century Moroccan hadith scholar Ahmad al-Ghumārī (d. 1960) exemplified later scholars' access to material out of the reach of an early critic by writing a book entitled (*Laysa kadhālik*)', (Not So), in which he rebuts a series of statements that early critics like Ibn Hanbal made about transmitters and hadiths based on new evidence.

Of course, while later critics could authenticate a hadith that had previously been considered unreliable, the opposite was theoretically very difficult. When al-Bukhārī judged a hadith to be *sahīh*, his decision was based on information about the hadith that may have been lost to history. As Ibn Taymiyya explains, 'whatever hadiths reached [early scholars] and that they deemed authentic may only have come down to us through unknown transmitters, broken *isnād*s or not at all.'[98] How, then, could a later scholar question the authentication of an earlier master?

Not all the previously inaccessible evidence to which later hadith critics had access, however, was reliable according to the hadith critical method. Scholars of the Late Sunni Tradition made large numbers of hadiths admissible in religious discourse by exploiting the tremendous range of questionable hadiths found in the late *musnad* collections of the tenth to twelfth centuries as well as the principle that weak hadiths were acceptable as proof on non-legal issues. Basing their argument on the above-mentioned stance of early masters like Ibn Hanbal, leading late Sunni scholars like al-Nawawī and al-Suyūtī all agreed that as long as a hadith was not forged it could be used in any discussion not concerning the prohibition and permissibility of an act.[99] In order to raise a hadith to the level of admissibility in such cases, all a scholar had to do was prove that it was not forged – proving that it was merely 'weak' sufficed. This was the course of action that al-Suyūtī admitted to taking when he presented hadiths supporting his argument that the Prophet's parents were destined for Heaven even though they had never known Islam during their lives.

In order to rehabilitate a hadith that critics had earlier declared a forgery, one had to provide evidence that it had some 'basis (*asl*)' in the early Islamic tradition. For example, even though there might not be enough evidence to trace a hadith authentically to the Prophet, a weak hadith might be the result of a Companion's statement or an early legal ruling that had accidentally been attributed to Muhammad. It was still a legitimate indicator of proper Islamic values.

The most frequently cited sources for finding such an '*asl*' for a hadith were the *Musnad al-Shihāb* of al-Qudāʿī and the *Musnad al-Firdaws* of al-Daylamī, both late works infamous for the unreliability of their contents. When Mullā ʿAlī Qārī argued for accepting the hadith **'Wiping one's neck [during ablutions] is protection against fetters [on the Day of Judgment]** (*mash al-raqaba amān min al-ghill*),' which al-Nawawī had said was forged and which other critics had declared a Companion statement, he announced that a Prophetic version was found in the *Musnad al-Firdaws* and thus that the hadith was weak, not forged. 'And weak hadiths,' he added, 'are acted on by consensus for establishing the virtues of actions.'[100]

When attempting to raise a weak hadith to the status of '*hasan* due to other narrations,' the evidence to which later critics often resorted were the narrations that earlier critics like Ibn ʿAdī or al-Bukhārī had listed in their weak transmitter collections to show a certain person's flawed hadiths! (See Case Study Two in this chapter). Although the early masters Ibn Maʿīn, al-Bukhārī, Abū Zurʿa al-Rāzī, al-Tirmidhī, Ibn ʿAdī, al-Dāraqutnī, and al-Khatīb al-Baghdādī all declared that various versions of the hadith **'I am the city of knowledge and ʿAlī is its gate'** were baseless, later critics such as al-ʿAlāʾī (d. 761/1359), Ibn Hajar, and al-Suyūtī all agreed that, when taken together, these narrations made the hadith *hasan*.[101]

The final means by which hadiths achieved exaggerated authority in the Late Sunni Tradition was the exploitation of the concept of *mutawātir* reports. It was accepted by consensus among Sunni scholars that if a report had reached the level of *mutawātir* it was utterly certain that the Prophet had said it. Although scholars like Ibn al-Salāh had declared that no such hadith existed in actuality, al-Suyūtī composed a collection titled *al-Azhār al-mutanāthira fī al-ahādīth al-mutawātira* (The Scattered Flowers of Massively Transmitted Hadiths) in which he included 111 hadiths he declared *mutawātir* because ten or more Companions had narrated it from the Prophet. But a *mutawātir* hadith had to have such a number of *isnād*s at every level of transmission, and not all the chains of transmission that al-Suyūtī used as evidence were reliable to begin with. Because the concept of *mutawātir* was so ambiguous, later critics frequently abused the label to argue for the undeniable authenticity of a hadith they were citing. Although earlier scholars had agreed that the hadith **'My community will not agree on an error'** lacked any fully *sahīh isnād*s, 'Abdallāh al-Ghumārī (d. 1993) claimed that it was *mutawātir*.

How do we explain seemingly deceptive tactics like the exploitation of weak hadiths by late Sunni scholars? Were they not pious defenders of the hadith tradition, whose whole purpose was 'to ward off lies from the Prophet of God'? Although we might note that the Late Sunni Tradition was very permissive with hadiths, scholars like al-Suyūtī felt they were on firm ground. In the case of the Prophet's parents going to heaven, after all, al-Suyūtī did not just have hadiths in mind when attempting to prove his case. He had the whole heritage of Islamic thought at his disposal, such as Quranic verses saying that 'No bearer of burdens will bear the burdens of another' and theological principles such as the Sunni tenet that people born in a community before its prophet arrives will not be held accountable for ignorance of God's religion. As we shall see in Chapter 5, in the early period of Islam, if the Muslim community's practice agreed with a hadith then that hadith was considered reliable even if its *isnād* was poor. This was the same approach taken by the Late Sunni Tradition; if centuries of Muslim scholars had agreed that the meaning of a hadith was accurate, then ascribing it to the Prophet was acceptable as well. As Ibn al-Qayyim said, such a hadith, 'even if it has not been established as reliable, the fact that it has been acted on in all regions and eras with no rejection is sufficient for us to act on it.'[102] Of course, this assumes that those centuries of Muslim scholars were right.

AUTHENTICATING HADITHS BY DREAMS OR INSPIRATION

Islamic civilization has accorded great credence to dreams or inspired visions in which Muslims encounter the Prophet. This is based on two *sahīh* hadiths: **'Nothing of prophethood will remain after me except righteous nightly dreams,'**[103] and **'Whoever has seen me in a dream has seen me while awake, for indeed Satan does not assume my form.'**[104] Seeing the Prophet in a dream is thus a reliable experience with probative value. Muslim jurists and legal theorists, however, have agreed unanimously that, while a vision of the Prophet may reveal truths to someone concerning personal matters, it cannot have any effect on law or formal relationships. It cannot excuse you from work or school.[105]

In the first few centuries of the hadith tradition, dreams and visions therefore played a colorful but ultimately superficial role in hadith authentication. Al-Tabarānī had a dream in which he asked the Prophet about the status of the hadith, **'The believers in their mercy towards one another are like a man part of whose body is in pain – the rest of his body feels the pain.'** The Prophet replied '*Sahīh, sahīh, sahīh*!' This hadith, however, had already been authenticated by al-Bukhārī and Muslim, so al-Tabarānī's inspired vision effected no change in its standing.[106]

The Late Sunni Tradition was characterized by a more prominent and novel method of facilitating hadith authentication: illuminating inspiration, or '***kashf***' (literally, 'unveiling'). This method was developed by the influential and highly controversial Sufi systematizer Ibn 'Arabī (d. 638/1240). For Ibn 'Arabī, receiving revelatory inspiration (*kashf*) from contact with God's ultimate truth as reflected in the 'Muhammadan reality' (see Chapter 7), was one of the three means by which a human could acquire sound religious knowledge. Unlike the other two methods, rational investigation and prophetic revelation, however, *kashf* allowed the saint on whom God bestowed this power to place the knowledge attained by these other methods in their proper place.[107]

As Ibn 'Arabī explained, weak hadiths are not valid proofs because they lack a reliable *isnād*. But some of these reports might in fact be real sayings of the Prophet that have gone unrecognized because of poor transmitters. If one could find a reliable *isnād* for such a hadith, then it could be acted on. A saint who receives direct, unveiling knowledge from God is like a Companion hearing this hadith from the Prophet, except that he hears it from the eternal Prophetic light. His inspiration can inform him that the Prophet actually said that hadith since, like a Companion, the saint is actually in the Prophet's presence.

Like other legal theorists, however, Ibn 'Arabī acknowledges that a hadith authenticated by *kashf* cannot be used in legal arguments. But he does contend that *kashf* can reveal to a saint that a certain hadith that had been authenticated by traditional hadith criticism was in fact forged.[108]

Hadith critics of the Late Sunni Tradition adopted Ibn 'Arabī's belief that inspiration provided proof that a hadith was authentic provided that it did not affect law, although the technique has found little use outside the work of a few scholars like the North African Sufi 'Abd al-'Azīz al-Dabbāgh (d. 1719) (who claimed to have heard hadiths from the Prophet via the sole intermediary of the enigmatic character of Muslim legend, Khidr).[109] Almost no critics have accepted that *kashf* could overrule a *sahīh* ruling arrived at by the traditional methods of hadith criticism. Some scholars have squarely rejected any allowance for *kashf* in hadith – the Egyptian Mālikī scholar Muhammad 'Illaysh (d. 1882) stated, 'There is no room for such laxity in the religion of God, and sainthood and miracles have no role in this issue [of hadith authentication]. Rather, recourse is to the hadith masters knowledgeable about this matter.'[110]

APPLYING HADITH CRITICISM TO THE REST OF ISLAMIC CIVILIZATION: *TAKHRĪJ* AND *MUSHTAHIR* BOOKS

By the 1200s the collection of hadiths had come to an end, and hadith scholars devoted themselves to consolidation, commentary, and criticism. With the hadith canon firmly established, hadith critics turned their attention away from hadith collections and towards the manner in which other areas of Islamic scholarship used hadiths. In books of ***takhrīj***, a rash of which appeared during the 1300s and 1400s, a hadith scholar took a book from another genre and discussed the status of the hadiths it contained. Since few books outside hadith collections featured *isnād*s when they quoted hadiths, *takhrīj* books first provided all the hadith collections that provided chains of transmission for a hadith and then discussed its reliability.

The earliest known *takhrīj* book was the work that 'Abd al-'Azīm al-Mundhirī (d. 656/1258) devoted to the *Muhadhdhab*, a major work of Shāfi'ī law written by Abū Ishāq al-Shīrāzī (d. 476/1083). Many *takhrīj* books devoted to works of Islamic law followed. The Hanafī al-Zayla'ī produced his famous *Nasb al-rāya* (Erecting the Standard), a *takhrīj* of the hadiths in the *Hidāya*, a formative Hanafī law book by al-Marghīnānī (d. 593/1196–7). Ibn al-Mulaqqin (d. 804/1401) and Ibn Hajar wrote their *Badr al-munīr* and *Talkhīs al-habīr* respectively, both devoted to the hadiths included in the major Shāfiʿī legal text of al-Rāfiʿī. Several *takhrīj* books dealt with the hadiths cited in prominent books of legal theory, such as Ibn Kathīr's *Tuhfat al-tālib*, which addressed the contents of Ibn al-Hājib's abridged treatise on legal theory. Ibn Hajar also devoted a *takhrīj* work to the *Kashhāf*, the famous Quranic commentary by al-Zamakhsharī (d. 538/1144). Renowned Sufi texts also attracted *takhrīj*'s. Ibn Hajar's teacher Zayn al-Dīn al-ʿIrāqī (d. 806/1404) wrote a very critical *takhrīj* of the hadiths that the great Sufi al-Ghazālī had used as proof in his famous but controversial opus, the *Ihyā' ʿulūm al-dīn* (Revival of the Religious Sciences). Ibn Hajar's student, Shams al-Dīn al-Sakhāwī (d. 902/1497), wrote a *takhrīj* of al-Sulamī's popular Forty Hadith collection on Sufism.

Later hadith scholars also directed their hadith criticism towards Muslim society as a whole. A whole genre of books emerged that took *takhrīj* 'to the streets,' examining hadiths that were widespread in Muslim society. Ibn al-Jawzī, Ibn Taymiyya, and al-ʿIrāqī each wrote a book analyzing and criticizing the often baseless hadiths recited by popular storytellers (*qussās*). Books of '*mushtahir*,' or 'well-known,' hadiths examined hadiths popular in everyday Muslim life in order to determine if they had any basis in the Prophet's speech and judge their reliability. Badr al-Dīn al-Zarkashī (d. 794/1392) wrote the first known book in this genre. Al-Sakhāwī's *al-Maqāsid al-hasana* and Ismāʿīl al-ʿAjlūnī's (d. 1748-9) *Kashf al-khafā'* are the most famous books on *mushtahir* hadiths.

HADITH CRITICISM CASE STUDY ONE: CAN YOU PUT YOUR SHOES ON STANDING OR NOT?

Having traced the origins and development of Sunni hadith criticism, let us take a look at their methods in action. Our first case study is the report **'The Prophet forbade people from putting on their shoes while standing** (*nahā Rasūl Allāh ʿan yantaʿila al-rajul qā'iman*),' which appears in the *Sunan*s of Ibn Mājah, al-Tirmidhī, and Abū Dāwūd, as well as the *Tārīkh al-kabīr* of al-Bukhārī and the *Musnad* of Abū Yaʿlā al-Mawsilī.

This was not seen as an extremely important legal issue. Even those who upheld the authenticity of the hadith maintained that the Prophet

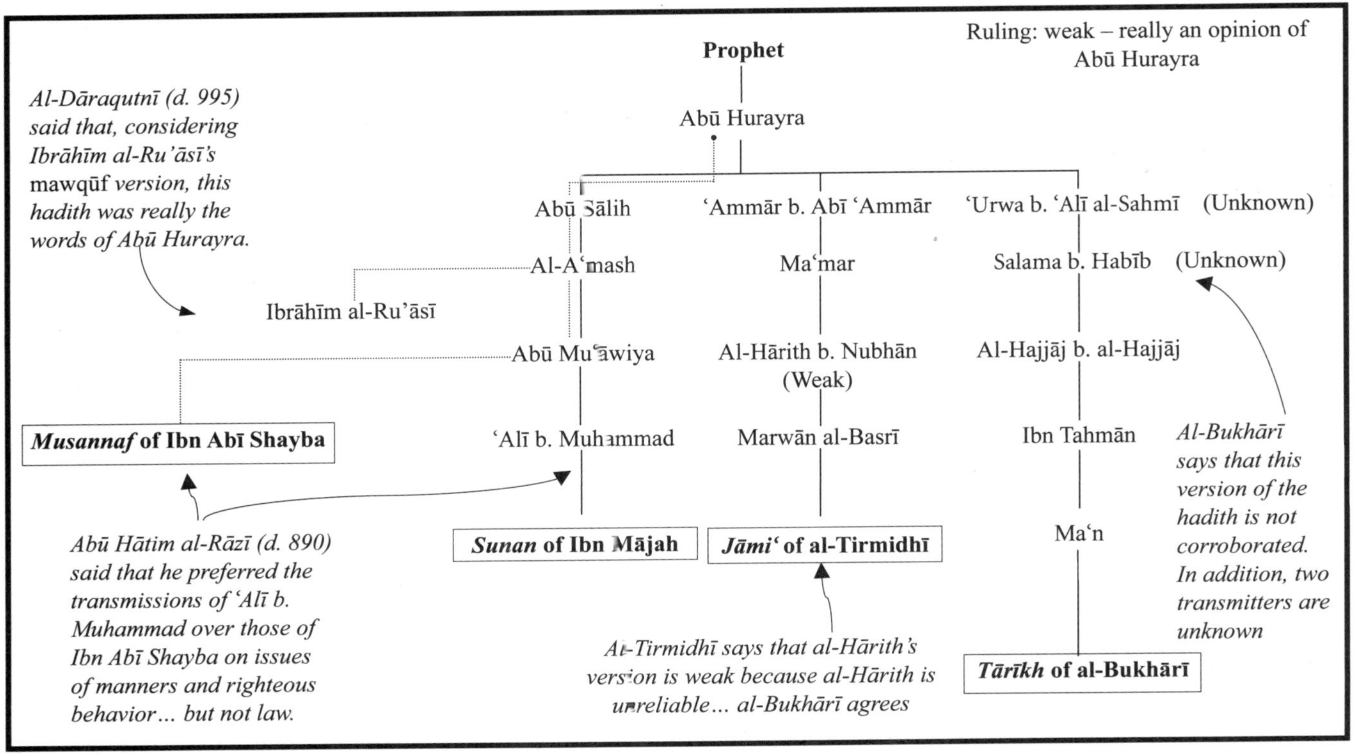

Figure 3.4 Hadith Prohibiting Putting on one's Shoes while Standing: the Transmission of Abū Hurayra

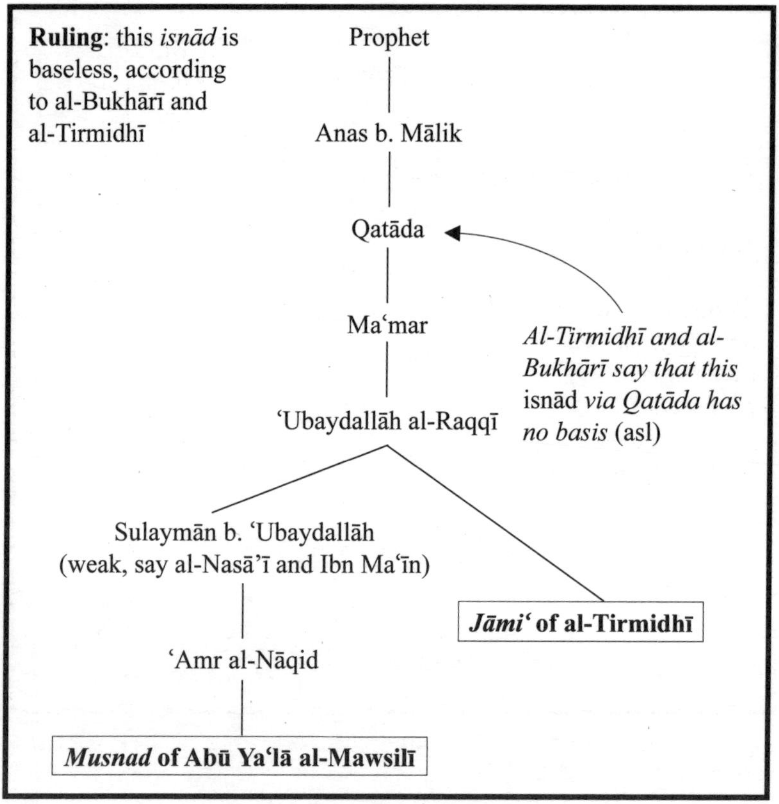

Figure 3.5 Hadith Prohibiting Putting on one's Shoes while Standing: the Transmission of Anas b. Mālik

was suggesting that people put on their shoes while seated because this was easier. But the question was the subject of some disagreement: the *Tabaqāt* of Ibn Sa'd and the *Musannaf*s of Ibn Abī Shayba and 'Abd al-Razzāq al-San'ānī include reports that Aisha and the prominent Successor scholars Ibn Sīrīn, Ibrāhīm al-Nakha'ī, and al-Hasan al-Basrī all saw no problem with putting on one's shoes while standing. The Companion Abū Hurayra and the early scholar Yahyā b. Abī Kathīr, however, are reported to have discouraged the practice.

The Muslim hadith critic's first step in evaluating a Prophetic tradition would be to collect all the available narrations of the report. These could be scattered everywhere from hadith collections to books of law, history, or Quranic exegesis. Once this was done, the critic would organize all these narrations according to the Companions who

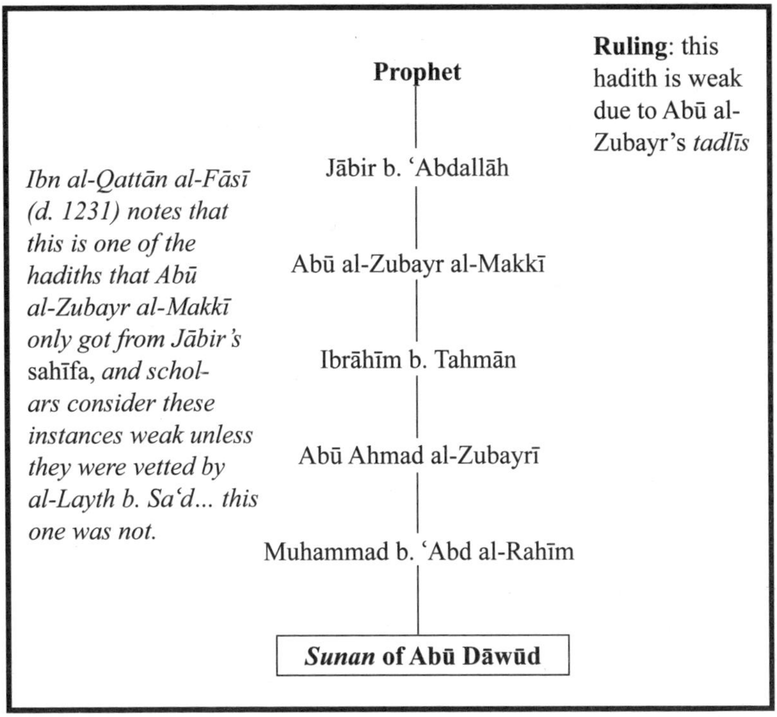
Prophet
Jābir b. ʿAbdallāh
Abū al-Zubayr al-Makkī
Ibrāhīm b. Tahmān
Abū Ahmad al-Zubayrī
Muhammad b. ʿAbd al-Rahīm
Sunan of Abū Dāwūd
Ruling: this hadith is weak due to Abū al-Zubayr's *tadlīs*
Ibn al-Qattān al-Fāsī (d. 1231) notes that this is one of the hadiths that Abū al-Zubayr al-Makkī only got from Jābir's sahīfa, *and scholars consider these instances weak unless they were vetted by al-Layth b. Saʿd... this one was not.*

Figure 3.6 Hadith Prohibiting Putting on one's Shoes while Standing: the Transmission of Jābir b.ʿAbdallāh

narrated them, since the transmission of each Companion is technically a hadith distinct from those of other Companions, who might have heard the report from the Prophet at another time. The critic would then examine the hadith of each Companion one by one to establish its reliability.

To accomplish this, the critic would trace the different narrations of the various Successors from the Companion in question, then the narrations from the next generation after the Successor, *et cetera*, starting with the latest person in the *isnād* and working towards the source to evaluate the quality of the *isnād*. The critic would ask: is each link reliable? Did each link hear hadiths from their supposed source? If any narration from the Companion has a fatal flaw, such as a seriously weak transmitter or a clear break in the *isnād*, then it would be inadmissible as evidence. If a narration had a transmitter who was criticized for a lesser failing such as occasional errors or a bad memory, the critic

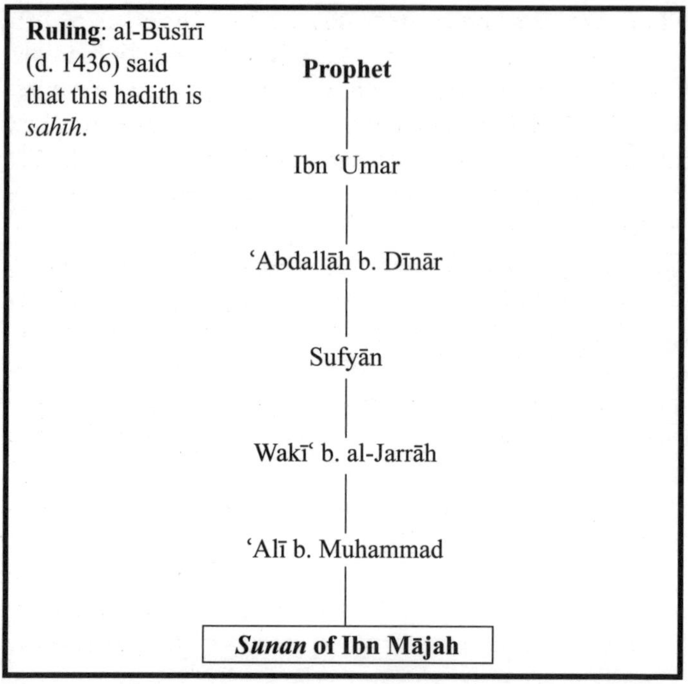

Figure 3.7 Hadith Prohibiting Putting on one’s Shoes while Standing: the Transmission of Ibn ‘Umar

would keep this narration in mind for consideration in comparison with the other narrations from the Companion or the Successor.

If there were some disagreement in wording or form between the different versions of the narration from the Companion, then the critic would use the various strengths and weaknesses of the competing narrations, along with any data gleaned from weaker versions maintained for consideration, to choose the most reliable version. This task would then be performed for the next Companion’s transmission from the Prophet. Once one Companion’s hadith has been verified, the hadith is considered *sahīh* or *hasan* depending on its strength. If, in addition to one Companion’s *hasan* narration, another Companion’s narration was acceptable as well, then this could raise the tradition as a whole to the level of *sahīh*.

Let us first examine the narration of Abū Hurayra (see Figure 3.4). We see that three Successors supposedly narrated this hadith from Abū Hurayra: Abū Sālih, ‘Ammār b. Abī ‘Ammār and ‘Urwa b. ‘Alī al-Sahmī. We can immediately dismiss the narrations of ʿAmmār b. Abī ʿAmmār and ʿUrwa b. ʿAlī al-Sahmī, for al-Tirmidhī and al-Bukhārī agree that the former is weak because of the presence in its *isnād* of al-Hārith b. Nubhān, who critics agree was unreliable. The narration of ʿUrwa b. ʿAlī is similarly baseless, for al-Bukhārī says it enjoys no corroboration, and there are two unknown transmitters in the *isnād*.

This leaves us with the narration of Abū Sālih from Abū Hurayra. Here, however, we find disagreement among the two narrations from Abū Sālih's *isnād*. The version that Ibn Abī Shayba recorded from Abū Muʿāwiya in his *Musannaf* is not a Prophetic hadith at all, but rather the opinion of Abū Hurayra. The version that Ibn Mājah recorded from his teacher ʿAlī b. Muhammad, from Abū Muʿāwiya, however, is a Prophetic hadith. Which version is correct? Both Ibn Abī Shayba and ʿAlī b. Muhammad are respected and reliable hadith scholars; is there any way to judge whose version should be taken?

Ibn Abī Shayba was one of the most prominent hadith transmitters of his generation, while ʿAlī b. Muhammad served only as a source for hadith collectors in the northern Iranian cities of Rayy and the Qazvin, where he became an important source for Ibn Mājah. Although the rigorous critic Abū Hātim al-Rāzī, who studied with both Ibn Abī Shayba and ʿAlī b. Muhammad, felt that ʿAlī was more reliable for hadiths concerning the virtues of actions and righteous behavior, Ibn Abī Shayba was in general in command of more hadiths and possessed of a better understanding of his craft. Because the hadith of putting on one's shoes is a legal issue, Abū Hātim's testimony would lead us to incline towards Ibn Abī Shayba's *mawqūf* (Companion) version of the report. More important, however, is the conclusion of the great critic al-Dāraqutnī, who introduces another Companion version of the report narrated from al-Aʿmash by Ibrāhīm al-Ru'āsī. Since it is the Companion version that enjoys corroboration and the preponderance of evidence, al-Dāraqutnī concludes that the hadith is really the opinion of Abū Hurayra and not a Prophetic hadith.

Turning to the narration of the hadith from the Prophet by Anas b. Mālik (see Figure 3.5), found in al-Tirmidhī's *Jāmiʿ* and the *Musnad* of Abū Yaʿlā al-Mawsilī, we see that al-Tirmidhī and al-Bukhārī categorically state that this narration by Maʿmar from Qatāda has no basis (*asl*). Al-Tirmidhī does not even think the narration is worthwhile enough to inform us of his immediate source for this particular version. In the case of Abū Yaʿlā's narration, it seems probable that

Sulaymān b. ʿUbaydallāh, deemed weak by many critics, erred in his narration from his father and turned a Successor opinion transmitted by Maʿmar into a Prophetic hadith.

The transmission of the report from Jābir b. ʿAbdallāh is also not admissible as proof of the hadith's reliability (see Figure 3.6). The hadith was transmitted from Jābir by Abū al-Zubayr al-Makkī, who did not hear all the *sahīfa* of Jābir from him through direct transmission. This means that, unless Abū al-Zubayr explicitly states that he heard this hadith aurally from Jābir, there is too much chance that Abū al-Zubayr could commit an error in his reception of the report for his testimony to be reliable.

Of the three versions we have examined so far, one has turned out to be a Companion opinion in reality and two are unreliable. This is not the case, however, for the hadith narrated by the Companion Ibn ʿUmar in Ibn Mājah's *Sunan* (see Figure 3.7). The *isnād* of this narration seems to be extremely strong – all its transmitters were highly respected, and there are no evident breaks in the *isnād*. So far the first two steps of the three-tiered hadith critical method (Is there an *isnād*? Who is in the *isnād*?) have proceeded successfully.

But there seems to be no corroboration for this transmission. This seems very odd in light of how famous the scholars in the *isnād* were and how prolifically they transmitted hadiths. It seems very unlikely that only one person would transmit this from Sufyān al-Thawrī, who was the most sought-after scholar of his day. It is equally bizarre that only one person would transmit this hadith from Wakīʿ, who was another pillar of hadith transmission.

Should this lack of corroboration from scholars who, it would seem, should have students spreading this hadith far and wide, lead us to doubt the reliability of this report from Ibn ʿUmar? The nature of these transmitters' relationships with one another lessens our worries. Wakīʿ was the leading disciple of Sufyān, so much so that he was called 'The Transmitter of Sufyān (*rāwiyat Sufyān*),' and when Sufyān died Wakīʿ took up his place teaching in the mosque. Although ʿAlī b. Muhammad was not as famous as these two earlier generations, he was in Kufa for many years with Wakīʿ and did not emigrate from the city to his new home in Qazvin until after Wakīʿ's death. None of the transmitters in the *isnād*, then, were students who studied only briefly with their sources for the hadith; all were long-term students or senior disciples, so it is not surprising that they might have heard some hadiths from their teachers that other students who had less exposure to them did not. The report from Ibn 'Umar thus seems reliable. Its lack of corroboration may cause us enough concern, however, to deem it *hasan* instead of *sahīh*.

This is, in fact, how many later hadith critics judged this hadith. Al-Nawawī and al-'Irāqī called it *hasan*. Al-'Irāqī's student, the famous Ibn Hajar, notes that while some of the transmissions of the report are weak the tradition is 'established (*ma'rūf*).' Al-Būsīrī states that the hadith is *sahīh* based mainly on the transmission of Ibn 'Umar in the *Sunan* of Ibn Mājah. The modern hadith scholars al-Albānī and Khaldūn al-Ahdab also deem the hadith authentic.

HADITH CRITICISM CASE STUDY TWO: CONDEMNING BELIEF IN FREE WILL

This case study deals with a much more controversial topic: do human beings have free will or has God preordained their actions? Some Muslim schools of theology, such as the Mu'tazila, affirmed free will because they insisted that God was totally just (how could He punish people for deeds He ordained for them?). For Sunni Islam, however, the question was more one of power than justice. Sunni theologians wanted to protect the notion of God's power (*qadar*), namely His power to know eternally what all human actions would be. If humans were free to choose, they thought, this would give humans power beyond God's knowledge. Sunni scholars thus insisted that God predestined a person's fate in the womb. How this could be reconciled with the justice of God punishing the bad and rewarding the good in the afterlife was a divine mystery beyond human ken.

The two traditions discussed here address the early Islamic school of thought that believed in free will, referred to by Sunnis as the *Qadariyya* (or Qadarites). One hadith refers to them as Zoroastrians (*majūs*) because Zoroastrians believe in two deities, a benevolent creator god and a god of darkness. For Sunnis, believing that humans possessed a power beyond the control of God was tantamount to elevating them to godlike status; hence, a second god. The second group referred to in one of the hadiths, the *Murji'a*, was a school of thought that believed in suspending judgment about people's fate in the afterlife.

Chapters condemning the Qadarites were commonplace in the Sunni hadith collections of the ninth and tenth centuries, and a huge number of elaborate hadiths were forged denigrating that theological position. Here we will examine two of the more reliable (from a Sunni perspective) hadiths on the subject. They are instructive because they illustrate well the difference between the criticism of *narrations* and those of the *traditions* they constitute. We also see how later critics could take advantage of this distinction in their rulings on authenticity. As we shall see, all but two of the following narrations were declared decidedly 'weak' or even forged by hadith critics in the early period, and even the one narration that might rise to the level of *hasan* still suffered from serious flaws. Early critics like al-Bukhārī, Ibn 'Adī, and al-'Uqaylī (d. 323/934) pointed out the flaws in these individual narrations, assuming their learned audience would know that such errors had no bearing on other narrations of the same traditions. When the twelfth-century scholar Ibn al-Jawzī wrote his influential collection identifying forged hadiths, however, he declared both the traditions examined here to be forged altogether.

The first hadith is the Prophet's statement 'Two types from my community have no share in Islam: the Murji'ites and the Qadarites,' with some narrations including variations such as the phrase that these two groups 'will not gain my intercession.' As Figure 3.8a illustrates, a main narration of this tradition comes through the Companion Ibn 'Abbās via his student 'Ikrima. This narration is only transmitted from 'Ikrima by Nizār and Sallām, both of whom are harshly criticized by a wide range of hadith critics. Moreover, the individual narrations from transmitters like 'Abdallāh al-Laythī have each been identified as unacceptable (*munkar*), due to a lack of corroboration, or declared false by early critics such as Ibn 'Adī and al-'Uqaylī. As a result of all this, the tradition from Ibn 'Abbās has uniformly been declared weak by scholars such as al-Khatīb al-Baghdādī, al-'Alā'ī, Ibn Hajar, al-Suyūtī, al-Albānī, and others.

As Figure 3.8b shows, there were other narrations of this 'Two types…' tradition as well. Like the version through Ibn 'Abbās, all these narrations were declared unreliable by Muslim scholars at various times. For several of the narrations, we see the problem of a lack of corroboration. This raised suspicions because it might be an instance of a sinister forger 'stealing' an *isnād* from an existing hadith and attaching it to a concocted *matn*. Or it might be the result of a careless transmitter accidentally creating a whole new, baseless

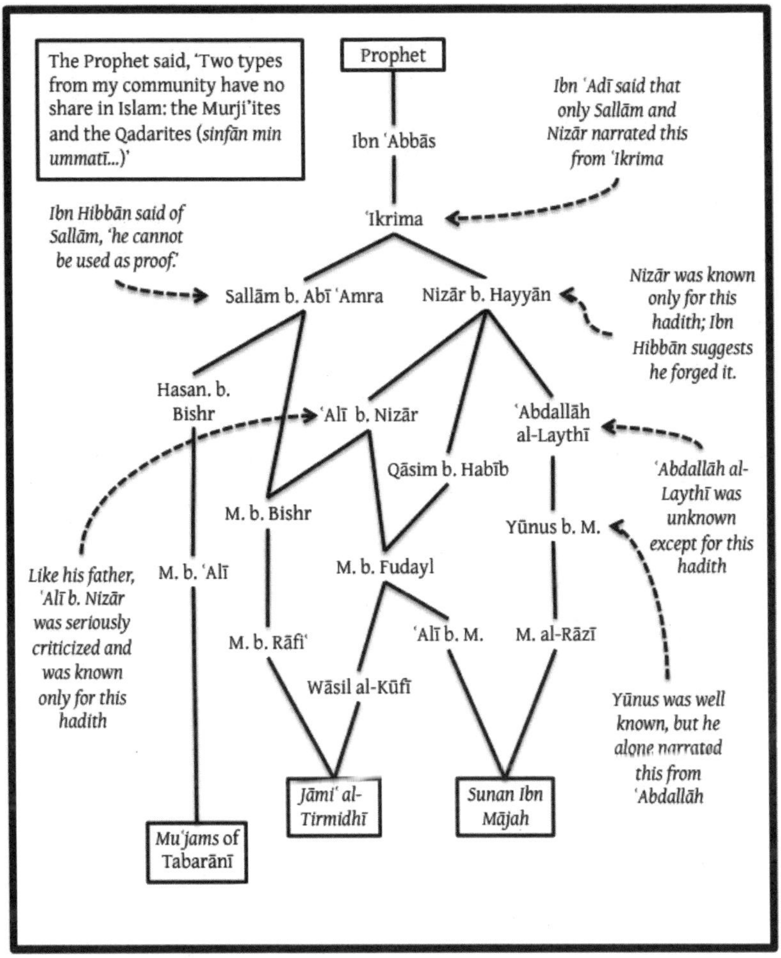
The Prophet said, 'Two types from my community have no share in Islam: the Murji'ites and the Qadarites (sinfān min ummatī...)'
Prophet
Ibn 'Abbās
Ibn 'Adī said that only Sallām and Nizār narrated this from 'Ikrima
'Ikrima
Ibn Hibbān said of Sallām, 'he cannot be used as proof.'
Sallām b. Abī 'Amra
Nizār b. Hayyān
Nizār was known only for this hadith; Ibn Hibbān suggests he forged it.
Hasan. b. Bishr
'Alī b. Nizār
'Abdallāh al-Laythī
Qāsim b. Habīb
'Abdallāh al-Laythī was unknown except for this hadith
M. b. Bishr
Yūnus b. M.
Like his father, 'Alī b. Nizār was seriously criticized and was known only for this hadith
M. b. 'Alī
M. b. Fudayl
M. b. Rāfi'
'Alī b. M.
M. al-Rāzī
Wāsil al-Kūfī
Yūnus was well known, but he alone narrated this from 'Abdallāh
Jāmi' al-Tirmidhī
Sunan Ibn Mājah
Mu'jams of Tabarānī

Figure 3.8a Hadith 1 on the Qadarite Heresy: 'Two types…' – the Narration of Ibn 'Abbās

transmission for a hadith. Looking at each narration from left to right on the chart, we see:

- The narrations from the Companion Anas b. Mālik found in the *Hilyat al-awliyā'* (Ornament of the Saints) of Abū Nu'aym al-Isbahānī (d. 430/1038) and the *Ibāna al-kubrā* (Greater Clarification) of the Hanbalī theologian Ibn Batta (d. 387/997) each depend on transmitters who are either wholly unidentified or whose reliability is unknown (*majhūl al-hāl*).

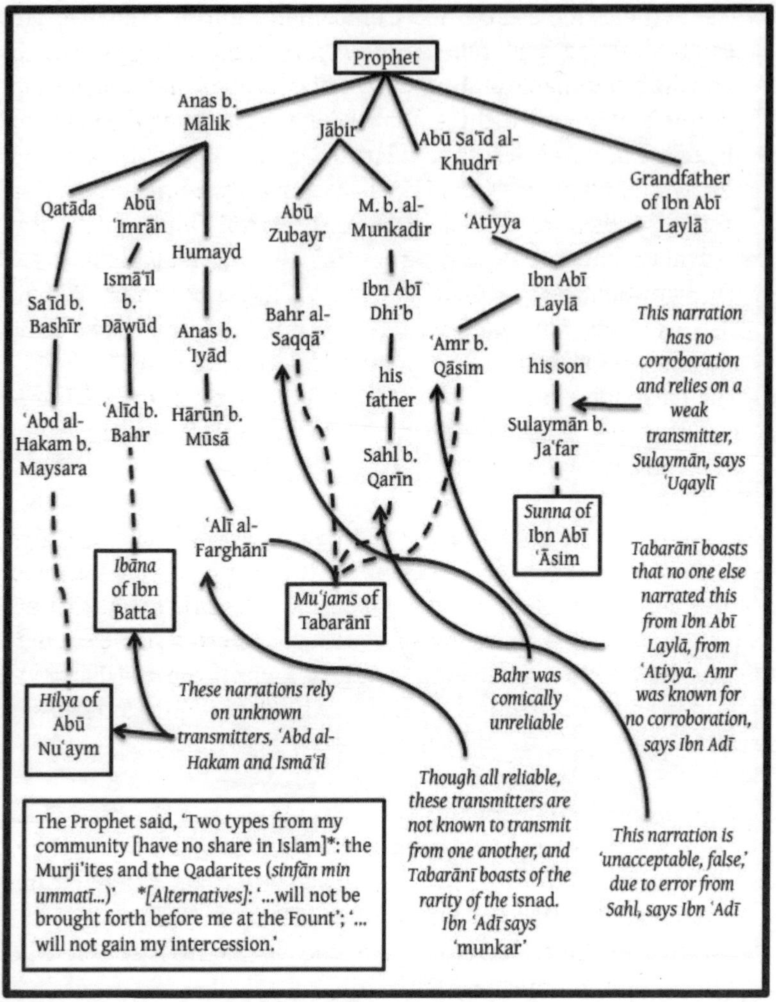

Figure 3.8b Hadith 1 on the Qadarite Heresy: Sundry Narrations

- The narration through Anas → Humayd in the *Muʿjam al-awsat* of al-Tabarānī comes via transmitters who are all reliable, according to al-Haythamī. But they are not common transmitters from one another, and al-Tabarānī himself boasts of how no one besides Abū Damra Anas b. ʿIyād narrated this from Humayd, and no one besides Hārūn narrated it from Abū Damra. Because of the total lack of corroboration from this transmission, Ibn ʿAdī calls this narration 'unknown (*munkar*).'

- The two narrations from the Companion Jābir b. ʿAbdallāh are also both found in al-Tabarānī's *Muʿjam*. Bahr al-Saqqā' was so incredibly unreliable that one early critic recalled that, after he had written down some hadiths from Bahr, a cat, sensing the value of the material, came and urinated on the pages. As for the narration via Sahl b. Qarīn, al-Tabarānī boasts that only Sahl narrated this from his father, from the famous jurist Ibn Abī Dhi'b. But, as Ibn ʿAdī notes, this narration is a gross error on the part of Sahl.
- The narration via the Kufan jurist Ibn Abī Laylā → ʿAmr b. Qāsim, also in al-Tabarānī's *Muʿjam al-awsat*, is unreliable because ʿAmr was known for lacking corroboration for his narrations.
- The narration from Ibn Abī Laylā that is found in the *Kitāb al-sunna* of Ibn Abī ʿĀsim (d. 287/900) is an isolated narration and relies on a weak transmitter, Sulaymān b. Jaʿfar.

The second tradition regarding Qadarites quotes the Prophet as saying, 'The Qadarites/those who deny God's power (*qadar*) are the Zoroastrians of my nation ....' Although al-ʿUqaylī noted that all its narrations are via weak transmitters, some were reliable enough to earn the tradition an overall rating of *sahīh* from al-Hākim al-Naysābūrī and *hasan* from al-Albānī. Looking at Figure 3.9, from left to right, we see:

- The most reliable narration is found in the *Sunan* of Ibn Mājah and comes from the Companion Jābir b. ʿAbdallāh, via a chain of strong transmitters, until Baqiyya b. al-Walīd. Although Ibn ʿAdī noted that Baqiyya would often narrate from Ibn Jurayj via unmentioned intermediaries – a major violation – in this case he names as his intermediary the leading jurist and hadith transmitter of Syria, al-Awzāʿī.
- The narrations from Ibn ʿUmar via Salama b. Dīnār (Abū Hāzim) → Zakariyyā b. Yahyā b. Manzūr, found in the *Muʿjam al-awsat* of al-Tabarānī and the *Kitāb al-sunna* of Ibn Abī ʿĀsim, are dismissed as unreliable because al-Bukhārī, Ibn Maʿīn, al-Nasā'ī, and others said Zakariyyā was very weak.

  Moreover, as Ibn ʿAdī notes, only Zakariyyā's narration from Salama includes Salama specifying that he heard the hadith from Nāfiʿ. This is important, since Ibn Hajar states that it is largely agreed upon that Salama did not hear directly from the Companion Ibn ʿUmar. If the narration from Nāfiʿ → Salama is unreliable,

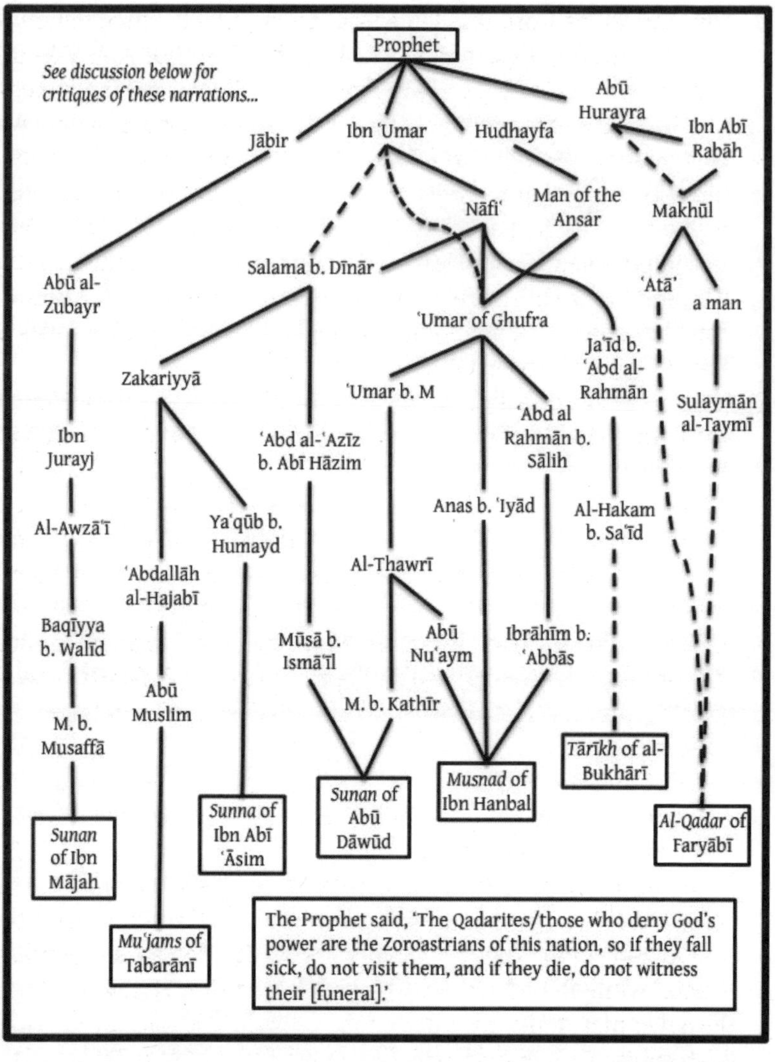

Figure 3.9 Hadith 2 on the Qadarite Heresy: 'The Zoroastrians of my nation ...'

then the only remaining narrations from Salama come through Ibn 'Umar → Salama, which includes a break in the *isnād*. Some critics, such as al-Hākim al-Naysābūrī and Ibn al-Qattān of Fez (d. 628/1230), considered this narration *sahīh* provided (and this is a big provided!) that Salama had heard hadiths directly from Ibn 'Umar.

- The narrations from Ibn 'Umar via 'Umar b. 'Abdallāh, the freeman of Ghufra, appear in works like the *Sunan* of Abū Dāwud and the *Musnad* of his teacher Ibn Hanbal. 'Umar the freeman of Ghufra was a moderately respected transmitter whose main fault was frequent *mursal* narrations, i.e., quoting a Companion without specifying that he heard the hadith from an intermediary (as in the case of one narration in the *Musnad* of Ibn Hanbal). This is compensated for by his specifying in another narration in the *Musnad* that he heard the hadith from Ibn 'Umar → Nāfi'. But, as Ibn 'Adī and al-Albānī point out, the lack of clarity constitutes a flaw (*'illa*) in the narration.
- There is also a narration through 'Umar of Ghufra via an unnamed man from the Medinan Ansār, from the Companion Hudhayfa b. Yamān, found in the *Sunan* of Abū Dāwūd and Ibn Hanbal's *Musnad*. It includes an additional clause in the *matn*: '... and they are the party of the Antichrist, and it befits God to join them with him.' This narration is unreliable because of the unidentified transmitter.
- One narration via Nāfi' bypasses the problem of 'Umar of Ghufra. According to al-Bukhārī and Ibn 'Adī, however, it is fatally flawed (*munkar*) because it is known only through the unreliable al-Hakam b. Sa'īd.
- Finally, the narrations of the hadith from the Companion Abū Hurayra are hopelessly tangled. These are found in several works from the tenth century, but the earliest source for them is the *Kitāb al-qadar* of Ja'far al-Faryābī (d. 301/913) and the *Kitāb al-sunna* of Ibn Abī 'Āsim (narrations not shown). They all come through the Syrian Successor Makhūl. But one comes through an unidentified 'man,' while the others have Makhūl citing Abū Hurayra, whom he never met, and come through the problematic transmitter 'Atā' al-Khurāsānī. The one narration that features Makhūl narrating from Abū Hurayra via an intermediary, the prominent Successor of Mecca, Ibn Abī Rabāh, is known to us only via Maslama b. 'Alī, who is criticized for this uncorroborated narration.

Conclusion: Rating these Two Hadiths

With the exception of the narration of the 'Qadariyya are the Zoroastrians...' hadith from Jābir in the *Sunan* of Ibn Mājah, every narration of these two traditions is either impugned for weak transmitters, lack of corroboration, or both. Looking at these narrations as particulars, Ibn al-Jawzī thus considered the two hadiths to be complete forgeries.

Most later scholars, however, defended the overall acceptability of our two hadiths. Responding to what they thought was an extreme ruling by Ibn al-Jawzī, al-'Alā'ī, Ibn Hajar, al-Suyūtī, and most recently Ahmad al-Ghumārī and al-Albānī all defended these two hadiths. They argued that most of the narrations are weak, but they do not merit the label of outright forgeries. When they are aggregated, the hadiths even rise to the level of *hasan*. Several scholars took a middle ground. Al-Munāwī labeled both hadiths as weak, and the Hanafī scholar Ibn Abī al-'Izz (d. 792/1390) declared simply that all hadiths on the Qadariyya are weak.[111]

SUGGESTIONS FOR FURTHER READING

For further information on hadith criticism and its historical development, see Ignaz Goldziher's *Muslim Studies II*, Muhammad Siddiqi's *Hadith Literature* (Cambridge, 1996), Eerik Dickinson's *The Development of Early Sunnite* Ḥadīth *Criticism* (Leiden, 2001), and Jonathan Brown's *The Canonization of al-Bukhārī and Muslim* (Leiden, 2007). For a work specifically discussing the contributions of Sunni hadith critics, see Scott Lucas, *Constructive Critics, Ḥadīth Literature and the Articulation of Sunnī Islam* (Leiden, 2004). See also Brown, 'Critical Rigor versus Juridical Pragmatism,' *Islamic Law and Society* 14, no. 1 (2007), pp.1–41. For more depth on the issue of content/*matn* criticism of hadiths, see J. Brown, 'How We Know Early Hadith Critics Did *Matn* Criticism and Why It's So Hard to Find,' *Islamic Law and Society* 15 (2008), pp.143–184 and the same author's 'The Rules of *Matn* Criticism: There Are No Rules,' *Islamic Law and Society* 19 (2012), pp. 356–396. For more on how sure Muslims scholars were that the Prophet had said something and debates over using hadiths scholars knew were unreliable, see the author's 'Did the Prophet Say It or Not?: the Literal, Historical and Effective Truth of Hadiths in Sunni Islam,' *Journal of the American Oriental Society*, 129, no. 2 (2009), pp. 1–27; and 'Even if it's not True it's True: Using Unreliable Hadiths in Sunni Islam,' *Islamic Law and Society* 18 (2011), pp. 1–52.

Two useful primary sources for the method of hadith criticism in the early period are G.H.A. Juynboll's 'Muslim's Introduction to His Sahih,' republished in *Studies on the Origins and Uses of Islamic Hadīth* (Variorum, 1996) and J. Brown's translation of *The Kitab al-'Ilal of Imam al-Tirmidhi* (Madina Institute, 2018). Eerik Dickinson has translated one of the most important Muslim texts on the technical terms of hadith study, the *Muqaddima* of Ibn al-Salāh, into English under the title *An Introduction to the Science of Hadith* (Reading, UK, 2005). James Robson has also translated an earlier and shorter manual on hadith criticism by al-Hākim al-Naysābūrī entitled *An Introduction to the Science of Tradition* (London: Luzac & Co., 1953). A recent example of traditional Muslim hadith criticism is Zafar Ahmad al-Tahānawī's (d. 1974) *Qawa'id fi Ulum al-Hadith: Principles of the Sciences of Hadith* (London: Turath Publishing, 2014). A translation of a representative book of *mawdū'āt* (forged) hadiths is Mullā 'Alī al-Qārī's *Encyclopedia of Hadith Forgeries*, trans. G.F. Haddad (Beacon Books, 2013). Ibn al-Jawzī's fascinating book on storytellers, popular preachers, and their abuse of hadiths has been translated into English by Merlin Swartz as *Ibn al-Jawzī's Kitāb al-Quṣṣāṣ wa'l-Mudhakkirīn* (Beirut: Dar El-Machreq, 1986).

ENDNOTES

1 Benjaminson and Anderson, *Investigative Reporting*, p. 30.
2 'Pet food: too posh to eat pooch,' *The Economist*, June 20, 2015.
3 Al-Dhahabī, *Mīzān al-i'tidāl*, vol. 2, p. 293.
4 Ibid., vol. 3, p. 517.
5 Cited from al-Madā'inī's *Kitāb al-ahdāth*; Ahmad b. Sa'd al-Dīn al-Miswarī, *Al-Risāla al-munqidha min al-ghiwāya fī turuq al-riwāya*, pp. 51–55.
6 'Abdallāh b. al-Zubayr al-Humaydī, *Al-Musnad*, vol. 1, p. 2.
7 'Abd al-Razzāq al-San'ānī, *Musannaf*, vol. 10, p. 381.
8 *Sahīh Muslim*: *kitāb al-janā'iz, bāb al-mayyit yu'adhdhabu bi-bukā' ahlihi 'alayhi*.
9 *Musnad Ibn Hanbal*: vol. 6, p. 246.
10 Abū Zur'a al-Dimashqī, *Tārīkh Abī Zur'a al-Dimashqī*, p. 270.
11 For an example, see al-Dhahabī, *Mīzān al-i'tidāl*, vol. 2, p. 369.
12 Ismā'īl b. Ahmad al-'Ajlūnī, *Kashf al-khafā'*, vol. 1, p. 227.
13 '*Kuntu 'ind al-nabī dhāt layla qāl: unzur hal tarā fī al-samā' min shay' ...*'; *Musnad Ibn Hanbal*: vol. 1, p. 209.
14 Al-Suyūtī, *al-La'ālī' al-masnū'a fī al-ahādīth al-mawdū'a*, vol. 1, p. 357.
15 Al-Rāfi'ī, *al-Tadwīn fī akhbār Qazwīn*, vol. 1, p.452.

16 Osama al-Syed Mahmoud, personal communication 2/06.
17 Al-Suyūtī, *al-La'ālī al-masnū'a*, vol. 1, p. 16; vol. 2, p. 221.
18 Al-Khatīb, *Tārīkh Baghdād*, vol. 9, p. 334; vol. 2, p. 379.
19 Mullā 'Alī Qārī, *al-Asrār al-marfū'a fī al-akhbār al-mawdū'a*, p. 442.
20 Ibid., p. 236; Ibn al-Jawzī, *Kitāb al-mawdū'āt*, vol. 1, p. 41.
21 Al-Dhahabī, *Mīzān al-i'tidāl*, vol. 1, p. 187; Qādī 'Iyād, *Kitāb al-shifā*, p. 226.
22 Al-Hākim al-Naysābūrī, *Kitāb al-madkhal ilā ma'rifat kitāb al-iklīl*, pp. 134–135.
23 Ibn 'Adī, *al-Kāmil fī du'afā' al-rijāl*, vol. 1, p. 151.
24 Al-Dhahabī, *Mīzān al-i'tidāl*, vol. 1, p. 141.
25 Ibn al-Jawzī, *Kitāb al-mawdū'āt*, vol. 1, p. 39.
26 Ibn Hajar, *Fath al-bārī*, vol. 1, p. 266.
27 Al-'Ajlūnī, *Kashf al-khafā'*, vol. 1, pp. 412–413.
28 Mullā 'Alī Qārī, *al-Masnū' fī ma'rifat al-hadīth al-mawdū'*, p. 121.
29 Al-'Ajlūnī, *Kashf al-khafā'*, vol. 1, pp. 319–320; Ibn Abī Hātim al-Rāzī, *'Ilal al-hadīth*, vol. 2, p. 342.
30 *Sahīh Muslim*: *muqaddima*, *bāb al-isnād min al-dīn*.
31 Al-Albānī, *Silsilat al-ahādīth al-da'īfa wa al-mawdū'a*, vol. 1, p. 53.
32 Jonathan Brown, 'How We Know Early Ḥadīth Critics Did *Matn* Criticism,' pp. 170–171.
33 *Sahīh Muslim*: *muqaddima*, *bāb al-isnād min al-dīn*.
34 Al-Hākim, *Kitāb al-madkhal ilā ma'rifat kitāb al-iklīl*, p. 58.
35 Lucas, *Constructive Critics*, pp. 143–156.
36 Abū Ghudda, ed., *Arba' rasā'il fī 'ulūm al-hadīth*, p. 180.
37 Abū Ja'far al-'Uqaylī, *Kitāb al-du'afā' al-kabīr*, vol. 1, p. 13.
38 *Sahīh Muslim*: *muqaddima*, introduction.
39 Al-'Uqaylī, *Kitāb al-du'afā' al-kabīr*, vol. 1, p. 13.
40 Al-Khatīb, *Tārīkh Baghdād*, vol. 10, p. 260.
41 Al-Dhahabī, *Mīzān al-i'tidāl*, vol. 1, pp. 218 ff.
42 Muhammad Ibn al-Amīr al-San'ānī, *[Question and Answer]*, 38b.
43 Muhammad b. 'Aqīl, *al-'Atb al-jamīl 'alā ahl al-jarh wa al-ta'dīl*, p. 92.
44 Al-Dhahabī, *Mīzān al-i'tidāl*, vol. 2, p. 205.
45 Ibn Abī Hātim, *al-Jarh wa al-ta'dīl*, vol. 2, p. 37.
46 Al-Mundhirī, *Jawāb al-hāfiz al-Mundhirī*, p. 89.
47 Al-Dhahabī, *Mīzān al-i'tidāl*,vol. 4, p. 237.
48 Al-'Irāqī, *al-Taqyīd wa al-īdāh*, p. 231.
49 *Sahīh al-Bukhārī*: *kitāb fadā'il al-sahāba*, *bāb* 1.
50 Al-Khatīb, *al-Kifāya*, vol. 1, p. 188.
51 Ibn Taymiyya, *Majmū'at al-fatāwā*, vol. 27, p. 223.
52 'Alī Jum'a, personal communication, 8/27/03.
53 Jum'a, *Qawl al-sahābī 'ind al-usūliyyīn*, p. 34.
54 For example, the Prophet's stepson Hind b. Abī Hāla; al-Bukhārī, *Kitāb al-du'afā' al-saghīr*, p. 123.
55 Abū Ghudda, *Arba' rasā'il fī 'ulūm al-hadīth*, pp. 111, 207; J. Brown, 'Crossing Sectarian Boundaries in the 4th/10th Century,' pp. 55–58.
56 Abū Zur'a al-Dimashqī, *Tārīkh Abī Zur'a al-Dimashqī*, p. 93.
57 Ibn Abī Hātim al-Rāzī, *al-Taqdima*, p. 127.
58 Salāh al-Dīn al-'Alā'ī, *Jāmi' al-tahsīl fī ahkām al-marāsīl*, p. 80.

59 *Jāmiʿ al-Tirmidhī: kitāb al-ʿilal, bāb al-mursal.*
60 Ibn Hibbān al-Bustī, *Sahīh Ibn Hibbān*, vol. 1, pp. 144–145.
61 *Sahīh Muslim*: *muqaddima*, introduction.
62 Al-Dhahabī, *Mīzān al-iʿtidāl*, vol. 2, pp. 440–441.
63 *Sahīh Muslim*: *muqaddima*, introduction.
64 *Jāmiʿ al-Tirmidhī: kitāb al-jihād, bāb mā jā'a fī al-mighfar.*
65 *Jāmiʿ al-Tirmidhī: kitāb al-ʿilal; kitāb al-birr wa al-sila, bāb mā jā'a fī adab al-walad.*
66 Al-Khalīlī, *Al-Irshād*, p. 21.
67 J. Brown, 'Critical Rigor versus Juridical Pragmatism,' p. 21 ; 'Alī b. 'Umar al-Dāraqutnī, *Kitāb al-ilzāmāt wa'l-tatabbuʿ*, ed. Muqbil al-Wādiʿī (Medina, al-Maktaba al-Salafiyya, [1978]), pp. 266–7.
68 J. Brown, 'Critical Rigor,' pp. 38–41.
69 Badīʿ al-Sayyid al-Lahhām, *al-Imām al-hāfiz Jalāl al-Dīn al-Suyūtī*, pp. 460–463.
70 Al-Dhahabī, *Mīzān al-iʿtidāl*, vol. 3, p. 306.
71 Al-Bukhārī, *al-Tārīkh al-awsat*, vol. 2, pp. 109–110.
72 Muslim, *Kitāb al-tamyīz*, p. 147.
73 Ibn al-Murtadā, *Tabaqāt al-muʿtazila*, p. 81.
74 This is attributed to 'Alī b. al-Madīnī; Ibn 'Adī, *Al-Kāmil*, vol. 1, p. 131.
75 *Sunan al-Nasā'ī: kitāb al-janā'iz, bāb al-niyāha ʿalā al-mayyit.*
76 Ibn Qutayba, *Ta'wīl mukhtalif al-hadīth*, p. 208.
77 Ibn 'Abd al-Barr, *Kitāb al-tamhīd*, vol. 1, p. 58.
78 *Jāmiʿ al-Tirmidhī: kitāb al-ʿilal.*
79 Al-Dhahabī, *Mīzān al-iʿtidāl*, vol. 1, p. 119.
80 Al-Husayn b. Ibrāhīm al-Jawzaqānī, *al-Abātīl wa al-manākīr*, pp. 89–90.
81 Ibn al-Jawzī, *Kitāb al-mawdūʿāt*, vol. 1, p. 106.
82 J. Brown, 'The Rules of *Matn* Criticism,' pp. 364, 376–80.
83 Ibn Khuzayma, *Sahīh Ibn Khuzayma*, vol. 1, p. 3.
84 Ibn Hajar, *al-Nukat ʿalā kitāb Ibn al-Salāh*, p. 134.
85 Ibn Taymiyya, *Majmūʿat al-fatāwā*,vol. 18, p. 23.
86 *Jāmiʿ al-Tirmidhī: kitāb al-ʿilal.*
87 Hamd al-Khattābī, *Maʿālim al-sunan*, vol. 1, p. 6.
88 Ibn Abī Hātim, *al-Jarh wa al- taʿdīl*, vol. 2, pp. 30–31.
89 Al-Khatīb, *al-Kifāya fī maʿrifat usūl ʿilm al-riwāya*, vol. 1, p. 399.
90 Al-Khatīb, *al-Jāmiʿ*, vol. 2, p. 195.
91 J. Brown, 'The Rules of Matn Criticism,' pp. 362–64
92 Abū Bakr al-Jassās, *Usūl al-Jassās*, vol. 1, pp. 504 ff., 2, pp. 3–6, 14.
93 Ibn al-Salāh, *Muqaddima*, p. 454.
94 Ibn Hibbān, *Sahīh Ibn Hibbān*, vol. 1, p. 145.
95 Jamāl al-Dīn al-Zaylaʿī, *Nasb al-rāya li-ahādīth al-Hidāya*, vol. 1, p. 342.
96 Al-Dhahabī, *Siyar aʿlām al-nubalā'*, vol. 17, p. 175.
97 Al-Nawawī, *al-Adhkār*, p. 214.
98 Ibn Taymiyya, *Majmūʿat al-fatāwā*, vol. 19, p. 144.
99 Al-Nawawī, *Sharh Sahīh Muslim*, vol. 1, p. 240; al-Suyūtī, 'al-Taʿzīm wa al-manna fī anna abawayh rasūl Allāh fī al-janna,' p. 2.
100 Mullā 'Alī Qārī, *Al-Asrār al-marfūʿa*, p. 305.
101 Al-ʿAjlūnī, *Kashf al-khafā'*, vol. 1, pp. 236–237.
102 Ibn Qayyim al-Jawziyya, *Kitāb al-rūh*, p. 32.

103 Mālik, *al-Muwatta'*: *kitāb mā jā'a fī al-ru'ā.*
104 *Sunan Ibn Mājah*: *kitāb ta'bīr al-ru'ā, bāb ru'yat al-nabī.*
105 See 'Abd al-Rā'ūf al-Munāwī, *Fayd al-qadīr sharh al-Jāmi' al-saghīr*, vol. 11, pp. 5805–6.
106 Al-Rāfi'ī, *al-Tadwīn fī akhbār Qazwīn*, vol. 1, p. 309.
107 William Chittick, *Imaginal Worlds*, p. 10.
108 Chittick, *The Sufi Path of Knowledge*, pp. 251–252.
109 John Voll, 'Two Biographies of Ahmad Ibn Idris al-Fasi (1760–1837),' p. 641.
110 Mullā 'Alī Qārī, *Al-Masnū'*, p. 216. See also, al-Sakhāwī, *Maqāsid*, p. 424.
111 Ibn al-Jawzī, *Kitāb al-Mawdū'āt*, vol. 1, pp. 275–278; Ibn Abī al-'Izz, *Sharh al-'Aqīda al-Tahāwiyya*, p. 273; Ibn Hajar, *Hidāyat al-ruwāt*, vol. 1, p. 102; al-Suyūtī, *al-La'ālī al-masnū'a*, vol. 1, pp. 236–240; al-Munāwī, *Fayd al-qadīr*, vol. 7, p. 3743, vol. 8, p. 4398; Ahmad al-Ghumārī, *al-Mudāwī*, vol. 4, p. 638; al-Albānī, *Da'īf Sunan Ibn Mājah*, p. 11, idem, *Silsilat al-ahādīth al-da'īfa*, vol. 12, pp. 481–482.

4

PROPHETIC TRADITIONS IN SHIITE ISLAM

INTRODUCTION

Muhammad's authority to interpret definitively the meaning of the Quran and instruct Muslims did not disappear when he died. It continued in the form of an inheritance left to the Muslim community. To a large extent, sectarian divisions in Islam have revolved around competing claims over who should assume this role of authoritative interpreter. The tradition that became Sunni Islam offered one answer: the community as a whole, represented by the ulema (the Muslim scholarly class), was heir to Muhammad. Their collective interpretation of Islam, expressed through consensus (*ijmāʿ*), was as definitive as the Quran or the Prophet's edicts.

The tradition that would become Shiite Islam proposed a different answer: the family of the Prophet had inherited his authority, which was held by select members of the family known as **imams**. The first imam was ʿAlī b. Abī Ṭālib (d. 40/660), Muhammad's cousin and the husband of his daughter Fatima, through whom all descendants of the Prophet trace their ancestry. Shiites maintain that the Prophet had imparted his knowledge to ʿAlī, and through ʿAlī to his descendants. When one of these revered descendants, Mūsā al-Kāẓim (d. 183/799), was asked if the Prophet had brought mankind all the knowledge they would require to understand their religion and if any of that had been lost, he replied, 'No, it is with his family.'[1] Mūsā's father, Jaʿfar al-Ṣādiq (d. 148/765), had given the same answer. The Quran contains the answers to all questions, he said, 'but men's minds cannot grasp them.' For an imam in whose veins the Prophet's esoteric knowledge of God's will runs, however, he can see these answers in the Quran 'as easily as he looks at his own palm.'[2]

Hadiths were one medium for transmitting the Prophet's legacy through the generations of his community as they expanded outwards from Medina in time and space. Since Shiism had a different vision of the heirs to the Prophet's authority, it is no surprise that the Shiite hadith tradition differs greatly from its Sunni counterpart. As the majority of the world's Shiites subscribe to the **Imami**, or *Ithnaʿasharī* ('Twelver,' so called because it traces the Prophetic authority through twelve imams) creed, and since Imami hadith scholarship has dwarfed that of other Shiite sects, in this chapter we will focus mainly on the Imami Shiite hadith tradition. We will then turn our attention briefly to Zaydi Shiite hadith scholarship. As in the previous chapters, mention of 'authentic' or 'forged' hadiths refers to Muslim standards for reliability, not Western historical ones.

In Sunni Islam, hadiths were reports transmitted from the only individual that Sunnis deemed infallible: the Prophet Muhammad. In Imami Shiite Islam, the infallibility of the Prophet lived on in the form of the imams, each one appointing one of his sons as the next imam. Not only were these imams therefore the best source for sayings of the Prophet, they themselves were sources of their own hadiths. The vast majority of Imami Shiite hadiths thus occur in one of three forms:

1 A hadith of the Prophet is transmitted through an *isnād* made up of the imams after him.
2 The saying of an imam is transmitted from him by later imams.
3 The saying of an imam is transmitted from him via an *isnād* of his followers.

1. ʿAlī b. Abī Tālib
2. al-Hasan 3. al-Husayn
4. ʿAlī Zayn al-ʿĀbidīn
5. Muhammad al-Bāqir
6. Jaʿfar al-Sādiq
7. Mūsā al-Kāzim
8. ʿAlī al-Ridā
9. Muhammad al-Taqī
10. ʿAlī al-Naqī
11. al-Hasan al-ʿAskarī
12. Muhammad al-Mahdī: the Hidden Imam

Figure 4.0 The Twelve Imams

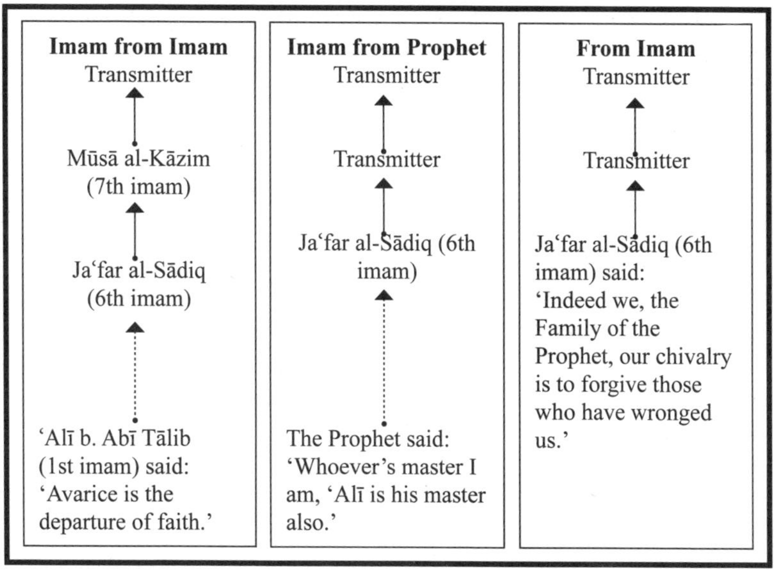
Imam from Imam
Transmitter
Mūsā al-Kāzim (7th imam)
Ja'far al-Sādiq (6th imam)
'Alī b. Abī Tālib (1st imam) said: 'Avarice is the departure of faith.'
Imam from Prophet
Transmitter
Transmitter
Ja'far al-Sādiq (6th imam)
The Prophet said: 'Whoever's master I am, 'Alī is his master also.'
From Imam
Transmitter
Transmitter
Ja'far al-Sādiq (6th imam) said: 'Indeed we, the Family of the Prophet, our chivalry is to forgive those who have wronged us.'

Figure 4.1 Forms of Imami Shiite Hadiths

Whether a hadith originated with the Prophet or an imam, or whether or not the *isnād* between an imam and the Prophet was complete was of no importance. After all, imams were infallible and spoke with the inherited authority of the Prophet. A famous Shiite hadith makes this amply clear. The sixth imam, Ja'far al-Sādiq, is reported to have said:

> My hadiths are the hadiths of my father, and the hadiths of my father are the hadiths of my grandfather, and the hadiths of my grandfather are the hadiths of al-Husayn, and the hadiths of al-Husayn are the hadiths of al-Hasan, and the hadiths of al-Hasan are the hadiths of the Commander of the Faithful ('Alī b. Abī Tālib) (s), and the hadiths of the Commander of the Faithful are the hadiths of the Messenger of God (s), and the hadiths of the Messenger of God are the words of God most high.[3]

Shiites also sometimes narrated hadiths from the Prophet *via* his Companions in the same manner as Sunnis. But as we will discuss below, this was generally done for polemical purposes. There was little reason for Shiites to rely on the all-too-fallible Companions of the Prophet when they believed that the imams who descended from him were immune to deception or misguidance.

THE DEVELOPMENT OF EARLY SHIITE HADITH LITERATURE

Three major events defined the Imami Shiite community and had a formative influence on its hadith tradition. First, the failure of the early Muslims to acknowledge collectively that ʿAlī and his descendants should have been the rightful political and religious rulers in Islam made the idealistic Sunni vision of the early Muslim community untenable. Unlike the categorical trust that Sunnis placed in the reliability of the Companions as hadith transmitters, Shiites believed that even this founding generation had failed. Any Companion who did not support ʿAlī's claim to succeed the Prophet was at best complicit with injustice, at worst an active denier of the truth.

Second, for the Imami Shiites, like other Shiite groups who identified religious leadership with the Prophet's descendants, this reliance on the family of the Prophet resulted in a crisis when the line of imams seemed to come to an end. In 260/874, Hasan al-ʿAskarī, the eleventh imam, died in captivity in the Abbasid court. A young man, he had no heir that the public knew of. The Shiite imams had served as the authoritative interpreters of the Quran, the Prophet's legacy, and Islam in general for their followers. Who now would meet this need? Some members of the Shiite community claimed that the eleventh imam had indeed had a son, who had been hidden away by the community from the Abbasid caliph. Tired of the unjust and iniquitous world, the infant boy had vanished in an underground cave in Samarra, to return in the future as the rightly guided Messiah (*Mahdī*) and 'fill the world with justice as it had been filled with injustice.' In the coming decades, certain members of the community claimed to be in contact with the 'Hidden Imam,' even delivering questions posed by members of the community to him. Eventually the prominent Shiite noble Ibn Rawh al-Nawbakhtī formalized this function, announcing that he and two predecessors were 'ambassadors (*safīr*)' of the Hidden Imam.[4]

In 329/941 the third formative event occurred: the last of the 'ambassadors' died. This controversial office, claimed disputably by many, proved too problematic to both the Hidden Imam and his community, and all contact between the two would be cut off until the Imam's return. The last 'ambassador' informed his followers soon before his death that the Hidden Imam had instructed him that anyone from that point on who claimed contact with the Imam was a fraud.[5] The Shiite community, who had held that God would not leave His community without an authoritative interpreter of His religion, found itself completely alone. This duty would now fall upon the shoulders of the scholars. Although not in contact with him, they would act as the Hidden Imam's regents until his return.

It is in this period of crisis, beginning with the initial disappearance of the twelfth imam and reaching a crescendo with his ultimate occultation (passing into a state of supernatural seclusion), that we find the earliest development of Imami Shiite doctrine and hadith. First, the Imami community, with its centers at Qumm and Rayy in Iran, would have to distinguish itself from other Shiite groups who believed that it was in fact earlier imams who had represented the end of the earthly Alid line and would return as the awaited *Mahdī*. Hasan b. Mūsā al-Nawbakhtī's (d. between 300–310/912–922) and Sa'd b. Abdallāh al-Qummī's (writing 292/905) ninth-century books on various sects of the Shiites are the first surviving articulations of Imami doctrine. These books seek to carve out a doctrinal identity for the Imami Shiites that distinguishes them from both the earlier Shiite extremist groups, such as those that believed that 'Alī was divine, as well as the groups such as the Ismailis (many of whom awaited the return of the imam Ismā'īl, the brother of the seventh imam Mūsā al-Kāzim, whom they claimed was in occultation) and the Waqifiyya sect, who believed that it was Mūsā al-Kāzim who had gone into occultation.

Furthermore, who was this twelfth 'Hidden' imam, unknown to all but a few prominent Shiites, and what was the nature of his occultation? Even many of the Shiite families who had believed in the imamate of the Hidden Imam's father al-Hasan al-'Askarī did not know the answer to these questions. The scion of a great Shiite family of Qumm, Ibn Bābawayh (d. 381/991), attempted to clarify these points to his community in his *Epistle on Beliefs*, which comprehensively formulated the doctrine of Imamis.[6]

What heritage did Imami Shiite scholars like Ibn Bābawayh have to draw on in their efforts to define Imami law and doctrine? Like many pious Muslims in the first three generations of Islam, those individuals who believed that the family of the Prophet enjoyed a special status or religious authority collected the sayings and rulings of the imams in order to preserve their legacy. In particular, the students who flocked around the sixth imam, Ja'far al-Sādiq (The Truthful), in Medina collected their notes of his teachings. The legacy of his son, the seventh imam, Mūsā al-Kāzim, was also collected in numerous small books by his students. Even until the time of the eleventh imam, devotees of the family of the Prophet labored to record their teachings, rulings, and interpretations of the Quran.[7]

A notebook of sayings of imams like Ja'far al-Sādiq was called an *asl* ('source,' pl. *usūl*). Hundreds (Imami Shiites have traditionally talked of the 'four hundred *usūl*,' but other numbers have been mentioned as well) of these *usūl* were compiled, sometimes by a student of the imam recording his teachings directly and sometimes through an *isnād* from the imam to a slightly later collector. The *usūl* contained the material essential for formulating a religious and communal vision: elaborations of doctrine, answers to legal queries and polemics against those who opposed the rightful station of the *ahl al-bayt* (The Family of the Prophet).

In addition, early Shiite compilers collected books on the virtues (*fadā'il*, *khasā'is*) of 'Alī and his progeny as well as the history of their careers. Zayd b. Wahb (d. 96/714–15), a Kufan devotee of the family of the Prophet, compiled a book of the sermons of 'Alī (*Kitāb khutab amīr al-mu'minīn*).[8]

Like the Sunni hadith tradition, some of these early books may really have been written after the deaths of their supposed authors by some later figure. Even some Shiite scholars, for example, doubt the authenticity of a book of hadiths attributed to the Successor Sulaym b. Qays al-'Āmirī called *Kitāb al-saqīfa*.[9] Some of the *usūl* drew on these dubious early books, like the 'Book of the Sunna, Rulings and Judicial Cases' (*Kitāb al-sunan wa al-ahkām wa al-qadāyā*) of the Companion Ibrāhīm Abū Rāfi' and *al-Sahīfa al-sajjādiyya* attributed to the fourth imam, 'Alī Zayn al-'Ābidīn.[10] These early books may have really existed, or they may have been conjured up by later Shiites eager to show that 'Alī and his descendants truly had some special knowledge, in book form, that no other Companions possessed.

For the Imami community, eager to elaborate a clear doctrine, ritual, and law in the absence of its imam, however, these *usūl* were not very useful. They needed to be reorganized according to topic. Starting in the early eighth century, Shiite scholars began making selections of hadiths and organizing them into 'compendia' (*jāmi'*, pl. *jawāmi'*) and 'topical books' (*mubawwab*). These books could either address one issue or, like the *musannaf* and *sunan* books of the Sunnis, a whole range of subjects. For example, Ja'far al-Sādiq's student Ghiyāth b. Ibrāhīm had compiled a book of the imam's teachings organized along the lines of what was permitted or forbidden for various legal topics.[11] Ibn al-Qaddāh (d. *c.* 180/796–7) collected a book of hadiths specifically on the nature of heaven and hell.[12]

These early topical collections by students of the imams provided a foundation for the Imami Shiite community to draw from and build on. Muhammad b. al-Hasan al-Saffār al-Qummī (d. 290/903) wrote the famous *Basā'ir al-darajāt*, which specifically dealt with the virtues and prerogatives of imams.[13] Ibn Bābawayh's *Kitāb al-jāmi' li-ziyārat al-Ridā* provided reports on the virtues of the eighth imam and the importance of visiting his grave, while the *Kitāb al-jāmi' al-kabīr fī al-fiqh* by Ibrāhīm b. Muhammad al-Thaqafī (d. 283/896) more closely resembled a comprehensive *sunan* book.[14] A *tafsīr* replete with reports about why verses of the Quran were revealed was attributed to the eleventh imam al-Hasan al-'Askarī (although Shiite scholars debate whether or not the imam actually wrote it).

Even as the *usūl* and early books were broken up to create these topical works, some Shiite scholars like Ahmad Ibn 'Uqda (d. 332/944), who were deeply committed to hadith transmission, continued to transmit the *usūl* in their original form – approximately thirteen survive today.[15] It is interesting that, as Ron Buckley has noted, Shiites started compiling topical collections of hadiths as part of developing their law at approximately the same time that great Sunni scholars such as Mālik b. Anas and al-Bukhārī were doing the same.[16]

THE SHIITE HADITH CANON

These topical works of law, ritual, and doctrine formed the basis for what became the four books of the Shiite hadith canon: the *Kāfī fī 'ilm al-dīn* of Muhammad b. Ya'qūb al-Kulaynī (d. 329/939), the *Man lā yahduruhu al-faqīh* of Ibn Bābawayh (d. 381/991) and the two collections of Abū Ja'far Muhammad b. al-Hasan al-Tūsī (d. 460/1067), the *Tahdhīb al-ahkām* and the *Istibsār fīmā ukhtulifa fīhi al-akhbār*. While the Sunni hadith canon is made of books very similar to one another in structure and purpose (they are all from the *sunan* genre), the components of the Shiite canon represent varying tools for different visions of the role of hadith in religious rulemaking.[17]

Al-Kulaynī offered his massive *al-Kāfī fī ʿilm al-dīn* (The Sufficient Book in the Knowledge of Religion) as a source for Shiites who could not find scholars possessing true knowledge of Islam or sort out the tangled web of reports narrated from the Prophet and the imams. Al-Kulaynī says that this dearth of knowledge was due to the unwillingness of scholars to resort only to 'the Quran and the Prophet's sunna with true knowledge and understanding.' Instead, they have turned to blind imitation (*taqlīd*), what they saw as their own best judgment (*istihsān*) and baseless interpretation (*ta'wīl*). The *Kāfī*, al-Kulaynī says, is the answer. It will suffice for 'those who want knowledge of the religion and to act on it according to authentic reports from the Truthful Ones [i.e., the imams] and the established Sunna that is the basis for right legal action.'[18] The *Kāfī* covers the whole range of legal topics applicable in Muslim life as well as the issues of the origins and nature of the imamate. Like al-Bukhārī's *Sahīh*, the very structure of the books explains the lessons the reader should derive from it; the titles of each subchapter instruct the reader how to understand the hadiths it includes. The author trusts the book to be its own explanation.

A generation later, the great Ibn Bābawayh compiled another comprehensive topical hadith collection designed to assist Imami Shiites who had no other source for understanding Islam properly. His *Man lā yahduruhu al-faqīh* (He Who Has No Legal Scholar at Hand) is even more consciously a reference work than the *Kāfī*. Unlike al-Kulaynī, Ibn Bābawayh does not provide full *isnād*s for each hadith. He does not want the reader to concern himself with such specialized details, but rather assures his audience that he has only included reports that are authentic.[19]

Ibn Bābawayh and early Imami scholars sought to meet the immediate challenges facing the community with reports from the Prophet and imams alone as evidence. Ibn Bābawayh's most famous student, Muhammad b. al-Nuʿmān al-Hārithī (d. 413/1022), called al-Shaykh al-Mufīd, however, was a Muʿtazilite rationalist who saw hadiths as only a limited component of elaborating law and doctrine for the Imami community. Hadiths should be part of a larger framework for understanding Islam, used properly and supervised by a more authoritative master: reason. As a follower of the Muʿtazilite school in Baghdad, al-Shaykh al-Mufīd believed that rational investigation was an essential tool for determining correct belief, and he abandoned his teacher Ibn Bābawayh's reliance on using *āhād* reports from the imams as evidence in many issues.[20]

It was one of al-Shaykh al-Mufīd's students in Baghdad who would be responsible for half of the Shiite hadith canon and become one of the most influential scholars in Shiism: Muhammad b. al-Hasan al-Tūsī (d. 460/1067). While al-Kulaynī and Ibn Bābawayh had assured their readers that their books consisted of only authentic hadiths, al-Tūsī's two hadith works made this authentication process more transparent. Furthermore, for him hadiths were clearly just one part in a larger process of deriving law. Al-Tūsī's first book, the *Tahdhīb al-ahkām*, is in fact not a true hadith collection at all. It is a commentary on a legal work by al-Shaykh al-Mufīd (called *al-Muqni'*), structured along its lines but focusing on its hadiths. Al-Tūsī's *al-Istibsār fīmā ukhtulifa fīhi al-akhbār* (Seeking Clarity on that which Reports Differ) resembles much more closely the books that Sunni scholars like al-Shāfi'ī devoted to sorting out and reconciling hadiths that seemed to contradict one another: books of *ikhtilāf al-hadīth* (see Chapter 5).

Western scholars refer to these four collections as the Shiite hadith 'canon' because Shiites consider them the most authoritative sources for hadiths.[21] In effect, with the compilation of these four works, the earlier *usūl* and topical hadith collections became practically obsolete.[22] The authority of the canonical collections does not, however, entail that criticizing the authenticity of hadiths in them is unseemly or impermissible. Their canonicity derives from their widespread acceptance and use, not their infallibility.

CONTINUED HADITH LITERATURE AND THE MEGA-COLLECTIONS

Of course, the formation of the Shiite hadith canon did not mean an end to Shiite hadith literature. Ibn Bābawayh devoted several books to explaining the legal reasoning behind a selection of hadiths as well as explaining the meanings of controversial or confusing hadiths (his *'Ilal al-sharā'i'* and *Ma'ānī al-akhbār*). We also have the surviving records of great Shiite scholars like Ibn Bābawayh giving dictation sessions (*amālī*) to students in which they would narrate a selection of hadiths from the Prophet, the imams, and even Sunni hadith transmitters for teaching purposes. Of course, Shiite scholars continued to write about the virtues of the imams in books like *Khasā'is amīr al-mu'minīn* by al-Sharīf al-Radī (d. 406/1015) and the *Kitāb al-irshād fī ma'rifat hujaj Allāh 'alā al-'ibād* by al-Shaykh al-Mufīd. Although not strictly a hadith collection, al-Sharīf al-Radī's *Nahj al-balāgha* (The Path of Eloquence), a collection of what are said to be the speeches of 'Alī b. Abī Tālib (of which some are clearly among the oldest surviving pieces of Arabic writing), is seen as a literary masterpiece by Shiites and Sunnis alike (although Sunnis consider much of the book to be forged).[23] Also frequently cited is Ibn Shahrāshūb's (d. 588/1192) collection of all the literature on the lives, virtues and feats of the imams: the massive *Manāqib Āl b. Ābī Tālib*.

The greatest transformative step that the Shiite hadith tradition took after its canon had formed, however, occurred much later. In the early seventeenth century, a movement arose among Shiite scholars in the Hijaz, Iraq, and Iran that opposed what it viewed as the overly rationalist character of Imami Shiite thought as well as the overly hierarchical structure of the Shiite clergy. Followers of this trend believed that Imami Shiites should reaffirm their reliance on the hadiths of the Imams as the only true way to understand law and dogma properly, and they were thus known as the *Akhbārī* school (because of its reliance on *akhbār*, reports). This led to a renewed interest in collecting and commenting on Shiite hadiths in the seventeenth century.[24]

Although Shiites did not develop as extensive a tradition of penning massive commentaries on their hadith collections as did Sunnis, in this period they did amass several mega-collections that combined and commented on existing hadith works, and some of which are more gigantic than even the largest Sunni commentary.[25] Three of these mega-collections are extremely well known. The first is the *Wasā'il al-shī'a ilā ahādīth al-sharī'a* (The Paths of the Shiites to the Hadiths of the Holy Law) by Muhammad b. al-Hasan al-'Āmilī (d. 1104/1693). Second, Mullā Muhsin Fayd al-Kāshānī (d. 1091/1680) wrote a massive digest and commentary on the four canonical hadith collections, entitled *al-Wāfī*. The last is a work astounding not only in its vast size, but also in the great accuracy with which its author drew on and cited earlier books. The mammoth *Bihār al-anwār* (Oceans of Light) by Muhammad Bāqir al-Majlisī (d. 1110/1700), one hundred and ten printed volumes, is so enormous that one needs a guidebook, the *Safīnat al-biḥār* (The Ship of the Seas) by ʿAbbās al-Qummī (d. 1936) to navigate it effectively. The *Biḥār* covers almost all the topics pertinent to Shiite history, belief, and law. Not only does Majlisī's huge collection include the material found in earlier hadith books, the author also unearthed old manuscripts of *uṣūl* that survive only in his book.[26] Majlisī's work is encyclopedic, not critical, and he left his readers to decide what material is authentic or not.

SHIITE HADITH CRITICISM

Shiite hadith criticism began much later than its Sunni counterpart, appearing in full force only in the early eleventh century. While the imams were alive, there was no need to worry about forged hadiths – any reports attributed to an earlier imam would be checked by his descendants.[27] In the immediate wake of the twelfth imam's disappearance, however, Shiites like al-Kulaynī, and later Ibn Bābawayh, understood that it was now the responsibility of scholars to assure that the Shiite community only acted on reports authentically traced to the imams. The failure of scholars to distinguish between reliable and unreliable hadiths had been a leading motivation for the writing of al-Kulaynī's and Ibn Bābawayh's collections. Writing in the decades after the final occultation of the twelfth imam, Ibn Bābawayh already acknowledged that the two *uṣūl* books of Zayd al-Zarrād and Zayd al-Narsī were forged.[28]

Early Shiite hadith scholars like al-Kulaynī and Ibn Bābawayh had believed that the *uṣūl* of the imams contained all the knowledge necessary for the Shiite community to survive during the Hidden Imam's absence. This school of thought, later known as the *Akhbārī* school, considered the four canonical collections to be totally reliable records of the earlier *uṣūl* books. With the rise of the Shiite Muʿtazilite school of al-Shaykh al-Mufīd in Baghdad (later the origin of the *Uṣūli* school, which advocated the use of independent legal reasoning and a more critical use of hadiths), Shiite scholars began to look more skeptically at the contents and use of these collections. Their contents sometimes created serious liability for what had emerged as Imami orthodoxy. Al-Kulaynī's *Uṣūl*, for example, contained a report that the existing Quran was only one third of the original revealed book. In the decades after al-Kulaynī's death, however, Ibn Bābawayh had established the historical integrity of the Quranic text as a tenet of Imami belief.[29] Imami scholars acknowledged that some reports in these books could have been inserted by Shiites with deviant beliefs. Moreover, even a pious and well-intentioned *usūl* compiler could have made an error in including one report instead of another. Like the Sunnis, some Imami Shiites forged hadiths to help reinforce communal identity. One forged hadith, for example, said that visiting the grave of the eighth imam, ʻAlī al-Ridā, in Mashhad was worth seventy pilgrimages to Mecca.[30]

Transmitter Criticism

Like the Sunni tradition, Shiite hadith criticism centered on evaluating transmitters and then using this information to help decide the reliability of *isnād*s. Proper belief was the centerpiece of Shiite transmitter criticism. Before the occultation of the twelfth imam and the formation of a distinct Imami Shiite community, there was a sense that a Muslim's realization that the family of the Prophet was the sole religious authority was testament enough to his reliability. It was thus reported that Jaʻfar al-Sādiq had said, 'Know the status of people by the extent to which they narrate from us (*iʻrifū manāzil al-nās ʻalā qadr riwāyatihim ʻannā*).'[31]

As the Shiite scholarly tradition grew more elaborate, however, this would not suffice. Al-Shaykh al-Mufīd's student, the famous al-Tūsī (d. 460/1067), began developing a system of transmitter criticism to weed out reports from unreliable people and ensure that Shiites were only taking hadiths from 'the party of truth.'[32] Although al-Tūsī seems to have been the first Shiite to employ a system of rating the reliability of transmitters, like the Sunnis, Shiite hadith scholars had long been keeping records in order to identify the myriad of people who made up their *isnād*s to the imams. Ahmad Ibn ʻUqda (d. 332/944) devoted a large book to identifying all the people who studied with and transmitted the teachings of Jaʻfar al-Sādiq, Ahmad b. Muhammad al-Hamdānī (d. 333/944–5) wrote a book entitled 'The Book of Dates and Those Who Narrated Hadiths (*Kitāb al-tārīkh wa dhikr man rawā al-hadīth*),' and later Ahmad b. Muhammad al-Jawharī (d. 401/1010–11) compiled a work called 'The Comprehensive Book on Identifying Hadith Transmitters (*Kitāb al-ishtimāl ʻalā maʻrifat al-rijāl*).'[33] Although these books have been lost, the earliest surviving book on Shiite transmitters, that of Muhammad b. ʻUmar al-Kashshī (d. *c.*

340/951), focuses on laying out the full names of transmitters, their relationships to other transmitters and, if possible, when they lived. Like many early Sunni books of hadith transmitters, these books were concerned more with identifying transmitters than criticizing them.

When he began his efforts to make sure no fraudulent material had crept into the *usūl* since the disappearance of the twelfth imam, al-Tūsī had to ensure that Shiites had received material from Muslims with the proper beliefs. Certainly, Imami Shiites needed to be on guard against hadiths forged or propagated by anti-Shiite Sunnis. But the more immediate danger was sifting out reports from Shiites who had extremist beliefs like the deification of 'Alī and those who believed that the line of the Prophet had ended with an earlier imam going into occultation. Before worrying about Sunni opponents, the Imami community had to demonstrate that it was not extremist and to distinguish itself from other Shiites.

Al-Tūsī's book of transmitter criticism (*Rijāl al-Tūsī*) is thus more concerned with identifying Shiite transmitters who believed that it was actually an earlier imam, like Mūsā al-Kāzim, who had disappeared and ended the imamate than with criticizing anti-Shiite Sunnis. Ibn Hanbal, a fierce critic of Shiism, is mentioned in the books with no disapproving comment, while many Shiites are dismissed for their belief in the occultation of an earlier imam or their extremist Shiite beliefs. Al-Tūsī tries to list those transmitters who collected *usūl* from the imams, determining whether they are 'trustworthy (*thiqa*)' or not.

Abū al-'Abbās al-Najāshī (d. 450/1058) followed al-Tūsī in compiling an influential book of Shiite transmitter criticism, the *Rijāl al-Najāshī*. Unlike al-Tūsī, however, he aimed his book at a Sunni audience. Tired of his opponents accusing Shiites of having no tradition of hadith transmission and hadith books, he offers example after example of accomplished Shiite hadith authors and the *isnād*s in which he found them. He even uses books of Sunni transmitters to help in his evaluation. It appears, in fact, that al-Najāshī was consciously imitating the methods and language of Sunni transmitter criticism; he frequently called narrators 'weak (*da'īf*),' or 'having accurate transmissions (*sahīh al-samā'*),' just like his Sunni contemporaries.

Isnād *and* Matn *Criticism*

Al-Tūsī not only seems to have been the first Imami scholar consistently to evaluate hadith transmitters, he was also the first to apply these criticisms to authenticate or dismiss hadiths. In the *Istibsār* he uses *isnād* criticisms to show how what seems to be two contradictory hadiths is really just an unreliable hadith clashing with a reliable one.[34] The Shiite science of *isnād* criticism was further developed by Jamāl al-Dīn b. Tāwūs (d. 673/1274) of Baghdad and the great founder of the Hilla school in Iraq, 'Allāma Muhammad b. Idrīs al-Hillī (d. 726/1325).

Shiite hadith criticism continued to draw on and in effect mirror Sunni hadith criticism. The first major book defining the technical terms and methods of Shiite hadith criticism, written by al-Shahīd al-Thānī (d. 965/1558) (entitled 'Knowledge of Hadith, *Dirāyat al-hadīth*'), is basically a digest of the Sunni Ibn al-Salāh's famous *Muqaddima*. Only on a few important issues does the Shiite method diverge from its Sunni counterpart. For example, a hadith is defined as the report transmitted from any 'infallible (*ma'sūm*)' individual, not just the Prophet. This allows for the Shiite reliance on the hadiths of the imams.[35] The concern for avoiding extremist Shiites or believers in earlier vanished imams appears clearly in the labels that Shiites use to indicate unreliable narrators: 'extremist (*ghāl*)' and 'believing in the occultation of an earlier imam (*Wāqifī*),' from whom one can accept hadiths only before he adopted deviant beliefs.[36]

Allowance is made for occasionally narrating from Sunnis: one of the sub-grades of *hasan* hadiths, 'trustable (*muwaththaq*),' is defined as a hadith that is reliable even though a Sunni is in the *isnād*.[37] Al-Shahīd al-Thānī sharply critiques his Sunni brethren by noting how they concerned themselves only with the outward signs of a transmitter's upright character ('*adāla*), ignoring the need for an appropriate belief in the family of the Prophet. Hence, he says with an air of tragedy, there is such a plethora of supposedly 'authentic' hadiths in Sunni eyes.[38]

As the Sunnis knew well, Mu'tazilism had always held an examination of the contents of a hadith to be the final arbiter in determining its authenticity. The Shiite adoption of the Mu'tazilite framework in the eleventh century thus meant that content criticism would enjoy a more prominent role in Shiite hadith criticism than it did among Sunnis. Just because the *isnād* was reliable did not mean the report was authentic or legally compelling.[39] Al-Sharīf al-Murtadā (d. 436/1044) maintained that every report attributed to the Prophet or imams had to be authenticated by reason.[40] Influential scholars like 'Allāma al-Hillī would not even accept the medium grade of reports, *hasan*, because they were too unreliable.[41]

Interestingly, even the earlier *Akhbārī* scholars like al-Kulaynī had reserved an important role for content criticism. The *Kāfī* cites a number of hadiths from the Prophet and Jaʿfar al-Sādiq with statements like 'Everything is compared to the Book of God and the Sunna, and any hadith that does not agree with the Book of God is but varnished falsehood.'[42] While Sunni scholars had uniformly rejected statements such as Jaʿfar's because they contradicted the important role of hadiths in explaining and modifying the Quran (see Chapter 5), Shiites embraced them as an indication of the importance of content criticism.

THE RELATIONSHIP BETWEEN SUNNI AND SHIITE HADITHS

Although we have seen some of the important differences between the Sunni and Shiite traditions of hadith study, they have never been totally separate. They share common origins, overlap, and have interacted with one another over the course of Islamic history. The chief factors for the commonalities or interactions between the two have been the decidedly non-sectarian beliefs of many early Shiites, the lingering (and sometimes burgeoning) devotion to the family of the Prophet among Sunnis, and the Shiite need to draw on Sunni hadiths in their defense of Shiite doctrine.

To what extent can we talk about separate bodies of Sunni and Shiite hadiths? In the first two hundred years after the death of the Prophet, the majority of early Shiites did not espouse a doctrine that differed dramatically from the majority of Muslims. Of course, there were those supporters of ʿAlī and his family who despised or totally rejected the legitimacy of the first two rulers after the Prophet – Abū Bakr and ʿUmar – who were lionized by mainstream Sunni Islam. Sunnis could generally not accept such Shiites as Muslims in good standing. Other early Shiite extremists believed that ʿAlī was God incarnate and were thus ostracized uniformly by other Muslims, Sunnis and Shiites alike. There was also a germinating Imami community who looked to the Shiite imams for sole religious guidance. Most early Shiites, however, were merely characterized by 'an enhanced reverence' for the descendants of the Prophet, an attraction to their charisma and support for their general disapproval for the less-than-ideal regimes of the Umayyads and early Abbasids.[43] Love for the family of the Prophet was particularly intense in Kufa, 'Alī's adopted capital and the setting for many 'Alid revolts against the Umayyads. In fact, Sunni hadith critics accepted that, in the case of a Kufan transmitter, such loyalties did not mean the transmitter was necessarily Shiite. It was just part and parcel of being Kufan.

Although never considered infallible religious authorities or the perennial rightful rulers of Islam, the family of the Prophet has always been venerated in Sunni Islam. Certainly, in times of intense Sunni/Shiite conflict or in the writings of diehard Sunnis like Ibn Taymiyya (d. 728/1328), Sunnis have deemphasized this. Even the notoriously anti-Shiite Shams al-Dīn al-Dhahabī (d. 748/1348), however, warned 'May God curse those who do not love 'Alī.'[44]

Especially in the first two centuries of Islam, many scholars later glorified by Sunni Muslims, such as Abū Hanīfa and al-Shāfi'ī, displayed pronounced affection for the family of the Prophet. Brought before the Abbasid caliph on charges of being an extreme Shiite, al-Shāfi'ī composed a verse of poetry proclaiming that, if loving the family of the Prophet was being a heretic, then he would proudly admit to that charge. Even the most trusted Sunni hadith collections contain hadiths urging Muslims to love and honor the Prophet's family and descendants. Al-Bukhārī included in his famous *Sahīh* the report in which the Prophet said, **'Fatima is part of me, so whoever has angered her has angered me** (*Fātima bad'a minnī fa-man aghdabahā aghdabanī*).'[45]

In the seventh and eighth centuries, much of what would make up the Shiite hadith corpus was just hadiths expounding the virtues of 'Alī.[46] Sunni hadith critics embraced much of this material. Ibn Hanbal himself commented that 'there has not appeared via authentic *isnād*s, hadiths testifying to the virtues of any Companion like what has appeared testifying to the virtues of 'Alī b. Abī Tālib.'[47]

In the eighth century, however, as the sayings of imams like Ja'far al-Sādiq were compiled, we see the emergence of an independent body of specifically Shiite hadiths.[48] By the time of the twelfth imam's final disappearance in 941 CE, the body of material that made up the Shiite hadith corpus was effectively complete.[49] What sorts of hadiths did this corpus consist of?

First, we find hadiths that are simply not found among Sunnis, such as hadiths in which the Prophet is quoted as explicitly foretelling the coming of the twelve imams and ordering Muslims to follow them, or the hadiths of the imams themselves. Sunnis would never accept hadiths requiring them to believe in the Twelver imamate, nor would they even consider the reports of the imams as counting as 'hadiths.' With their collection of the hadiths of the imams, the Shiites thus built up a body of material totally absent in Sunni hadith collections even though they might dovetail perfectly with Sunni themes. Reports in the *Kāfī* in which Mūsā al-Kāzim curses those who use analogical reasoning to derive Islamic law would fit seamlessly into the writings of Ibn Hanbal or al-Bukharī, but the fact that they were the hadiths of an imam put them outside the pale of Sunni Prophetic hadiths.[50]

Second, we find pro-Shiite hadiths that appear in Sunni books but without the sectarian element. In the collection of Ibn Bābawayh's dictation sessions (*Amālī*), he narrates a hadith that the pro-'Alid Companion Jābir b. 'Abdallāh narrated from the Prophet: **' 'Alī b. Abī Tālib is the earliest to embrace Islam in my community, the most knowledgeable of them, the most correct in his religion, the most virtuous in his certainty, the most prudent, generous and brave of heart, and he is the imam and caliph after me.'**[51] We find that many Sunni hadith collections, even early ones such as the *Musannaf* of 'Abd al-Razzāq al-San'ānī (d. 211/827) and the *Musnad* of Ibn Hanbal, include the section of this hadith that says that 'Alī is 'the earliest to embrace Islam in my community, the most knowledgeable of them.' The sections ordaining him as caliph and imam, however, are absent.

Third, we find hadiths with a distinct pro-'Alid content that both Sunnis and Shiites accept equally. For example, the famous hadith of Ghadīr Khumm, in which the aging Prophet stops his followers by the pool of Ghadīr Khumm and tells them **'Whoever's master I am, 'Alī is his master.'** The vaunted Sunni hadith critics al-Tirmidhī and al-Hākim al-Naysābūrī both considered this report to be authentic. In another hadith that al-Hākim, Ibn Khuzayma, and even the great Muslim b. al-Hajjāj include in their *Sahīh* collections, the Prophet tells his followers, **'Indeed I am leaving you with two things of great import (*thaqalayn*) ... you will not go astray as long as you hold fast to them: the Book of God and my family.'**

Of course, Sunnis and Shiites have upheld two very different interpretations of these hadiths. Shiites view them as clear evidence that Muhammad wished 'Alī and his descendants through Fatima to succeed him both in temporal and religious leadership of the Muslim community. Sunnis view them as two exhortations to honor 'Alī and the Prophet's family, but contextualize such hadiths with the plentiful pool of reports in which the Prophet praises his leading Companions like Abū Bakr and 'Umar using the same language and appears to reserve places of leadership for them.

Some Sunnis were less patient with such pro-'Alid hadiths than others. Al-Hākim al-Naysābūrī, who was so accepting of pro-'Alid reports that he was accused of Shiism, declared authentic the hadith in which the Prophet supposedly said, **'O Fatima, God is angered when you are angered, God is pleased when you are pleased.'** Al-Hākim's teacher, al-Dāraqutnī (d. 385/995), however, was not so generous. He exposed it as a hadith that the fifth imam Muhammad al-Bāqir attributed directly to the Prophet – a typical and laudable Shiite *isnād*, but a case of broken transmission (*mursal*) according to Sunnis.[52] Al-Tabarānī's collections featured a hadith in which the Prophet reversed the sun so that 'Alī could make up a prayer he had missed. Ibn al-Jawzī, Mullā 'Alī al-Qārī and others ruled it a forgery by Shiites, while other prominent Sunnis like Qādī 'Iyād and al-Suyūtī declared it *sahīh*.[53]

Finally, many Shiite hadiths appear in the Sunni collections that aimed merely at collecting as many hadiths as possible and made no pretension at any critical stringency. Many of these collections, such as the *Hilyat al-awliyā'* (The Ornament of the Saints) of Abū Nu'aym al-Isbahānī (d. 430/1038), were works devoted to documenting the rich heritage of Sufism and therefore included a great deal of pro-'Alid material. 'Alī was, after all, seen as the progenitor of the Sufi tradition and the beginning of most of the *isnād*s though which the Sunni Sufi orders traced their teachings to the Prophet (see Chapter 7). These reports were generally innocuous, with no sectarian edge, and urged goodly and pious behavior. While Ibn Bābawayh quoted the fifth imam Muhammad al-Bāqir that the Prophet had said that the best of God's slaves are those **'Who, when they seek perfection in their acts, hope for good tidings, seek forgiveness when they do wrong, are thankful to God when they give, persevere when they are tried, and forgive when they are angered,'** Abū Nu'aym cites it through a very Sunni *isnād* in his *Hilyat al-awliyā'*.[54]

The biggest factor in the Sunni embrace of many Shiite hadiths was the veneration for the family of the Prophet that gained great currency among the Sunni Muslim majority of Egypt, Iraq, Iran, and Central Asia beginning in the eleventh century. In that time, almost every village and town 'discovered' its own *imāmzāde*, or the tomb of a pious descendant of the Prophet, to serve as a local pilgrimage and miracle center.[55] The Sunni fascination with the family of the Prophet as a medium for ***baraka*** (blessing) led to a widespread study and transmission of hadiths narrated through the Shiite imams, even if professional hadith scholars like al-Dhahabī and Mullā ʿAlī Qārī (d. 1014/1606) decried such books as forgeries. In the Iranian city of Qazvin in particular, the *Sahīfa* of the eighth imam ʿAlī Ridā (d. 203/818), who traced his *isnād*s back through the imams to the Prophet, became widely transmitted for pietistic purposes. Most of its contents were harmless pieces of advice, such as **'Knowledge is a treasure, and questions are its key.'**[56]

The religious power of an *isnād* through the imams sometimes manifested itself in bizarre and miraculous reports. The great Sunni hadith critic Ibn Abī Hātim al-Rāzī (d. 327/938) is reported (falsely, in my opinion) to have said that once, when he was in Syria, he saw a man unconscious in the road. He remembered that one of his teachers had once told him, 'the *isnād* of ʿAlī Ridā, if it is read over a senseless person, he'll recover.' Ibn Abī Hātim tried out this cure, and the man returned immediately to health.[57]

As we found in our discussion of Sunni hadiths, for Sunni critics a hadith transmitter's sectarian affiliation ultimately took the back seat to his or her reliability in transmission. If you consistently transmitted hadiths that were corroborated by other experts, even deviant beliefs would not disqualify you from participating in the Sunni hadith tradition. Individuals with pronounced Shiite leanings, such as ʿAbd al-Rahmān b. Sālih (d. 235/849–50) and Saʿīd b. Khuthaym (d. 180/796–97), thus served as respected and valued transmitters in mainstay Sunni hadith books such as the *Sunan*s of al-Nasāʾī and al-Tirmidhī. In theory, Sunni hadith critics restricted themselves from accepting the transmissions of Shiite narrators who tried to convert others to their cause (since this might provoke them to forge pro-Shiite hadiths) or, at the very least, not accepting those hadiths with a pro-ʿAlid message from such Shiite transmitters. In reality, however, even the great Muslim b. al-Hajjāj included in his *Sahīh* a report from a known Shiite, ʿAdī b. Thābit (d. 116/734), in which the Prophet announced that only a believer could love ʿAlī and only a hypocrite could hate him.

As such, we find a marked overlap of transmitters between the Sunni and Shiite hadith traditions. Abān b. Taghlib (d. 140/757) was a well-known and devoted Kufan Shiite who appears as a narrator from the imams in al-Kulaynī's *Kāfī*, but all the Sunni Six Books except *Sahīh al-Bukhārī* included his hadiths as well.

On rare occasions, there was also overlap between Sunnis and Shiites on influential hadith critics. Ibn 'Uqda (d. 332/944) was the most important collector of the Shiite *usūl* and a pioneer in compiling the names of Shiite transmitters.[58] Yet he was praised by the most prominent Sunni critics of his day, like al-Dāraqutnī and Ibn 'Adī, and later the scholar al-Subkī (d. 771/1370) called him 'one of the hadith masters of the Shariah;'[59] this, even though he was such a staunch Shiite that he occasionally disparaged Abū Bakr and 'Umar. He commanded one the most impressive memories of his day, either having memorized or being current with 850,000 hadiths, 3,000 from the family of the Prophet alone. When he wanted to move from his native Kufa, he found that his personal library of six hundred camel-loads of books prevented him. Not only did Sunnis appreciate Ibn 'Uqda's command of hadith transmissions, they also valued his opinions on evaluating transmitter criticism. In fact, the earliest evaluation of al-Bukhārī's and Muslim's famous *Sahīhayn* comes from Ibn 'Uqda.[60]

SHIITE USE OF SUNNI HADITHS

Imami Shiism matured under the looming shadow of the Sunni Abbasid caliphate and had to survive under Sunni states such as the Seljuq Turks, the Ilkhanid Mongols, and the Ottoman Empire. Even during periods in which Shiites achieved political ascendancy, such as the tenth century (called the 'Shiite Century' because the Shiite Buyids ruled Iraq and Iran, with the Shiite Fatimids in Egypt and Syria), Shiites still lived as a minority among the Sunni masses. Shiite scholars very much appreciated the use of Sunni hadiths, especially reports with a pro-'Alid bent, as tools for either debating their Sunni opponents or convincing them that Imami Shiism presented no threat to Sunni Islam. The Shiite scholar Radī al-Dīn Ibn Tāwūs (d. 664/1266) kept a digest of the *Sahīhayn* in his library for such uses.[61] In such cases, Shiites would abandon their own method of hadith criticism and play by Sunni rules in the hopes of convincing Sunnis on their own terms.

Ibn Bābawayh, for example, began one of his dictation sessions in the mosque with a hadith narrated from the Prophet by Abū Hurayra, whom Shiites considered an arch-liar who had covered up 'Alī's right to the caliphate by forging hadiths to the contrary. In this hadith, however, Abū Hurayra is quoted telling the Muslims to fast on the eighteenth of the month Dhū al-Hijja because that was the day of Ghadīr Khumm – the day when the Prophet had announced to his followers that 'Alī was to be their master after him.[62] In his efforts to prove that no one in history had ever been named 'Alī before 'Alī b. Abī Tālib, the Shiite scholar of Qazvin, Abū al-Husayn Qazvīnī (d. *c.* 560/1165), invoked as evidence the *Sahīhayn* and other Sunni hadith books that 'are relied upon.' Qazvīnī tells his opponents to 'take up the *Sahīhayn*' and find the hadith that says that 'Alī's name is written on the leg of God's throne and on the doorway to Paradise as the brother of Muhammad. Since both these structures existed before the creation of the world, 'Alī is doubtless the first person to have been so named.[63] Qazvīnī's attempt was admirable, but it did not convince his opponents; the hadiths he cited were nowhere to be found in the *Sahīhayn* or any reputable Sunni collection.[64]

THE ZAYDI HADITH TRADITION

Zaydism is a branch of Shiism associated with Zayd b. 'Alī (d. 122/740), son of the fourth imam 'Alī Zayn al-'Ābidīn, who rebelled unsuccessfully against the Umayyads in the twilight days of their rule. Although Zaydi Islam is a relatively small sect, flourishing in classical times in Kufa and northern Iran but now limited to northern Yemen, its hadith tradition deserves attention due to both its originality and influence.

Zaydis believe that the true teachings of Islam, as a religious system and a message of political justice, have been preserved by members of the family of the Prophet who rose up against the tyrannical and impious rule of the Umayyads, Abbasids, and later dynasties. Unlike Sunnis, Zaydis do not see early Islamic history as an idealized expansion of the pure faith under ultimately legitimate Muslim rulers. Zaydis believe that 'Alī should have been the first caliph, but, unlike Imami Shiites, they believe that the Prophet's instruction on this matter was ambiguous.[65] Zaydis also break with Imami Shiism by not attributing a specific line of infallible, divinely specified imams with any special access to the esoteric truths of Islam and the Quran.

Nor do they pay any special attention to the awaited Hidden Imam. Instead, Zaydis believe that the family of the Prophet is the historical protector and preserver of the true teachings of Islam and that it is their duty to stand up for justice in the face of oppressive rulers. Any member of the family of the Prophet who combines a mastery of Islamic scholarship with an ability to stand up against injustice has the right to call himself the imam. In many ways, Zaydism is a middle ground between Sunni and Imami Shiite Islam.

In their outlook on hadiths, Zaydis can be distinguished from Sunnis by four features: 1) an enhanced reverence for the family of the Prophet, 2) a case-by-case evaluation of the Companions, 3) a more cynical view of early Islamic history, and 4) their Muʿtazilite thought. Zaydis summarize this with a quote from their Imam al-Hasan b. Yahyā b. al-Husayn b. Zayd b. ʿAlī:

> The solution to disagreements over what is permissible and prohibited is to follow the clear and established texts from the Quran and to draw on those well-known, consistently transmitted reports from the Prophet which have no chance of being conspired forgery, as well as reports from the righteous members of his Family that agree with the clear indications of the Book of God. In addition, we must follow the just and pious members of the Family of the Messenger of God. These are the compelling proofs for Muslims, and it is not permitted to follow other than these.[66]

The Zaydi Imam al-Murtadā Muhammad b. Yahyā (d. 310/922) said:

> Indeed many hadiths disagree with the Book of God most high and contradict it, so we do not heed them, nor do we use them as proof. But all that agrees with the Book of God, testified to by it as correct, is authentic according to us, and we accept it as evidence. And also what our ancestors narrated, father from son, from ʿAlī, from the Prophet, we use as proof. And what was narrated by the reliable (*thiqāt*) people of the Prophet's Companions, we accept and apply it. And what disagrees with [all] this we do not see as correct, nor do we espouse it.[67]

Zaydis feel that there is undeniable evidence from the Quran and Sunna that ʿAlī and his descendants through the Prophet's daughter enjoy unique virtues and leadership responsibilities. The legal rulings and consensus of scholars from the Family of the Prophet and the hadiths they transmit are authoritative for Zaydis. Like Imamis,

Zaydis accept the *mursal* hadiths of imams (their narrations from the Prophet without citing a full *isnād*). In addition, as Imam Sharaf al-Dīn (d. 965/1557–8) stated, whatever scholars from the Family of the Prophet declare to be authentic hadiths is so. Although Zaydis foreswear those who openly opposed the Family of the Prophet, they generally allow the narration of hadiths from Sunni transmitters either in order to use their hadiths as evidence against them or because those specific hadiths have been verified by Zaydi scholars. One of the Zaydi criticisms of the Sunni hadith tradition is the relatively small reliance on hadiths transmitted through the family of the Prophet. Zaydi scholars, for example, blame al-Bukhārī for narrating hadiths via Khārijites known for their hatred of ʿAlī but not through the revered imam Jaʿfar al-Sādiq.

Zaydi Islam also upholds a unique stance on the Companions of the Prophet. Both Sunni and Imami Shiite Islam espouse absolute positions – either anyone who saw the Prophet even for a moment was upstanding or only those who actively supported ʿAlī were. For Zaydis, only those individuals who enjoyed prolonged exposure to the Prophet and remained loyal to his teachings after his death are worthy of the title 'Companion.' Individuals known for impious behavior, like Walīd b. ʿUqba, or those who actively fought against ʿAlī, such as Muʿāwiya, are not considered to be Companions at all. Zaydis take Sunnis to task for naively believing that anyone who met the Prophet could serve as a reliable hadith transmitter.

Zaydis maintained this more cynical perspective in their approach to early Islamic history in general. The political agendas of Umayyad and Abbasid rule, they assert, left lasting affects on Sunni Islam. They believed that the Umayyads had encouraged the forgery of anti-Alid hadiths as well as hadiths praising other less worthy Companions. The Abbasids cultivated the four Sunni *madhhab*s as a means to stem any loyalty to the Family of the Prophet, making a dismissal of the Prophet's Family a hallmark of early Sunni Islam.

As influential to their hadith worldview as their Alid loyalties is the Zaydi commitment to the Muʿtazilite school of theology and legal theory. Like other Muʿtazilites, Zaydis believe that passing the tests of the Quran and reason is essential for determining the authenticity of hadith. Zaydis often require hadiths to be massively transmitted (*mutawātir*) or accepted by the consensus of scholars in order to be used in defining theological stances. But Zaydis also accepted hadiths on these subjects if they were approved by imams. The Muʿtazilite rejection of anthropomorphism has led Zaydis to dismiss any hadith that describes God in overly human terms in a manner that could not be interpreted figuratively. Zaydis thus hold that hadiths like the ones stating that when God sits on his throne it squeaks like a saddle or that Muhammad is physically seated next to God on His throne are elements of Jewish and Christian lore that crept into the Islamic tradition through early converts like Ka'b al-Ahbār.

Major Zaydi Hadith Collections and Critics

The specifically Zaydi corpus of hadith is not as vast as either its Sunni or Imami Shiite counterparts. Its foundation is the *Musnad* of Zayd b. 'Alī, which Zaydis claim to be the first book of hadiths written in Islam. It consists of 228 Prophetic hadiths, 320 reports from 'Alī, and two reports from al-Husayn.[68] Interestingly, many of the reports that Zayd narrates from his great-great grandfather 'Alī appear as Prophetic hadiths in Sunni collections, such as the statement **'The ulema are the heirs of the prophets. The prophets have not left a dinar or a dirham; rather, they left knowledge as an inheritance among the scholars.'**[69] Small *amālī*, or dictation session, collections are very important in Zaydi Islam. Two famous ones are the *Amālī* of Abū Tālib Yahyā b. Husayn (d. 424/1033) and the *Amālī al-sughrā* of Imām al-Mu'ayyad Ahmad b. al-Husayn al-Hārūnī (d. 421/1030). Another central work of hadith and law is the *Jāmi' al-kāfī* of Abū 'Abdallāh Muhammad b. 'Alī of Kufa (d. 445/1053–4).

Zaydis have generally drawn heavily on what we would define as the Sunni and Imami Shiite hadith reservoirs. Zaydi scholars regularly quote mainstream Sunni hadith collections as well as Imami works like the *Usūl al-kāfī* of al-Kulaynī and the *Nahj al-balāgha* of al-Sharīf al-Radī, choosing material that they feel conforms to Zaydi doctrine. Zaydis can draw from such eclectic sources because of the intermediate position that their school occupies between Sunni and Imami Shiite Islam. Sunni scholars that the Sunni tradition saw as favoring or cultivating a great affection for the Family of the Prophet are seen by Zaydis as pious Shiites. The Zaydi scholar Sārim al-Dīn al-Wazīrī (d. 914/1508) thus declares that al-Nasā'ī, who refused to write a book on the virtues of Mu'āwiya, al-Hākim al-Naysābūrī, who declared the hadith of Ghadīr Khumm to be *sahīh*, and al-Tabarī are all Shiites.[70]

The most important works of Zaydi hadith criticism appeared relatively late in Islamic history. Although these books draw at great length from earlier works of Zaydi hadith scholarship, few early works have survived intact. Zaydis view Ibn ʿUqda (d. 332/944) (mentioned above as a Sunni and an Imami hadith critic, an indication of how elastic these sectarian identities could be) as the progenitor of their formalized study of hadith transmitters and criticism, citing his many lost books on the various students who transmitted from imams like Jaʿfar al-Sādiq.[71] The most frequently cited later works are *al-Falak al-dawwār fī ʿulūm al-hadīth wa al-fiqh wa al-āthār* (The Orbiting Heavenly Body on the Sciences of Hadith, Reports and Law), an ambitious one-volume work by the fifteenth-century scholar Sārim al-Dīn Ibrāhīm al-Wazīrī that lays out the basics of the Zaydi world-view, hadith criticism, important transmitters, and stances on major legal issues, as well as the *Kitāb al-Iʿtisām* of al-Qāsim b. Muhammad b. ʿAlī (d. 1059/1620).

SUGGESTIONS FOR FURTHER READING

A further study of Shiite hadiths should begin with more involved reading on Shiism in general. Heinz Halm's *Shīʿism* (2nd ed., New York, 2004) is both succinct and comprehensive, discussing all the branches of Shiism. Moojan Momen's *An Introduction of Shiʿi Islam* (New Haven, 1985) is a classic guide to Imami Shiism in particular. For specific discussions of Shiite hadith, see Etan Kohlberg's chapter 'Shīʿī Hadīth' in *The Cambridge History of Arabic Literature: Arabic Literature until the End of the Umayyad Period* (London, 1983) as well as his article 'Al-Usūl al-Arbaʿumi'a' in *Jerusalem Studies in Arabic and Islam* 10 (1987). Ron P. Buckley's article 'On the Origins of Shīʿi Hadīth' in *Muslim World* 88, no. 2 (1998), Robert Gleave's 'Between *Hadīth* and *Fiqh*: The "Canonical" Imāmī Collections of Akhbār' in *Islamic Law and Society* 8, no. 3 (2001), and Andrew Newman's *The Formative Period of Twelver Shīʿism: Hadīth as Discourse between Qum and Baghdad* (Richmond, Surrey, 2000) are also very informative. Anyone interested in the early period of Shiism under the imams should consult Hossein Modaressi's encyclopedic *Tradition and Survival: A Bibliographical Survey of Early Shīʿite Literature Vol. 1* (Oxford: Oneworld, 2003). For a summary of the circumscribed Ismaili hadith tradition, see Ismail Poonwala, 'Hadith Ismaʿilism' in the *Encyclopedia Iranica.*

For an analysis of Imami Shiite hadith criticism, see Asma Afsaruddin's article 'An Insight into the Hadīth Methodology of Jamāl al-Dīn Aḥmad b. Ṭāwūs,' *Der Islam* 72, no. 1 (1995): 25–46.

For original works of Shiite hadith scholarship in translation, see a fascinating section of al-Kulaynī's *Al-Kāfī*, trans. Muhammad Hasan al-Rizvani (Karachi, 1995) and 'Abd al-Hādī al-Fadlī and al-Shahīd al-Thānī, *Introduction to Hadīth, including Dirāyat al-Hadīth*, trans. Nazmina Virjee (London, 2002).

ENDNOTES

1 Muhammad b. Ya'qūb al-Kulaynī, *Al-Kāfī* (Karachi), p. 150.
2 Ibid., pp. 158–160.
3 Ibid., pp. 136–137.
4 Heinz Halm, *Shi'ism*, p. 36.
5 Ibid., pp. 36–37.
6 Ibid., p. 42.
7 Etan Kohlberg, 'Shī'ī Hadīth,' p. 301.
8 Hossein Modaressi, *Tradition and Survival*, p. 81.
9 Kohlberg, 'Shī'ī Hadīth, pp. 300–301.
10 Ibid., p. 306.
11 Modaressi, *Tradition and Survival*, p. 228.
12 Ibid., p. 147.
13 Kohlberg, 'Shī'ī Hadīth,' p. 304.
14 Kohlberg, 'Al-Usūl al-Arba'umi'a,' p. 133.
15 Ibid., p. 170.
16 Ron Buckley, 'On the Origins of Shī'i Hadīth,' p. 182.
17 Robert Gleave, 'Between *Hadīth* and *Fiqh*: The "Canonical" Imāmī Collections of Akhbār,' p. 351.
18 Al-Kulaynī, *al-Usūl al-kāfī*, vol. 1, pp. 45–49.
19 Ibn Bābawayh, *Man lā yahduruhu al-faqīh*, vol. 1, p. 71.
20 Al-Sharīf al-Murtadā, 'al-Man' min al-'amal bi-khabar al-wāhid,' in *Masā'il al-Murtadā*, p. 81.
21 Gleave, p. 352.
22 Kohlberg, 'Al-Usūl al-Arba'umi'a,' p. 135.
23 See al-Dhahabī, *Mīzān al-i'tidāl*, vol. 3, p. 124.
24 Devin Stewart, 'The Genesis of the Akhbārī Revival,' p. 188.
25 Kohlberg, 'Shī'ī Hadīth,' p. 306.
26 Kohlberg, 'Al-Usūl al-Arba'umi'a,' p. 137.
27 Ibid., pp. 139–140.
28 Ibid., p. 141.
29 Mohammed Amir Moezzi, *The Divine Guide in Early Shiism*, pp. 89–90.
30 Halm, p. 58.
31 Al-Kulaynī, *al-Kāfī* (Karachi), pp. 129–130.

32 Kohlberg, 'Al-Usūl al-Arba'umi'a,' pp. 139–141.
33 Ahmad b. 'Alī al-Najāshī, *Rijāl al-Najāshī*, vol. 1, pp. 225, 240.
34 Gleave, p. 372.
35 'Abd al-Hādī al-Fadlī and al-Shahīd al-Thānī, *Introduction to Hadīth, including Dirāyat al-Hadīth*, p. 25.
36 Ibid., p. 34.
37 Ibid., p. 26.
38 Ibid., p. 25.
39 Cf. Kohlberg, 'Shī'ī Hadīth,' p. 303.
40 Halm, p. 51.
41 Al-Fadlī and al-Thānī, p. 26.
42 Al-Kulaynī, *al-Kāfī* (Karachi), p. 179–180.
43 Buckley, p. 168.
44 Al-Dhahabī, *Mīzān al-i'tidāl*, vol. 4, p. 357.
45 *Sahīh al-Bukhārī: kitāb fadā'il ashāb al-Nabī, bāb manāqib qarābat Rasūl Allāh.*
46 Buckley, p. 168.
47 Ibn Abī Ya'lā, *Tabaqāt al-hanābila*, vol. 2, p. 156.
48 Kohlberg, 'Shī'ī Hadīth,' p. 299.
49 Ibid., p. 303.
50 Al-Kulaynī, *Al-Kāfī* (Karachi), p. 147.
51 Ibn Bābawayh, *Amālī al-sadūq*, p. 7.
52 Al-Dhahabī, *Mīzān al-i'tidāl*, vol. 2, p. 492; al-Hākim, *al-Mustadrak*, vol. 3, p. 154.
53 Al-Suyūtī, *al-La'ālī al-masnū'a*, vol. 1, pp. 308–313; idem, *al-Khasā'is al-kubrā*, vol. 2, p. 82; al-Albānī, *Silsilat al-ahādith al-da'īfa*, vol. 2, p. 395.
54 Ibn Bābawayh, *Amālī*, p. 9; Abū Nu'aym al-Isbahānī, *Hilyat al-awliyā' fī tabaqāt al-asfiyā'*, vol. 6, p. 120.
55 Cf. Halm, pp. 58–59.
56 '*Musnad 'Alī Ridā*,' p. 446.
57 Al-Rāfi'ī, *Al-Tadwīn fī akhbār Qazwīn*, vol. 3, p. 482; *Sunan Ibn Mājah: muqaddima, bāb fī al-īmān.*
58 Kohlberg, 'Al-Usūl al-Arba'umi'a,' pp. 130–131.
59 Tāj al-Dīn al-Subkī, *Tabaqāt al-shāfi'iyya al-kubrā*, vol. 1, pp. 314–316.
60 J. Brown, 'Crossing Sectarian Boundaries,' pp. 55–58.
61 Kohlberg, *A Medieval Muslim Scholar at Work*, pp. 324–325.
62 Ibn Bābawayh, *Amālī*, p. 2.
63 Nāsir al-Dīn Qazvīnī, *Ketāb-e naqd*, pp. 576–578.
64 The hadith of 'Alī's name being written on the doorway to Paradise does, however, appear in the *Kitāb fadā'il al-sahāba* of Ahmad b. Hanbal; Ibn Hanbal, *Kitāb fadā'il al-sahāba*, vol. 2, p. 665.
65 Muhammad Yahyā al-'Azzān, *Al-Sahāba 'ind al-zaydiyya*, p. 56.
66 'Abdallāh Hamūd al-'Izzī, *'Ilm al-hadīth 'ind al-zaydiyya* p. 42.
67 Al-Miswarī, *Al-Risāla al-munqidha*, pp. 60–62.
68 Al-'Izzī, *'Ilm al-hadīth 'ind al-zaydiyya*, p. 271.
69 Zayd b. 'Alī, *Musnad Zayd b. 'Alī*, p. 383.
70 Sārim al-Dīn Ibrāhīm al-Wazīr, *Al-Falak al-dawwār fī 'ulūm al-hadīth wa al-fiqh wa al-āthār*, pp. 69, 222.
71 Al-'Izzī, *'Ilm al-hadīth 'ind al-zaydiyya*, p. 225.

5

THE FUNCTION OF PROPHETIC TRADITIONS IN ISLAMIC LAW AND LEGAL THEORY

THE AUTHORITY OF THE SUNNA IN LAW

All Muslims believe that the Quran is the primary source of Islamic law. Throughout Islamic history, the vast preponderance of Muslims have also affirmed that the teachings of the Prophet adjust, augment and explain the Holy Book, although they have disagreed on how and to what extent it occurs. The Quran is not a detailed legal manual. Only about five hundred of the book's verses provide legal injunctions, and even on major questions such as ritual prayer the Quran is often vague. For both Sunni and Shiite Islam, the Prophet's Sunna has thus proven an essential resource for explaining and supplementing the Quranic message. As the Companion 'Imrān b. Husayn supposedly told a person who wanted to take religious law only from the Holy Book and not from the Sunna, 'Indeed you are an idiot, do you find in the Book of God prayer explained!? Do you find in it fasting explained!? Indeed the Quran ordains this, but the Sunna explains it.'[1]

As the lens through which the Quran was understood, the Sunna of the Prophet has controlled the way in which Muslims have interpreted the Quranic revelation. Although no Muslim would claim that the word of Muhammad is *ontologically* equal or superior to the word of God, early Sunnis such as Yahyā b. Abī Kathīr (d. 129/747) long ago acknowledged that 'The Sunna came to rule over the Quran, it is not the Quran that rules over the Sunna.'[2] This was not in any way an admission of any deficiency in the Quran – rather it recognizes that the book required the Prophet's example and teachings in order to explain its verses and unlock its manifold meanings to an evolving community. As many early Muslims such as Ayyūb al-Sakhtiyānī (d. 131/748) noted, 'The Quran needs the Sunna more than the Sunna needs the Quran.'[3] Muslim schools of thought at various times have insisted, out of principle, that the words of a mere mortal, even Muhammad, could never conceivably carry more interpretive weight than the word of God. Yet they have all historically recognized that, whichever way one chooses to phrase it, the Prophet's legacy has profoundly informed and altered the way the Quran's legal message has been understood.

The word 'Sunna,' of course, is not fully synonymous with 'hadith.' In the first century and a half of Islamic history, '*sunna*' was often understood as the accepted set of practices and beliefs of the Muslim community as passed on from the Companions. A 'hadith' was merely a report from the Prophet that may or may not have actually been acted on as a rule in daily Muslim life. Shu'ba b. al-Hajjāj was thus considered a master of hadiths but not of *sunna*, while Sufyān al-Thawrī (d. 161/778) was considered a master of both.[4] We have already seen that Mālik believed that the practice of the people of Medina, which he felt had been transmitted *en masse* from the time of the Prophet, was a much more reliable source for discovering the Prophet's Sunna than a solitary hadith narrated by one *isnād*. By the time of Mālik's student al-Shāfi'ī, however, among the *ahl al-hadīth* a concerted study of hadiths had become the essential route for learning and implementing the Sunna of the Prophet.

The importance of hadiths in the Sunni derivation of Islamic law is clear from the sources from which the different Sunni schools of law drew. Hanafīs ranked the sources of law as 1) the Quran, 2) sound hadiths, 3) Companion opinions, and 4) methods of legal reasoning based on the Quran and Sunna. Al-Shāfi'ī consulted 1) the Quran and reliable hadiths, 2) the consensus of scholars, 3) Companion opinions, and 4) analogical reasoning based on the Quran and Sunna. Mālikīs described their sources of law as 1) the Quran, 2) the Prophet's Sunna, which was understood through hadiths, Companion rulings, and the practice of Medina, 3) consensus, 4) legal reasoning and communal needs. Hanbalīs described Ibn Hanbal's sources of law as 1) the Quran and reliable hadiths, 2) the consensus of the early community, 3) Companion opinions, 4) weak hadiths, and 5) analogical reasoning based on the Quran and Sunna.[5]

It is worth noting that accepting the Sunna and hadiths as an essential source of Islamic law was not uncontested. In the first two centuries of Islam (and indeed, in the modern period as well, see Chapter 10), there were schools of thought that rejected the use of hadiths in Islamic law entirely. The works of al-Shāfiʿī record his disputations with these scholars, known to Sunnis as the 'People of Speculative Theology (*ahl al-kalām*),' who could not accept the idea of taking their religion and its laws from reports transmitted merely 'from so-and-so, from so-and-so.'[6] This was a function fit for something as historically reliable as the Quran alone. This extreme skepticism towards hadiths, however, died out in classical Sunni and Shiite Islam, although its traces will be seen below in the Muʿtazilite approach to hadiths. Sunni Islam in particular followed the reasoning with which al-Shāfiʿī had confronted the 'People of Speculative Theology': without the Sunna and hadiths, how could Muslims know the details of prayer or of the Ramadan fast?[7]

THE INTERACTION OF THE SUNNA WITH THE QURAN IN LAW

Al-Shāfiʿī offered a succinct description of the manner in which the Sunna could affect interpretation of the Quran. First, the Prophet could demonstrate that the meaning of a general Quranic verse was more specific than it appeared. The Quran, for example, states 'The thief, male or female, cut off their hand in retribution for what they have done, an exemplary punishment from God, for God is mighty and wise' (Quran 5:38). We learn from a hadith narrated from the Prophet by Aisha, however, that we should **'not cut off someone's hand for an item whose value is less than a quarter dinar'** (1/4 dinar is approximately $25). From other hadiths we learn that the punishment also does not apply in cases of stealing things from unsecured locations, embezzlement or taking things publicly.[8] The Sunna also clarified ambiguous or vague Quranic commands. The Quran orders Muslims to pray and fast, but only the Sunna explains how these rituals are performed. The Sunna could also abrogate or add entirely new information to the Quran. The Quran forbids Muslims from eating carrion, but in a famous hadith the Prophet approves of a group of Muslims who had eaten the meat of a dead whale they had found on the beach, for he reminds them that everything that comes from the sea is permissible to eat. Hadiths also inform Muslims that they can eat dead grasshoppers they find. The Quran forbids men from marrying their mothers, sisters, daughters, or aunts (with the corresponding male relationships for women implied as well), saying that women 'other than these are permissible' (Quran 4:24). Hadiths add that a man cannot marry a woman and her aunt at the same time.

Traditional Sunni scholars have uniformly rejected the hadith, invoked by Muʿtazilites, that orders Muslims to reject hadiths that differ with the Quran. As al-Shāfiʿī said, such an idea was 'pure ignorance,' since the purpose of hadiths was to explain, modify, and add to the Quran. Hadiths could thus by definition break with the evident meaning of Quranic verses.

Coming from the *ahl al-ra'y* tradition, the Hanafīs also recognized these interactions between the Sunna and the Quran, although as we will see they maintained different standards for when hadiths could fulfill these functions. Hanafī legal theorists discussed how hadiths could reinforce Quranic rulings (called an 'affirming indication,' or *bayān taqrīr*), add explanatory information to a Quranic ruling (called an 'explanatory indication,' or *bayān tafsīr*), or replace and restrict a Quranic ruling (called an 'abrogating indication,' or *bayān tabdīl*).'[9]

DIFFERENT CONDITIONS FOR THE USE OF HADITHS IN LAW

The *ahl al-hadīth* movement (the original core of Sunni Islam) was built on the premise that a report established as coming from the Prophet was legally compelling. As al-Shāfiʿī famously stated, 'If the hadith is reliable, then that is my ruling (*in sahha al-hadīth fa-hādhā madhhabī*).'[10] Both *sahīh* and *hasan* hadiths were considered admissible in law, and we have seen that early *ahl al-hadīth* jurists like Ibn Hanbal sometimes acted on weak hadiths if they could find no other evidence whatsoever on a particular issue.

When Sunni legal theory matured in the eleventh century, it was accepted that, although *āhād* (i.e., non-massively transmitted) hadiths did not yield epistemological certainty (*yaqīn*) that the Prophet had made that statement, they did yield a very strong probability (*zann*). This was sufficient for fixing law and ritual. While almost all legal hadiths were *āhād*, the Quran was epistemologically certain, massively transmitted from the time of the Prophet. This posed a problem for proponents of the majority Ash'arī school of legal theory (subscribed to by Shāfi'ī, Mālikī, and many Hanbalī scholars). These legal theorists could not accept that an *āhād* hadith, which conveyed mere probability, could replace a Quranic ruling. They therefore rejected the doctrine that *āhād* hadiths could abrogate (*naskh*) the Quran. But if this were the case, then how could they explain rulings such as allowing eating dead fish or the prohibition on marrying a woman and her aunt? As the Ash'arī legal theorist Ibn Fūrak (d. 406/1015) cleverly explained, this was possible because such a ruling could be phrased as an *āhād* hadith *specifying* or *adjusting* Quranic verses, not replacing their rulings.[11]

The various groups that made up the Partisans of Legal Reasoning (*ahl al-ra'y*) also accepted the compelling power of hadiths. In principle, no Muslim could argue that the Prophet's words merited anything short of obedience. Abū Hanīfa is quoted as saying, 'Whoever says that we prefer our own legal reasoning (*qiyās*) to a revealed text [from the Prophet] has lied, by God, and defamed us. For what need is there for legal reasoning in the presence of such a text!?'[12] The crux of the difference between the *ahl al-hadīth* and the *ahl al-ra'y* was how one determined if a hadith was reliable enough to be accepted in law.

As a rule, the Hanafī school of law does not allow hadiths to abrogate or specify the evident meaning of Quranic verses unless the report is *mashhūr* (widespread and accepted by jurists). They viewed specification (*takhsīs*) of a Quranic verse as a form of abrogation (*naskh*) of the holy book and therefore did not permit it by *āhād* hadiths. For example, the other three Sunni schools of law require a Muslim to have the intention to perform his ritual ablutions before he starts washing on the basis of the famous hadith **'Indeed deeds are [judged] by intentions** (*innamā al-a'māl bi'l-niyyāt*).' But because this hadith is only narrated by one solitary chain of transmission for four stages in the *isnād* (Prophet → 'Umar b. al-Khattāb → 'Alqama b. Waqqās → Muhammad b. Ibrāhīm → Yahyā b. Sa'īd al-Ansārī), the Hanafīs do not consider it widespread enough to adjust the Quran, which simply instructs Muslims to wash certain parts of their bodies for ablutions (Quran 5:6). For Hanafīs, then, one can take a shower and then retroactively count that as one's ablutions even if one had not intended to do so while showering.

In the case of a hadith that is not widely enough transmitted to be deemed *mashhūr*, Hanafīs do not accept it in legal discussions if it deals with a case of *'umūm al-balwā*, or an issue of great importance to Islamic law. If the issue addressed by the hadith were crucial for Muslims' understanding of their religion, then God and His prophet would have assured that it was transmitted by more reliable means. Hanafīs also do not accept a non-*mashhūr* hadith if the early scholars who transmitted it did not act according to its ruling. If the hadith truly represented the Prophet's Sunna, then why would a pious narrator not follow it? Finally, until the 1000s CE many Hanafī jurists favored their own legal reasoning over a non-*mashhūr* hadith if its transmitters were not considered skilled in legal analysis. A hadith from *Sahīh al-Bukhārī* quotes the Prophet permitting parties in a sales transaction to change their minds up until 'the two part company.' Although accepted as a rule in the Shāfi'ī and Hanbalī schools, this broke with the Hanafī school's principle that sales are finalized upon agreement, barring some fraud or defect. Hanafīs did not reject this hadith outright. Rather, they turned to comments on it by the Kufan authority Ibrāhīm al-Nakha'ī (d. 96/717), who explained that 'parting company' was understood not in the physical sense but as the verbal end of the negotiation.[13]

The Mālikī school of law was also considered by some to be part of the *ahl al-ra'y* movement. It is very difficult, however, to determine exactly what the early Mālikī stance on hadiths was. Mālik himself often rejected hadiths that contradicted the practice of the people of Medina. For example, Mālik also did not act on the evident meaning of the 'parting company' hadith because it was not acted on in Medina. He also took the meaning of 'parting company' as ending the negotiation. Mālik also chose not to act on hadiths that he recognized as reliable if he feared they would lead to misunderstandings or facilitate prohibited acts (a concept known as *sadd al-dharā'i'*, or 'blocking means'). He did not allow acting on a *sahīh* hadith that recommended that Muslims fast for six days in the month immediately following the obligatory month-long fast of Ramadan because he feared people would confuse this optional fast with the required one.[14]

The Mu'tazilite school of theology and legal theory, of course, retained the most rigorous standards for accepting hadiths for use in law. According to later Mu'tazilites, the founder of the school, Wāsil b. 'Atā' (d. 131/750), would only accept hadiths if they were agreed upon as authentic by the whole community of scholars.[15] For matters of law, the Mu'tazilite master Abū Hudhayl (d. 200/815) required a hadith to have four separate narrations, although later members of the school required only two.[16]

WEAK HADITHS AND PRACTICE: DIFFERENT PROOFS FOR THE AUTHENTICITY OF LEGAL HADITHS

During the formative first three centuries of the Sunni legal tradition, there was a diversity of approaches to weighing the evidence provided by *isnād*s against the accepted practice of legal scholars. Despite their obsession with the *isnād* as the only means of authenticating hadiths, early *ahl al-hadīth* jurists affirmed that the widespread acceptance of a legal ruling could offset a lackluster *isnād*. In such a case, it is actually the accepted practice of Muslim scholars that justifies the ruling. The hadith only embodies it in the Prophetic word. The Quran specifies certain family relations who automatically inherit if a family member dies (Quran 4:11–12). In a hadith that appears in the Four *Sunans* of al-Tirmidhī, al-Nasā'ī, Abū Dāwūd and Ibn Mājah, the Prophet states that 'The killer does not inherit,' meaning that if someone murders someone from whom they stand to inherit, they will not inherit anything. Despite being widely quoted, al-Tirmidhī notes that 'this hadith is not sound,' an opinion with which later critics agree. Yet al-Tirmidhī adds, 'practice has been based on this hadith amongst the people of knowledge.' Indeed, though this hadith is the only scriptural basis for this position, the ruling has been agreed upon by all schools of law in Islam.[17]

Another famous example occurs in the case of inheritance as well. The Quran and hadiths set detailed regulations for how much a person must leave to each of his or her inheritors – a person can distribute no more than one third of the estate to people of his or her own choosing. In a famous hadith, however, the Prophet declares, **'No bequest to an inheritor unless the inheritors all agree** (*lā wasiyya li-wārith illā in shā'a al-waratha*)'; in other words, one cannot leave part of this third to someone who already inherits automatically. Every one of the many narrations of this hadith suffers from some flaw in the *isnād* according to Muslim hadith critics. But as al-Shāfi'ī and the Mālikī hadith scholar of Lisbon, Ibn 'Abd al-Barr (d. 463/1070), declared, 'With reports like this that became well established among all the scholars, it is not necessary to provide an *isnād*. For its widespread transmission and well-known status among them is stronger than any *isnād*.'[18]

Some also maintained that juridical mastery obviated the need to cite an *isnād* at all. From the early Islamic period onward, jurists from the Hanafī school held that a competent scholar of the early period need not provide an *isnād* for a hadith he cited. Unlike the Partisans of Hadith, they therefore considered *mursal* hadiths (hadiths in which an early scholar such as a Successor quoted the Prophet without an *isnād*, see Chapter 3) to be acceptable proofs in legal discourse. They argued that when Abū Hanīfa cited the Prophet's words or deeds as legal proof without providing any *isnād*, this was because he was so confident in the authenticity of the hadith that he did not bother with a chain of transmission.[19] In addition, in the time of Abū Hanīfa (who was considered a Successor because he had seen the Companion Anas b. Mālik as a boy) it had not become predominate practice for scholars to provide *isnād*s. Mālik thus frequently included *mursal* hadiths in his *Muwatta'*.

Al-Shāfiʿī, however, led the Partisans of Hadith attack on *mursal* hadiths and insisted on providing an *isnād* in order to prove the reliability of one's hadith. He stated that he had examined the *mursal* hadiths in circulation and found that only those of the senior Successor Saʿīd b. al-Musayyab were reliable, since it was assumed that he had heard them all through his father-in-law Abū Hurayra.[20] Because there was a break in the *isnād*s of *mursal* hadiths, the *ahl al-hadīth* considered them to be unreliable. Scholars from the Shāfiʿī and Hanbalī schools of law thus only used *mursal* hadiths as evidence if they came from Saʿīd b. al-Musayyab, when they were backed up by the legal rulings of Companions or to tip the balance in the case of two competing hadiths.[21]

THE EVOLVING USE OF HADITHS IN THE SUNNI SCHOOLS OF LAW

Although hadiths have played an undeniably crucial role in constructing Islamic law, that role has not remained static since the early period of Muslim legal thought. As we saw in the *musannaf* period, early legal scholars like Mālik b. Anas relied on Companion opinions and the rulings of early jurists from the Successor generation more often than Prophetic hadiths. Companion opinions and analogical legal reasoning ranked highly among the sources of law that the Shāfiʿī, Mālikī, Hanafī, and Hanbalī schools identified. By the ninth century, however, it had become necessary for schools of law to find Prophetic hadiths to justify their stances. In his massive book of substantive law, the *Umm*, al-Shāfiʿī had cited only about four thousand three hundred hadiths with full *isnād*s to the Prophet as evidence. The eleventh-century Shāfiʿī scholar Abū Bakr al-Bayhaqī, however, filled his massive *Sunan al-kubrā* (The Great Sunan) with over twenty thousand narrations from the Prophet in order to back up every detail of Shāfiʿī law.

The history of Sunni legal thought, however, was not a linear process of collecting more and more hadiths to justify a certain legal position. The Sunni schools of law were evolving interpretive traditions that presented evidence in different ways depending on their needs. Each *madhhab* (school of law) represented a tradition of transmitting, explaining, reexamining, adjusting and adapting the body of law originated by its founding figures.

In the case of the Hanbalī school of law, for example, the legal opinions given by Ibn Hanbal were collected from his senior students by Abū Bakr b. al-Khallāl (d. 311/923–4). His student al-Khiraqī (d. 334/945–6) sifted through the many and sometimes seemingly contradictory opinions of Ibn Hanbal, attempting to place each one in its proper context. His work, known as the *Mukhtasar* (The Abridgement), was the foundational text of the Hanbalī school.

Later scholars transformed this work to fit various needs. Ibn Qudāma (d. 620/1223), for example, channeled the *Mukhtasar* into four works of increasing size and complexity: the *ʿUmda* (The Pillar), designed to introduce students of the school to its principal rulings; the *Muqniʿ* (The Convincing Book), which introduced Hanbalī students to the various differences of opinion among the school's major figures; the *Kāfī* (The Sufficient Book), which introduced students to the evidence and argumentation for these positions; and finally the huge *Mughnī* (The Obviating Book), which added more evidence and the opinions of other schools of law as well. The *Muqniʿ* was digested by Mūsā al-Hajjāwī (d. 968/1560) into a small and easily memorized text called the *Zād al-mustaqniʿ* (Provisions for One Seeking Certainty), which provided the official Hanbalī stances on issues of law. This work was then explained by Mansūr al-Buhūtī (d. 1051/1641) in his *al-Rawd al-murbiʿ* (The Abundant Garden), in which the author expanded the work and also provided the reader with evidence for its rulings.

In these works, the Hanbalī school's use of hadiths expanded and contracted according to the purpose of a particular book. We can see this clearly in the example of the Hanbalī position on how someone should pray if he is too weak to stand or even sit up straight: he should lie on his side facing the direction of prayer, nodding with his head to represent the normal bowings and prostrations of prayer. The *Mukhtasar* of al-Khiraqī does not concern itself with providing evidence on this – it merely seeks to identify Ibn Hanbal's stances on legal issues. The lengthy *Mughnī* of Ibn Qudāma, however, provides a myriad of Quranic verses, hadiths, and early scholarly opinions to justify Ibn Hanbal's choice. We find Ibn Qudāma citing a hadith that Ibn Hanbal had included in his famous *Musnad*: The Prophet said to 'Imrān b. Husayn: '**Pray standing, and if you cannot, then sitting, and if you cannot, then on your side** (*salli qā'iman wa in lam tastati' fa-qā'idan wa in lam tastati' fa-'alā janb*).' This was excellent evidence for the Hanbalī opinion, since the hadith had been included in the *Sahīhayn* and was thus extremely reliable. Ibn Qudāma also lists other hadiths transmitted by al-Nasā'ī that add that the person should lie down fully if unable to lie on his side.[22]

Centuries later, however, when al-Buhūtī was providing evidence for the Hanbalī position in his *Rawd al-murbī'*, he omitted these reliable hadiths and instead used an otherwise very weak hadith from the *Sunan* of al-Dāraqutnī. The reason for this was clear: this one hadith lays out the Hanbalī position word for word! It reads:

> The Prophet said: **The sick person should pray standing if he can. If he cannot, he should pray sitting down. If he is unable to prostrate, he gestures with his head and makes the gesture of prostration lower than the gesture representing bowing. If he is unable to pray sitting, he should pray on his right side facing the direction of prayer, and if he is unable to do that he should lie with his legs facing the direction of prayer**.[23]

In the *Mughnī*, Ibn Qudāma sought to collect the most reliable hadiths as evidence to support the Hanbalī school. For al-Buhūtī, the school's position was already justified. He only wanted to provide his reader with one concise piece of evidence that summarized it even if that hadith was unreliable.

IKHTILĀF AL-HADĪTH: DISAGREEMENT AND DIFFERING INTERPRETATION OF HADITHS AMONG JURISTS

The Prophet taught thousands of followers, interacted with his community for twenty-three years, and acted as a judge and political leader for the last ten. As a result, sifting through his Companions' sundry recollections of his words in order to determine his precedent (Sunna) was a monumental task. The vast number and complex meaning of the hadiths with which jurists had to contend in their attempts to derive Islamic law made the hadith tradition fertile ground for disagreement and varying interpretations.

Even a cursory reading of major hadith collections illustrates the difficulty of reaching definitive conclusions based on hadiths. In al-Tirmidhī's *Jāmi'*, for example, we find one section listing hadiths forbidding drinking while standing up followed by another section with hadiths describing how the Companions saw the Prophet drinking while standing up! In addition to determining which hadiths to act on, a Muslim scholar had to place these hadiths within the framework of Quranic injunctions and the specific interests of the Muslim community. A common saying among Muslim scholars thus identifies hadith critics with pharmacists, who provide the medicine, and legal scholars with doctors, who know how to use this medicine properly.[24]

Disagreement was often the outcome of limited access. As we have seen, in its first two centuries the hadith tradition was highly localized. In Medina, Mālik did not have access to the same hadiths as Abū Hanīfa in Kufa. These two jurists were thus working from different bodies of hadiths. Al-Shāfi'ī is reported to have said that the hadiths that provide the basis for all legal rulings (*usūl al-ahkām*) are only fifty or so in number. He adds that his teacher Mālik only had thirty, while his teacher Sufyān b. 'Uyayna (d. 196/811) in Mecca had all but six.[25]

Assuming that scholars had access to the same hadiths, what are the factors that could lead Muslim jurists to reach different legal conclusions on their basis? Why might a scholar ignore a hadith or take one over another? The fourteenth-century analyst Ibn Taymiyya (d. 728/1328) explained that disagreements over the Prophet's Sunna as communicated by the hadith literature revolved around three points.[26]

First, a scholar might not have thought that a certain hadith was reliable. Instead, he might have chosen another narration over it. For an example, let us turn to al-Tirmidhī's *Jāmi'*, which documented legal disagreement as well as hadiths. In his section on how one should say 'Amen' in prayer, al-Tirmidhī writes:

> It was reported to us by Bundār Muhammad b. Bashshār: it was reported to us by Yahyā b. Sa'īd al-Qattān and 'Abd al-Rahmān b. Mahdī: it was reported to us by Sufyān, from Salama b. Kuhayl, from Hujr b. 'Anbas, from Wā'il b. Hujr: he said, **'I heard the Prophet read [the Quranic verse in prayer] "And not those rejected by God nor those who have gone astray" and then he said, "Amen," stretching out his words.'** And on that issue there are also hadiths from 'Alī b. Abī Tālib and Abū Hurayra.
>
> The hadith of Wā'il b. Hujr is a *hasan* hadith, and that is the position of more than one of the people of knowledge from among the Companions of the Prophet, the Successors and those after them. They hold that a person raises his voice in saying 'Amen' and does not say it silently. This is the opinion of al-Shāfi'ī, Ahmad b. Hanbal and Ishāq b. Rāhawayh.
>
> But Shu'ba b. al-Hajjāj narrated this hadith from Salama b. Kuhayl, from Hujr b. al-'Anbas, from 'Alqama b. Wā'il, from his father, that **'the Prophet read [the verse] "Not those rejected by God nor those who have gone astray," and said "Amen" but lowered his voice.'**
>
> I heard Muhammad [al-Bukhārī] say, 'the first hadith, [that] of Sufyān, is more authentic than the [second] hadith, [that] of Shu'ba on that issue. And Shu'ba erred at several points in the hadith, saying "from Hujr b. al-'Anbas", when it is really 'Hujr b. 'Anbas … and he added in the hadith "from 'Alqama b. Wā'il" when that is not part of the hadith's [*isnād*]. Rather it is "from Hujr b. 'Anbas, from Wā'il b. Hujr." Finally, [Shu'ba] said, "and he lowered his voice," when really it is "and he extended his voice in saying Amen."
>
> I asked Abū Zur'a [al-Rāzī] about that hadith and he said, 'Sufyān's hadith on that issue is more authentic than Shu'ba's.' He added, 'And there is [a hadith of] al-'Alā' b. Sālih al-Asadī, from Salama b. Kuhayl, like the narration of Sufyān. It was reported to us by Abū Bakr Muhammad b. Abān: it was reported to us by 'Abdallāh b. Numayr: it was reported to us by al-'Alā' b. Sālih al-Asadī, from Salama b. Kuhayl, from Hujr b. 'Anbas, from Wā'il b. Hujr, from the Prophet, the likes of Sufyān's hadith, from Salama b. Kuhayl.'[27]

Here we see the debate surrounding two narrations of the same hadith, one through Sufyān, from Salama b. Kuhayl, which describes the Prophet saying 'Amen' out loud during prayer; and one through Shu'ba, from Salama b. Kuhayl that says the opposite. Jurists like al-Shāfi'ī and Ibn Hanbal chose Sufyān's narration, which describes the Prophet saying 'Amen' out loud, rejecting Shu'ba's version.

Al-Tirmidhī provides the opinions of the influential hadith critics al-Bukhārī and Abū Zur'a al-Rāzī to explain why: Shu'ba's narration includes an error (a very minor one!) in the name of the transmitters and adds another transmitter incorrectly into the *isnād*. More importantly, al-'Alā' b. Sālih al-Asadī's narration of the hadith from Salama b. Kuhayl corroborates Sufyān's narration of 'Amen' being said out loud. The hadith scholars' critical method, focusing on the reliability of the *isnād* and corroboration, thus led many jurists to uphold saying 'Amen' out loud in prayer.

Second, a jurist might conclude that one hadith had abrogated another one, annulling and replacing its ruling. All hadith scholars and jurists acknowledged an authentic hadith in which the Prophet instructed Muslims to perform ablutions after eating food cooked by fire. Al-Suyūtī even declared it *mutawātir*.[28] Sunni scholars, however, agreed on hadiths transmitted by Ibn 'Abbās and Abū Bakr that during the last few years of his life in Medina the Prophet had been served a cooked lamb shoulder and then had prayed his afternoon prayer without performing ablutions. The Companions therefore understood that the earlier requirement for ablutions had been nullified.[29]

Several hadith scholars penned books devoted to listing and analyzing hadiths that abrogated or were abrogated. Ibn Hanbal's student Abū Bakr Ahmad al-Athram (d. 261/875) wrote his *Nāsikh al-hadīth wa mansūkhuhu* (Abrogating and Abrogated Hadiths), Ibn Shāhīn (d. 385/996) of Baghdad and Abū Bakr al-Hāzimī (d. 584/1188–89) also wrote large and widely studied works on hadith abrogation.

Finally, a jurist might not have thought that a hadith addressed a particular issue or may have weighed it against other evidence in a manner that differed from other jurists. We have already seen that Hanafīs did not allow hadiths to modify or abrogate Quranic rulings unless they were well established. This led Hanafīs to break with the other Sunni schools of law in not requiring Muslims to declare their intentions before performing ritual ablutions. Mālik, for his part, favored the practice of Medinans over many hadiths. In the case of the apparent contradiction between hadiths in which the Prophet instructed his followers not to drink while standing up and hadiths describing the Prophet doing just that, many jurists understood this as meaning that drinking standing up was discouraged but nonetheless permissible.[30]

The context in which a hadith appeared could have tremendous impact in its implications. We find, for example, two narrations of a hadith narrated from ʿUrwa b. al-Zubayr, from his aunt Aisha, from the Prophet. In one the Prophet states '**Whoever is tried by having daughters and perseveres with them, they will veil him from the Hellfire [on the Day of Judgment].**' This report does not leave a very positive impression of daughters! In the second narration, however, we find illuminating details. Aisha recounts how 'A woman entered asking me [for food] and had two daughters with her. But all I had with me was a date, so I gave it to her, and she split it between her two daughters without eating any herself. When the Prophet came I told him of this, and he said, '**Whoever is tried by these daughters, they will be a veil from Hellfire [on the Day of Judgment].**'[31]

In the modern period, context has strongly informed the use of another gender-related hadith. In his defense of women's right to hold public office, the Egyptian scholar Muhammad al-Ghazālī (d. 1996) noted that the majority of classical scholars had objected to women serving as judges on the basis of the *sahīh* hadith, '**The people who entrust their affairs to a woman will not succeed** (*lan yufliha qawm wallū amrahum imra'a*).' Al-Ghazālī, however, retorts that the context in which this hadith was said clarifies its meaning. The Persian Sassanid Empire was experiencing internal political crises as well as military defeats at the hands of the Byzantines. In the midst of this trouble, the Sassanids brought a woman to the throne. The Prophet was merely noting that this would not prevent the empire's downfall.[32]

Ever creative, Jalāl al-Dīn al-Suyūtī (d. 911/1505) wrote a book on the 'reasons for the appearance of hadiths' (*Asbāb wurūd al-hadīth*, the book had that same title), as did Ibrāhīm b. Hamza (d. 1708). These books, however, did not introduce any new information about hadiths. The context and motivations for the Prophet's statements were already found either within hadith collections or in commentaries on these works. Books like al-Suyūtī's simply culled that information from these sources and reorganized it.

The different reasons for disagreement over interpreting hadiths could coincide. Al-Shāfiʿī described how scholars should address such situations. In a case of clashing hadiths, one should first examine which hadiths have the most reliable *isnāds*. First, he states unequivocally that no two reliable hadiths can be contradictory, since it is impossible for the Prophet to have an inconsistent Sunna. Instead, one must determine the proper relationship between the contrasting hadiths. Al-Shāfiʿī states that hadiths that convey different rulings on an issue may indicate that the Prophet intended there to be latitude and flexibility. If this is not the case, then the one hadith might address certain circumstances and the second one other circumstances. If neither of these options is possible, one hadith must abrogate the other. The scholars who emerged amongst the early generations of Muslims were key resources in fitting the data provided by individual, reliable hadiths into a coherent system. As Abū Dāwūd wrote in his *Sunan*, 'If two reports from the Messenger of God clash, one looks to what the Companions and those who came after them acted on.'[33]

We can see the way in which reconciliation and abrogation interacted in the question of 'the Two Prostrations of Error (*sajdatā al-sahw*).' When Muslims perform their canonical prayer – done five times daily – their prayers consist of a fixed cycle of actions and utterances including bowing, prostrations, and kneeling. In the last prayer cycle of the prayer, the worshipper performs the '*Taslīm*', or turning one's head to the right and left and saying 'May the peace and mercy of God be upon you (*al-salām 'alaykum wa rahmat Allāh*)' to the person to the right and left. This marks the end of the prayer. If a worshipper errs in the proper procedures of the prayer, they can touch their foreheads to the ground twice while seated at the end of the prayer. These two prostrations are called 'The Two Prostrations of Error.'

The Shāfiʿī school holds that these prostrations should be done before the *Taslīm*, while Hanafīs maintain that they should be performed afterwards. Mālikīs and Hanbalīs take more subtle positions. The following is al-Tirmidhī's discussion of the different hadiths dealing with this issue and the different ways that scholars have interpreted them. He mentions a hadith affirming that the Two Prostrations are made before the *Taslīm*, only alluding to another famous one in which the Prophet prays them afterwards:

> It was reported to us by Qutayba [b. Saʿīd]: it was reported to us by al-Layth [b. Saʿd], from Ibn Shihāb [al-Zuhrī], from al-Aʿraj, from ʿAbdallāh b. Bujayna al-Asadī, associate of the Banū ʿAbd al-Muttalib [family], that the Prophet stood up in the Noon prayer when he should have remained seated, so when he finished his prayer he prostrated twice, saying 'God is most great (*Allāhu akbar*)' for both prostrations, before saying the final *Taslīm* [to exit the prayer]. And the congregation following the Prophet in prayer did the same as him.

He had done this to make up for forgetting to remain seated during part of the prayer.

. . .

The hadīth of Ibn Bujayna is a *hasan sahīh* hadith, and it is acted on by some of the people of knowledge, being the opinion of al-Shāfiʿī. He holds that the Prostrations of Error are always before the *Taslīm*, saying that this hadith abrogates the other hadiths on this issue. Al-Shāfiʿī mentions that this hadith represents the practice of the Prophet in the last stage of his career. Ahmad Ibn Hanbal and Ishāq b. Rāhawayh say that if someone stands up in prayer in the midst of his normal two prostrations he should perform the two Prostrations of Error before the *Taslīm* as per the hadith of Ibn Bujayna.

The scholars have disagreed on when one should perform the two Prostrations of Error, before the *Taslīm* or after it? Some hold that one should perform them after the *Taslīm*; this is the position of Sufyān al-Thawrī and the Kufans [in other words, the Hanafīs]. Some have said 'before the *Taslīm*,' and this is the position of most the Medinan jurists like Yahyā b. Saʿīd, Rabīʿa [al-Ra'y] and others. This is the opinion of al-Shāfiʿī.

Others have said that if the mistake is adding something to the prayer then the Prostration of Error is after the *Taslīm*, and if it is an error of omission then before the *Taslīm*. This is the opinion of Mālik b. Anas.

Ahmad Ibn Hanbal said, 'All the hadiths related from the Prophet concerning the two Prostrations of Error should be employed, each according to its specific context.' He sees that when the Prophet stood up incorrectly in the hadith of Ibn Bujayna, he prayed the two Prostrations **before** the *Taslīm*. When the Prophet accidentally prayed five prayer cycles during the Noon prayer (which consists of four) he prayed the two Prostrations **after** the *Taslīm*. And when the Prophet accidentally said the *Taslīm* after only two prayer cycles in the four-prayer-cycle Noon or Afternoon prayers, he did the two Prostrations after the *Taslīm*. So every report is acted on according to its specific context, and every error in prayer that is not mentioned in one of these hadiths, then the two Prostrations of Error should be before the *Taslīm*.[34]

On this issue, we see that al-Shāfiʿī concluded that the hadith of the Prophet performing the two Prostrations of Error before the *Taslīm* abrogated all earlier hadiths and represented the Prophet's final Sunna. Mālik and Ibn Hanbal, however, attempted to reconcile the contrasting hadiths on the issue.

Several influential works were devoted to examining and attempting to reconcile seemingly contradictory hadiths. The first and most famous was al-Shāfiʿī's *Ikhtilāf al-hadīth*. The Hanafī scholar Abū Jaʿfar al-Tahāwī (d. 321/933) also wrote his voluminous *Sharh mushkil al-āthār*. Ibn Qutayba (d. 276/889) devoted his *Ta'wīl mukhtalif al-hadīth* to defending and reconciling hadiths that Muʿtazilites had dismissed as contradictory or irrational.

THE FUNCTION OF HADITHS IN ISLAMIC LEGAL THEORY

Hadiths did not just provide much of the substance of Islamic law, they also informed the theories through which that law was understood and derived. The Prophet's legacy shaped the manner in which Muslim legal theorists discussed law and epistemology, and these theorists also turned to hadiths as justification for their own ideas. In Chapter 3 we saw how Islamic legal theory (*usūl al-fiqh*) affected hadith criticism. Now let us examine how hadiths influenced Islamic legal theory. Interestingly, many of the most important hadiths in legal theory are considered weak (*daʿīf*) by Muslim hadith critics.

Genealogy of Knowledge and the Transmission of Authority from the Prophet

The Sunni tradition portrays itself as a genealogy of transmission in which each generation of scholars inherits its knowledge and methods of reasoning from its teachers. Paralleling the *isnād* exactly, this chain continues back to the Prophet. It is this transmission from teacher to student that creates and passes on interpretive authority.

The hadith that expressed this worldview and was frequently invoked to bolster it was narrated from the Prophet by the Companion Abū Dardā' and is found in the three *sunan*s of Abū Dāwūd, al-Tirmidhī, and Ibn Mājah: '**Indeed the scholars are the inheritors of the prophets** (*al-ʿulamā' warathat al-anbiyā'*).' Books in the Sunni tradition (written, of course, by members of the scholarly class) frequently refer to the ulema by this honorific. The great thirteenth-century Sufi master Abū Hafs al-Suhrawardī (d. 632/1234) wrote to one of the most vaunted legal theorists of his day, Fakhr al-Dīn al-Rāzī (d. 606/1210), that the religious knowledge of the Muslim scholars is 'the greatest inheritance. For earthly inheritors received the inheritance of the world according to the rules of the people of the earthly world, while the prophets bequeath as their legacy divine wisdom. So know that, just as there is no station higher than that of prophethood, there is no honor above that of those who inherit this station.'[35] Even the early scholar of the Successors, Abū al-Zinād (d. 130/748), used to tell his students that, just as the Quran ordered Muslims not to raise their voices over that of Muhammad, 'Silence in the presence of the scholars and respecting them is incumbent upon those learning, for the scholars are the inheritors of the prophets.'[36] This hadith thus served to justify the Muslim scholarly class's role as the sole interpreters of the Prophet's message. Interestingly, most scholars, such as al-Suyūṭī, consider this hadith to be weak.[37] Ibn Hajar, however, notes that there are enough reports conveying this meaning to prove that the hadith has some basis in the Prophet's speech.[38]

The Companions were the first essential link in the Sunni genealogy of knowledge. They transmitted the Prophet's legacy in the form of hadiths. Moreover, in their own approaches to questions of law and dogma the Companions demonstrated the principles and methods of reasoning of the early Muslims. The Companions were the medium and lens through which the Prophet's teachings passed on to later generations. Not only were the actual legal rulings of senior Companions such as ʿAlī, ʿUmar, and Zayd b. Thābit an important legal source for later scholars like Abū Ḥanīfa and al-Shāfiʿī, but the Sunni worldview and notion of religious authority depended on a veneration of the Companions. If they could not be trusted, then how could one have confidence in the Shariah?

A hadith commonly employed to affirm the Companions' suitability as the conduit for the transmission of this legal authority was '**My Companions are like the stars, which ever of them you follow, you will be rightly guided** (*ashābī ka'l-nujūm bi-ayyihim iqtadaytum ihtadaytum*).' This hadith was commonly found in books of legal theory in order to prove that any Companion was a worthy representative of the Prophet's legal teachings. Both the *ahl al-hadīth* and *ahl al-ra'y* bent the hadith to their own purposes, however. Al-Shāfiʿī's student al-Muzanī (d. 264/878), who wrote the most important abridgement of al-Shāfiʿī's *Umm*, contended that it meant that the Companions were all upstanding hadith transmitters.[39] The Hanafī legal theorist Fakhr al-Islām al-Bazdawī (d. 482/1089) argued that the hadith demonstrates that, like the Companions, Muslim scholars should employ their individual legal reasoning (*ra'y*).[40] Yet this hadith is also considered unreliable or even forged by Muslim hadith critics.

The manner in which these hadiths about the inheritance of knowledge in Islam were woven together by scholars can be seen in a work of the Damascene scholar Ibn Taymiyya (d. 728/1328), who wrote that, after believing in God and the Prophet, it is the duty of all Muslims to follow the scholars 'who are the inheritors of the prophets and whom God made like the stars, by whom one seeks guidance on land and sea.'[41]

The Authoritative Consensus of the Muslim Community (ijmāʿ)

The most powerful expression of authority in the Sunni tradition is not the Quran or even the Prophet's Sunna. Rather, it is *ijmāʿ*, or the consensus of the community. As an adage of Cairo's al-Azhar University puts it, 'Consensus is the stable pillar on which the religion depends (*al-ijmāʿ al-rukn al-rakīn yastanidu ilayhi al-dīn*).' If the Sunna controls the interpretation of the Quran, then consensus controls the interpretation of the Sunna. In the controversial modern debate over whether or not Islam requires Muslim women to wear headscarves, some argue that this law is not found in the Quran and that the hadiths ordering it are not reliable. But since the community of Sunni scholars has historically declared that it is 'agreed upon by consensus' that the headscarf is required, arguing otherwise means breaking with the Sunni schools of law. The role of *ijmāʿ* in Islamic law began in the early Islamic period. The Successor al-Musayyab b. Rāfiʿ (d. 105/723–4) stated, for example:

> The community, if an event occurred for which they could find no reports from the Prophet, would come together on it and reach a consensus. And the truth was in what they agreed on, the truth was in what they agreed on.[42]

Consensus received more formal justifications in books of legal theory. Because the Quran did not provide any unambiguous evidence that the consensus of the Muslims was authoritative, scholars turned to hadiths. One of the most commonly cited proofs is a famous hadith, the most well-known version of which can be found in the *Sunan* of al-Tirmidhī through Ibn 'Umar, that the Prophet said, '**Indeed God most high will not bring my community together on an error, and the hand of God is over the collective, and who splits away**

splits away into the Hellfire (*Inna Allāh taʿālā lā yajmaʿu ummatī ʿalā dalāla wa yad Allāh ʿalā al-jamāʿa, wa man shadhdha shadhdha ilā al-nār*).'[43] Ibn Hajar al-ʿAsqalānī notes that 'this is a well-known hadith narrated *via* many paths, but none of them are free of some criticism,' although al-Suyūṭī declares the hadith to be *hasan* because of its many narrations.[44]

In addition to such criticisms of the hadith, legal theorists actually found themselves in an even direr predicament: an *āḥād* hadith such as this one did not yield the certainty that scholars required to establish an important principle of legal theory. Unfortunately, the usual tool that Sunni legal theorists used to turn an *āḥād* hadith into absolute certainty was to claim that the community had come to consensus on its accuracy! Since Sunni scholars were at risk of lapsing into circular reasoning here, legal theorists like al-Ghazālī (d. 505/1111) argued that the authenticity of this hadith was not guaranteed by consensus but rather by 'the general rules governing reality (*al-ʿāda al-jāriya*).' If Muslim scholars from Spain to Central Asia agreed on this hadith, it was realistically impossible for it not to have a true basis in the Prophet's teachings.[45]

Creating Islamic Law outside the Quran and Sunna

In the Sunni tradition the Quran and Sunna are known as 'the two bases (*al aslūn*)' and are the only constitutive sources of law. Consensus derives its authority from them, and legal analogy refers new cases back to known rules from the Holy Book and the hadiths. Muslims, however, have maintained avenues for legal reasoning outside the letter of these scriptures. Various Sunni schools of law have reserved the right to rule on legal issues based on the best judgment of legal scholars or in pursuit of the Muslim community's best interest (with the general stipulation that such rulings cannot contradict the Quran and Sunna). Both these procedures are based on and legitimized by hadiths. Like the other hadiths in this section, however, these reports do not measure up to the standards of Muslim hadith critics.

In fact, the famous report '**Whatever the Muslims see as good is good according to God; and whatever the Muslims see as reprehensible is reprehensible according to God** (*mā ra'āhu al-muslimūn hasanan fa-huwa ʿind Allāh hasan wa mā ra'āhu al-muslimūn sayyi'an fa-huwa ʿind Allāh sayyi'*)' is not really a Prophetic hadith at all. Hadith critics determined that it was a statement of the Companion

Ibn Masʿūd. Yet the early Hanafī scholar of Baghdad, Muhammad b. al-Hasan al-Shaybānī (d. 189/805), one of Abū Hanīfa's leading disciples, attributed it to the Prophet in his argument for Muslims instituting new practices that they felt enhanced their religious life but did not exist during the time of the Prophet. Specifically, he was defending ʿUmar b. al-Khattāb's decision to organize voluntary communal nightly prayers in the mosque during the month of Ramadan.[46] This was not practiced during the Prophet's lifetime but was quickly embraced and became ubiquitous in the Muslim world.

An even more famous hadith is the Prophet's saying '**No harm and no harming** (*lā darar wa lā dirār*),' which Abū Dāwūd, the author of one of the Six Books, called one of the four pillars of legal hadiths.[47] Mālik and his student al-Shāfiʿī narrated this hadith as a *mursal* report, while Ibn Mājah had it *via* a full *isnād* from the Companion ʿUbāda b. Sāmit in his *Sunan*. It has generally been considered *hasan*. Regardless of its authenticity in the eyes of hadith scholars, however, this hadith became a central principle in Islamic legal thought. Muslim legal theorists used the phrase to elaborate what they saw as one of the principal goals of Islamic law, namely 'Promoting benefit and preventing harm.' They have also used it to justify the widely accepted notion of 'public interest (*maslaha mursala*),' which posited that Muslim scholars could rule in the interest of their community as long as they did not contravene any explicit injunctions from the Quran or Sunna. The Hanbali scholar Najm al-Dīn al-Tūfī (d. 716/1316) used this hadith to craft the controversial argument that if the public interest of the Muslim community clashed with scripture, public interest should take precedence.[48]

SUGGESTIONS FOR FURTHER READING

The most interesting book to read on this topic is the recently translated Muhammad 'Awwama, *The Influence of the Noble Hadith upon the Differences of Opinion Amongst the Jurist Imams* (London: Turath, 2014). To see how Mālik used hadiths in his *Muwatta'*, see Aisha Bewley's translation of the book, entitled *Al-Muwatta of Imam Malik ibn Anas* (London: Kegan Paul Intl., 1989) and Umar F. Abd-Allah's *Malik and Medina* (Brill, 2013). For the manner in which al-Shāfiʿī placed hadiths in his system of legal theory, see the translation of his extremely influential *Risāla* entitled, *The Epistle on Legal Theory*, trans. Joseph Lowry (New York: NYU Press, 2015). For more reading on the use of hadiths in early Sunni law, see Harald Motzki, *The Origins of Islamic Jurisprudence: Meccan Fiqh Before the Classical Schools*, trans. Marion Katz (Leiden: Brill, 2002); Yasin Dutton's *The Origins of Islamic Law: The Qur'an, the Muwatta' and Medinan 'Amal* (London: Curzon, 1999); Scott Lucas's 'Abu Bakr Ibn al-Mundhir, Amputation and the Art of Ijtihād,' *International Journal of Middle Eastern Studies* 39 (2007): 351–368, and Christopher Melchert's 'The Traditionist-Jurisprudents and the Framing of Islamic Law,' *Islamic Law and Society* 8, no. 3 (2001): 383–406. For a general discussion of the legal implications of hadiths in mature Sunni law, see Ibn Rushd's *The Distinguished Jurist's Primer*, trans. Imran Ahsan Nyazee (Reading, UK: Garnet Pub., 1994).

For in-depth discussions of mature Sunni legal theory, see Wael Hallaq's *A History of Islamic Legal Theories* (Cambridge: Cambridge University Press, 1997) and Bernard Weiss's *The Search for God's Law* (Salt Lake City: University of Utah, 1992). For a translation of a short book that Ibn Rajab al-Hanbalī (d. 795/1392) devoted to the 'Scholars are the inheritors of the prophets' hadith, see Ibn Rajab al-Hanbalī, *Heirs of the Prophets*, trans. and introduction Zaid Shakir (Chicago: Starlatch Press, 2001).

ENDNOTES

1 '*Inna al-Qur'ān ahkama dhālik wa al-sunna tufassiru dhālik*'; Abū Sa'd al-Sam'ānī, *Adab al-imlā' wa al-istimlā'*, p. 4.
2 *Sunan al-Dārimi*: introductory chapters, *bāb al-sunna qādiya 'alā kitāb Allāh.*
3 '*Al-Qur'ān ahwaj ilā al-sunna min al-sunna ilā al-Qur'ān*'; Abū Muhammad al-Barbahārī, *Sharh al-sunna*, p. 71.
4 Ibn Abī Hātim al-Rāzī, *al-Jarh wa al-ta'dīl*, p. 2:20.
5 Abū Zahra, *Abū Hanīfa*, p. 235; idem, *Al-Shāfi'ī*, p. 166; idem, *Ibn Hanbal*, p. 205; idem, *Mālik*, p. 224.
6 Al-Shāfi'ī, *Al-Umm*, p. 7:256.
7 Al-Shāfi'ī, *Al-Risāla*, p. 177.
8 *Jāmi'al-Tirmidhī: kitāb al-hudūd, bāb fī kam tuqta' al-yad; Sunan Abī Dāwūd: kitāb al-hudūd, bāb man saraqa min hirz, bab al-qat' fī al-khulsa ....*
9 Abū Zahra, *Abū Hanīfa*, p. 266.
10 Ibn Hibbān, *Sahīh Ibn Hibbān*, p. 5:498.
11 Brown, *The Canonization of al-Bukhārī and Muslim*, p. 191.
12 'Abd al-Wahhāb al-Sha'rānī, *Al-Mīzān al-kubrā*, p. 1:71.

13 *Jāmiʿ al-Tirmidhī: kitāb al-buyūʿ, bāb mā jāʾa fī al-khiyār*; Anwar Shāh Kashmīrī, *al-ʿArf al-shadhī* (Karachi, Qadīmī Kutubkhāne), p. 304.
14 Abū Zahra, *Mālik*, p. 259; *al-Muwattaʾ: kitāb al-buyūʿ, bāb bayʿ al-khiyār*.
15 Abū Hilāl al-ʿAskarī, *Kitab al-awāʾil*, p. 2:119.
16 Brown, *The Canonization of al-Bukhārī and Muslim*, pp. 178 ff.
17 *Jāmiʿ al-Tirmidhī: kitāb al-farāʾid, bāb mā jāʾa fī ibtāl mīrāth al-qātil.*
18 Ibn ʿAbd al-Barr, *al-Tamhīd*, p. 24:290.
19 Al-Tahāwī, *Sharh mushkil al-āthār*, p. 15:39.
20 Al-ʿAlāʾī, *Jāmiʿ al-tahsīl fī ahkām al-marāsīl*, p. 40.
21 See Muhammad ʿAwwāma, *Athar al-hadīth al-sharīf fī ikhtilāf al-aʾimma al-fuqahāʾ*, pp. 30 ff.
22 Ibn Qudāma al-Maqdisī, *al-Mughnī*, p. 2:570; *Musnad Ibn Hanbal*: 4 :426.
23 Mansūr al-Buhūtī, *Al-Rawd al-murbiʿ*, p. 108.
24 Al-Khatīb, ʻNasīhat li-ahl al-hadīth,ʼ p. 124.
25 Al-Khalīlī, *Al-Irshād*, p. 6.
26 Ibn Taymiyya, *Majmūʿat al-fatāwā*, pp. 19:128 ff.
27 *Jāmiʿ al-Tirmidhī: kitāb al-salāt, bāb mā jāʾa fī al-taʾmīn.*
28 Al-Suyūtī, *Al-Azhār al-mutanāthira fī al-ahādīth al-mutawātira*, p. 12.
29 *Jāmiʿ al-Tirmidhī: kitāb al-tahāra, bāb mā jāʾa fī al-wudūʾ mimmā ghayyarat al-nār; bāb tark al-wudūʿ min al-nār.*
30 Badr al-Dīn al-Zarkashī, *Al-Bahr al-muhīt fī usūl al-fiqh*, p. 3:268.
31 *Jāmiʿ al-Tirmidhī: kitāb al-birr wa al-sila, bāb mā jāʾa fī al-nafaqa ʿalā al-banāt wa al-akhawāt.*
32 Muhammad al-Ghazālī, *Al-Sunna al-nabawiyya bayn ahl al-fiqh wa ahl al-hadīth*, pp. 56–57; Ibn Hajar, *Fath al-bārī*, p. 13:70–71.
33 Ibn ʿAdī, *Al-Kāmil*, p. 1:125; *Sunan Abī Dāwūd: kitāb al-salāt, bāb man qāla lā yaqtaʿu al-salāt shayʾ.*
34 *Jāmiʿ al-Tirmidhī: kitāb al-salāt, bāb mā jāʾa fī sajdatay al-sahw qabl al-taslīm.*
35 Al-Munāwī, *Fayd al-qadīr*, vol. 8, p. 4:4101.
36 Ibn Battāl, *Sharh Sahīh al-Bukhārī*, vol. 1, p. 196.
37 Al-Suyūtī, *Al-Jāmiʿ al-saghīr*, p. 352.
38 Al-ʿAjlūnī, *Kashf al-khafāʾ*, vol. 2, p. 83.
39 Ibn Hajar, *Fath al-bārī*, vol. 4, p. 70.
40 Fakhr al-Islam al-Bazdawī, *Usūl al-Bazdawī*, vol. 1, p. 236.
41 Ibn Taymiyya, *Majmūʿat al-fatāwā*, vol. 19, p. 128.
42 *Sunan al-Dārimī*: introductory chapters, *bāb al-tawarruʿ ʿan al-jawāb fīmā laysa fīhi kitāb wa lā sunna.*
43 *Jāmiʿ al-Tirmidhī: kitāb al-fitan, bāb mā jāʾa fī luzūm al-jamāʿa.*
44 Ibn Hajar, *Talkhīs al-habīr*, p. 3:141; al-Suyūtī, *al-Jāmiʿ al-saghīr*, p. 113.
45 Wael Hallaq, ʻOn the Authoritativeness of Sunni Consensus,ʼ pp. 434 ff.
46 Muhammad b. al-Hasan al-Shaybānī, *Muwattaʾ Mālik*: *bāb qiyām shahr Ramadān wa mā fīhi min al-fadl.*
47 Al-Khatīb, *al-Jāmiʿ*, vol. 2, p. 301.
48 Najm al-Dīn al-Tūfī, *Risāla fī riʿāyat al-maslaha*, p. 23.

6

THE FUNCTION OF PROPHETIC TRADITIONS IN THEOLOGY

INTRODUCTION

Throughout their history, Muslims have rarely doubted that hadiths should play *some* role in understanding what *actions* were acceptable or unacceptable in God's sight. Even the most intransigent rationalists of ninth-century Baghdad accepted that hadiths could be used as a source for law if narrated by two or four chains of transmission. Law has always been a central part of the Islamic faith tradition, but it has not required *total* certainty. The different Sunni legal schools, for example, accepted that differences of interpretation could exist regarding the sources of the law, and the dubious authenticity of some of those sources itself left room for further doubt.

Since the eleventh century, mainstream Sunni opinion has held that, even if considered reliable, hadiths narrated by only a limited number of chains of transmission (termed *āhād* hadiths, which are the vast preponderance of reports that make up the hadith collections) yield only strong probability (*zann rājih*) and not total certainty (*yaqīn*) that they were truly the commands of the Prophet. This strong probability has been deemed acceptable for deriving Islamic law, so in practice both scholars and lay Muslims have treated *sahīh* hadiths as being the authenticated words of the Prophet.

But what about theology, those tenets of what Muslims should believe about God, the cosmos, and a person's fate after death? Did the Quran not lambast earlier communities who had made pronouncements about God and religion based not on revelation but merely on their own beliefs? The Quran had proclaimed that 'they have no knowledge of this, they do but conjecture' (Quran 45:24). If Muslim scholars held that the reports found in the great hadith compilations of the ninth century only yielded 'strong probability' as opposed to the total certainty yielded by the Quran, what should be the role of hadiths in theology?

THE ORIGINAL SUNNIS AND THE PRIMACY OF HADITHS IN THEOLOGY

By the twelfth century, Sunni Islam had become a very adaptive religious tradition that could accommodate four varied schools of law, divergent schools of both literalist and speculative theology, and numerous Sufi orders all under one 'big-tent' of deference to the Quran and the Prophet's legacy. Since that time, Sunni scholars have been able to adopt the rational methods of Greek logicians and the thought of Gnostic Christians into the Islamic tradition, all the while sincerely professing their loyal adherence to the Prophet's Sunna and rejection of *bid'a,* or heretical innovation in religion.

The Sunni worldview, however, was not always so flexible. Sunni Islam began as the small and strictly conservative *ahl al-ḥadīth* (Partisans of Hadith) sect in the eighth and ninth centuries. For these original Sunnis 'the *isnād* is part of religion,' and they preached that if anyone 'impugns reports from the early community or denies anything from the hadiths of the Messenger of God, then doubt his Islam.'[1] Even great scholars like Abū Hanīfa, who promoted using independent legal reasoning, were heretics in the eyes of these original Sunnis.[2]

For these original Sunnis, in whose ranks we find early pillars of the hadith tradition like Ibn Hanbal, al-Bukhārī, Muslim, Abū Dāwūd, and al-Tirmidhī, hadiths were not only reliable enough to inform Muslims of proper theology – they were its primary source. As early Sunnis proclaimed, 'Islam is the Sunna, and the Sunna is Islam,' and 'the Sunna of the Messenger of God is not known by reason, but by transmission.'[3]

Some of the theological beliefs that these early Sunnis upheld (and have since become part of Sunni Islam) included:

A belief that God knew before creation whether a person would enter Heaven or Hell and that humans cannot comprehend the true nature of free will and predestination.

A belief in the 'punishment of the grave' (*'adhāb al-qabr*), or the notion that the dead are punished for their sins or rewarded for their good deeds in the grave even before they are resurrected on the Day of Judgment. This recompense will be determined by a test administered by two angels, Munkar and Nakīr, who will appear to a person in his grave and ask him about God, the true religion, and the Prophet.

A belief that Jesus will return at the end of time along with another Messianic figure known as the *Mahdī* (The Guided One) and that together they will vanquish the Antichrist (*Dajjāl*).

A belief that late at night God descends to the lowest heavens to answer the prayers for forgiveness of those Muslims who have stayed up late in worship (see the hadith examined at the end of Chapter 9).

A belief that on the Day of Judgment believers will be rewarded for their faith by actually seeing God.

A belief that there will be certain landmarks on the Day of Judgment. One of these is the Fount (*al-Hawd*), a pool where Muhammad will meet his community. Another is the Bridge (*al-Sirāt*). This bridge crosses Hellfire, and, although the believers will cross it easily, for the unbelievers it will become narrower than a hair and sharper than a sword, causing them to fall into Hell.

None of these articles of faith is clearly laid out in the Quran. There are vague or ambiguous references to some of these tenets; the holy book contains verses such as 'On that Day [of Judgment] their faces will be pleased, gazing at their Lord' (Quran 75:22–23), which Sunnis have argued establish seeing God. But the only unambiguous description for these beliefs, and the only mention at all of others such as the Antichrist and the *Mahdī*, come from hadiths such as the following:

The hadith from the Companions 'Abdallāh b. Mas'ūd, Hudhayfa b. Yamān, Jundub, and others in various permutations that the Prophet said, **'I will be the first of you to the Fount [on the Day of Judgment], with some from among you raised up with me but then falling back trembling. I will say, "O my Lord, these are from my community!" but it will be said, "You do not know what wrongs they committed after you!"** ' (From the *Sahīhayn* of al-Bukhārī and Muslim)

The hadith of the Companion Abū Sa'īd al-Khudrī: We were afraid that there would come after our prophet some catastrophe, so we asked the Prophet of God and he said, **'Indeed in my community there will be the Messiah (*mahdī*), he will come and live five or seven or**

nine (the transmitter was not sure).' We asked the Prophet, 'Five or seven or nine what?,' and he said, 'years.' Then the Prophet continued, 'And a man will come to the Messiah and say, 'Give me, give me,' and he will dispense whatever he can from his own clothing.' (From the *Sunan* Ibn Mājah and the *Jāmi*ʿ of al-Tirmidhī)[4]

The hadith of Abū 'Ubayda b. al-Jarrāh, that 'the Messenger of God said, **"Indeed every prophet since Noah has warned his community of the Antichrist (*Dajjāl*), so indeed I warn you of him." Then he described him and said, "It may be that some of those who have seen me or heard my words will live to see him." '** (From the *Jāmi*ʿ of al-Tirmidhī)[5]

The hadith of the Companion Abū Hurayra, from the Prophet: **'Indeed the dead person goes to the grave, and the righteous man sits in his grave with no fear or terror. It is said to him, "What [religion] were you?" and he replies, "Islam." And it is said to him, "Who is that man?" and he replies, "Muhammad the Messenger of God, he came to us with clear evidence from God and we believed in him." It is said to him, "Did you see God?" and he replies, "It is not for anyone to see God." Then a small glimpse of Hell is given to him, and he sees its people bound to one another, and it is said to him, "Behold what God has spared you!" Then he is given a glimpse of Heaven and sees its splendor and all within. It is said to him, "This is your place, you believed in truth and died with that belief, so you will be resurrected in truth, God willing." The iniquitous man, however, sits in his grave terrified. It is said to him, "What [religion] were you?" and he replies, "I do not know." And it is said to him, "Who is that man?" and he replies, "I heard the people saying things about him so I said them too." Then he is shown a glimpse of Heaven and its splendor, and it is said to him, "Look at what God has denied you." Then he is shown a glimpse of Hell, and he sees its inhabitants bound to one another, and it is said to him, "This is your place, you were in doubt, in doubt you died and in doubt you will be resurrected, God willing." '** (From the *Sunan* of Ibn Mājah)[6]

The hadith narrated by Abū Hurayra in which the Prophet says: **'Adam and Moses argued, and Moses said, "O Adam, you whom God created with His hands and breathed His spirit into have led the people astray and exiled them from Paradise." Adam replied, "And you, O Moses, whom God purified with His own speech, do you blame me for committing an act which God had fated for me before the creation of the heavens and the earth?" So Adam bested Moses in the argument.'** (From the *Sahīh Muslim*)[7]

> The hadith narrated by Abū Hurayra that **'The Messenger of God (s) came out to us while we were debating free will and predestination (*al-qadar*) and was angered to the point that his face turned red, as if a pomegranate had burst on his cheeks. He said, "Is this what you have been taught to do?! Is this what I was sent with!? Indeed those who came before you perished when they began debating this matter, so I have ordered you not to contend over it."** ' (From the *Jamī*ʿ of al-Tirmidhī)[8]

The elaborate **epistemological** (having to do with the study of knowledge and its sources) classification of sources into those yielding probability or certainty, introduced into Sunni Islam in the tenth century by Muslim rationalists, was totally foreign to the early Sunnis. Hadiths that early Sunnis deemed authentic according to their system of criticism were the words of the Prophet and compelling in every sense. As Ibn Hanbal said about the hadith in which the Prophet foretells that Muslims will literally see God on the Day of Judgment, 'We believe in it and we know that it is the truth.'[9] When al-Tirmidhī presents a hadith describing how God will take people's charitable donations 'with His right hand,' the author explains:

> More than one scholar has said that this hadith and other narrations like it dealing with God's attributes and the Lord most high's descending every night to the lowest heavens, that these narrations have been established [as reliable] and are to be believed. They say that one should not fall into error concerning them and say 'How could this be?' It has been reported that Mālik b. Anas, Sufyān b. 'Uyayna, and 'Abdallāh b. al-Mubārak all said about such hadiths, 'Take them as is without asking "How".' Such is the stance of the scholars from the People of the Sunna and the Early Community (*Ahl al-Sunna wa al-Jamāʿa*).[10]

Contrast this with the stance of early Muslim rationalists like the great Muʿtazilite author al-Jāhiz (d. 255/869), who wrote 'If not for reason, religions would never be upheld for God, and we would never have been able to distinguish ourselves from the atheists, and there would be no distinction between truth and falsehood.'[11] For these rationalists, the idea that God could be seen or move from place to place, they felt, belittled the omnipotent and unknowable creator of the universe. Claims that people would be punished in their graves had no basis in the Quran and were only transmitted by glorified rumors – precisely what the Quran had warned Muslims against.

LATER SUNNISM AND THE RECONCILIATION OF REASON AND HADITHS IN THEOLOGY

The tenth century witnessed a merging of the strict, literalist Sunni theological beliefs of Ibn Hanbal and the rationalist Muʿtazilites' theories of knowledge. The individual most responsible for this was Abū al-Hasan al-Ashʿarī (d. 324/935–6), who was born in Basra in southern Iraq and became a prominent member of the Muʿtazilite rationalist school there. In 300/912–13, however, he had a series of dreams in which the Prophet appeared to him and instructed him to take care of his community, to follow the Sunna but not to abandon the ways of rationalist theology. He understood this as meaning that he should embrace the beliefs of the Sunnis but express and defend them with the tools of rational and speculative argument.

Al-Ashʿarī's strategy of forcing the rationalist methods of the Muʿtazilites into service for Sunni beliefs became hugely influential. It allowed a merging of the Sunni and Muʿtazilite schools, and in the century after al-Ashʿarī's death three Sunni scholars, Abū Ishāq al-Isfarā'īnī (d. 418/1027), Ibn Fūrak (d. 406/1015), and Abū Bakr al-Bāqillānī (d. 403/1013), combined hadith scholarship and the rationalist tools of the Muʿtazilites into what became the dominant Ashʿarī school of theology. Because the ways in which knowledge is derived affect law as well as theology, this school was also a way of looking at legal theory. It is often referred to as the Ashʿarī, or 'Majority (*Jumhūr*)' school of theology and legal theory. Along with the surviving *ahl al-hadīth* school of the early Sunnis (discussed below), which still generally rejected all use of rationalist tools, the Ashʿarī/Majority school constitutes one of the two great Sunni theological and legal-theory orthodoxies.[i]

Abū al-Hasan al-Ashʿarī embraced all the tenets of the early Sunni theology, such as the punishment of the grave, seeing God on the Day of Judgment, and the denial of unrestricted free will, proclaiming that these were the beliefs of true Sunnis.[12] Merging Sunni beliefs and the Muʿtazilite vision of knowledge, however, presented serious challenges.

As we saw in Chapter 3, with the contributions of legal theory to hadith criticism, Muʿtazilite legal theory and its Ashʿarī succes-

[i] There is a third Sunni school, the Māturīdī school, which closely resembles the Ashʿarī school and thus will not be discussed in this book.

sors divided reports transmitted from the past into two distinct levels, each conveying its own level of certainty and suited to its appropriate tasks. *Āhād* reports, or those transmitted by only a few chains of transmission, yielded probable knowledge (*zann*) and were only suitable for establishing Islamic law or the details of ritual. The second type of reports was a massively transmitted (*mutawātir*) one, or a report transmitted by such a vast number of people in so many different places that it is impossible to imagine that anyone could have made it up or conspired to forge it.

Although the hadiths establishing the beliefs mentioned above by al-Ashʿarī appear in highly respected Sunni hadith collections such as the *Sahīhayn* of al-Bukhārī and Muslim, they were only *āhād* hadiths. The Muʿtazilite and Ashʿarī traditions of epistemology had made clear the requirements that reports had to meet in order to convey absolute certainty. Legal theorists required that a hadith be transmitted by anywhere from five to forty transmitters at every stage in its transmission in order to be considered *mutawātir*. Other influential Ashʿarīs, like al-Juwaynī (d. 478/1085), avoided this focus on specific numbers. Instead, they argued that a hadith was *mutawātir* as long as it was transmitted *via* circumstances that made conspiring to forge it impossible and allowed it to convey immediate certainty to anyone who heard it. But as we saw in Chapter 3, Sunni hadith scholars admitted that no (or at most one) hadith actually met these requirements for being *mutawātir*.

How could the Sunnis who followed the new Ashʿarī tradition of theology and epistemology, then, justify their beliefs in things like the punishment of the grave or the coming of the Antichrist? They found two solutions: first, legal theorists like Abū Ishāq al-Isfarāyīnī and Hanafī contemporaries like Abū Bakr al-Jassās (d. 370/981) developed a middle tier of reports between *āhād* hadiths and the almost unattainable certainty of *mutawātir* ones. This middle tier was called 'well-known (*mashhūr*)' or 'widespread (*mustafīd*)' and was defined as those hadiths that might have started out with only a few chains of transmission but then became massively transmitted as time went on. Their authority was guaranteed not by the breadth of their transmission, but rather by the fact that the Muslim community had agreed on their authenticity.[13]

Second, in the eleventh century, Ashʿarī hadith scholars and legal theorists like al-Khatīb al-Baghdādī (d. 463/1071) and Abū Hāmid al-Ghazālī (d. 505/1111) articulated the notion of reports that were '*mutawātir bi'l-ma'nā*', or 'massively transmitted in their meaning.' Even if one particular hadith, they said, was not transmitted widely enough to meet the requirements for being *mutawātir*, what happened if you had a number of different hadiths that all shared one common element? Maybe no one hadith about the Messiah (*Mahdī*) could be considered *mutawātir*, but what if we collected all the hadiths mentioning him? We find a hadith in the books of al-Tirmidhī, Ibn Mājah, al-Bayhaqī, and al-Hākim al-Naysābūrī transmitted by several Companions in which the Prophet says, **'When the black banners come from eastern Iran, go join that army, for indeed the Messiah is among them.'** We find another hadith from two Companions in which the Prophet tells his followers that, even if only one day were remaining before the end of the world, God would lengthen that day so that He could send a messiah from the descendants of the Prophet with the same name as him. In another hadith through 'Alī, the Prophet predicts the coming of one of his descendants who will fill the earth with justice as it has been full of injustice. Even in the comments of the Companions, we find Ibn 'Abbās saying that a ruler will come from the family of the Prophet, bringing justice so absolute that under his rule flocks of sheep will be safe from predators.[14]

If we take all these hadiths together they all agree on one common element: there is a Messiah who will come. According to Ash'arī scholars, just as it is impossible to imagine that one massively transmitted hadith could have been forged, so it is impossible to imagine that all these separate hadiths could be forged with one common theme if that theme were not really representative of the Prophet's words. By creating a middle tier of non-*mutawātir* hadiths whose certainty was assured by the consensus of the Muslim community or whose meanings appeared in many different hadiths that together could be considered *mutawātir*, Muslims from the mainstream Ash'arī school of theology could justifiably believe in articles of faith found not in the Quran, but rather in their hadith collections.[15]

THE OTHER SUNNI ORTHODOXY: THE SURVIVING *AHL AL-HADĪTH* SCHOOL

The Ash'arī school of theology is often called the Sunni 'orthodoxy.' But the original *ahl al-hadīth*, early Sunni creed from which

Ash'arism evolved has continued to thrive alongside it as a rival Sunni 'orthodoxy' as well. While Ash'arīs proclaimed the theological beliefs of the early Sunnis like Ibn Hanbal, the influence of Mu'tazilite rationalism had led them to decline some of the most extreme early Sunni beliefs. Certainly, Ash'arīs affirmed that believers would 'see God' on the Day of Judgment, but this could not involve actually *seeing* God as we see objects in front of us today. Rather, God will create an optical image of God in their minds. How could an omnipotent creator, wholly outside creation, be seen? The Quran says that our vision 'cannot grasp Him' (Quran 6:103). Yes, authentic hadiths left no doubt that God does indeed 'descend to the lowest heavens' at some point in the night, but how could an unencompassable being engage in *physical* movement? Rather, it was God figuratively 'approaching' the believers by responding to their prayers.[16]

Ash'arī theologians had accepted the Mu'tazilite principle of content criticism. As al-Ghazālī said, any hadith describing God in an anthropomorphic way or assigning Him some physical location must be interpreted figuratively or rejected as false.[17] In a famous hadith known as the Hadith of the Slave Girl (*hadīth al-jāriya*), the Prophet tests to see if a slave girl was Muslim by asking her if he was a prophet and asking her where God was. She replied by saying 'In the sky (*fī al-samā'*)'. The Prophet acknowledged this as a correct profession of faith and ordered that the girl be freed.[18] Ash'arī theologians, however, said that, although it is recognized as authentic, this hadith is only *āhād* and is not sufficient to establish belief.[19] Extreme Ash'arīs have gone so far as to say that anyone who assigns a direction to God or believes that He actually moves is an unbeliever.[20]

In the wake of the tenth-century Ash'arī synthesis, some Muslim theologians still maintained the strict details of the early Sunni creed. This continuation of the original Sunni theological school is often referred to as the **Salafī** school of theology (because they claim to follow the righteous early Muslim community, or the *Salaf*) or as followers of 'Traditional (*Atharī*)' or *ahl al-hadīth* theology. Famous adherents of this school include the Sufi 'Abdallāh al-Ansārī (d. 481/1089) of Herat and the Damascene scholar Ibn Taymiyya (d. 728/1328).

For this Salafī school, reason has no role in determining theological beliefs. It is 'nothing more than a tool for distinguishing things.'[21] If the Prophet described God as descending during the night, who are we to insist that this descent occurs in one form as opposed to another? Ibn Taymiyya argues that the early Muslim community had no compunction about assigning a direction to God. He asserted that the Quran, the Sunna, and the practice of the righteous early community provided undeniable evidence that it was acceptable to point upward when referring to God (although he maintained that this meant that God was *above* the heavens, not in them).[22]

Adherents of the Salafī school of theology felt that the Ash'arīs had allowed the influence of rationalism to lead them astray from the true beliefs of Muhammad. How could they claim that a *sahīh* hadith cannot provide a reliable basis for belief, demanded the Salafī scholar Abū Nasr al-Wā'ilī of Mecca (d. 444/1052), but that frail human reason can?[23] Hadiths like the Hadith of the Slave Girl that address theological tenets, al-Wā'ilī continues, have been transmitted by numerous chains of transmission that are more than enough to make one's heart feel at ease with believing in them.[24] Unlike the wayward Ash'arīs, al-Wā'ilī boasts, his school of theology is that of the true 'People of the Sunna (*ahl al-sunna*), who stand fast on what the early generations (*salaf*) had transmitted to them from the Messenger of God.'[25] Today this school of *ahl al-hadīth* theology is espoused by the Wahhābī movement in Saudi Arabia and the various other hadith-based Salafī movements (see Chapter 10 for more on this).

SUGGESTIONS FOR FURTHER READING

For an accessible discussion of the Mu'tazilite rationalist school, including the translation of one of their texts, see Yahyā Nātiq bi'l-Haqq, *Basran Mu'tazilite Theology*, ed. Wilfred Madelung et al. (Leiden: Brill, 2011); *Defenders of Reason in Islam: Mu'tazilism from Medieval School to Modern Symbol*, by Richard Martin et al. (Oxford: Oneworld, 1997). A selection of different theological creeds, including one attributed to Ibn Hanbal, is translated in Montgomery Watt's *Islamic Creeds* (Edinburgh: Edinburgh University Press, 1994). Another excellent selection can be found in John Alden Williams, ed., *The Word of Islam* (Austin: University of Texas, 1994, Chapter 5). Two of al-Ash'arī's short treatises on theology have been translated in *The Theology of al-Ash'ari*, trans. Richard McCarthy (Beirut: Imprimérie Catholique, 1953). For a discussion of apocalyptic visions in Islam, see David Cook, *Studies in Muslim Apocalyptic* (Princeton: Darwin Press, 2002).

ENDNOTES

1 Al-Barbahārī, *Sharh al-sunna*, p. 81.
2 Al-Khatīb, *Tārīkh Baghdād*, vol. 2, p. 176.
3 Al-Barbahārī, *Sharh al-sunna*, p. 59; Abū Nasr al-Wā'ilī, *Risālat al-Sijzī ilā ahl Zabīd*, p. 99.
4 *Jāmi' al-Tirmidhī: kitāb al-fitan, bāb mā jā'a fī al-mahdī.*
5 *Jāmi' al-Tirmidhī: kitāb al-fitan, bāb mā jā'a fī al-dajjāl.*
6 *Sunan Ibn Mājah: kitāb al-zuhd, bāb dhikr al-qabr wa al-bilyā.*
7 *Sahīh Muslim: kitāb al-qadar, bāb hijāj Ādam wa Mūsā* (s).
8 *Jāmi' al-Tirmidhī: kitāb al-qadar, bāb mā jā'a fī al-tashdīd fī al-khawd fī al-qadar.*
9 Ibn al-Farra, *Al-'Udda fī usūl al-fiqh*, vol. 3, p. 900.
10 *Jāmi' al-Tirmidhī: kitāb al-zakāt, bāb mā jā'a fī fadl al-sadaqa.*
11 Al-Jāhiz, *Rasā'il al-Jāhiz*, vol. 1, p. 285.
12 Abū al-Hasan al-Ash'arī, *Maqālāt al-islāmiyyīn*, vol. 1, pp. 346–348.
13 Brown, *The Canonization of al-Bukhārī and Muslim*, pp. 183–193.
14 See Ahmad al-Ghumārī, *Ibrāz al-wahm al-maknūn min kalām Ibn Khaldūn*, p. 113.
15 Al-Sarakhsī, *Usūl al-Sarakhsī*, vol. 1, p. 329.
16 Al-Kawtharī, *Maqālat*, p. 145. Al-Bayjūrī (d. 1860) held that the hadith referred to the descent of God's angels, not God himself; al-Bayjūrī, *Sharh Jawharat al-tawhīd*, p. 158.
17 Abū Hāmid al-Ghazālī, *al-Mankhūl min ta'līqāt al-usūl*, p. 286.
18 *Sunan Abī Dāwūd: kitāb al-ayman wa al-nudhūr, bāb al-raqaba al-mu'mina.*
19 Taqī al-Dīn al-Subkī, *al-Sayf al-saqīl fī al-radd 'alā ibn al-Zafīl*, p. 94.
20 See, for example, al-Kawtharī, *Maqālāt*, p. 146. Ibn Hajar al-Haytamī, *al-Fatāwā al-hadīthiyya*, p.152.
21 Al-Wā'ilī, *Risāla*, p. 85.
22 Ibn Taymiyya, *Majmū'at al-fatāwā*, vol. 3, p. 97; Abū Zahra, *Ibn Taymiyya*, p. 269.
23 Al-Wā'ilī, *Risāla*, p. 101.
24 Al-Wā'ilī, *Risāla*, pp. 187–190.
25 Al-Wā'ilī, *Risāla*, p. 99.

7

THE FUNCTION OF PROPHETIC TRADITIONS IN SUFISM

INTRODUCTION

The Islamic mystical tradition, or Sufism, has historically been one of the religion's most important components. Sufism has played a dual role in Islamic history. It has served as the medium through which a spiritual elect has achieved and described direct experience with God. At the same time, through popular rituals and the veneration of saints, Sufism has allowed those unsung masses in Islamic civilization, whether villagers in India or merchants in the Balkans, to feel closer to God and more intimately ensconced in their faith.

As the tradition of seeking and describing direct mystical experiences with God, Sufism is 'the art of knocking' on the door of the Divine.[1] Because for Muslims Muhammad was the human closest to God, practitioners of Sufism also see it as the science of understanding and applying the Prophet's message in the fullest and most perfect way. As the process of fulfilling the duties of the pious Muslim and gaining proximity to God, the famous Sufi Abū Bakr al-Shiblī (d. 334/945–6) described Sufism as 'comforting the heart with the fan of purity, clothing the mind with the cloak of faithfulness, acquiring generosity and rejoicing in meeting God.'[2] As the perfection of character, Sufism is 'all proper manners, for every time and every place.'[3]

As in other domains, in Sufism hadiths have served as a source of guidance and a medium of connection to the Prophet. In one sense, in Sufism the *isnād* of the hadith is all-important, for it establishes the transmission of the Prophet's teaching, his excellence of character as well as esoteric knowledge inherited from him and taught by the pious elite. In another sense, however, *isnāds* and their authenticity mean nothing in Sufism – those Sufi masters for whom the door has been opened have been able to access God's truth directly without the medium of prophecy or Muhammad's teachings. For them, truths about the reality of God and man are true whether actually said by the Prophet or phrased in his words. The tension has been a constant one in the Sufi tradition. One early Sufi, al-Dārānī (d. 204/820) taught that, even if you are inspired to perform some act of worship, you should not do so until you find a hadith justifying it. Ironically, another Sufi took a similar statement from Ibn Hanbal and tacked on a forged *isnād* to the Prophet.[4]

THE FOUNDATION OF SUFISM IN HADITH: THE HADITH OF GABRIEL

Hadiths have always played an important role in Muslim etiquette and pious ethics. The famous hadith scholar Abū Dāwūd once wrote that a Muslim only needed to know four hadiths, none of which involve dogmatic or legal strictures: '**Actions are judged only by intentions**,' '**Part of a person perfecting their Islam is to leave aside matters that do not concern them**,' '**What is prohibited is clear, what is permissible is clear, and what is other than that is uncertain**,' and '**No one's faith is complete until he wishes for his brother what he wishes for himself.**'[5]

From its early coalescence in the ninth century, the Sufi tradition has employed hadiths to instruct those seeking the Sufi path and to justify its teachings. The Forty Hadith collection devoted to Sufism written by the famous Iranian Sufi Abū 'Abd al-Rahmān al-Sulamī (d. 412/1021) was one of the most widely transmitted books in the centuries after its author's death and served as a primer for Sufism among Muslim students. It contained hadiths urging piety, generosity, and asceticism, such as '**Whoever wants to join me, let him suffice from the goods of this world with only what a traveler needs. And beware of mixing with the rich.**'[6]

The hadith that has historically essentialized the Sufi tradition and provided its most firm foundation in the Prophet's teachings is the famous Hadith of the Angel Gabriel. This report is extremely well known and met Muslim hadith critics' highest standards of authenticity. It appears in the *Sahīhayn* of al-Bukhārī and Muslim, as well as the three *Sunan*s of Abū Dāwūd, al-Tirmidhī, and Ibn Mājah, narrated from the Prophet by the Companions 'Umar b. al-Khattāb, Talha b. 'Ubaydallāh, Anas b. Mālik, or Abū Hurayra. The version from Abū Hurayra appearing in al-Bukhārī's *Sahīh* reads:

> ←Ishāq ←Jarīr ← Abū Hayyān ← Abū Zur'a ←Abū Hurayra: One day the Prophet was out before the people when a man came walking up to him and said, 'O Messenger of God, what is faith (*īmān*)?' [The Prophet] said, 'Faith is to believe in God, His angels, His messengers, that you will meet Him, and to believe in the resurrection.' [The man] said, 'O Messenger of God, what is Islam (submission)?' [The Prophet] replied, 'Islam is to worship God, not associate anything with Him, to perform the prayer, render the poor tithe, and fast Ramadan.' The man asked, 'O messenger of God, what is *ihsān* (perfection)?' [The Prophet] said, '*Ihsān* is to worship God as if you could see Him, for indeed even if you cannot see Him, He sees you.' [The man] said, 'O messenger of God, when is the Hour [of Judgment]?' [The Prophet] said, 'The one being asked is no more knowledgeable about that than the one asking, but I will tell you about its signs: when women give birth to their mistresses, that is one of the signs; when the naked and barefoot rule the people, that is one of the signs; one of five things that only God knows "Indeed God knows the Hour, he sends down the rain and knows what is in the wombs" (Quran 31:34). Then the man left, and the Prophet ordered that he be brought back to him, but no one could find him. Then the Prophet said, 'That was Gabriel, he came to teach the people their religion.'[7]

The Hadith of Gabriel has served as a formative expression of how Muslims broadly conceive of their religion. The hadith structures Islam in three tiers: it consists first of select articles of belief, followed by the outward submission to God through the performance of set rituals and deeds. Beyond these two basic levels of religious commitment lies the level of supererogatory piety sought by those who truly want to live in a state of constant God-consciousness: *ihsān*. Sufism has defined itself as the quest for *ihsān*, to be continually in a state of remembering God and acting accordingly. Sufis have therefore considered their path to be an optional one. Those who do not choose to pursue it still remain fully Muslim in faith and practice. Sufis elect to go beyond what is required. 'For this elite of the elite,' explains the great theologian and mystic Abū Ḥāmid al-Ghazālī (d. 505/1111), 'the verse "And God is better and more enduring" (Quran 20:73) has become manifest, and they have chosen a place "in an assembly of truth in the presence of an omnipotent Lord" (Quran 54:55).'[8]

THE ISSUE OF THE AUTHENTICITY OF SUFISM AND THE *ISNĀD* OF SUFI TEACHINGS

From its inception, Islam has been an iconoclastic faith opposed to erecting intermediaries between God and man, founded on the premise that only revelation can shape the contours of faith and ritual. This extremely conservative approach to tenets of belief and ritual (as opposed to law) explains why Muslims from China to Great Britain, Sunni and Shiite, all pray their daily prayers in the same way, differing only in details. This conservative spirit has also meant that, although Sufism has played an undeniably prominent role in Islam, it has also been one of the most controversial dimensions of the faith tradition.

The central objection launched by Muslim critics of Sufism has been that it contains elements of heretical innovation (called *bid'a*) or belief not originally part of Islam. Some Muslim scholars have found three aspects of Sufism to be problematic: 1) ritual practices and prayers that are viewed as imported innovations not originating in the Sunna of the Prophet or his Companions, 2) the institution of Sufi brotherhoods in the twelfth century with formalized relationships between a spiritual guide (Arabic '*shaykh*' or Persian/Turkish '*pīr*') and his disciples, and 3) a theosophical cosmology that upholds the 'Unicity of Existence (*wahdat al-wujūd*),' or the notion that only God actually exists and that creation is a mere illusion.

The first point was unacceptable to many Muslim scholars because it seems to break with the fundamental Islamic principle that only the Quran and Sunna can serve as the basis for ritual and belief. As Ibn Qayyim al-Jawziyya (d. 750/1351), a famous critic of Sufism, explained, in Islam 'the presumption about claims of ritual is that they are false until some proof is provided, whereas the presumption in contracts and personal interactions is that they are valid until proven otherwise.'[9] The second point caused concern because Sufi brotherhoods and the veneration of *shaykh*s seemed to create formalized institutions and invest certain people with authority unacknowledged in the Prophet's message. As Ibn Taymiyya objected, 'It is not for anyone to belong to a *shaykh* by swearing to be his follower … but rather he should take as a guide anyone who is from among the people of faith without specifying anyone with an excessive position of spiritual authority.'[10] Finally, for many, 'the Unicity of Existence' was a theological perspective similar to pantheism, or the belief that the divine was present in creation and objects of nature – a position firmly rejected in Islam.

Architects and proponents of the Sufi tradition were aware from an early stage of these objections and sought to ground their ideas in the original revelation of the Prophet. Abū al-Qāsim al-Junayd (d. 298/910), the epicenter of classical Sufism in Baghdad, thus declared that 'Our science [of Sufism] is bounded by the Quran and the Sunna.'[11] Sufis admitted that practices such as ritual gatherings where the names of God are recited or specific liturgies said after prayers were innovations. But they were like flowers that had blossomed from seeds rooted in the Prophet's original teachings. As the Sufi Abū al-Hasan al-Fūshanjī (d. 348/959) said, 'Today Sufism is a name without a reality, it was once a reality without a name.'[12]

Al-Fūshanjī's quote raises another important point concerning objections to Sufism: many of Sufism's harshest critics, such as Ibn al-Jawzī (d. 597/1201) and Ibn Taymiyya, were themselves Sufis who only rejected certain corrupted components of Sufism, such as extremist beliefs or the excessive practices of some Sufis. They maintained the legitimacy of the ethical components of Sufism, what they called 'the science of purifying the heart.'

As in hadiths and law, the principal anchor for the authenticity of Sufism was the *isnād*. The Sufi tradition cultivated two kinds of *isnād*s to the Prophet. The first was known as the *isnād al-tazkiya* (*isnād* of purification) or the *isnād al-suhba* (*isnād* of discipleship) and was a commonsense feature of traditional Islamic piety. The second form of *isnād* represented a formal or mystical chain of transmission from teacher to student back to the Prophet.

The *isnād* of purification/discipleship was based on a very sensible premise. If the Companions spent many years around the Prophet, they would have learned his pious and God-fearing ways from his example. The Successors who studied at the Companions' hands would have learned this from them, and so would any committed students of the Prophet's teachings in subsequent generations. A sincere scholar's duty to his students did not stop at teaching them the Quran, the Sunna, and Islamic law. He also instructed them on proper etiquette and instilled in them a desire for *ihsān*. We can see an example of this with Ismāʿīl b. ʿUlayya (d. 193/809) of Baghdad, an early hadith scholar whose mother had brought him to a senior scholar and said, 'This is my son, let him be with you and take from your etiquette and character.'[13] As a youth the famous jurist and Sufi of Baghdad, Ibn al-Jawzī, would attend the hadith dictation sessions of one teacher who would recite a hadith and then start crying out of fear of God and love for the Prophet. Later in life Ibn al-Jawzī would write, 'I benefited more from his crying than his simply transmitting the hadith.'[14]

The earliest recorded *isnād*s for Sufi teachings go back through al-Junayd. One Jaʿfar al-Khuldī (d. 348 /959) said that he 'took' from al-Junayd, who took from al-Sarī al-Saqatī, from Maʿrūf al-Karkhī, from Farqad al-Sabakhī, from al-Hasan al-Basrī, from Anas b. Mālik and the other great Companions, from the Prophet.[15] The famous Sufi systematizer al-Qushayrī (d. 465/1072) traces his *isnād* through his teacher Abū ʿAlī al-Daqqāq, from Abū al-Qāsim al-Nasrābādī, from al-Shiblī, from al-Junayd, from Sarī al-Saqatī, from Maʿrūf al-Karkhī, from Dāwūd al-Tā'ī, from the Successors, from the Companions, from the Prophet.[16]

The second type of *isnād* in Sufism was understood as the transmission of esoteric knowledge – a weighty matter indeed – or something equally intangible but less serious: the transmission of blessings (*baraka*) from a saint to an aspirant. Many Muslims believed that the Prophet had chosen certain Companions with whom to deposit secret knowledge beyond the comprehension of normal Muslims and limited to the spiritual elite. The Companion Hudhayfa b. Yamān was told about all the strife and challenges that would afflict the Muslims until the Day of Judgment, and it was reported that Abū Hurayra said, 'I memorized two vessels [of knowledge] from the Prophet. As for the first, I made it known among the people. As for the second, if I made it known my throat would be cut.'[17]

This esoteric knowledge could be transmitted from the Prophet to a Companion, and later from saint to student, by a mere touch. As one report (admittedly very unreliable, according to Muslim hadith critics) has it, when ʿAlī was washing the Prophet's body for burial some water splashed from the body into ʿAlī's eyes, granting him in one instant 'the knowledge of the ancient and latter day sages.'[18] Many Sufis believed that this knowledge could be transmitted from such Companions through teacher to student. For many Sufis, however, and even for critics of Sufism, these *isnād*s were not conduits for any secret mystical knowledge. They were merely symbols for the transmission of blessings from a revered pious figure to his students.

Only in the eleventh and twelfth centuries did the Sufi tradition elaborate the *isnād* as a medium for transmitting the Prophet's mystical knowledge or his blessings, at which point 'Alī b. Abī Tālib first emerged as an important component in the Sufi chain of transmission.[19] 'Alī had always been seen as the Prophet's spiritual heir, leading al-Junayd to say, '*that* is a person who was granted '*ilm ladunnī*', or the directly, divinely granted wisdom that God gives to select people.[20] Sufis quoted the Companion Ibn Mas'ūd as saying that the Quran was revealed with 'an Outer and Inner meaning, and indeed 'Alī b. Abī Tālib has with him the knowledge of both.'[21]

The Sufi *isnād* through 'Alī became very famous after the eleventh century because of what was known as the 'Investiture with the Cloak (*libs al-khirqa*).' In this ritual, a Sufi master put a *khirqa* (a cloak or shawl) on a student being initiated into his Sufi order. The *khirqa* became the sign of 'taking the path' of a Sufi order and was often given to the student after he had fulfilled certain requirements such as a year of charity or of spiritual vigilance. Along with being told the special prayers of the order and giving his oath of allegiance to the *shaykh*, being invested with the *khirqa* was a crucial part of joining a Sufi order. Sometimes *khirqa*s were colored and served as the uniform for a particular Sufi order. In addition to the *khirqa* of initiation, Sufis also cultivated the tradition of the *khirqat al-tabarruk*, or the 'cloak of blessings,' which was given as a benediction to a layman who did not intend to join the order.[22]

The famous Hanbalī scholar and Sufi Ibn al-Mubrad (d. 909/1502) explains that the devoted student of knowledge should 'be invested with a *khirqa* to wear, for blessing is to be hoped for from that. And a group of the righteous early Muslims used to do this, asking the righteous to invest them with a cloak and seeking to learn from their behavior and actions.'[23]

Ibn al-Mubrad provides us with one of the *isnād*s for his *khirqa*, which we immediately note proceeds *via* the Family of the Prophet. He traces it back through a long chain of masters to:

> Abū Bakr al-Shiblī, who was invested with the *khirqa* by the hand of Abū al-Qāsim al-Junayd, who received it from the hand of Sarī al-Saqatī, who received it from the hand of Ma'rūf al-Karkhī, who was the spiritual disciple of 'Alī b. Mūsā al-Ridā, who was the disciple of [his father Mūsā] al-Kāzim, who was the disciple of [his father] Ja'far al-Sādiq, who was the disciple of [his father Muhammad] al-Bāqir, who was the disciple of [his father] Zayn al-'Ābidīn, who was the disciple of his father al-Husayn, who was the disciple of his father 'Alī b. Abī Tālib, who was the companion of the Prophet.[24]

The most famous *isnād* for the *khirqa*, however, was through the Successor al-Hasan al-Basrī, from 'Alī, from the Prophet.

Critics of Sufism pounced on the chain of transmission for the *khirqa* as a point of vulnerability. Because the Sufi tradition had invested so much of its legitimacy in this *isnād*, the methods of hadith criticism would become a central tool for those who wished to question that legitimacy or to defend it. Ibn al-Jawzī of Baghdad criticized the way the Sufis of his day wore the *khirqa* in order to appear pious and gain repute. In fact, he rejected the idea of having an *isnād* for receiving the *khirqa* from one's *shaykh*, calling it 'all a lie' that had no basis in the Sunna.[25] Ibn Taymiyya argued that, not only did the donning of a *khirqa* not come from the Prophet's practice, not even the early Sufis engaged in the practice (we can note in Ibn al-Muhrad's *isnād* (above) that all mention of receiving the *khirqa* goes no further back in time than Ma'rūf). 'Rather,' he writes, 'it resembles more a king passing on the trappings to his successor ... which is fine if done with good intentions. But as for making that a Sunna [of the Prophet] or a path to God most high, that is not the case.'[26]

Many critics of Sufism attacked a more technical aspect of the *khirqa isnād*. Many Sufis traced their *isnād*s through al-Hasan al-Basrī, from 'Alī to Muhammad. But hadith masters who did not support many Sufi practices, such as Ibn al-Salāh (d. 643/1245), Ibn Hajar (d. 852/1449), and al-Sakhāwī (d. 897/1402) all argued that al-Hasan al-Basrī had never met or heard hadiths from 'Alī.[27] How could he have received the *khirqa*, or any knowledge at all for that matter, from him?

Proponents of Sufism have tried to find evidence from the hadith tradition to bolster the claim of al-Hasan receiving the *khirqa* from 'Alī. Al-Suyūtī (d. 911/1505) points out that al-Hasan al-Basrī was born in Medina and grew up in the house of one of the Prophet's wives. He met many of the Companions and attended congregational prayers led by the caliphs 'Uthmān and 'Alī. Since 'Alī did not leave Medina until al-Hasan was fourteen years old, al-Hasan would have had ample time to study with 'Alī. Furthermore, al-Suyūtī finds examples of hadiths where al-Hasan al-Basrī explicitly states that he heard the report from 'Alī, such as the hadith from the *Musnad* of Abū Ya'lā al-Mawsilī that **'The parable of my community is like the rain: it is not known which is better, its beginning or its end.'**[28]

The debate over the strength of the *isnād* for the *khirqa* and al-Hasan's hearing hadith from 'Alī was intense and has lasted until the present day, when the Moroccan Ahmad al-Ghumārī wrote a book entitled 'The Evident Proof for Sufis Being Connected to 'Alī (*al-Burhān al-jalī fī intisāb al-sūfiyya ilā 'Alī*).' But ultimately this one point cannot settle the argument over the legitimacy of Sufism. As is clear from the *isnād*s listed above, Sufis cite many other *isnād*s for their teachings that do not involve al-Hasan al-Basrī, 'Alī, or the *khirqa*. More importantly, many of the hadith scholars, such as Ibn al-Salāh, who criticized the *isnād*s for the *khirqa* practice, themselves sought and received *khirqa*s from Sufi masters! Regardless of the authenticity of the practice, they did so because it had become an accepted tradition for receiving blessings (*baraka*) from pious Muslim saints. No matter how poor its *isnād*, the *khirqa* carried great weight as the sign of a relationship with a Sufi master as well as a token of his blessings.

HADITHS IN THEOSOPHICAL SUFISM

Since the early period of Sufism, mystics have underscored the absolute contrast between the ultimate reality of God and the transience of His creation. As the Quran states, 'All things perish except His face' (Quran: 28:68). Many Sufis stressed how all of creation is nothing more than an ephemeral reflection of God's magnificence and held that man's greatest accomplishment is to penetrate the veil of this world and 'become annihilated' in God in this life – as one forged hadith puts it, to **'die before you die.'**[29] A truly pious and perspicacious mystic grasps that God reveals His beauty (*tajallī*) in every object in this world and that the pinnacle of human awareness is to know God more and more intimately through His signs and perfectly reflect His attributes. Attaining this state of being dissolved in God is what led ecstatic Sufi mystics like Bayazid al-Bastāmī (d. 261/874) to declare 'Glory be to Me!' and the famous Sufi martyr al-Hallāj (d. 309/922) to pronounce 'I am the Ultimate Truth/God (*anā al-haqq*)!,' both phrases being otherwise reserved for God alone. To achieve this profound understanding was to reconnect completely with the source of all existence and fulfill the deepest yearnings of the soul. As the great Persian Sufi poet Jalāl al-Dīn Rūmī (d. 672/1273) wrote, like the reed flute whose song laments its separation from the reed bed:

> Every person who has long remained far from his source,
> Longingly seeks the day of his reunion.

This mystical worldview flourished in the writings of Sufis like al-Ghazālī but was first organized into a comprehensive cosmology, or view of the universe, by the seminal Sufi Muhyī al-Dīn Ibn 'Arabī (d. 638/1240), who hailed from Spain, traveled throughout the Middle East and eventually died in Damascus.

Ibn 'Arabī devised a conception of creation as a reflection of God's perfect attributes. Each of the manifold components and dimensions of the cosmos and the natural world mirrors His endless beauty, order, and creative capacity. The pinnacle and capstone of creation is mankind, the element that reflects God's most essential attribute: His unity. Humans embody within their souls and character all the multiplicity of the cosmos but are able to bring them into unified balance and proper proportion. A person who has achieved this state of enlightened balance not only embodies 'the spirit of the cosmos,' he or she also is the most perfect reflection of God's perfection. This is 'the perfect human being (*al-insān al-kāmil*),' who has purged him or herself of imperfections and grown closer and closer to God's attributes until he dissolves into non-existence. For only God truly exists at all.[30] For Ibn 'Arabī, investiture with the *khirqa* symbolizes 'putting on' the divine qualities.[31]

The function of revealed religion is similar. Each of the great prophets sent by God to their respective communities embodied and reflected one of His attributes. Their culmination, which Ibn 'Arabī refers to with the Quranic phrase 'the Seal of the Prophets' (Quran 33:40), was Muhammad. He was 'the perfect human' *par excellence*, the consummate reflection of God who represented the goal that all seekers of truth sought and the station attained by saints. His timeless reality, which Ibn 'Arabī called 'the Muhammadan Reality (*al-haqīqa al-muhammadiyya*)' was, in fact, the whole purpose of creation.

The theosophical Sufi tradition, brought to its height by Ibn 'Arabī, explained the reason for God's creation in the 'Hadith of the Hidden Treasure,' which Ibn 'Arabī cites many times in his massive treatise *al-Futuhāt al-makkiyya* (The Meccan Revelations). It is a hadith *qudsī*, in which the Prophet quotes God directly as saying **'I was a hidden treasure, and I wanted to be known. So I created the cosmos so that I might be known'** (*kuntu kanza makhfīyan fa-ahbabtu an u'raf fa-khalaqtu al-khalq li-u'rafa*).This hadith communicated an essential point of Ibn 'Arabī's cosmology: knowing God is the purpose of all creation. Humans exist because God wanted them to know Him and strive to become His flawless reflections. Although this sense is conveyed in Quranic verses such as the one reading 'I have not created the jinn or mankind except to worship me' (Quran 51:56, with Ibn 'Abbās glossing 'worship' as 'know'), the Hadith of the Hidden Treasure imbued this motivation with an almost emotional longing that conveys the themes of desire and intimate knowledge so key to the Sufi tradition.

A second hadith that served as an important piece of evidence in theosophical Sufism was known as the Hadith of Reason (*hadīth al-'aql*). It is another *qudsī* hadith, in which the Prophet explains:

> **Indeed God, when he created reason, He said to it, 'Come,' and it came. Then He said, 'Go back,' and it went back. So God said, 'By my glory and beauty, I have not created anything nobler than you. By you I will take and by you I will give'** (*Inna Allāh lammā khalaqa al-'aql qāla lahu: aqbil fa-aqbala, thumma qāla adbir fa'adbara, fa-qāla 'wa 'izzatī wa jamālī mā khalaqtu khalqan ashraf minka, fa-bika ākhudhu wa bika u'tī*).

This hadith established an important tenet of Sufism and speculative theology in Islam in general: man's reason is ultimately subordinate to God and serves the cause of grasping His truth. For Ibn 'Arabī and upholders of the theosophical Sufi tradition, there were three ways for humans to attain knowledge: prophetic revelation, inspiration from God (often called '*dhawq*,' 'tasting,' or *kashf*, 'unveiling'), and rational investigation. Yet the mainstream Sunni tradition, especially in its infancy during the ninth and tenth centuries, was highly suspicious of relying on reason. They considered it a loophole for human beings to meddle in matters of religion that God alone should define.

For Sufis, the Hadith of Reason established that reason obeyed God and prophecy.

Unfortunately, neither the Hadith of the Hidden Treasure nor the Hadith of Reason had any basis in the actual words of the Prophet, according to Muslim scholars. Opponents of Ibn ʿArabī's theosophical Sufism, such as Ibn Taymiyya, said that the Hadith of the Hidden Treasure 'has no *isnād*, weak or strong, to the Prophet,' and even moderate scholars who supported Sufism, like Ibn Hajar and Mullā ʿAlī Qārī, acknowledged that its attribution to the Prophet was baseless.[32] The Hadith of Reason actually did appear in some hadith collections, although highly unreliable ones. Ibn Hanbal's son ʿAbdallāh included it as a *mursal* hadith in his book of *zuhd*, and al-Tabarānī included it in his large *muʿjam*. However, every major Sunni hadith critic, from early figures such as al-ʿUqaylī (d. 323/934) and al-Dāraqutnī to later ones such as al-Sakhāwī and Mullā ʿAlī Qārī, agreed that the report was extremely weak or forged.[33]

Ibn ʿArabī himself was no amateur in hadiths; he had cultivated his own collection of hadiths with full *isnād*s back to the Prophet. He acknowledged that these two hadiths had no basis according to the methods of hadith critics. Rather, as he states in the case of the Hadith of the Hidden Treasure, it was known to be 'sound on the basis of unveiling (*kashf*)' (see Chapter 3 on Criticism through Unveiling).[34] What concern was it to Sufis if no reliable *isnād* could be found for an important hadith? Sufi masters like Ibn ʿArabī felt that their understanding of the cosmos superseded the mere probabilities generated by Sunni hadith criticism and its reliance on the *isnād*. As the early Sufi al-Bastāmī was quoted as saying, 'You take your knowledge dead from the dead, but I take my knowledge from the Living One who does not die.'[35]

SUGGESTIONS FOR FURTHER READING

Fortunately, a great deal has been written about Sufism in English. Helpful works include Annemarie Schimmel's *Mystical Dimensions of Islam* (Chapel Hill: University of North Carolina Press, 1975) and Sayyed Hosein Nasr's *Sufi Essays* (London: G. Allen & Unwin, 1972). Michael Sells' *Early Islamic Mysticism* (New York: Paulist Press, 1996) contains many original texts in translation. For a more specific discussion about the theosophical Sufism of Ibn ʿArabī, see Claude Addas, *The Quest for the Red Sulfur: The Life of Ibn ʿArabī* (Cambridge: Islamic Text Society, 1993) and William Chittick's *The Sufi Path of Knowledge* (Albany: State University of New York Press, 1989). For an edited collection of essays dealing with debates over Sufism within the Islamic tradition, see F. de Jong and Bernd Radtke's *Islamic Mysticism Contested* (Leiden: Brill, 1999). For a translation and discussion of many of the hadiths frequently used in Sufism, see Javad Nurbakhsh, *Traditions of the Prophet* (New York: Khaniqahi-Nimatullahi Publications, 1981). Ibn ʿArabī's *Mishkāt al-anwār* is translated as *Divine Sayings*, trans. Stephen Hirtenstein (Oxford: Anqa Publications, 2004).

ENDNOTES

1 Martin Lings, *What is Sufism?*, p. 7.
2 Al-Khatīb, *Tārīkh Baghdād*, vol. 14, p. 393.
3 This statement is from Abū Hafs al-Naysābūrī; Al-Sulamī, *Tabaqāt al-sūfiyya*, p. 119.
4 Al-Makkī, *Qūt al-qulūb*, vol. 1, p. 167; Abū Nuʿaym al-Isbahānī, *Hilyat al-awliyā'*, vol. 10, p. 15.
5 Ibn Nuqta, *Kitāb al-taqyīd*, p. 280.
6 Al-Sulamī, *Kitāb al-arbaʿīn fī al-tasawwuf*, p. 5.
7 *Sahīh al-Bukhārī*: *kitāb al-īmān*, *bāb* 38.
8 J. Brown, 'The Last Days of al-Ghazzālī and the Tripartite Division of the Sufi World,' p. 93.
9 Ibn Qayyim al-Jawziyya, *Iʿlām al-muwaqqiʿīn*, vol. 1, p. 344.
10 Ibn Taymiyya, *Majmūʿat al-fatāwā*, vol. 11, p. 289.
11 Al-Khatīb, *Tārīkh Baghdād*, vol. 7, p. 251.
12 ʿAlī Hujvīrī, *Kashf al-mahjūb*, p. 49.
13 Al-Dhahabī, *Mīzān al-iʿtidāl*, vol. 1, p. 217.
14 Ibn al-Jawzī, *Mashyakhat Ibn al-Jawzī*, p. 86.
15 Ibn al-Nadīm, *The Fihrist*, p. 455.
16 ʿAbd al-Ghāfir al-Fārisī, *Tārīkh Naysābūr*, pp. 513–514.
17 *Sahīh al-Bukhārī*: *kitāb al-ʿilm*, *bāb hifz al-ʿilm*.
18 Badr al-Dīn al-Zarkashī, *Al-Tadhkira fī al-ahādīth al-mushtahira*, p. 93.
19 J. Spencer Trimingham, *The Sufi Orders in Islam*, p. 261.
20 Abū Nasr al-Sarraj, *The Kitáb al-Lumaʿ fi'l-Tasawwuf*, p. 129.
21 Abū Nuʿaym al-Isbahānī, *Hilyat al-awliyā'*, vol. 1, p. 65.
22 Trimingham, *The Sufi Orders in Islam*; pp. 80, 183–185.
23 Ibn al-Mubrad, *Tahdhīb al-nafs li'l-ʿilm bi'l-ʿilm*, p. 86.
24 Ibid., p. 88.
25 Ibn al-Jawzī, *Talbīs Iblīs*, pp. 186, 191.

26 Ibn Taymiyya, *Majmūʿat al-fatāwā*, vol. 11, p. 289.
27 Shams al-Dīn al-Sakhāwī, *Al-Maqasid al-hasana*, p. 338.
28 Al-Suyūtī, *al-Hāwī li'l-fatāwā*, vol. 1, pp. 102–104.
29 Javad Nurbakhsh, *Traditions of the Prophet*, p. 66.
30 William Chittick, *Imaginal Worlds*, pp. 34–37.
31 Lings, *What is Sufism?*, p. 18.
32 Al-Sakhāwī, *Al-Maqāsid al-hasana*, p. 334; Mullā ʿAlī Qārī, *Al-Asrār*, pp. 269 ff.
33 Al-Albānī, *Silsilat al-ahādīth al-daʿīfa*, vol. 1, p. 53.
34 Chittick, *The Sufi Path of Knowledge*, p. 250.
35 ʿAbd al-Wahhāb al-Shaʿrānī, *Al-Tabaqāt al-kubrā*, p. 11.

8

THE FUNCTION OF PROPHETIC TRADITIONS IN POLITICS

If there is one area of the Islamic heritage familiar to the lay reader, it is that of politics. Yet this is a subject that the Quran does not address in any elaborate manner. The themes of power, obedience, of rise and fall that grace the pages of the holy book concern how human communities should relate to God's absolute dominion, not the proper modes of human governance. The Quran instructs Muslims to 'Obey God, and obey the Messenger and those in authority amongst you' (Quran 4:59), and it praises those who conduct their affairs by mutual consultation (*shūrā*) (42:38). 'Reconciliation is best,' the Quran teaches (4:128), but otherwise it is not a strikingly political text. The basic foundations of Muslim political life were laid not in the Quran but through the rapid and immediate experience of the early Muslim community: first as it consolidated power in Arabia towards the end of the Prophet's life; and then as it burst into the greater Middle East after his death in 632 CE.[1]

Many of the key, early traditions and institutions of the Muslim polity emerged from Arabian tribal life: the role of the leader as first amongst equals, cleverly balancing competing interests; the centrality of mutual oaths of allegiance (*bay'a*) between the leader and his subjects (see Quran 4:10); the significance of family relations and tribal politics; the temptations of conquest and the challenge of fairly distributing its spoils; and finally the hopeless suffering of civil war.

Both these ideals and instructions for dealing with political realities infused the hadith corpus as it formed in the early Islamic period. But in that formative era Muslims were only a small minority in their new empire (for example, even 230 years after the

Islamic conquests, only fifty percent of Iraq was Muslim and only forty percent of Iran).[2] They ruled over a diverse population with its own ancient political heritage. Within a century and a half of the Prophet's death, the massively expanded state he had founded had moved its capital from Medina, first to Kufa, then to Damascus, and then finally to Baghdad, 'The City of Peace' and 'The Navel of the World.' Arabian political tradition gave way as Muslim rulers adopted the Near Eastern Roman and Persian traditions of the ruler being, as one unreliable but still very popular hadith phrased it, **'the shadow of God on earth.'**[3]

THE CALIPH IS FROM THE QURAYSH

In June 2014, the Islamic State of Iraq and Sham (ISIS) issued a proclamation that it had 'established the Islamic caliphate and appointed a caliph for the state of Muslims.' It had chosen as the caliph a man known as Abu Bakr al-Baghdadi, one of its guerilla leaders. He was not the most expressive or powerful member of the organization, but he was a descendent of the Prophet's tribe of Quraysh. This bolstered his claim to Islamic leadership.[4] The Prophet had made it clear that this bloodline was a requirement for a claimant to the caliphate, as is described in famous hadiths in *Sahīh al-Bukhārī* and *Sahīh Muslim*, such as **'This matter will remain with the Quraysh as long as there are two of them,'** and other hadiths in which the Prophet states, **'Dominion is with the Quraysh,' 'The Quraysh are the authorities over the people in good and bad until the Day of Resurrection,'** and **'The leaders (*a'imma*) are from the Quraysh.'**[5]

Until its abolition in 1924, leadership in the Muslim community had been tied in some way or another to the institution of the caliphate (Arabic *khilāfa*, with caliph, *khalīfa*, meaning 'successor' or 'appointed representative'). Although various forms of this word are used in the Quran, in the holy book they generally convey the notion of succession in time. In two instances the Quran uses the term *khalīfa* to describe those whom God has placed on earth to exercise authority or to whom some authority has been delegated (Quran 38:26 and 2:30). But by the late 800s CE Muslim exegetes had elided all of these meanings and merged them with the notion of supreme political authority in the Abode of Islam.[6]

Nonetheless, surviving evidence – such as coins – leaves no proof of the title 'caliph' being used before the late 600s CE. At that point, well into the Umayyad dynasty, it appears alongside the primary title that had been used by Muslim rulers since the decade after the Prophet's death: 'Commander of the Faithful (*amīr al-mu'minīn*)' (this title is attested in a rock inscription dated 58/678, during the reign of the first Umayyad caliph, Mu'āwiya).[7] The title of caliph is, however, mentioned repeatedly in the hadith corpus, which also provides detailed guidance on the qualifications and conditions for Muslim rulers as well as the duties of their subjects.

The title of caliph has cast a long shadow in Islamic civilization. But neither the reality of this office nor perceptions of it have been static. Leadership of the Muslim community passed from the Prophet's close friend Abū Bakr, who had been selected through a contentious negotiation within the Muslim community, through three other close lieutenants of the Prophet, until 657 CE. At that point, the Muslim state fragmented in civil wars over who should hold the reins of power. This strife – as well as any notion of meritocratic rule – came to an end in 692 CE, when the Umayyad clan of the Quraysh tribe solidified their dynasty in Damascus, passing the mantle of caliph down within their family. In 750 CE, after several years of rebellion against the crumbling Umayyad regime, descendants of the Prophet's uncle, 'Abbās, seized the title and built the new caliphal capital of Baghdad. As spoils of war from raids or new conquests dwindled, however, the Abbasid caliphs lost control of their armies and provincial governors. By the mid 800s, the provinces of North Africa, Egypt, and what is today northeastern Iran and Central Asia were controlled by local dynasties bound only by nominal loyalty to the caliphs. In Baghdad itself, the Abbasid caliphs had become prisoners or pawns in the hands of the Turkic slave bodyguards originally imported to protect them. From the late ninth century onward, the Abbasid caliphs would enjoy the 'protection' of various Persian or Turkic warlord dynasties.

The caliphate survived despite its lack of military clout because it provided the symbolic aegis under which the Abode of Islam cohered. The various local dynasties that ruled in the caliph's name could only argue their legitimacy in the language of Islam. So compelling was the office of the caliphate that parallel claimants arose: the Shiite Fatimid ruler of North Africa declared himself caliph in 910 CE, and soon after the surviving Umayyad province of Andalusia declared itself a caliphate as well. In the central Islamic lands the prestige of the Abbasid caliphate waned. In 1258 CE the pagan Mongols sacked Baghdad and executed the Abbasid caliph and most of his family. A refugee member of the Abbasid clan fled to Cairo, where he and his descendants continue to 'rule,' and, more accurately, to bestow the formal right to rule in their name upon the Mamluk sultans of Egypt and Syria. Ironically, on the expanding peripheries of Islamic civilization the caliphate still carried great prestige. The warlord sultan of Delhi in the mid 1300s proudly had his appointment as the Abbasid caliph's legitimate deputy read aloud at Friday prayers. In 1498 CE the sultan of the Songhay Empire of Mali, Askia Muhammad, also obtained the blessings of the Abbasid caliph in Cairo to rule.[8]

The belief that the caliph had to hail from the Quraysh tribe was widely held during the early centuries of Islam. The widely respected scholar al-Nawawī (d. 676/1277) wrote that this was the consensus of the Prophet's Companions.[9] It was so important, in fact, that when the Abbasid caliphs fell under the actual control of the Persian Buyid state in 945 CE, and later under the control of the Turkic Seljuq dynasty, leading Sunni scholars like al-Ghazālī preferred to theorize a nominal Qurayshi caliph who 'delegated' authority to a Persian or Turkic warlord rather than to transfer the title of caliph to that warlord himself.[10] This formalistic effort to preserve a Qurayshi caliphate, however, soon lost out to a more pragmatic approach. Beginning with al-Ghazālī's own mentor, the famous Shāfiʿī jurist and theologian al-Juwaynī (d. 478/1085), Muslim scholars began to see that the caliph and the real holder of power had to be one and the same person, regardless of lineage.[11]

By the 1400s, however, the currency of political legitimacy had suffered staggering inflation. In the wake of the Mongol conquests, it was descent from the world conqueror Genghis Khan that granted a right to empire. Such favor of God, shown through conquest, obviated any need for recognition from the caliph, argued a prominent Sunni theologian of the era. In fact, he declared the Turkic warlord who ruled western Persia to be the caliph.[12] In the sixteenth century various sultans in Southeast Asia took the title of caliph and commander of the faithful as well.[13] When the Ottoman Empire conquered Egypt and Syria in 1517, the sultan received recognition from the last Abbasid caliph for his legitimate rule. But this was less than a formality. For the Ottoman sultans, conquest of Constantinople in 1453 bestowed upon them the title of Caesar. Moreover, the real anchor of their legitimacy was as supposed descendants from the great Oghuz Turkish clan that had conquered the Middle East in the eleventh century.[14] As the millennium of the Islamic calendar approached (1591 CE), the rulers of powerful Muslim states took on the title of the messianic *Mahdī*. Both the Ottoman Suleiman the Magnificent (d. 1566 CE) and the Mughal sultan Akbar the Great (d. 1605 CE) thus ruled as 'emperor of Islam, *Mahdī*,' etc. Caliph was but one of the titles they *both* claimed.

Had it mattered more, the Ottomans certainly had the strongest claim to the universal caliphate. The dynasty had formally received recognition from the last Abbasid caliph. Akbar's grandson, the Mughal emperor Shah Jahan (d. 1666 CE), praised the Ottoman sultan as 'successor' of the first four caliphs, known in Sunni Islam as the *Rāshidūn* (rightly guided) caliphs. But this was a diplomatic nicety.[15] Being *the* caliph in such a context granted little leverage. In the sixteenth century, the newly Muslim state of Aceh in Southeast Asia hailed the Ottoman sultans as 'God's caliph on earth.' But this was only because the Ottomans had sent crucial arms and military support in the Acehnese war against the Portuguese.[16]

In the mid nineteenth century, however, the claim of universal caliphate took on renewed utility for the Ottoman Empire. In the wake of conflicts in Russia and the Caucasus, the Ottoman sultan 'Abd al-'Azīz (r. 1861–76) reasserted his family's claim to the universal caliphate to act as the protector of Muslim refugees. The last powerful Ottoman sultan, 'Abd al-Hamīd II (r. 1876–1909), realized that even greater potential lay in foregrounding the Ottoman title. Encroached on from all sides by the colonial machinations of the European Great Powers, and with his empire being chipped away by nationalist movements in the Balkans, Sultan 'Abd al-Hamīd realized he could leverage his title as the caliph of *all* the world's Muslims, many of whom now lived under British, French, or Dutch rule, to protect himself from colonial pressures.[17]

Ironically, reviving the caliphate's Quraysh requirement may not have been a Muslim initiative. Eager to oppose what they considered to be the dangerous influence of Ottoman claims to global Muslim authority, elements within the British government began agitating against the legitimacy of the Ottoman claim to the caliphate. Beginning in 1877, numerous British Orientalists put forth arguments that the Ottomans could not be the caliphs since they were clearly not descended from the Quraysh. They happily pointed to the hadiths stating this condition. British authorities hoped to move the seat of the caliphate to friendlier areas that fell under British influence, such as Egypt or later to Mecca.[18] In March 1924, the Turkish Republic abolished the caliphate. That same month Sherif Husayn of Mecca, a proud Qurayshi descendant of the Prophet and also a British client, proclaimed himself caliph (only a few months later he fled Mecca into exile as Saudi armies conquered the Hejaz).[19] Two years later it was the turn of the king of Egypt, who was of Albanian-Turkish descent, to hold a caliphal congress in hopes of receiving nomination for the office. Though the king's hopes were ultimately dashed, his supporters countered those who argued that the caliph had to be of Qurayshi descent by pointing to the long precedent of non-Quraysh caliphs.[20]

They had a strong point. The Ottomans, Mughals, and many other claimants to the caliphate had all ignored the Quraysh requirement. But how could they have done so when it is so clearly stated in hadiths found in the premier Sunni hadith collections? In his argument against the Quraysh condition, al-Juwaynī notes regarding the hadith **'The leaders are from the Qurasyh (*al-a'imma min Quraysh*)'** that 'some leading scholars have ruled that it is widely transmitted (*mustafīd*), with its attestation known with certainty (*maqtū' bi-thubūtihi*).' Al-Juwaynī rebuts this by drawing on the epistemological standards developed in Sunni legal theory and theology: the hadith may be *sahīh*, but its narrations fall short of the number needed for massive parallel transmission (*tawātur*) and thus for certainty. Therefore no certainty (*'ilm*) exists as to the genealogical requirement. In fact, al-Juwaynī adds, God can, and has, granted temporal power to whomever He chooses.[21] Addressing the Ottoman lack of proper genealogy after that dynasty's claim to the caliphate in the early sixteenth century, the Ottoman grand vizier Lutfī Pasha wrote a treatise in 1544 CE in which he argued that the hadiths on the Quraysh requirement were only applicable to the first few decades of Islamic rule, namely the era of the four *Rāshidūn* caliphs.[22]

In fact, Lutfī Pasha had a strong argument. Terse hadiths like **'The leaders are from the Quraysh'** were among the least reliable reports on this subject in the eyes of Sunni hadith critics. The most reliable narrations specify *conditions* for the Quraysh claim to the caliphate. A hadith in *Sahīh Bukhārī*, narrated by Mu'āwiya, quotes the Prophet as saying, **'Indeed this matter lies among the Quraysh, and no one will oppose them but God will cause him to fall upon his face *as***

long as they uphold the faith' (emphasis mine).[23] Others, from less reliable collections such as the *Sunan* of al-Bayhaqī and the *Musnad* of Ibn Hanbal, include the condition **'as long as they obey God and are righteous in His rule,'** or that the Quraysh **'have a right upon you all as long as they do three things: as long as they are just; if mercy is sought from them, they grant it; and as long as, if they make a covenant, they fulfill it.'**[24]

According to the great historian, hadith scholar, and social philosopher Ibn Khaldūn (d. 808/1406), the conditional nature of the requirement for Qurayshi descent was clear from the reasoning behind the hadiths. The only reason God had placed leadership of the Muslim community in the hands of the Quraysh, Ibn Khaldūn argued, was because of the tribe's strong group solidarity (*'asabiyya*), which the philosopher considered to be the essential ingredient for a successful state. Following the natural cycle by which such a ruling group loses its solidarity (success breeds complacency and then weakness, observed Ibn Khaldūn), the reason for God having favored the Quraysh would no longer apply.[25]

THE LEGITIMACY OF REBELLION IN SUNNI ISLAM

Anyone who doubted the relevance of hadiths in the modern world had only to follow events in Egypt from 2011 to 2013, during the Arab Spring and its subsequent winter chill. Throughout this tumultuous period, invocations of the Prophet's words flew back and forth across various media as contending parties argued for or against protest, revolution, and finally various government responses, each invoking religious argument to prove the legitimacy of their claims. As the protests against the regime of Hosni Mubarak forced the leader out in late January 2011, Egyptians arguing that it was a Muslim's duty to protest cited the hadith that **'The best jihad is a word of truth spoken before an oppressive ruler (*kalimat haqq 'ind sultān jā'ir*).'**[26] Many ulama, including the then Grand Mufti of Egypt, 'Alī Jum'a, warned against the protests and the chaos and bloodshed that might result, quoting a hadith that had become well known despite being highly unreliable: **'Civil strife sleeps, and God curses whomever awakens it.'**[27] When a military coup finally toppled the president elected to replace Mubarak and the army massacred over a thousand civilians protesting the coup, Jumʿa also turned to hadiths to assuage any guilt on the part of the military and its supporters. He drew on the hadith that **'Whoever seeks to break apart this nation, when it is united, strike him with the sword whoever he may be.'**[28]

The Prophet's career passed from oppression, through exile and struggle, and finally to victorious return. Once he and his followers had been expelled from their home city of Mecca, the Quran granted the Muslims permission to fight the Quraysh lords of the city in order to regain what they had lost. Although the holy book notes several times the severity of warfare and killing, it stresses that the Muslims' cause was just. God commands the Muslims to fight those who had made war on them, who had driven them from their homes and who were trying to extirpate their religion. War is unappealing, the Quran affirms, but 'strife (*fitna*) is worse than killing' (Quran 2:191, 217). Fighting should be avoided, but there are causes that justify it: self-defense, securing religious freedom, and defense against injustice.[29] But what happens when these just causes clash with the Quranic command that Muslims should 'Obey God, and obey the Messenger and those in authority amongst you'? It is silent on whether this means Muslims should refrain from rebellion if threats against life, property, and justice come from their own rulers.

The Sunni hadith corpus, however, is not silent. As it gelled in the ninth century, Sunni Islam was dogmatically politically quietist. In this respect it stood out against the politically activist strains of Islam that eventually coalesced into the Zaydi Shiite tradition, which produced consistent rebellions against Umayyad and then Abbasid rule through the late 800s CE, when Zaydis retreated to redoubts in northern Iran and soon thereafter to Yemen. Very much unlike the Zaydi doctrine that a true imam proved himself in part by openly resisting tyranny, firm tenets of Sunni doctrine were that Muslims should 'pray behind every righteous and sinful leader' and that obedience to the ruler was an absolute requirement provided he did not command them to disobey God.[30]

These positions rested not on the Quran but on the myriad hadiths found in the mainstay Sunni hadith collections like the *Sahīhayn* of al-Bukhārī and Muslim. They conveyed a clear political message. Reports attributed to the Prophet include **'Whoever obeys the ruler has obeyed me, and whoever disobeys the ruler has disobeyed me,'** and **'Incumbent upon you is listening and obeying, in hard-**

ship and in ease, in what pleases and displeases, and even if your properties are taken unfairly.'[31] In one hadith, the Prophet is asked about rulers who would deny people their rights. After hesitating to answer several times, he replies, **'Listen and obey, for what they have taken on is upon them, and what has been put on you is upon you.'**[32] Perhaps the most extreme is the hadith, found in *Sahīh Muslim*, in which the Prophet tells the Companion Hudhayfa:

> **There will be after me leaders who will not be guided by my guidance, nor will they abide by my Sunna. Men will arise among them whose hearts are those of devils though they be in human bodies .... Listen and obey the commander, even if your back is beaten and your wealth taken. Listen and obey.**[33]

Yet there were limits. The hadiths commanding obedience even to unjust rulers draw a line at the ruler demonstrating 'egregious disbelief (*kufran bawāha*),' and the Prophet's order to listen to and obey rulers has the condition 'as long as they pray.'[34] In addition, Muslims should not obey commands that entail clearly disobeying God's law. When the commander of one raiding party sent out by the Prophet ordered his soldiers to jump into a fire to show their respect for his assigned command, they refused. They told the Prophet, who applauded them for their disobedience. **'Obedience is only in what is right,'** he explained, which Sunni scholars soon formulated into a maxim: 'There is no obedience to a creature if it means disobeying the Creator.'[35]

The Sunni tenet is clear: Muslims *must not* rebel against a ruler no matter how unjust or impious he is provided he is nominally Muslim. The reasoning behind the Sunni position, and presumably behind the sayings attributed to the Prophet, was simple. Injustice and oppression were evils, but they were markedly better than civil war and anarchy. A brutal and uncaring ruler was awful. But, in theory at least, Muslims who steered clear of posing any challenge to him could lead their lives in relative safety and security. It was *fitna* (civil, political, and misguided religious strife) that was the ultimate worldly evil, since it undermined all other areas of life, 'trading security for fear, spilling blood, freeing the hands of the foolish, launching attacks upon the Muslims and spreading corruption in the land,' as the famous scholar al-Qurtubī (d. 671/1273) wrote. A saying commonly repeated in Sunni works of political theory was 'An oppressive leader is better than unending strife (*imām ghashūm khayr min fitna tadūm*).'[36]

In hadiths, the strife (*fitna*) that the Prophet spoke of was understood to be the civil wars that ravaged the nascent Muslim polity in the decades after his death, the general decay of the Muslim polity over time, as well as the tribulations and temptations prophesied to afflict the world as the end of days approached. **'There will be *fitnas*,'** one famous hadith states, **'in which the one who stays seated is better than the one who stands, and the one who stands still is better than the one who walks ....'**[37] Countless hadiths of varied reliability preach the same message: do not involve yourselves in such strife. **'If there is *fitna* between the Muslims,'** states another hadith, **'then take up a sword of wood.'**[38] Al-Nawawī summarized the Sunni position: rebellion against the ruler is prohibited by the consensus of the Muslims even if he is sinful, due to a fear of strife (*fitna*) and anarchy. The only exception is if the ruler becomes an avowed unbeliever.[39] This tenet of political theory remained strong into the modern period. The most notable hadiths on the topic were brought together by the Ottoman judge Yūsuf al-Nabhānī (d. 1932), a passionate advocate of the last caliphs, in his *Forty Hadiths on the Obligation of Obeying the Commander of the Faithful*.

Sunni quietism, however, was at odds with the Quran's powerful imperative for ordaining justice in the public sphere. 'Indeed God commands justice, virtue and giving the near of kin their due, and He forbids indecency, wrong and wickedness,' states the Quran (16:90). It commands those who believe to 'be steadfast in upholding justice, witnesses to God, even against yourselves, your parents or your kin' (Quran 4:135). This theme of standing for justice is also stated most explicitly in well-known hadiths from the mainstay Sunni collections. When the Umayyad caliph Marwān tried to give the sermon on Eid before the prayer instead of after it, a man rose and objected that the caliph was changing the Sunna. The Companion Abū Saʿīd al-Khudrī then rose and reminded everyone of the Prophet's command, **'Whoever among you sees a wrong, let him change it with his hand. And if he is not able, then with his tongue. And if he is not able, then with his heart, but that is the weakest of faith.'**[40]

Outside the Sunni fold, other Muslims had long read the Quran as prohibiting the tolerance of unjust rulers. God tells Abraham that he is making him a 'leader (*imām*)' for all mankind but that, among his progeny, 'My covenant does not include the unjust (*ẓālimīn*)' (Quran 2:124). Some Muslims understood this as meaning that no tyrant could be a rightful ruler or authority. Adherents to this school of thought read the quietist hadith (found in the *Sahīhayn*) in which the Prophet states, **'We do not contest the authority of those holding it (*lā nunāzi'u al-amr ahlahu*),'** not as Sunnis did, namely 'we do not contest the authority of those in charge,' but rather that legitimate holders of authority must be 'befitting it (*ahluhu*).'[41]

Even some Sunnis trod a more nuanced path between political quietism and activism. This was particularly true amongst early figures, who predated the formation of classical Sunnism. Abū Hanīfa, for example, supported several rebellions against the Umayyads and Abbasids. The Hanafī scholar al-Jassās (d. 370/981) reminded his readers that Abū Hanīfa's position was 'well known on fighting oppressors and unjust leaders.' Al-Jassās shared the position of the Mālikī scholar Ibn Khuwayz Mindād (d. 390/1000), who explained that the Quranic verse stating that no one unjust can uphold God's covenant meant that, indeed, no unjust person could be the rightful caliph. But, he adds, Muslims should not rebel against such a ruler or try to remove him until the decision-making elite (*ahl al-hall wa'l-'aqd*) decided he should be removed.[42] Commenting on the above hadiths warning against involvement in *fitna*, the Shāfi'ī scholar Muhibb al-Dīn al-Tabarī (d. 694/1295) affirms that Sunnis all agreed that Muslims should not involve themselves in conflicts between parties driven by desire for power or worldly goods. But this does not entail remaining silent in any disagreement:

> ... since, if it were required to stay out of every disagreement between two parties among the Muslims, and to break the sword, then none of God's limits would be upheld. Falsehood would never be defeated, and the people of oppression and hypocrisy would find an easy path to declare licit people's inviolable property and to spill their blood ....[43]

Nor should we understand that Sunni Islam approved of unjust or despotic rulers. Hadiths clearly condemned unjust conduct on the part of the ruler, even if they urged Muslims to obey the ruler nonetheless. The *Sahīhayn* feature the hadith promising that God will deny Heaven to rulers who cheat their subjects of their rights.[44] Another hadith quotes the Prophet as saying, **'Indeed there will be rulers over you all, but do not aid them in their injustice or believe their lies ....'**[45]

The dogmatic quietism of the Sunni tradition, however, was able to elide the activist message found in some hadiths. The influential sixteenth-century Hanafī scholar Mullā 'Alī Qārī explained that the hadith calling on believers to right wrongs by force if needed should be understood as follows: 'Enjoining right with the hand is done by the state, with the tongue by scholars, and with the heart by the masses.' This was repeated by the Salafi scholar Muqbil bin Hādī al-Wādiʿī (d. 2001), who penned a whole book, intended for mass audiences, entitled *A Way out of Strife* (*Makhraj min al-fitna*). Al-Wādiʿī argues that not rebelling against the state is the key to escaping chaos and violence.[46]

In light of the intense debates sparked by the Arab Spring/Winter, contention has swirled around details of some of the hadiths advocating political quietism, in particular the Companion Hudhayfa's dramatic narration that Muslims should obey the ruler even if he beats their backs and takes their property (found in *Sahīh Muslim*). Interestingly, this clause of the hadith appears in only a few of the many, varied narrations of this tradition via Hudhayfa. It is also a rare instance of a hadith in the *Sahīhayn* being criticized. The tenth-century hadith master al-Dāraqutnī had concluded that this narration of the hadith suffered from a broken *isnād*, since the narrator who reported it from Hudhayfa, one Abū Salām, had never actually met him or even anyone around him.[47] Al-Nawawī argued that this flaw was compensated for by the collective strength of the tradition. But he did not address the specific wording of 'even if your back is beaten or your wealth taken.' Modern defenders of the hadith have argued that a similar wording is found in a narration in the *Sunan* of Abū Dāwūd and the *Musnad* of Ibn Hanbal and point to al-Albānī's conclusion that this narration is *hasan*.[48]

Depending on their political leanings, Muslim scholars have understood the meanings of this hadith as either supporting existing regimes or validating their opposition. The well-known Saudi scholar ʿAbd al-ʿAzīz al-Turayfī, who has shown himself to be more politically conscious than the generally quietist clerical establishment in his country, nonetheless offers that the details of the controversial added clause do not matter because they are merely examples of the overall injustice (*zulm*) that a ruler might visit upon his subjects. The Prophet's ruling is the same: do not rebel as long as the ruler is nominally Muslim.[49] One of the most outspoken scholarly critics of the quietist camp in and after the Arab Spring has been the Mauritanian hadith scholar Muhammad Hasan Didū. In a 2013 television appearance, he argues that Hudhayfa's tradition must be read in its entirety. Referring to the narration of it in the *Sunan* of Abū Dāwūd, which defenders use to substantiate the 'beating backs and taking wealth' clause, Didū notes how the Prophet precedes this remark with a condition: 'If God has a caliph in the world, even if he strikes your back or takes your wealth, obey him.' The viewer is left with the conclusion that extreme political quietism is only owed to the one, universal caliph of the Muslims, not to petty dictators. Didū reinforces this when he states that these dictators do not implement the Shariah and therefore do not enjoy the obedience due a true Muslim ruler.[50]

SUGGESTIONS FOR FURTHER READING

For an overview of Islamic political thought and its relation to law, see Ovamir Anjum's *Politics, Law, and Community in Islamic Thought* (Cambridge: Cambridge University Press, 2012), and for a comprehensive study of the caliphate and disputes around it, see Mona Hassan, *Longing for the Lost Caliphate* (Princeton: Princeton University Press, 2016). Yūsuf al-Nabhānī's forty hadith collection has been translated as *Forty Hadiths on the Obligation to Obey the Ruler*, trans. S. Z. Chowdhury (CreateSpace, 2015). For an excellent study on the heritage of political activism and quietism in Sunni Islam, see Ahmet Alibašic, 'The Right of Political Opposition in Islamic History and Legal Theory: An Exploration of an Ambivalent Heritage,' *Shajarah: Journal of ISTAC* 4, no. 2 (1999): pp. 231–295. For an important analysis of Muslim scholars articulating Shariah arguments for or against rising up against oppressive rulers in the Arab Spring, see Aria Nakissa, 'The Fiqh of Revolution and the Arab Spring: Secondary Segmentation as a Trend in Islamic Legal Doctrine,' *Muslim World* 105 (2015): pp. 398–421. For more on the *bay'a*, see Ella Landau-Tasseron, *The Religious Foundations of Political Allegiance: A Study of Bay'a in Pre-Modern Islam* (Washington, D.C.: Hudson Institute, 2010), available at https://www.hudson.org/content/researchattachments/attachment/1166/20100521_baya3may20.pdf.

ENDNOTES

1 Paul Heck, 'Politics and the Qur'ān,' in *Encyclopaedia of the Qur'ān*, ed. Jane Dammen McAuliffe (Leiden: Brill, 2001).

2 Richard Bulliet, 'Conversion to Islam and the Emergence of a Muslim Society in Iran,' in Levtzion, ed., *Conversion to Islam*, p. 31; idem, *Conversion to Islam in the Medieval Period*, p. 85.

3 Al-Albānī, *Silsilat al-ahādīth al-daʿīfa*, vol. 1, pp. 687–688; vol. 2, pp. 69–70; Ahmad al-Ghumārī, *al-Mudāwī*, vol. 4, pp. 269–270.

4 See 'Dāʿish yuʿlinu qiyām khilāfa islāmiyya wa yubāyiʿu al-baghdādī,' *Al-Hayat*, 29 June 2014, http://www.alhayat.com/Articles/3292478; and Ali Hashem, 'The Many Names of Abu Bakr al-Baghdadi,' *Al Monitor*, 23 March 2015, http://www.al-monitor.com/pulse/en/originals/2015/03/isis-baghdadi-islamic-state-caliph-many-names-al-qaeda.html; Cole Bunzel, 'From Paper State to Caliphate: The Ideology of the Islamic State,' Brookings Institute (2015), pp. 18, 23 and 26. Available at https://www.brookings.edu/research/from-paper-state-to-caliphate-the-ideology-of-the-islamic-state/.

5 For these hadiths, see *Sahīh al-Bukhārī*: *kitāb al-ahkām, bāb al-umarā' min Quraysh*; *Sahīh Muslim*: *kitāb al-imāra, bāb al-nās tabaʿ li-Quraysh*; *Jāmiʿ al-Tirmidhī*: *kitāb al-manāqib, bāb fī fadl al-yaman* (the author notes that the most reliable version is actually a Companion opinion); *kitāb al-fitan, bāb mā jā'a anna al-khulafā' min Quraysh*; *Musnad Ibn Hanbal*, vol. 3, p. 129.

6 Wadad Kadi, 'Caliph,' in *Encyclopaedia of the Qur'ān*.

7 See Ovamir Anjum, *Politics, Law, and Community in Islamic Thought*, p. 47; Ali Ibrahim Ghabban and Robert Hoyland, 'The inscription of Zuhayr, the oldest Islamic inscription (24 AH/AD 644–645), the rise of the Arabic script and the nature of the early Islamic state,' *Arabian Archeology and Epigraphy* 19 (2008): pp. 216–218.

8 John O. Hunwick, 'Muhammad b. Abī Bakr,' in *Encyclopaedia of Islam*, 2nd ed., P. Bearman, Th. Bianquis, C. E. Bosworth, E. van Donzel, W. P. Heinrichs, eds. First published online: 2012.

9 Al-Nawawī, *Sharh Sahīh Muslim*, vol. 12, p. 441.

10 See Abū Hāmid al-Ghazālī, *al-Iqtisād fī al-iʿtiqād*, p. 115.

11 Anjum, *Politics, Law, and Community in Islamic Thought*, pp. 111–112.

12 This theologian was the famous Jalāl al-Dīn Davānī (d. 908/1502); John Woods, *The Aqquyunlu*, pp. 103–105.

13 Howard M. Federspiel, *Sultans, Shamans and Saints*, p. 45.

14 Hakan Karateke, 'Legitimizing the Ottoman Sultanate: a Framework for Historical Analysis,' in *Legitimizing the Order: The Ottoman Rhetoric of State Power*, pp. 26–27.

15 Aziz Ahmad, *Studies in Islamic Culture in the Indian Environment*, p. 38.

16 Martin Kramer, *Islam Assembled: The Advent of the Muslim Congresses*, p. 4.

17 M. Şükrü Hanioğlu, *A Brief History of the Late Ottoman Empire*, p. 130. There is evidence that a message from 'Abd al-Hamīd prevented major Muslim forces from joining an uprising against the USA in the Philippines; Kemal Karpat, *The Politicization of Islam*, p. 235.

18 Tufan Buzpinar, 'Opposition to the Ottoman Caliphate in the Early Years of Abdülhamid II: 1877–1882,' pp. 59–89; Mona Hassan, *Longing for the Lost Caliphate*, pp. 9, 171–182.

19 Kramer, *Islam Assembled*, pp. 83–85.

20 Kramer, *Islam Assembled*, p. 101.

21 Al-Juwaynī, *Ghiyāth al-umam*, pp. 62–63.

22 Karateke, 'Legitimizing the Ottoman Sultanate,' p. 27.

23 *Sahīh al-Bukhārī: kitāb al-ahkām, bāb al-umarā' min Quraysh.*
24 Al-Bayhaqī, *al-Sunan al-kubrā*, vol. 8, p. 246; *Musnad Ibn Hanbal*, vol. 4, p. 424.
25 Ibn Khaldūn, *The Muqaddimah*, p. 159.
26 *Sunan al-Nasā'ī: kitāb al-bay'a, bāb fadl man takallama bi'l-haqq 'ind imām jā'ir.*
27 This hadith first appears in the thirteenth century, in al-Rāfi'ī's *Tadwīn fī akhbār qazwīn*, vol. 1, p. 291. Just a few decades later the hadith was used by the Ayyubid sultan to warn a scholar against making trouble; al-Subkī, *Tabaqāt*, vol. 8, p. 231. See also al-Suyūtī, *al-Jāmi' al-saghīr*, p. 370; al-'Ajlūnī, *Kashf al-khafā*, vol. 2, p. 108; Nakissa, 'The Fiqh of Revolution,' p. 412.
28 See https://www.youtube.com/watch?v=081BXWsGWhc, where Jum'a elides several hadiths from *Sahīh Muslim*: *kitāb al-imāra, bāb hukm man farraqa amr al-muslimīn wa huwa mujtami'*. See also the Human Rights Watch report on the massacres, available at https://www.hrw.org/report/2014/08/12/all-according-plan/raba-massacre-and-mass-killings-protesters-egypt.
29 See Quran 2:217; 2:190–193; 22:39–40; 60:7.
30 Abū Ja'far al-Tahāwī, *The Creed of Imam al-Tahāwī*, p. 68.
31 *Sahīh al-Bukhārī: kitāb al-fitan, bāb qawl al-Nabī s sa-tarawn ba'dī umūran tunkirūnahā*; *Sahīh Muslim*: *kitāb al-imāra, bāb wujūb tā'at al-umarā'* ....
32 *Sahīh Muslim*: *kitāb al-imāra, bāb fī tā'at al-umarā' wa in mana'ū al-huqūq.*
33 *Sahīh Muslim*: *kitāb al-imāra, bāb al-amr bi-luzūm al-jamā'a 'ind zuhūr al-fitan*. See also *Sunan* of Abū Dāwūd: *kitāb al-fitan wa'l-malāhim, bāb dhikr al-fitan wa dalā'ilihā.*
34 *Sahīh Muslim*: *kitāb al-imāra, bāb wujūb al-inkār 'alā al-umarā' fīmā yukhālifu al-shar' wa tark qitālihim mā sallū* ....
35 *Sahīh al-Bukhārī: kitāb al-ahkām, bāb al-sam' wa'l-tā'a li'l-imām mā lam takun ma'siya*; *Jāmi' al-Tirmidhī: kitāb al-jihād, bāb mā jā'a lā tā'a li-makhlūq fī ma'siyat al-khāliq.*
36 This is originally attributed to the Companion 'Amr b. al-'Ās; Abū Hāmid al-Ghazālī, *Ihyā' 'ulūm al-dīn*, vol. 4, p. 2616.
37 *Sahīh al-Bukhārī: kitāb al-fitan, bāb takūnu fitna al-qā'id fīhā khayr min al-qā'im.*
38 *Sunan Ibn Mājah*: *kitāb al-fitan, bāb al-tathabbut fī al-fitna.*
39 Al-Nawawī, *Sharh Sahīh Muslim*, vol. 12, pp. 466–470.
40 *Sahīh Muslim*: *kitāb al-īmān, bāb bayān kawn al-nahy 'an al-munkar min al-īmān* ....
41 Al-Qurtubī, *al-Jāmi' li-ahkām al-Qur'ān*, vol. 1, p. 520; *Sahīh al-Bukhārī: kitāb al-fitan, bāb qawl al-Nabī (s) sa-tarawn ba'dī umuran tunkirūnahā.*
42 Al-Qurtubī, ibid; Abū Bakr al-Jassās, *Ahkām al-Qur'ān*, vol. 1, pp. 85–87.
43 Al-Munāwī, *Fayd al-qadīr*, vol. 2, p. 842.
44 *Sahīh al-Bukhārī: kitāb al-ahkām, bāb man istar'ā ra'iyya fa-lam yansuh*; *Sahīh Muslim*: *kitāb al-īmān, bāb istihqāq al-wālī al-ghāshsh li-ra'iyyatihi al-nār.*
45 *Musnad Ibn Hanbal*, vol. 3, p. 24; vol. 6, p. 395.
46 'Alī Qārī, *Mirqāt al-mafātīh*, ed. Jamāl Aytānī (Beirut: Dār al-Kutub al-'Ilmiyya, 2001), vol. 9, p. 324; Muqbil bin Hādī al-Wādi'ī, *al-Makhraj min al-fitna*, pp. 143, 186; idem, *Majmū' fatāwā al-Wādi'ī*, p. 74.
47 Al-Dāraqutnī, *Kitāb al-Tatabbu'*, ed. Muqbil al-Wādi'ī (Medina: al-Maktaba al-Salafiyya, 1978), pp. 181–182.

48 *Sunan* of Abū Dāwūd: *kitāb al-fitan wa'l-malāhim, bāb dhikr al-fitan wa dalā'ilihā*; *Musnad Ibn Hanbal*, vol. 5, p. 403. The wording in this version is '… and if God has a caliph on earth, and he strikes your back and takes your wealth, obey him ….'; al-Albānī, *Silsilat al-ahādīth al-sahīha*, vol. 4, p. 400 (#1791). See http://www.ahlalhdeeth.com/vb/showthread.php?t=60584; http://www.almeshkat.net/vb/showthread.php?t=99133.

49 https://www.youtube.com/watch?v=utzUaboX-NI

50 https://www.youtube.com/watch?v=2ey9D2Konac; https://www.youtube.com/watch?v=2Lo3LD1wmhU

9

THE AUTHENTICITY QUESTION: WESTERN DEBATES OVER THE HISTORICAL RELIABILITY OF PROPHETIC TRADITIONS

INTRODUCTION

Thus far we have discussed hadiths and their functions in Islamic civilization as a tradition developed by a people who affirmed that Muhammad was a prophet, the last in a series sent to humanity by a God who created the universe and is its sole font of truth. So far, the hadith tradition has unfolded among Muslims. Though they might have disagreed on the proper use or interpretation of hadiths, Muslims have controlled the boundaries of the discussion. This book, however, does not assume that the reader believes that God influences the course of history or that Muhammad was a prophet. Instead, you may have noticed (assuming I've done my job) that this book discusses hadiths in a 'neutral' or 'objective' tone according to the methods of modern historians of a religious tradition.

Like Muslim hadith critics, however, our methods of historical criticism in the West have their own tradition with its own assumptions. What we must admit before any further discussion is that, because a book does not assume that God directly intervenes in human events, that Muhammad was a prophet, or that hadiths are in general authentic, then what it really assumes is that God does *not* directly interfere in historical events, that Muhammad was *just a man*, and that there are *real doubts* about the historical reliability of the entire hadith corpus. Few Western readers of this book, for example, would accept the explanation that we know the Muslim hadith tradition is an accurate record of Muhammad's words because God would never let his chosen religion go unpreserved (a standard Muslim explanation). As you can imagine, discussion of hadiths in the West differs dramatically from its indigenous Muslim counterpart.

This chapter explores the Western academic investigation of early Islamic history and its radical critiques of the Sunni hadith tradition. 'The Authenticity Question,' as we will term it, has two implications that we must bear in mind. First, Western scholars' critical examination of hadiths and the methods that Muslims used to authenticate them can be seen as laudably advancing our understanding of Islamic origins and as part of a larger human endeavor to expand all areas of knowledge. Second, however, Western criticism of the hadith tradition can be viewed as an act of domination in which one worldview asserts its power over another by dictating the terms by which 'knowledge' and 'truth' are established. From this perspective, one could ask why the 'light' that Western scholars shed on hadiths is necessarily more valuable to 'the advancement of human understanding' than what the Muslim hadith tradition has already offered. As the likes of Edward Said have shown, knowledge is power, and studying an object is an act of establishing control over it. It is thus no coincidence that four of the five main avenues through which the Western study of the Islamic world progressed grew out of European colonial or diplomatic interests (the French study of Islamic law and culture in colonial North Africa, similar Dutch studies in Southeast Asia, British studies of Persianate Islam in India, and European diplomatic interest in the Ottoman Empire). The fifth avenue, which proved most important for our subject, was that of Semitic studies, and stemmed from Biblical studies (as we shall discuss below).[1]

European diplomats in the late nineteenth century plotted how to promote a 'progressive' Islam among their colonial populations, much as their American successors have in the twenty-first. Western discussions about the reliability of the hadith tradition are thus not neutral, and their influence extends beyond the lofty halls of academia. When reports surfaced in 2008 that the Turkish government was preparing a 'radical revision' of the Sunni hadith canon, mainstream Western media applauded this move towards reformation (the rumor proved false).[2] The Authenticity Question is part of a broader debate over the power dynamic between 'Religion' and 'Modernity,' and between 'Islam' and 'the West.' Instead of approaching the Authenticity Question from a teleological perspective, where we assume that the native 'Muslim' vision of the hadith tradition is wrong and that

Western scholars have awakened it from its millennial slumber and are guiding it gradually forwards, we will assume what I think is a more accurate approach: the hadith tradition is so vast and our attempts to evaluate its authenticity so inevitably limited to small samples, that any attitudes towards its authenticity are necessarily based more on our critical worldview than on empirical fact. Because we ultimately cannot know empirically whether Muhammad was a prophet or a character formed by history, or whether or not God played any role in preserving his words for posterity, we will not look at the Authenticity Question as one to which there is a right and wrong answer. Instead, we will identify what the various schools of thought on this question have taken as their basic assumptions and how they have built on them. We will examine how some schools of thought reacted to others and how their assumptions cast doubt on those of others.

THE ORIGINS AND ASSUMPTIONS OF THE WESTERN STUDY OF HADITH VS. THE ISLAMIC TRADITION

The Muslim hadith tradition and the Western academic study of Islamic origins represent diametrically opposed approaches to evaluating the authenticity of reports about the past. Both are critical, in that they concern themselves with questions of the reliability of historical sources, but they proceed from two sets of assumptions that are at loggerheads. The following section is a digression from the subject of hadiths, but it is an essential one if we are to understand why Western and Muslim scholars view the study of hadiths so differently.

As we have seen, the Sunni tradition of hadith criticism was founded on a commitment to sifting reliable from unreliable hadiths based on criteria that examined both the sources of a report and its contents. In the absence of conflicting evidence or some strong objection, however, Muslim hadith scholars and jurists treated a report attributed to the Prophet *prima facie* as something he really said. Ibn Hanbal thus famously stated that even a hadith whose authenticity was not established was a better source for law than ruling by one's reason alone. A critical examination of a hadith was required only when a scholar had some compelling reason to doubt its authenticity. Even then, the charismatic authority of the Prophet could overwhelm any critical concerns. The famous Egyptian scholar Ibn al-Ḥājj

(d. 737/1336) ignored the legal ruling of a hadith and was subsequently afflicted by leprosy. When the Prophet appeared to him in a dream, the scholar asked him why he was being punished, since he had analyzed the hadith and concluded that it was not reliable. The Prophet replied, 'It suffices you to have heard it.' Ibn al-Hājj repented and was cured by the Prophet in his dream.[3] Furthermore, Muslim belief that the Prophet had been granted knowledge of the unseen and intended his legacy to form the basis for the civilization of Islam has meant that Muslims venerate statements attributed to the Prophet before they doubt them. Skepticism towards hadiths was not the default setting of Muslim hadith critics.

The approach of Western scholars has been the converse. According to the famous Lord Acton (d. 1902), the modern historian cannot believe in the presumption of innocence. His first reaction to any historical report must be suspicion.[4] The modern Western study of history, commonly referred to (despite its internal diversity) as the **Historical Critical Method (HCM)**, is an approach to the past that emerged from Renaissance humanism and the critical approach to the sources of history and religion that subsequently developed in Germany in the eighteenth and nineteenth centuries. Maintaining a 'historical critical' perspective towards the past means that we do not accept what historical sources tell us without question. Instead, we interrogate them and attempt to establish their reliability according to a set of assumptions about how human society functions. As the great German historian Leopold von Ranke (d. 1886) declared, history is about looking behind the sources to find out 'What really happened.'[5]

Numerous books have been written on the origins of the modern, historical critical worldview. In brief, its roots lie in 1) The Renaissance rediscovery of the Classical heritage of Greece and Rome; 2) The Age of Discovery, particularly the discovery of the New World; and 3) The Protestant Reformation. The rediscovery of the Classical heritage gave European scholars a sense of historical distance from the past and revealed the historical changes undergone by long revered texts like the Bible. At the same time, it affirmed a constant, unchanging human nature – an essential tool for how Western scholars authenticate stories from the past. Greek and Roman historians exuded a cosmopolitan skepticism that European minds found irresistible and introduced the model of the historian as detached analyst, as opposed to Christian chronicler. Ironically, reengaging with Classical philosophy did not energize rumination on metaphysics and theology as much as it led to a new focus on studying the rules governing the material world. Meanwhile, the discovery of the Americas exploded the established map of the world, which had been drawn from the genealogies and geographies of the Bible. The Protestant Reformation dismantled the Church's monopoly on interpreting scripture, ultimately resulting in a view of the Bible as a historical product bound in its own context rather than an inerrant and timeless spring of literal truth.

The roots of the HCM emerged from the fourteenth to the sixteenth centuries, when Italian and French humanist scholars were reintroduced to the range of the Classical Greco-Roman heritage through manuscripts brought from the Muslim world and Byzantium. This led Western European scholars to a new perspective towards their cultural heritage. Western Europe had always considered itself a continuation of the Roman tradition, looking to Roman law and literature as exempla. But this relationship lacked any notion of historical distance; pre-Renaissance medieval artists painted Biblical heroes in the armor of English knights and portrayed French kings in Roman regalia.[6] History was conceived according to the scheme articulated by St. Augustine (d. 430) and drawn from Biblical themes and markers. Since the time of Adam, history had been punctuated by one great cosmic event, the life of Christ, and since his crucifixion mankind had been in unrelenting decline, awaiting his second coming.

One effect of the Renaissance 'rebirth' of interest in Roman figures like Cicero (d. 43 BCE) was that Italian scholars like the poet Petrarch (d. 1374) developed a sense of historical depth. Far from Augustine's medieval synthesis of the Classics and Christianity, what Petrarch found as he fell in love with the prose of Cicero's Latin letters was a pagan outlook on religion. Cicero's writings revealed a culture of supercilious skepticism alongside public piety. The famous Roman Senator readily admitted how ridiculous Roman religious practices were but still demanded they be respected in public.[7]

Nowhere was historical distance more obvious than in the Latin language itself. Renaissance humanism was first and foremost a realization of how different (or, according to the humanists, how decadent) medieval Church Latin was from the language of Cicero. This fascination with recovering the pure Latin of the ancient Romans led the Italian scholar of language, or **philologist**, Lorenzo Valla (d. 1457) to realize how many Latin words had come to mean something other than their original meaning. Examining a document called *The*

Donation of Constantine, which the Roman emperor Constantine supposedly had written in the early fourth century granting the pope control over lands in the West, Valla pointed out that the presence of linguistic **anachronisms** (things that appear out of place in time – like a letter supposedly written by Jesus but mentioning mobile phones) meant that this document must have been a later forgery. The document mentions 'fiefs,' or land grants, but Valla points out that this word did not appear until much later.[8] Noticing how language changed over time had led Valla to unmask a historical forgery that had long served as a pillar of the papacy's claim to the right to act as a temporal power. Identifying anachronisms would serve as a pillar of the HCM.

The Renaissance fascination with language as a tool for rediscovering origins had even more stunning implications for the study of the Bible. One of Valla's successors in philology, the famous Desiderius Erasmus of Rotterdam (d. 1536) duplicated Valla's obsession with Classical Latin in the field of Greek. Erasmus devoted his career to producing the most reliable and accurate versions of ancient Greek texts by comparing the oldest possible manuscripts of the books and then purging them of mistakes made in copying and the linguistic misunderstandings or even insertions of later scholars. When producing a new edition of the original Greek text of the New Testament, Erasmus discovered that a verse that had long been part of the Latin Bible and used as a definitive proof of the Trinity was a later addition totally absent in the original Greek.[9]

Erasmus' life straddled stunning discovery and religious upheaval. In the span of his adult life, two new continents were added to the map. Not only had the great minds of the past never guessed their existence, but their inhabitants had no place in the Biblical genealogy based on Adam's children. With the globe as conceived by Church fathers shattered, a path was opened for novel scholarship. The French Protestant Isaac de la Peyrère (d. 1676) made the controversial argument that the Bible must have been more local than global. Adam was not the first man but merely the patriarch of one of many tribes (since Cain was able to flee and marry elsewhere, see Genesis 4:16). Similarly, Noah's flood was not global, just a local punishment for the land of Canaan.[10]

By Peyrère's time, the Protestant Reformation had opened new space for theological speculation in Protestant realms like England and the Netherlands. The revival of philosophy, or the notion that metaphysical truth can be attained by reason alone, led to the blossoming in seventeenth-century England of Deism, or the belief in a rational God knowable and bound by reason. In line with contempt for the papacy and the discovery of the human hand in shaping scripture, Deists like John Toland (d. 1722) argued that Christianity had originally been a purely rational religion but that the early Church had corrupted it with Roman superstitions.[11]

The great Protestant reformers had called for Christianity to be based on scripture alone, with the Holy Spirit, not Church tradition, guiding the believer to the proper understanding of the Bible. In contrast to Church fathers, who had long read Biblical passages in accord with Church doctrine or with select tenets of Aristotelian philosophy, Protestant founders like John Calvin (d. 1564) insisted on a reading of the Bible that adhered more closely to its literal sense.[12] Ironically, this approach produced an influential Protestant outgrowth whose perspectives on the Bible proved hugely consequential. The Quakers soon came to see the inspiration of the Holy Spirit as a more important guide to truth than scripture, so critiques of the Bible's historical integrity began losing their sting.[13]

By the late seventeenth century, such developments had raised a key question at the fringes of Protestant thought. If truth could be known from outside scripture, either through reason or inspiration, and if that scripture itself seemed more and more like a historical product of a flawed Church tradition, then was the Bible really a timeless vessel of universal truth? Benedict Spinoza (d. 1677) of Amsterdam gave the most influential answer. In his landmark *Theological-Political Treatise*, he argued that the Bible must be treated as the product of a particular time and place, phrased in the language and idiom of its original audience. The Old Testament's description of God walking with man (Genesis 5:24) or the miracles of Jesus in the New Testament were not universal theological claims or historical facts. They were expressions of how religion was understood by the Bible's original audiences. This did not mean that the Bible was pointless, but it no longer held the paramount place in the hierarchy of truth. The 'universal foundation' of all religion, wrote Spinoza, was to love God and love one's neighbor, to 'defend justice, assist the poor, not to kill, not to covet other men's property, etc.'[14] But the historically bound Bible only *shared in* this truth, it did not monopolize it. Contrast Spinoza's approach with the Muslim position that the Quran is, as Muslim scholars have held, 'the most truthful of speech, suitable for all times and all places.'[15]

The critical methods of Erasmus and the philosophical outlook of Spinoza and the Deists took root and blossomed in the university cities of Germany, where the HCM emerged as a clear scholarly methodology in the late 1700s. The philological study of ancient texts led to a myriad of critical revelations about Greco-Roman history and the Bible. Examining the style of Greek in Homer's *Iliad* and *Odyssey*, F. A. Wolf concluded in 1795 that the two works could not have been the product of one author.[16] Studies of the New Testament Gospels led German scholars to conclude that, far from being themselves eye witnesses to the events of Jesus' life, the gospel writers Luke and Matthew had both constructed their versions of Christ's life based on material from the book of Mark. As Voltaire (d. 1778) reported, scholars now knew that the many non-canonical gospels that had been discovered actually predated the four gospels of the New Testament.[17] One German scholar, Hermann Reimarus (d. 1768), made the controversial but ultimately influential contention that the first generations of Christians had invented much of the life of Jesus. Leading German scholars of theology adopted the position that the truth of religion was knowable first and foremost by reason, with both scripture and Church teachings constructed by human hands. The truth of biblical narrative was no longer assumed. It had to correspond to reason and fact.

Of course, some German scholars still maintained the inerrant and literal truth of the Bible. Others tried to rationalize its miracles (Jesus did not walk on water, for example, this was merely what the Apostles *perceived*). But what emerged as the conventional approach, exemplified by the theology professor Johann Semler (d. 1791), was that the true function of the Bible was to convey *spiritual* truth, not historical or scientific fact. The Biblical canon was a historical development, and its particular meanings were tied to the worldviews of its original audiences. The Bible was no longer the sole storehouse of truth for mankind. Rather, it was just a stage in man's journey towards a greater philosophical truth working its way through history.[18] The development of the HCM among German scholars culminated in David Friedrich Strauss's (d. 1874) controversial 1835 book *The Life of Jesus*. The work called for a total rejection of the historicity of the gospels (Jesus' miracles were just 'culturally conditioned myths') and a recognition that Christianity must be based on the Christ of faith not of history.[19]

By the mid nineteenth century, what had been controversial seventy years earlier had become mainstream scholarship. The primary focus of university scholarship in Germany had shifted from Christian theology to history (though controversy still raged in more conservative colleges in Scotland and America). Historians no longer served the Bible and theology, now these subjects were merely objects of historical study.[20] A crucial principle of the HCM was that the original founders of all religions were not actually responsible for the later, formalized teachings of those religions. This idea was already present in Voltaire's observation that the early Church fathers relied on non-canonical gospels.[21] But it was ultimately formalized by the German sociologist Max Weber (d. 1920), who argued that a religion's orthodoxy was organized by later generations in order to institutionalize the founder's charismatic religious authority. Contrast this with the Sunni belief that hadith scholars were merely *preserving* their Prophet's original teachings by 'fending off lies from the Sunna of God's Messenger.'

This new German school of history assumed that the first step of studying any text was to question its reliability and determine its authenticity. In other words, the default setting for scholars was to doubt the reliability of material transmitted about the past. Certainly, this principle of doubt did not mean that European historians doubted *everything* about the past. But as their criticisms of the textual integrity of Homer's epics or the historical veracity of the Bible illustrate, they were willing to indulge fundamental doubts about the cornerstones of Western history and religion based upon what they considered anachronisms or stylistic inconsistencies within a text. Contrast this with the statement of Sunni hadith critics like Mullā 'Alī al-Qārī (d. 1014/1606), who asserted that 'it is manifestly obvious that if something has been established by transmission [from the Prophet], then one should not heed any contradiction with sense perception or reason.'[22]

In contrast to the mission of Muslim chroniclers – to preserve God's message and recount the history of God's chosen community – from the eighteenth century onward European historians envisioned themselves as detached observers. They were inspired by the Classical historians whose works Petrarch and others had recovered in the Renaissance. In writing his monumental *Decline and Fall of the Roman Empire*, Edward Gibbon (d. 1794) channeled the Roman historians Tacitus (d. *circa* 117 CE) (whom he called the first historian who 'applied the science of philosophy to the study of facts')[23] and Polybius (d. 118 BCE), who insisted it was the historian's duty to criticize friend and foe impartially.[24] Far from defending some religious truth, historians like Gibbon saw themselves like Cicero, standing above and outside religion's benighted confessional traditions while remarking on the deeper, underlying constancies of human history.

Along with an *a priori* doubt about textual reliability and the human construction of religious orthodoxy, the HCM rested on other revolutionary methodological foundations. The Renaissance had reacquainted European scholars with the Classical skepticism of Sextus Empiricus (d. *circa* 210 CE), who dismissed inherent truth and universal morality as unknowable and who urged people to focus on their immediate moral and physical surroundings. In the sixteenth century, the Italian city of Padua emerged as a center for 'natural philosophy' (i.e., science) where Aristotle's empirical observations, not his metaphysics, were front and center. Based on this Classical foundation, scholars in Padua developed the procedure of hypothesis and demonstration that became the foundation of empirical investigation.[25]

The writings of the Roman philosopher Lucretius (d. *circa* 55 BCE), a materialist who believed that only the material world existed and that natural causes, not the gods, governed our affairs, became wildly popular in the seventeenth and eighteenth centuries. His poetic stanza 'Happy is he who understands the causes of things' became a mantra often quoted by Enlightenment scholars. It embraced a materialist understanding of the world in which events proceeded according to natural laws and not according to divine intervention. The most influential scientists of the seventeenth and eighteenth centuries, such as Blaise Pascal (d. 1662), were still committed Christians. But for them, in order to protect Christian belief from critics, faith had to be placed beyond the realm of reason and scientific study. The physical world, on the other hand, was created by God according to fixed laws that could be measured and relied on. In the late 1700s, a certain crass materialism emerged that did not just set the metaphysical respectfully aside. It mocked any belief in the supernatural (reminiscent of Lucretius himself). Particularly evident in the writings of the French encyclopedist Diderot (d. 1784), this crass materialism would become a dominant cultural theme in Europe by the late 1800s. Contrast this with the position of Muslim scholars (and, indeed, medieval Christians) that scripture and empirical observation had to be read in accord with one another, since both revelation and nature were 'signs' of God.

The scientific revolution sealed the assumption that miracles or God's direct involvement could not be called on to explain history and scripture. European historians embraced the Roman poet Horace's command 'Let no god intervene (*nec deus intersit*)'; it was the immutable laws of nature and human society that shaped human history. They followed their Greco-Roman exemplars, who adhered to the ancient position that human nature was an unchanging constant.[26] Herodotus (d. *circa* 420 BCE), the 'Father of History,' concluded that Helen could not actually have been at Troy because people would never choose fighting a ten-year war over surrendering a woman they had wrongly abducted in the first place.[27] Just as Newton discovered the laws of motion, Voltaire described human society as governed by its own, constant laws.[28]

One of the central principles of the HCM was thus the Principle of Analogy (sometimes called, clumsily, uniformitarianism), which dictates that, although cultures can differ dramatically from place to place and era to era, human societies always function in essentially the same way. As a result, we can reconstruct how and why events transpired in Greece thousands of years ago based on our understanding of how individuals and groups function in our own societies today. If people generally tend to pursue their own interests and advance their own agendas today, then they did so in Greek times or at the time of Christ, and no one can be realistically exempted from such motivations.[29] Contrast this with the Sunni Muslim view of history in which, as the Prophet supposedly said, **'The best generation is the one in which I was sent, then the next, then the next'** (or, indeed, contrast it with the pre-Renaissance Christian view of history). For Sunni hadith critics, the Prophet's time was 'free of evil.'[30] His Companions were incapable of lying about him and certainly not analogous to anyone else.

Along with the Principle of Analogy and the detection of anachronisms to identify unreliable reports, the HCM has also relied on a tool often referred to as the Principle of Dissimilarity. Articulated by the Dutch classicist Jakob Perizonius (d. 1715), this states that a report that seems to contradict or challenge orthodoxy is probably originally true, since no one trying to construct or defend that orthodoxy would have made it up.[31]

In the study of the Bible, these trains of thought led to the development of what was termed **Form criticism** in Germany in the first decades of the twentieth century. This method of criticism combined the presumed doubt in the integrity of texts with the modern critic's confidence that the construction of these texts was affected by very profane, worldly interests. Form critics identified smaller sections within Biblical books from which their larger narratives were composed. Each of these smaller components, termed forms, 'served a definite function in a concrete situation in the life of the early church.' 'The main purpose for the creation, the circulation, and the use of these forms was not to preserve the history of Jesus, but to strengthen the life of the church.'[32]

From the mid nineteenth century to the early twentieth, the various strands of European thought on science, history, and religion came together to form a worldview immediately familiar to us today. Often called Positivism, it held that through their newly developed methods of science and rigorous scholarship, humans were able to cast aside ignorance and superstition and uncover the truth about their surroundings and their past. Equally important, only truth so discovered was worth following. Although glimpses of it had appeared in the Renaissance and around the time of the French Revolution, one crucial pillar of Positivism was the notion of progress – that human civilization was *improving*. Unlike almost everything else mentioned so far, this belief was unprecedented. It was alien to the Greeks, the Romans, and St. Augustine alike. Despite two world wars, Positivism remains alive today. It is immediately exemplified by the popular character Sherlock Holmes, whose detailed scientific method allows him to reconstruct past events and determine the exact character of any person.

As summarized neatly by Voltaire, historians applying the HCM believed reports coming from people in the past if 'what they say of themselves is to their disadvantage, when their stories have some resemblance of truth, and they do not contradict the normal order of nature.'[33] The important basic assumptions and methods that together made up the Historical Critical Method of scholars in Europe and later America are:

1 a presumption of doubt about the authenticity or reliability of a historical text or historical reports;
2 a general suspiciousness towards orthodox narratives presented in such texts or reports;
3 the conviction that by analyzing historical sources using the methods noted above a scholar can sift the reliable from

unreliable by identifying which parts of the text served which historical agendas.

The development of the Historical Critical Method would have immediate consequences for the questions of authenticity in the Islamic tradition. The nineteenth century in particular saw French and British scholars begin investigating the life of Muhammad and Islam's origins as part of their efforts to dominate colonized Muslim populations. For German scholars of the ancient Near East, studying Islam was a byproduct of Biblical studies. In his efforts to better understand the historical development of the Old Testament, the German Biblical scholar Julius Wellhausen (d. 1918) saw studying Islam as the best way to approximate the Bible's Semitic context. But, in seeking to 'uncover' the origins of Islam and its scripture, these German scholars were engaging in a conscious, if well-intentioned, act of domination. As it was announced proudly in 1902 at a German Orientalist conference, 'the darkness of antiquity has been illuminated' and 'light has been carried into the dusky forests' of India, Africa, and the Middle East by Europeans uncovering the origins and developments of these peoples' religions. As one scholar has put it, Theodor Nöldeke's (d. 1930) influential 1860 book on the origins of the Quran typified 'Europe's newfound confidence in its superior knowledge of oriental texts and traditions.'[34] More important for our purposes, these Orientalists were making an imposing assumption: that what had proven true of Christianity and the Bible must be true of all other religions and all other sacred texts as well. Soon the methods of Biblical scholars would be brought to bear on the Arab-Islamic tradition.

THE STAGES OF WESTERN CRITICISM OF EARLY ISLAMIC HISTORY

Unlike Muslims, who developed a distinct and independent science of hadiths, Western scholars have studied hadiths as part of a broader investigation of early Islamic history and the origins of the religion. We can divide these studies into three general areas, all of which touch upon the reliability of hadith literature: early Islamic political and sectarian history, the origins of the Quran, and the origins of Islamic law.

In the Western study of early Islam and the Authenticity Question we can discern four stages that are either chronologically or thematically distinct:

1. *The Orientalist Approach*: the initial application of the Historical Critical Method to early Islamic history, which challenges many features of the traditional Islamic legal and historical narratives but accepts its general structure.
2. *The Philo-Islamic Apology*: the arguments of some non-Muslim and Muslim scholars trained in the West responding to Orientalist critiques of hadiths.
3. *The Revisionist Approach:* beginning in the late 1970s, this approach applied the critical assumptions of the Orientalist Approach at a more basic level and questioned the greater narrative of early Islamic history, the origins of the Quran and of Islamic law.
4. *The Western Revaluation:* since the 1980s, this approach has rejected the extremes of the Revisionist Approach while continuing criticism of the early Islamic period according to the Historical Critical Method. Rejecting the radical skepticism of the Revisionists, however, has led some Western scholars to recognize both that the Orientalist method involves some questionable assumptions and also that the Muslim hadith tradition is much more sophisticated than previously believed.

THE HISTORICAL CRITICAL METHOD AND THE *MATN*: GOLDZIHER'S REVOLUTIONARY CRITICISM OF HADITHS

One of the first Western writers to question the reliability of the hadith corpus as a source for Muhammad's life and deeds was the Scotsman William Muir (d. 1905), who served as a colonial administrator and educator in British India. In his *Life of Mohamet* (1861) he rejects the hadith corpus as clearly biased and unreliable. Hadiths merely promoted the Muslim 'chorus of glory to Moḥammad' as well as the political, sectarian, and scholarly ambitions of the early Muslim community.[35] Only the Quran was a reliable source for the Prophet's teachings, Muir claims. Although he feels that 'European critics' must reject at least half of the material in *Sahīh al-Bukhārī*, Muir admits that some hadiths can be considered reliable. These include hadiths on issues on which independent reports are in general agreement as well as hadiths that portray the Prophet unfavorably (an example of the Principle of Dissimilarity at work).[36] He also notes that classical hadith criticism was useless because it focused only on the *isnād* and not the content of the hadiths themselves.[37] Although with Muir we see the application of the Historical Critical Method to hadith literature, it was the Hungarian Ignaz Goldziher (d. 1921) who applied this on a larger scale and with more academic rigor.

Faithful to the German school of history, Goldziher approached the textual sources of early Islamic history and thought with 'skeptical caution.' The fact that there was no historical documentation of the Prophet's life written in his own time, and that material about him had been transmitted through the very flexible medium of oral traditions, meant that hadiths could not be viewed as documentary evidence. They were eminently subject to forgery and manipulation.

Like Valla and the German biblical scholars, the critical keys that Goldziher used to sift true from false reports about the Prophet were anachronism and the Principle of Analogy; hadiths that seemed to address conflicts and concerns that emerged only after the Prophet's death must be propaganda created by parties involved in these conflicts, not the actual words of the Prophet. As a result, the contents of many hadiths not only prove they were forged, but they also allow the historian to determine who forged them and when.[38] For Goldziher, then, hadiths serve not as a document of the Prophet's actual legacy, but rather as 'a direct reflection of the aspirations of the Islamic community.'[39]

Goldziher notes that the Prophet's authority was immediately both compelling and appealing to Muslims. He concludes that the limited writing down of hadiths was a very early process, but the very power of the Prophet's precedent meant that Muslims also quickly found manipulating hadiths for their own purposes irresistible.[40] The fact that the Prophet could have had knowledge of future events served as a license for anachronism among early hadith forgers. Events unfolding in the nascent Muslim community could be 'described' or 'judged' by attributing statements to the Prophet, who had been informed about them by God.[41] (The hadith on the Qadarites examined in Chapter 3 is an example of this).

Goldziher lays out four main stages and motivations for the forgery of hadiths by Muslims during the first three hundred years of

Islam: political agendas, legal agendas, sectarian agendas, and communal/historical agendas. For Goldziher, the original and most potent motivation for the forgery of hadiths was politics. Specifically, he argues that many hadiths and the nature of the early hadith tradition as a whole leave no doubt that the Umayyad dynasty pursued a program of political propaganda in which hadith forgery played an important part.

Unlike the Muslim community during the Prophet's lifetime and the pious inhabitants of Medina after his death, in Goldziher's opinion Umayyad rule from Syria was entirely secular with no inherent Islamic legitimacy.[42] The Umayyads thus arranged for hadiths to be forged which legitimized their rule and political practices. Goldziher argues, for example, that during the Second Civil War (680–92), when the Umayyads' enemy 'Abdallāh b. al-Zubayr (d. 73/692) was in control of Mecca and the pilgrimage routes, the Umayyads circulated a hadith that urged Muslims not **'to remove the saddles from their mounts [in other words, to visit] except at three mosques,'** the Haram Mosque in Mecca, the Prophet's Mosque in Medina and the Al-Aqsa Mosque in Jerusalem. Goldziher infers that this hadith was an attempt to establish an alternative annual pilgrimage location in Umayyad-controlled territory in Palestine.[43] When the Umayyad caliphs wanted to appear more majestic before the congregation by delivering sermons while seated at Friday prayers, agents of the dynasty forged a hadith that the Prophet had given his sermons while seated.[44]

The Umayyads were able to forge and circulate these hadiths successfully, Goldziher argues, because they patronized and sponsored the early collection of hadiths in general. Goldziher points out that the early pivot of hadith collection in the Hejaz and Syria, al-Zuhrī, served as a tutor to Umayyad princes and a judge for the state. He even wore the uniform of the Umayyad military. Goldziher thus does not find it surprising that al-Zuhrī appears in the *isnād* of the above-mentioned hadith of the three mosques suitable for visiting.[45] He notes that many other early hadith masters, such as al-Sha'bī al-Himyarī (d. 103–10/721–8), were also associated with the Umayyad court. To a large extent, he suggests, the study of hadiths on a large scale occurred *because of* Umayyad interest in political propaganda.

Just as political concerns drove forgery of hadiths in the Umayyad period, Goldziher continues, they continued to motivate forgery under the Abbasids. Unlike the 'secular' Umayyads, the Abbasid state was built on a religious message: the return of rule to the family of the

Prophet, the Quran, and the Sunna.[46] He argues that under Umayyad rule, many of the Muslims living in their newly conquered realms had very little knowledge about the ritual and legal details of their religion.[47] Under Abbasid patronage, the pious religious scholars whose voices had been subdued during Umayyad times had to produce a comprehensive legal, dogmatic, and communal vision for the new Islamic empire. It was under the Abbasids that the Sunna of the Prophet became seen as the norm for all areas of life and that hadiths began to be used in religious law.[48]

Since the Quran contained very little legal material, these Muslim scholars had to resort to other means to construct Islamic law. The Partisans of Reason (*ahl al-ra'y*) turned to the legacy of Roman provincial law where, for example, Goldziher claims Muslims acquired the notion that a defendant in a case may clear himself of charges by swearing an oath. As for the Partisans of Hadith (*ahl al-ḥadīth*), 'the path followed by them was a less honest one.' They invented whole swathes of hadiths on issues of Islamic law and dogma in order to provide the raw material for their construction of Islamic tradition. With the Abbasids promoting such activities, he concludes, 'it may be imagined how greatly the fabrication of ḥadīths flourished under these circumstances.' In addition to forging a vast number of hadiths, Goldziher claims that the Abbasid-era Partisans of Hadith also invented the system of hadith criticism wholesale as a tool for rebutting any hadiths that their opponents might use against them in debates.[49]

Like the Umayyads, the Abbasids and their partisans also forged hadiths to legitimize their rule. Concerning a hadith in which the Prophet gives the spoils of war to his clan, the Banū Hāshim, from whom the Abbasids claimed descent, while giving none to the Banū 'Abd Shams, the clan of the Umayyads, Goldziher remarks that the 'dynastic-legitimistic character of this ḥadīth is obvious.'[50]

Throughout the early Islamic period, he asserts, pious Muslims also forged hadiths that allowed them to make sense of the turmoil and strife wracking their community. Thus we find the hadith in which the Prophet says that his is the best of generations and that all subsequent ones will diverge further and further from his golden age.[51] These pious scholars similarly forged hadiths urging political quietism – a cause no doubt supported by the government – with hadiths such as **'Blessed is he who avoids public agitations** (*inna al-saʿīd man junniba al-fitan*).'[52]

Forging hadiths became a way for religious scholars to narrate the course of Islam's history, as well as to predict its future, through the Prophet's words. Goldziher states that the Partisans of Hadith 'do not restrain themselves at all when they make the Prophet speak about the general development of the Islamic empire.' Hence we find hadiths describing how the Prophet, while digging the defensive ditch around Medina, saw visions of the faraway castles of Syria and Persia that the Muslims would conquer.[53]

Of course, Goldziher noted how more strictly sectarian conflicts also led to the forgery of large numbers of hadiths.[54] Shiites eager to prove 'Alī's claim to leadership forged the hadith of Ghadīr Khumm, in which the Prophet is made to announce to his Companions that **'Whoever's master I am, 'Alī is his master.'** Sunnis countered by forging exact counterparts to such hadiths featuring Abū Bakr or 'Umar instead of 'Alī, or circulating reports emphasizing that the Prophet had in fact made no will at all assigning a successor.[55] He also identified some less idealistic motivations for forging hadiths. Individual cities, tribes, and schools of law would forge chauvinistic hadiths in which the Prophet would foretell or affirm their prominence.[56]

Since Goldziher's work provides the foundation for later Western criticisms of hadiths, we must pause to examine some of his assumptions. As we saw with the German school of historical criticism, Goldziher maintains an attitude of pronounced skepticism towards the orthodox Muslim narrative of Islamic history. It is neither shaped by God's will nor immune from the profane motivations that afflict humans everywhere. The early Muslim community was not some morally upright polity but a series of self-interested parties that exploited the authority of the Prophet to their benefit. At the root of his reasoning lies the critical assumption that, if a hadith serves the purposes of a group, it was forged by that group. This is especially clear if the hadith contains some anachronism.

His willingness to indulge in skepticism is crucial for his conclusions about the hadith tradition. Describing the hadith activity of the early transmitter 'Abd al-Rahmān b. Khālid, Goldziher states confidently that 'there are presumably many [of his hadiths] which were to benefit the prevailing political tendencies, because this 'Abd al-Rahmān was for years an important official of Umayyad princes.'[57] In other words, the simple fact that 'Abd al-Rahmān served as an Umayyad functionary meant that he *must* have forged hadiths to support Umayyad causes. Less skeptical scholars might not feel comfortable with this reasoning, since a person can work for a state or company without lying on its behalf. In the above-mentioned case of the Prophet giving his clan more of the spoils of war than he gave to the Umayyad clan, why should we assume that this is forged simply because it seems to support the anti-Umayyad agenda of the Abbasids? It is not inconceivable that the Prophet actually did grant his clan the lion's share of booty, especially since the chief of the Umayyad family, Abū Sufyān, had been a diehard opponent of Islam in Mecca.

Sometimes Goldziher's vision of the hadith tradition as inherently manipulative and unreliable leads him to misinterpret evidence. As proof that Abbasid-era hadith scholars forged reports for the benefit of the state, he discusses the case of Ghiyāth b. Ibrāhīm, who made up a hadith in which the Prophet allowed raising pigeons for competition because Ghiyāth knew that the Abbasid caliph al-Mahdī was fond of them. Goldziher concludes that, although the caliph caught on to the forgery, 'the tale nonetheless shows what a court theologian was capable of doing in matters of the tradition.'[58] This story, however, is only found in Muslim sources as a textbook example of the sin of forging hadiths. Sunni hadith critics reviled Ghiyāth b. Ibrāhīm as a forger and referred to the incident as an example of how one person forged a hadith and how the network of critics immediately caught it. Goldziher, on the other hand, uses a story designed to illustrate an exception to represent the rule.

Goldziher's investigation of forgery in the hadith tradition nonetheless leads to some tremendous insights as to how pious Muslims could concoct lies about their Prophet. He describes how after the Prophet's death even his Companions forged hadiths 'which were thought to be in accord with his sentiments and could therefore, in their view, legitimately be ascribed to him.'[59] Under the Umayyads and Abbasids, he suggests, hadith scholars could justify forging hadiths because phrasing statements as the words of the Prophet was the idiom in which authority was expressed. 'The end sanctified the means.' The widespread circulation of hadiths such as one in which the Prophet instructs Muslims that, if they hear a hadith whose meaning accords with the Quran, **'then it is true whether I said it or not,'** demonstrate that some Muslims found no conflict in preserving what they felt were legitimate components of the Prophet's teachings by attributing false hadiths to him (Note: Muslim scholars considered this hadith to be unreliable or forged).[60]

Like Muir, Goldziher concluded that content criticism played no discernable role in the work of Muslim hadith critics. Even if the text of a hadith is replete with suspicious material, he observes, 'Nobody is allowed to say: "because the *matn* contains a logical contradiction or historical absurdity I doubt the correctness of the *isnād*." ' From this he concludes that 'Muslim critics have no feeling for even the crudest anachronisms provided that the *isnād* is correct.'[61] Goldziher's conclusion that examining the contents of reports was not a component of early hadith criticism has been consistently echoed by Western scholars.

DATING HADITH FORGERY BY *ISNĀD*S: THE SCHOOL OF JOSEPH SCHACHT

Goldziher had brought the European historical critical tradition to bear on hadith literature and had concluded that a significant number of hadiths that Muslims believed were authentic were actually forged as part of the articulation of Islamic political, legal, dogmatic, and historical worldviews. Western criticism of hadiths was brought to a new level by a German scholar named Joseph Schacht (d. 1969), who built on Goldziher's skepticism towards the reliability of hadith literature. Schacht also concludes that hadiths cannot be assumed in any way to actually describe the Prophet's life.[62] While Goldziher focused on political propaganda and sectarian agendas, Schacht focused specifically on the function of hadiths in Islamic law. Whereas Goldziher had utilized the *matn* of hadiths to determine when and why they were forged, Schacht examined the *isnād*s and the diachronic (literally, 'across time') tradition of hadith collection and use.

Legal hadiths, Schacht argues, do not represent the actual details of the Prophet's life. Rather, they were attributed to the Prophet by later schools of law to lend support to their doctrines.[63] He presents one simple observation that underlies his entire criticism of the hadith corpus. If we look at admittedly early Muslim scholarly writings, such as the letter that al-Hasan al-Basrī (d. 110/728) addressed to the Umayyad caliph 'Abd al-Malik (d. 86/705) warning him not to adopt a predestinarian outlook, we find that al-Hasan does not mention hadiths as part of his argument. Instead, he draws on the Quran and stories of earlier prophets.[64] Since Sunni hadith collections contain plentiful hadiths that al-Hasan al-Basrī could have used as evidence in his treatise, Schacht concludes, the fact that he did not use them in his polemics means that these hadiths must not have existed at the time.[65] This type of argument is known as an argument *e silentio*, or 'from silence.'

Schacht argues that the original study and elaboration of Islamic law, which he calls 'the ancient schools of law,' developed in cities such as Kufa and Medina around the practice of that local community and the opinions of its senior Muslim religious figures, such as Abū Hanīfa, Mālik b. Anas, and al-Layth b. Sa'd. The Prophet's Sunna was not an immediately revered source for law. Debates among these scholars, however, caused a great deal of contention because none of these ancient schools of law possessed arguments that their opponents found compelling enough to follow. Schacht thus concludes that by the late eighth and early ninth centuries, Muslim scholars of these ancient schools attempted to resolve this interpretive chaos by investing the legal precedent of the Prophet and his Companions with more authority. Schacht associates this transition with al-Shāfi'ī (d. 204/820), whose famous *Risāla* documents his campaign to identify the notion of authoritative precedent (*sunna*) solely with Prophetic hadiths.[66]

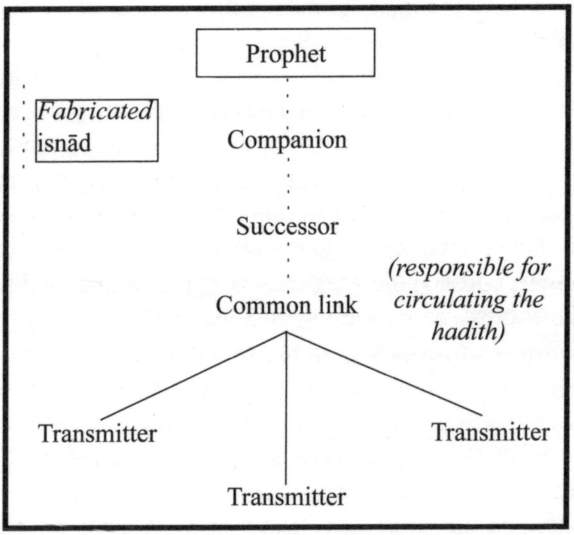

Figure 9.0 Schacht's Common Link

According to Schacht's thought, the movement away from the precedent of numerous authoritative figures such as the Companions and Successors to the Prophet himself manifested itself in the 'back-growth' of *isnād*s. Schacht's reasoning was simple and clear. Books surviving from the ancient schools of law, like Mālik's *Muwatta'*, include far more reports from later figures than from the Prophet himself.[67] The collections compiled after al-Shāfi'ī, however, such as the canonical Six Books, were undeniably focused on Prophetic reports.[68] Furthermore, these collections often included reports attributed to the Prophet that the authors of earlier hadith collections had attributed to Companions or Successors. A report in the *Muwatta'* may be attributed to a Companion, while a generation later al-Shāfi'ī attributes the same report to the Prophet through a defective *mursal isnād* (in which there exists a gap in the *isnād* between the Prophet and the person quoting him). Two generations later, in the *Sahīh* of al-Bukhārī, we find the same hadith with a complete *isnād* to the Prophet.[69] Schacht contended that the Prophetic versions of these reports had clearly been forged after the compilation of works such as the *Muwatta'*, since if they had existed earlier, then scholars like Mālik no doubt would have included them in their writings to trump their adversaries in legal debates.[70]

In Schacht's view, the development of law in the first centuries of Islam was thus a slow process of finding more and more compelling sources of authority for legal or doctrinal maxims. Statements from Successors were the oldest and thus most historically accurate.[71] In debates between early legal scholars, however, the problem of competing Successor reports was solved by disingenuous experts attributing these statements to the next highest rung on the ladder of authority: the Companions of the Prophet. We should thus treat these Companion reports as historical fabrications.[72] By the mid eighth century, the problem of competing reports from the Companions resulted in such statements being pushed back to the Prophet himself. Al-Shāfi'ī proved the greatest champion of this total reliance on Prophetic hadiths. Since the major Sunni hadith collections consist almost entirely of reports from the Prophet, much of their material must have been put into circulation after al-Shāfi'ī's time.[73] Schacht's conclusions yielded a simple rule: the farther back the *isnād* of a hadith goes, the more assured we should be of its fabrication and the later the date that this fabrication occurred.[74]

But how do we know who was responsible for the backgrowth of an *isnād* and when they had attributed a statement to the Prophet?

For the legal hadiths that Schacht studies, he posits the theory of the Common Link (see Figure 9.0). Schacht notices that for the hadiths he selected for analysis, the report is transmitted by only one chain until a certain point several generations after the Prophet. After this transmitter, whom Schacht terms the 'Common Link,' the hadith spreads out to more chains of transmission. Since the eighth century witnessed a process of *isnād*s growing backwards, then it seems reasonable to assume that this Common Link is responsible for fabricating his *isnād* back to the Prophet. Everything before the Common Link is thus made up, which explains why the hadith only spreads out widely after him.[75]

Schacht adds that, in addition to the backgrowth of *isnād*s leading to a massive increase in the number of 'hadiths,' jurists and hadith scholars also created 'parallel' *isnād*s to help avert the arguments made by Mu'tazilites who rejected the use of hadiths with a limited number of chains of transmission.[76] To avoid the stylistic awkwardness of putting what were clearly legal statements made by early Muslim scholars in the mouth of Muhammad, Schacht explains that the circumstances and contextual details of legal hadiths were added to provide 'an authentic touch.'[77]

Schacht's understanding of the early Islamic legal tradition and his Common Link Theory became the dominant vision of the hadith tradition among Western scholars and has exercised tremendous influence. This approach was elaborated further by the Dutch scholar G.H.A. Juynboll (d. 2010), one of the leading proponents of what we have termed the Orientalist school.

While acknowledging that the origins of what became hadith literature no doubt occurred in the life the Prophet, Juynboll adds that 'surely it is unlikely that we will ever find even a moderately successful method of proving with incontrovertible certainty the historicity of the ascription of such to the prophet but in a few isolated instances.' Too many of the Companions, he continues, were credited 'with such colossal numbers of obviously forged traditions that it is no longer feasible to conceive of a foolproof method to sift authentic from falsely ascribed material.'[78]

If it is beyond the historian's means to prove that the Prophet did say something, Juynboll certainly believes that one can prove that he did *not* say something. He does this by dating when the hadith came into existence. Building on Schacht's Common Link Theory, Juynboll asserts that the more people transmit a hadith from a scholar, 'the more historicity that moment has.' In other words, the more people narrated a hadith from a transmitter, the more attestation there is that the hadith actually existed at the time.[79] It must therefore have been forged at some earlier date.

Any links in an *isnād* that lack such multiple attestations are of dubious historical reliability, especially in light of the supposed adoration that early Muslims had for hadiths and their preservation. Juynboll asks, if the Prophet had really uttered a certain hadith in the presence of his devoted followers, how do we explain why he 'should choose to convey his saying about [a topic] to just one companion, and why this companion should choose to convey it to just one successor?'[80] For Juynboll, then, the only historically verifiable 'moment' in the transmission of a hadith occurs with a Common Link. Because it is inconceivable that a real hadith could be transmitted by only one *isnād* from the Prophet, anything before this Common Link must have been fabricated by him or her.[81]

Juynboll feels that concluding that a hadith must have been forged because more transmissions of it do not exist (an argument *e silentio*) is well justified. Since Muslim hadith scholars habitually collected all the available transmissions of a hadith they could find, their omission of any transmission must entail that it did not exist.[82]

In his case-by-case analysis of many hadiths, Juynboll develops a jargon for describing the different phenomena of *isnad* fabrication. As is illustrated in Figure 9.1, we see that the hadith has a clear Common Link, whom Juynboll would accuse of attributing the hadith to the Prophet along with a suitable *isnād*. We also find two other transmissions of the hadith besides that of the Common Link, one through the Common Link's source and another through a second Companion. Since there is no historical way to verify the existence of these two alternative transmissions (they lack a Common Link), they must have been forged by a transmitter or collector to provide an alternative chain of transmission, perhaps with a more elevated *isnād*, to that of the Common Link. Juynboll terms these alternative transmissions 'Diving' *isnād*s.[83] A hadith that has no Common Link, only a set of unrelated 'diving' chains (which Juynboll terms a 'spider'), is not historically datable in any sense.[84]

Juynboll's judgment on 'diving' chains of transmission leads him to dismiss the whole notion of corroborating transmissions (*mutāba'a*) among Muslim hadith scholars. Because these chains of transmission appear independently and lack any Common Link, they cannot be

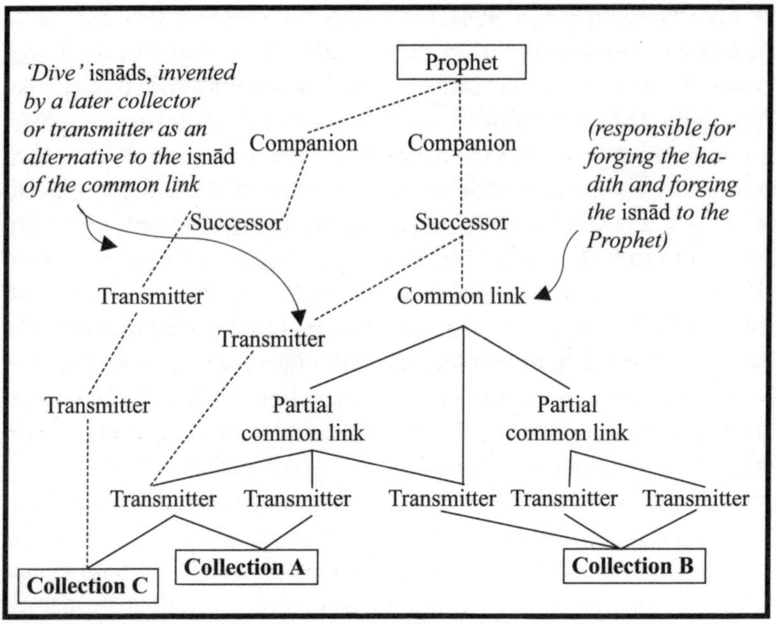

Figure 9.1 Juynboll's Common Link Theory

verified and should be assumed to be forgeries. They are simply plagiarisms of the Common Link's *isnād*s to make the hadith seem more reliable. Juynboll notes that it 'never ceases to astonish' him that master Muslim hadith scholars like Ibn Hajar al-'Asqalānī did not realize that corroborating *isnād*s were in fact groundless fabrications.[85]

As his treatment of corroborating transmissions suggests, Juynboll feels that the Muslim methods of hadith criticism were wholly ineffective at weeding out forged hadiths. First of all, he says, the science of hadith criticism emerged far too late to judge with any reliability what transpired in the early period of hadith forgery in the late seventh and early eighth centuries. Second, the methods of hadith critics did not consider the possibility that *isnād*s could be made up wholesale, a fact that rendered the proof value of any corroborating *isnād*s null. Juynboll notes that the phenomenon Muslim critics called *tadlīs* (obfuscation in transmission, see Chapter 3) would have allowed disingenuous forgers to attribute a hadith to an earlier respected scholar. He claims that *tadlīs* 'was hardly ever detected.' Finally, he follows Goldziher in asserting the 'near absence of application of suitable criteria' for content criticism by early hadith critics.[86]

Like Goldziher and Schacht, Juynboll concludes that the 'programmatic' production of hadiths started after the death of the Companions, with the standardization of the *isnād* format taking place in the 680s and 690s.[87] Following those earlier Orientalists, he agrees that hadiths originated as the exhortatory material of storytellers and preachers and only later addressed topics of Islamic law. Most of what Muslims considered to be the most reliable hadiths probably emerged in the 700s to 720s, when Muslim scholars began to invest the Sunna of the Prophet with ultimate authority and when the backgrowth of *isnād*s allowed material to be manufactured to furnish the Prophet's legacy. While Schacht had identified the backgrowth of an *isnād* if he found a Prophetic hadith in a collection like *Sahīh al-Bukhārī* that had appeared in an earlier collection as a statement of a Companion or Successor, Juynboll generalized this conclusion. Even if you cannot find a Companion/Successor opinion that corresponds to a Prophetic hadith, the fact that so many hadiths seem to have originated from these kinds of non-Prophetic statements makes 'any "prophetic" saying suspect as also belonging to that genre.'[88]

Using information provided by Muslim hadith critics and collectors themselves, Juynboll offers proof for the massive multiplication of hadiths in this period. In the earliest sources available, he says, major hadith transmitters like Ibn 'Abbās were described as narrating as few as nine hadiths from the Prophet. Yet by the time Ibn Hanbal compiled his vast *Musnad* in the first half of the 800s he collected 1,710 narrations from Ibn 'Abbās (although Juynboll admits that these included repetitions of the same hadith).[89]

Beyond the backgrowth of *isnād*s, in his numerous articles Juynboll criticized a variety of other concepts developed by Muslim hadith critics. He challenges the provenance of the *isnād* that Muslim critics considered one of the most reliable: Mālik ← Nāfi' ← Ibn 'Umar ← Prophet, by claiming that the transmitter Nāfi', the client of Ibn 'Umar, did not really exist as a major hadith narrator. Arguing that Nāfi' cannot be established as a Common Link, and pointing to the fact that the early transmission critic Ibn Sa'd (d. 230/845) did not describe him as a noteworthy hadith transmitter, Juynboll concludes that Mālik and other early scholars simply invented Nāfi' as a useful tool for anchoring their own legal opinions in the words of the Prophet.[90]

Juynboll also challenges the notion that attaining the level of *mutawātir* in the eyes of Muslim critics in any way guaranteed the authenticity of a hadith. Using his Common Link method on the famous hadith of **'Whoever lies about me intentionally, let him prepare a seat for himself in Hell,'** Juynboll claims that Common Link analysis cannot establish it as reaching back to the Prophet. He thus concludes that if the most famous *mutawātir* hadith cannot be proven to be authentic according to his methods, then the whole idea of *mutawātir* hadiths 'is **no guarantee** for the historicity of a *ḥadīth*'s ascription to the prophet.'[91]

THE PHILO-ISLAMIC APOLOGY

Orientalist criticisms of hadiths quickly elicited responses from Muslim scholars. Although he affirmed many of Muir's critiques of the hadith tradition, the Indian Islamic modernist, Sir Sayyid Ahmad Khan (d. 1898) retorted that Muir's assumption that the bulk of hadith transmitters were engaged in deliberate misrepresentation stemmed from his anti-Muslim bias. Furthermore, Khan accuses Muir of supporting his accusations of the political and sectarian motivations behind hadith forgery using as evidence the same reports he had deemed historically unreliable.[92]

Later, more in-depth responses to Orientalist criticisms came from scholars working and trained in Western universities who did not wholly agree with Goldziher, Schacht, and their followers. From the 1960s to the 1980s, a number of scholars, most of them from Muslim or Middle Eastern backgrounds, challenged Orientalist conclusions either wholly or in part. The most influential challenge came from Nabia Abbott (d. 1981) (a Christian from Iraq and later professor at the University of Chicago) who based her book *Studies in Arabic Literary Papyri II: Qur'ānic Commentary and Tradition* (1967) on a selection of early Arabic papyrus documents from the second half of the eighth and the early ninth centuries.

Abbott presents an interesting challenge to Goldziher's theory that the Umayyad government, with its agents like al-Zuhrī, instituted hadith collection and actively fabricated a substantial component of the hadith corpus pursuant to their political agenda. Evidence from our earliest sources on the origins of hadith study, she contends, portrays the Umayyads as concerned first and foremost with collecting the Prophet's teachings on administrative issues like taxes and charity, not with material connected to the political image of their rule. She notes how the first state attempt to collect hadiths, ordered by the caliph 'Umar b. 'Abd al-'Azīz (d. 101/720), was limited to administrative hadiths. The hadiths that al-Zuhrī collected for the Umayyads for promulgation in the provinces dealt only with charitable tithes (*sadaqa*).[93] Abbott argues that the 'family *isnād*s' like those from Nāfi' ←Ibn 'Umar or al-'Alā' b. 'Abd al-Rahmān ← his father ← Abū Hurayra emerged far earlier and were far more numerous than previously imagined. Umayyad rulers were attempting to make these private collections public, not ordering the forgery and circulation of baseless hadiths.[94]

Abbott also rebuts the argument that the exponential increase in the number of hadiths in the eighth and ninth centuries proves that hadiths were being forged *en masse*. First of all, she notes that even early written collections of hadith could be sizable: al-Hasan al-Basrī's *sahīfa* was a scroll six inches in diameter. Certainly, however, early written collections were much smaller than the great hadith compendia of the ninth century. Al-Zuhrī's library could be carried in one bag, while Ibn Hanbal's was twelve and a half camel loads, and al-Wāqidī's (d. 207/822) six hundred boxes.[95]

The explanation for this growth, however, was not necessarily forgery. Papyrus and parchment were extremely expensive, and scholars could only use them to record the most basic information about their hadiths, such as the *matn* with perhaps one *isnād*. With the arrival of cheap paper in the Middle East at the end of the eighth century, scholars could afford to write down every hadith narration they came across. In his famous *Musnad*, for example, Ibn Hanbal tried to include an average of seven narrations for every tradition he listed.[96] As the science of hadith collection and criticism developed in the mid eighth century, a 'hadith' became identified with its *isnād*, not with its *matn*. As ninth-century scholars obsessively collected all the various transmissions (each called a 'hadith') of one tradition, the number of 'hadiths' multiplied rapidly. As *isnād*s developed and became interlaced, this number increased even more, while the actual number of Prophetic traditions remained relatively small.[97]

Abbott's challenging some of the Orientalist attacks on the Sunni hadith tradition, however, did not mean that she embraced it fully. She notes that the widespread disagreement between Muslim critics on the reliability of a transmitter or *isnād* 'nullified' the real effectiveness of the Muslim science of hadith as a critical tool.[98] Abbott provides perhaps the most insightful explanation of how so much forged material did appear. Since Muslim hadith critics treated hadiths dealing with law much more severely than those that they used in exhortatory preaching (*al-targhīb wa al-tarhīb*), the type of *matn* greatly affected the critical stringency with which the hadith was treated. Much of the material forged in areas such as exhortatory preaching thus survived because Muslims allowed it to.[99]

A vigorous rebuttal of Orientalist scholarship came from an Indian scholar who studied at Cambridge University, Muhammad Mustafa al-Azami. In two books, *Studies in Early Ḥadīth Literature* (1978) and *On Schacht's Origins of Muhammadan Jurisprudence* (1984), Azami attacked Schacht's work (and also that of Goldziher) and those who had relied on his conclusions. One of the points for which Azami takes Goldziher and Schacht to task is the substantial inferences they make without any conclusive evidence. Goldziher, for example, had concluded that the Umayyad state had sponsored hadith forgery based on the fact that certain hadiths seemed to support Umayyad interests and that certain transmitters were linked to the court. Certainly, Azami acknowledges that the Umayyads fought groups like the Shiites. But he contends that there is no evidence of an official or unofficial Umayyad directive to fabricate hadiths for the cause of the state (here we should note that the historian al-Madā'inī did adduce evidence for this; see Chapter 3).[100]

One of Azami's principal objections to Schacht is his reliance on a small number of sources to reach broad generalizations. Azami begins his discussion by pointing out how few sources Schacht had relied on and drawing attention to the numerous early Arabic manuscripts that had been discovered since his time. Western scholars of hadiths, he states, should update their data instead of parroting Schacht uncritically.[101] Azami states that Schacht based his conclusions on the *Muwatta'* of Mālik and the *Umm* of al-Shāfi'ī, but he 'imposed the results of his study on the entire *ḥadīth* literature.'[102] Moreover, one of the *isnād*s that Schacht relies on for his evidence that *isnād*s grew backwards in Mālik's case was an instance in which later Muslim hadith critics believed Mālik had made a mistake. Schacht thus took an error on Mālik's part as an example of the rule instead of an exception to it.[103]

Azami also accuses Schacht of fundamentally misunderstanding the realities of early Islamic legal scholarship.[104] Schacht's argument *e silentio*, where a scholar failing to mention a hadith or a complete *isnād* meant that the hadith or that complete *isnād* must not have existed at that time, is flawed. A legal expert (*muftī*), Azami argues, often answered questions without documenting the evidence he had used in arriving at his conclusion or without providing a full *isnād* for his hadiths. Azami provides an example from al-Shāfiʿī's famous *Risāla*, where al-Shāfiʿī provides an incomplete *isnād* for a hadith but excuses himself because he did not have with him the book that included his more complete *isnād* for that hadith.[105]

Finally, Azami devotes a large portion of his books to attempting to prove that Muslims had begun writing down hadiths and even using the *isnād* during the time of the Prophet and his Companions. Here, he relies on surviving sources from the eighth and ninth centuries which mention earlier written sources. He does this in order to disprove Schacht's claim that Prophetic hadiths only appeared as *isnād*s grew backwards, a claim Schacht based in part on a lack of books surviving from the first two centuries of Islam that could serve as evidence that Muslims had recorded hadiths during that time.[106] Of course, here Azami relies on Muslims' testimony about their own thoroughness in hadith collection – a biased source that some Orientalists would not believe to begin with.

THE REVISIONIST APPROACH AND THE CATEGORICAL REJECTION OF THE MUSLIM NARRATIVE

Orientalists such as Goldziher, Schacht, and Juynboll had questioned the authenticity of individual hadiths and established a skeptical outlook towards hadith literature as a genre, but they did not doubt the overall narrative of the Prophet's life and Islamic origins. Muhammad was still assumed to have been a merchant from Mecca who had preached the monotheistic 'religion of Abraham' to his peers in Mecca before fleeing the city to establish a new Muslim community in Medina. Orientalists never questioned that he had claimed to receive revelations in the form of the Quran and had engaged in known conflicts with his enemies with the help of his famous cadre of Companions.

From 1977 to 1979, however, a series of studies demanded that the Historical Critical Method be applied fully and consistently to early Islamic history. If historians were supposed to adopt a skeptical attitude towards obviously biased sources and attempt to rely on the earliest, best documented evidence possible, why had Western historians believed the grand Muslim narrative of Islam's origins at all? After all, the history of the Prophet's life, message, and community was told solely by Muslims, and there were no surviving textual sources from before the mid 700s, a full century after the Prophet's death. This would have provided ample time for Muslim scholars and historians – certainly not impartial in their activities – to construct whatever legacy they wanted for their 'Prophet' from scratch. This Revisionist criticism of the Orientalists applied equally to scholars like Azami who had objected to their critiques, for Azami had also relied on sources written down long after the first generations of Islam to reconstruct the early collection of hadiths.

Two scholars, Patricia Crone (d. 2015) and Michael Cook, proposed rewriting early Islamic history using the earliest written sources on Islam, which had the added benefit of not being written by Muslims. On the basis of a set of surviving Christian religious writings dating from as early as 634 CE, Crone's and Cook's book *Hagarism* (1977) proposed that Islam had actually been a late version of apocalyptical Judaism in which the Arabs of the Hejaz had rediscovered their Abrahamic roots and sought to retake the Holy Land of Palestine. Clearly, this was a very different history than the detailed account of Muhammad's life and teachings given in the ḥadith literature!

The novel contribution of the Revisionist approach was not the mechanics of criticizing the hadith tradition, but the scale of skepticism. Crone, for example, espouses Schacht's and Juynboll's theory about the backgrowth of *isnād*s and the conclusion that hadiths cannot really tell us anything about Islam before the year c. 100/720. Crone seconds the Orientalist critique that hadiths transmitted by Muslims reflect 'what the Prophet meant to *them*, not what the generation before them had taken him to say, let alone what he had said or done in his own particular time and place.'[107]

In her work on the origins of Islamic law, *Roman, Provincial and Islamic Law* (1987), Crone's severe doubt about the reliability of the Islamic historical tradition leads her to a new degree of skepticism towards the hadith corpus as a whole. '[I]n the field of substantive law,' she argues, 'traditions attributed to the Prophet must indeed be presumed to be inauthentic.'[108] As an example, she takes one hadith

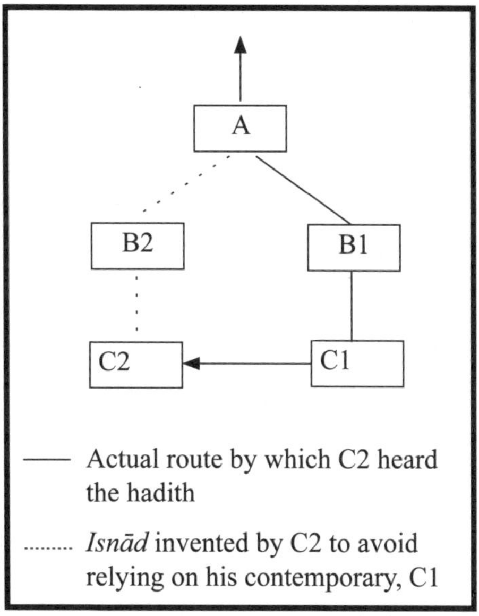

Figure 9.2 Cook's Theory of *Tadlīs* and Spread of *Isnāds*

that 'practically all' Orientalists had considered authentic: the famous 'Constitution' of Medina, the agreement between Muhammad and the Jews of Medina in which all parties agreed to be part of one 'community (*umma*)'. (Orientalists regarded this as authentic in part because it seems to contradict the orthodox Islamic notion that non-Muslims could not join Muslims in their religious polity, an example of the Principle of Dissimilarity at work.) Concerning the legal issue of patronage (*walā'*), early scholars like Ibn Jurayj (d. 150/767) and Maʿmar b. Rāshid (d. 153/770) had forbidden its sale or transfer, but they narrated no Prophetic hadiths to that effect. Based on Schacht's and Juynboll's argument *e silentio*, that would mean that no hadiths on that topic existed at their time. In the 'Constitution' of Medina found in the *Sīra* of Ibn Ishāq (d. 150/767), however, we find a statement by the Prophet banning the transfer of *walā'*. This hadith must have therefore been altered to meet this legal agenda sometime around the 770s CE.[109]

If even a report that Orientalists had felt confident about was not historically reliable, then what hadith could have escaped the ingenuous designs of early Muslim scholars? 'The chance of authentic material surviving at their hands is exceedingly small,' Crone contends. 'Indeed, in purely statistical terms it is minute.' She reminds her readers of figures Juynboll had collected about the growth of the numbers of hadiths supposedly narrated by Ibn 'Abbās. If there had been this massive increase, how do we know which ones Ibn 'Abbās really transmitted? 'Under such circumstances it is scarcely justified to presume ḥadīth to be authentic until the contrary has been proven.' Since this is very difficult indeed, 'then the presumption must be that *no* ḥadīth is authentic.'[110]

Crone (*Meccan Trade and the Rise of Islam*, 1987), and the scholars John Wansbrough (*Quranic Studies*, 1977) and John Burton (*Introduction to Hadith*, 1994) also stressed the exegetical origins of hadiths. In other words, hadiths were often created by Muslim scholars to help them explain the meaning of the Quran. Early Muslims disagreed on the meanings of many Quranic verses, so the hadiths produced to explain its meaning differed too.[111]

Although Revisionists generally built on the conclusions of the Orientalists, Michael Cook argues that even a key concession they had made – that a Common Link was a historically reliable moment in transmission – was wrong. Cook offers a novel argument as to how Muslim hadith transmitters were able to multiply the number of narrations of a hadith and, in essence, fabricate a Common Link. Juynboll had noted how *tadlīs* allowed disingenuous forgers to attribute a hadith to an earlier scholar by falsely inserting his name in the *isnād*. Cook saw an even more prominent role for *tadlīs*. In a traditional society, Cook explains, 'the relevant issue is not originality, but authority: sharp practice consists in falsely *ascribing* my view to a greater authority than myself.'[112]

Tadlīs was the means by which a hadith transmitter accomplished this. As shown in Figure 9.2, if C2 hears a hadith from his contemporary C1, who had heard it from his teacher B1 from A, and so on from the Prophet, C2 does not want to appear to be deriving religious knowledge from a peer. He therefore attributes it to the generation of his teachers, citing the hadith from his instructor B2 and extending the *isnād* back to A, *et cetera*. If history preserves both C1's and C2's *isnād*s, then it seems as though two chains of transmission emanated from A, when in reality there was only one. This accounts for the fraudulent spread of *isnād*s. By asserting that the *matn*s of certain eschatological hadiths clearly emerged later than the Common Link in their *isnād*s, Cook argued that dating by Common Links was naive.[113]

THE WESTERN REVALUATION

The fundamental doubts that Revisionist scholarship raised about early Islamic history prompted an unprecedented defense of the traditional narrative of hadiths and Islamic origins on the part of certain Western scholars. In a sense, regardless of the specific criticisms Western scholars might have launched at individual hadiths, they had heavily invested in the basic outline of Islamic history provided by Muslim historians and hadith scholars. To defend the overall integrity of the hadith tradition was to defend the vision of early Islamic history on which generations of Western scholars had relied.

What we are calling here 'Revaluation' scholars have challenged two main aspects of Orientalist and Revisionist criticisms of hadiths. First, they have argued that many of the basic assumptions made by these two groups are inherently inaccurate. Second, Revaluation scholars have demonstrated that earlier Western criticisms did not take into account the massive breadth and complexity of the Islamic hadith tradition. When hadiths are looked at from this more humble perspective, many of the arguments advanced by Orientalists and Revisionists lose their efficacy.

This does not mean that Revaluation scholars have accepted the Sunni vision of hadiths and their authenticity outright. While rejecting the Revisionist arguments, Fred Donner and others have espoused a theory that until the time of the Umayyad caliph 'Abd al-Mālik (d. 86/705), Islam as a religious ideology was very pluralistic and allowed both Christians and Jews to follow Muhammad's teachings without abandoning their own religions.[114] Nonetheless, the tone of Revaluation scholars is less combative than earlier generations. They speak more of 'dating' when we can be sure a hadith was in circulation than deeming it forged and identifying who forged it.

The most basic objection to the Revisionist recasting of the whole Muslim narrative of early Islamic history is that it simply asks us to believe too much. We might find it difficult to believe that Muslims could avoid all the pitfalls of historical manipulation, propagandizing, and error in their collection of hadiths, but it seems even harder to believe that a scholarly community stretching from Spain to Central Asia and plagued by intense internecine conflicts could have orchestrated such a colossal historical conspiracy in a time of premodern communication. As Fred Donner states in his rebuttal of the Revisionists, it is inconceivable that the divided and decentralized early Muslim community could somehow orchestrate a 'comprehensive redaction of the [Islamic] tradition as a whole into a unified form'[115] without leaving ample historical evidence. Similarly, Harald Motzki notes that the forgery of hadiths on the massive scale suggested by Orientalists and Revisionists would have been prevented by the communal oversight of hadith scholars.[116]

Some scholars have revaluated the standing assumptions that Orientalists and Revisionists had made about the overall authenticity of hadiths. Crone had stressed what Goldziher, Schacht, and Juynboll had implied: no hadith could be assumed to be the authentic words of Muhammad. This point is contested most overtly by David Powers, who is also an early pioneer of what can be termed the 'large-scale' identification of Common Links, or the notion that when one collects *all* the available transmissions of a hadith, its Common Link is much earlier than those supposed by Schacht and Juynboll.

In an article about wills and bequests in early Islamic law, Powers challenged Crone's and Cook's dismissal of a famous hadith in which the Prophet tells the Companion Sa'd b. Abī Waqqās that he may only specify one third of his wealth for his daughter (the rest is automatically divided by existing Islamic inheritance law). Powers argues that examining the *isnād*s and *matn* of the hadith suggests that it did in fact originate with Sa'd b. Abī Waqqās. In light of her error in evaluating the hadith, Powers concludes that Crone's statement that Prophetic hadiths should be assumed to be inauthentic 'hardly inspires much confidence.' Quite the opposite, Powers asserts that the burden of proof 'lies on those who would deny the authenticity of reports attributed to the Prophet.'[117] The default assumption is that a hadith is actually authentic.

Power's argument for dating this hadith at the very latest during the time of the Companions rested on an examination of all the extant transmissions of the report – something that Crone had neglected. He admits that trying to authenticate an *isnād* and find a Common Link is delving into the 'realm of conjecture and speculation,' but he argues that it seems very unlikely that the Sa'd b. Abī Waqqās tradition is forged. He collects all the narrations of the tradition, which emanate from six different individuals who all converge on Sa'd as the Common Link. Powers states that it is:

> either strange or a remarkable coincidence that half a dozen Successors, living in different cities of the Umayyad empire and pre-

sumably working independently of one another, adopted the same story to illustrate the origins of the one-third restriction, tracing it back to the Prophet by means of fabricated *isnāds*, all of which converge on one and the same Companion.[118]

The 'large-scale' analysis of transmission and fundamental questioning of Orientalist and Revisionist assumptions has continued in force in the scholarship of the German Harald Motzki. In a sense, Motzki is the first Western scholar to treat hadiths with the same 'respect' as Muslim hadith masters did. Like figures such as Ibn Hajar al-ʿAsqalānī, his judgments about hadiths depend on collecting *all* the available narrations of the report, not just the ones easily accessible in well-known collections.

Motzki's work proffers three main criticisms of previous Western hadith scholarship. First, he argues that the argument *e silentio* relied upon by Schacht, Juynboll, and Crone is invalid. Second, he demonstrates that Common Links are much earlier than previously thought, dating some to the time of the Companions in the second half of the seventh century. Finally, Motzki argues that, rather than being consummate forgers of hadiths, major hadith transmitters such as al-Zuhrī and Ibn Jurayj were in general reliably passing on reports from the previous generation.

Orientalists and Revisionists had relied on the premise that an early scholar's failure to employ a Prophetic hadith, or the best possible version of that hadith, in a debate in which it would have been pertinent proves that this Prophetic hadith did not exist at that time or in that form.[119] Motzki argues that this assumption is both unreasonable and inaccurate. A scholar could decide not to mention a hadith because he did not feel that it actually addressed the issue at hand. Especially in the time of early legal synthesists like Abū Hanīfa and Mālik, hadiths were still distributed regionally. We already saw the example of Mālik's Egyptian student informing him of a reliable hadith about washing one's feet that Mālik, who never left the Hejaz, had never heard.

As for the assumption that if a hadith was transmitted via only one *isnād* in the early period then it must have been forged, Motzki argues that we should not expect to find numerous *isnād*s from figures like the Successors back to the Prophet. *Isnād*s, after all, only came into use during the Successors' generation in the late 600s/early 700s. Even for those early hadith transmitters and legal scholars who provided *isnād*s to the Prophet at that time, it was only necessary to provide one *isnād* for a hadith, not a bundle as became common in the second half of the 700s and the 800s.

As for Juynboll's argument that Muslims obsessively transmitted hadiths, with hundreds of students attending their teachers' dictation sessions, common sense tells us that there are many reasons why history preserved one person's transmission from that teacher instead of those of many students. Just as only a small percentage of a teacher's students go on to become teachers themselves, so it is not inconceivable that only one of a hadith transmitter's students would go on to become a transmitter as well. Juynboll had argued that only the transmission of one to many can be considered a historically documented 'moment' in the life of a hadith. But, Motzki counters, if we only consider transmission from one person to a number of people historically reliable, then why do we have only a few hadith collections or Partial Common Links (Common Links that form in the transmission of a hadith after the Common Link, see Figure 9.1)? If we have established that the hadith came into existence with the Common Link, and that any hadith that actually existed must have been transmitted by all those who heard it from a teacher, then after the Common Links we should find thousands of chains of transmission in the fourth and fifth generations. The fact that we find so few Partial Common Links strongly suggests that Common Links and Partial Common Links were the exception rather than the rule in the transmission of hadiths. Their absence thus cannot be construed as proof for a hadith not existing at that time.

One of Motzki's central criticisms of Schacht's and Juynboll's work is the small number of sources from which they drew hadiths in determining the Common Link. In collecting transmissions of a hadith to locate a Common Link, for example, Juynboll relied principally on the *Tuhfat al-ashrāf* of Jamāl al-Dīn al-Mizzī (d. 742/1341), a work that collects together all the chains of transmission for a hadith but is limited to the traditions and transmissions found in the Six Books (and a few other small books). Motzki draws on a much larger and more diverse body of sources including early ones, such as the *Musannaf* of 'Abd al-Razzāq al-San'ānī (d. 211/827), and later ones, such as al-Bayhaqī's (d. 458/1066) *Dalā'il al-nubuwwa*. By consulting a much wider range of sources than these earlier scholars, Motzki demonstrates that the Common Links for the hadiths he analyzes actually belong to the time of the Companions in the second half of the seventh century.

Motzki lays out his rebuttal of Schacht's and Juynboll's Common-Link-as-forger argument most clearly in an article devoted to studying the hadiths related to the Prophet's order that a prominent Jewish leader in Khaybar, Ibn Abī Huqayq, be assassinated. By gathering together a tremendous array of chains of transmission from a wide variety of sources, Motzki demonstrates that this hadith has not one Common Link but several who were working independently and thus must have relied on some earlier common source. In the case of the killing of Ibn Abī Huqayq, Motzki concludes that the common link transmitters of hadiths relating to the event probably received their reports no later than the last third of the seventh century.[120] The hadith was circulating during the time of the Companions.

Motzki's 'large-scale' analysis of hadith transmission is based on a method of analyzing the *isnād* and *matn* together (termed *isnād cum matn* analysis). He explains that this process relies on three premises:

1 Variants of a tradition are (at least partially) the result of a process of transmission.
2 The *isnād*s of the variants reflect (at least partially) the actual path of transmission.
3 If variant texts (*matn*s) of a tradition emanating from the same common link are in fact similar enough, then it seems to be an authentic moment of transmission. If they are not similar, this is the result of either carelessness or intentional manipulation of the material.[121]

In order to determine whether the basic information found in the text of the hadith originated from before a Common Link, you must see if different Common Links all have the same basic *matn*. This requires a two-step process: 1) analyzing the elements of the different *matn* variants from all the chains of transmission emanating from one Common Link; 2) comparing the conclusions about the common material from that Common Link to the *matn* elements of other Common Links.[122] One must then ask whether the differences between the versions of the *matn* from the two Common Links are significant enough to preclude the possibility that one copied from the other and then provided his hadith with a different *isnād*.[123] If two variants of the same text from two separate Common Links are too disparate to be dependent on each other, then they *must* stem from an earlier common source. In order to verify this conclusion, one must determine whether variants on the common *matn* correlate with the chains of transmission. In other words, do the variants of the common story (*matn*) match the *isnād* tree?[124]

We can demonstrate this method of *isnād cum matn* analysis with a famous hadith stating that God descends at some point in the night to answer prayers (see Figure 9.3). Strictly speaking, *isnād cum matn* analysis must take into consideration *all* the extant transmissions of a hadith. Since that would be far too time-consuming for our purposes, we will only focus on those narrations that yield the sort of benefit associated with this type of analysis. In particular, we will look at two narrations of the hadith, one from Abū Hurayra and one from another Companion, Abū Saʿīd al-Khudrī.

We find the narration of Abū Hurayra recorded earliest in the *Muwatta'* of Mālik, which means that we know that the hadith was in existence at the very latest during the mid eighth century when Mālik was writing. Mālik's fellow student of al-Zuhrī, Maʿmar b. Rāshid, had this transmission as well as the other version from Abū

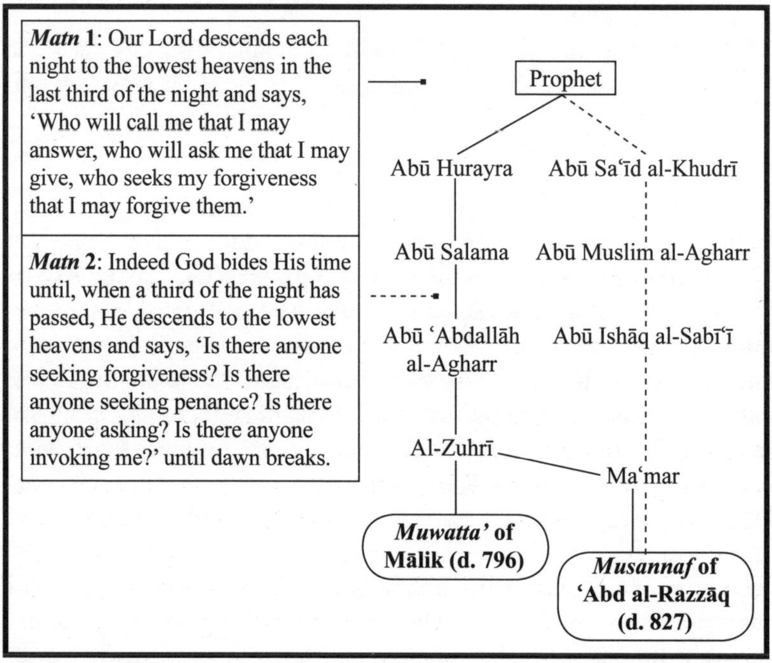

Figure 9.3 *Isnād/Matn* Analysis

Saʿīd al-Khudrī. Examining, the two *matn*s, we find that they contain the same general tradition but also feature noticeable differences. *Matn* 1, for example, states that God descends in the last third of the night, while *Matn* 2 says He descends after the first third. *Matn* 2 also includes the unique wording 'God bides His time.' Since we know the tradition existed with Maʿmar, but the differences between his two versions of the hadith preclude him having copied one from the other, he must have obtained the Abū Saʿīd version from an earlier source other than al-Zuhrī. If al-Zuhrī's source and Maʿmar's second source (presumably Abū Ishāq al-Sabīʿī) both had two different versions of the same general hadith, they must have received them from a common source, especially as Abū Ishāq was from Kufa and al-Zuhrī from the Hejaz. Since al-Zuhrī and Abū Ishāq, both Successors, died in 742–3 CE and 744–6 CE respectively, their common source must have lived in the late seventh century, which demonstrates that the hadith was in existence during the time of the later Companions.

One of the key sources that Motzki uses in his investigation is the *Musannaf* of ʿAbd al-Razzāq al-Sanʿānī (d. 211/827). In a series of articles in the early 1990s, Motzki used the *Musannaf* to prove that Schacht's conclusions about the reliability of legal hadiths were tainted by the narrow range of sources he consulted and a hypothesis-driven analysis by which Schacht judged the provenance of early legal material based on flawed assumptions about the nature of early Islamic legal scholarship.

In one article, Motzki takes up the material that ʿAbd al-Razzāq included in his *Musannaf* through the well-known *isnād* of Ibn Jurayj (d. 150/767) ← the famous Meccan Successor ʿAtāʾ b. Abī Rabāh (d. 114/732). Motzki argues that both ʿAbd al-Razzāq's and Ibn Jurayj's material and their manner of presenting it exhibits two startling characteristics that dispel the likelihood that they forged or intentionally misrepresented reports they transmitted. First, the characteristics of transmissions via the *isnād* are entirely consistent both in their form and content. Thus, both ʿAbd al-Razzāq and his source Ibn Jurayj always use the term 'I heard it from (*samiʿtu*) …' for some of their sources, while they use 'on the authority of (*ʿan*)' consistently for others. If either of these authorities were 'back projecting' their own legal views on to earlier authorities, Motzki argues, it is improbable that they could have maintained such formal consistency in their forgery.[125] Second, ʿAbd al-Razzāq admits to not knowing the exact origins of some of the hadiths in his collection, and Ibn Jurayj often admits to not understanding either the meaning or the wordings of the reports he transmits.[126] Moreover, in his narrations from ʻAṭā' b. Abī Rabāh, Ibn Jurayj sometimes posed questions directly to this scholar and sometimes heard his opinions second or even third hand. Including less direct transmissions when he could have easily claimed to have heard ʻAṭā' first hand suggests that Ibn Jurayj was forthcoming about such transmissions.[127]

Based on this evidence, Motzki argues that ʻAbd al-Razzāq and Ibn Jurayj both faithfully transmitted the material they received. Since there is thus little likelihood that the hadiths narrated by Ibn Jurayj from Atā' b. Abī Rabāh were forged, they can be seen as authentic representations of Muslim legal scholarship in Mecca in the late seventh and early eighth centuries.[128]

In another 1991 article, Motzki continues to use the *Musannaf* of ʻAbd al-Razzāq as a tool to correct Schacht's conclusions about early Islamic legal hadiths, in particular legal material ascribed to the famous al-Zuhrī. Motzki compares the legal hadiths narrated by al-Zuhrī's students Maʻmar b. Rāshid and Ibn Jurayj from their teacher with material found in the book of another of al-Zuhrī's students, Mālik. By proving that both the hadiths from Maʻmar/Ibn Jurayj and Mālik came from a common source, presumably al-Zuhrī, Motzki suggests that material attributed to al-Zuhrī actually came from him. Especially in the case of Maʻmar and Ibn Jurayj, their narrations bear no signs of intended forgery. These scholars drew on very diverse sources, and they readily transmitted hadiths or scholarly opinions that disagreed with their own stances. If they were using these transmissions only as a means to promote their own legal agenda, why would they transmit reports that disagreed with them?

Motzki devotes special attention to a bizarre report that al-Zuhrī attributes to one of the Prophet's Companions who allowed grown men to become related to women by breast-feeding from them. By establishing the transmission from al-Zuhrī and then showing that the material that al-Zuhrī reported was in itself compiled from several sources, Motzki argues that the Common Link for this report is in fact the Companion who supposedly said it in the second half of the seventh century. That al-Zuhrī personally disagreed with the Companion ruling he transmits (he did not approve of the practice of grown men suckling) testifies to his integrity as a transmitter.[129]

CONCLUSION: QUESTIONS ABOUT ASSUMPTIONS

Motzki raises some other interesting questions about the assumptions made by Schacht and Juynboll, assumptions that, I think, we can trace back to the Historical Critical Method itself. Extreme skeptics of the hadith tradition are motivated by the historical-critical approach of the Western tradition, which asks whether we should believe what historical sources tell us. However, sometimes doubting these sources obliges us to believe things more fantastical than simply accepting that the source might be authentic. Juynboll assumes that all 'diving' chains of transmission, all corroborating chains, and in fact any chain of transmission that does not emanate from a Common Link are forged (see Figure 9.1). But why? In the example of the hadith of God's descent at night, the only Common Link is the Companion Abu Hurayra. There are seven other chains of transmission through other Companions (not listed in Figure 9.3); are we to suppose that all these other chains coming from the Prophet, *via* different Companions, all with slight variations in the *matn* that are dispersed with total consistency among these different chains, are all fabricated? All this in a period of a hundred and fifty years (about the time that the earliest surviving written source for this hadith, the *Muwatta'*, was produced) within a circle of scholars who exerted a great deal of effort to prevent material from being forged wholesale about the Prophet? It seems more likely that the Prophet actually said that God descends at night to answer men's prayers. As Motzki points out, there is a certain *a priori* doubt about the reliability of the Muslim hadith tradition that may be totally groundless.

Western historians are of course totally right to point out the suspicious anachronism in a hadith in which the Prophet says, **'If you see Mu'āwiya on my pulpit, kill him,'** or the even more outrageous hadith of **'There will be in my community a man named Muhammad b. Idrīs [al-Shāfi'ī], and the strife he brings will be worse than Satan.'** But prominent Muslim hadith critics like Ibn 'Adī, al-Jawzaqānī, and al-Dhahabī also considered the hadith about Mu'āwiya to be unreliable or fabricated outright, and the hadith condemning al-Shāfi'ī was used by Muslim scholars as a textbook example of forgery.[130]

Even though many Muslim scholars considered them unreliable, the hadiths condemning the Qadarites (*qadariyya*) appear in collections like the respected Four *Sunan*. Certainly, it seems that the proper name Qadarite did not develop for over a century after the death of the Prophet.[131] But jumping to dismiss these hadiths as forgeries due to the anachronism of the Prophet 'foretelling' this sect's emergence is hasty. Western scholars might not accept that the Prophet could know the future, but the Quran clearly engages the questions of free will and predestination. Some Muslims in Muhammad's time could well have angered him by advocating the idea that God did not control human actions, so it is not unreasonable that he might have warned them against this. Crucially, for every hadith in which the Prophet condemns the Qadarites by this proper name there is a corresponding, non-anachronistic narration in which he refers to them as 'the people of *qadar*' or 'those who disbelieve in *qadar*.' In fact, these non-anachronistic narrations are the most reliable ones according to Muslim scholars. What seems like a clear case of anachronism to Western scholars might actually be a case in which the Prophet condemned an existing heresy, then some later transmitters of those hadiths lazily replaced 'the people of *qadar*/those who disbelieve in *qadar*' with the conventional label Qadarite as it had emerged in their time.[132]

Western critics from Goldziher onwards rebuked Muslim hadith scholars for not taking the contents of a hadith into consideration when analyzing its authenticity. But as we have seen, Muslim critics like al-Bukhārī did in fact use the contents of hadiths to prove that they were unreliable, although their degree of skepticism never approached that of the HCM.

Certainly, Muslim hadith critics differ from modern Western criticism in that they believe that the Prophet could know the future, but perhaps Western scholars could benefit from their cautious approach. Western reasoning for why the hadith about visiting the three mosques must be forged rested on the fact that it seemed to promote an Umayyad agenda and that al-Zuhrī, who was associated with the Umayyad court, is in the *isnād*.[133] But there are other early *isnād*s for this hadith that do not have al-Zuhrī in them.[134] Should we reconsider our conclusion or assume, quite without reason, that these other *isnād*s were forged as well? The Al-Aqsa Mosque is mentioned in the Quran, so is it so inconceivable that the Prophet would order his followers to pay special attention to it along with the Haram Mosque in Mecca and his mosque in Medina?

There is a certain 'chicken and the egg' logic to the Western approach to the reliability of hadiths. Goldziher and others have regularly criticized the hadith, considered *sahīh* by Muslims, **'When**

you see the black banners approaching from Khurasan, go to them, for indeed the Messiah (*mahdī*) is among them,' which they consider to be a product of Abbasid revolutionary propaganda (the Abbasids both had black banners and emerged from Khurasan).[135] But we must accept the fact that Muhammad, prophet or not, might actually have acted like a prophet and prophesied occasionally. Did the Abbasids forge this hadith about the black banners and the *Mahdī*, or did they take advantage of an existing hadith and simply tailor their banners to fit the messianic image that the Prophet had actually described?

Looking outside the Islamic tradition, the Old Testament Book of Zechariah reads, 'Rejoice greatly, O Daughter of Zion! Shout, Daughter of Jerusalem! See, your king comes to you, righteous and having salvation, gentle and riding on a donkey, on a colt, the foal of a donkey' (Zechariah 9:9). Does the fact that the Gospels describe Jesus entering Jerusalem on a colt or donkey (Mark 11:1–11; Matthew 21:1–4) mean that Christians made up this part of the Book of Zechariah to bolster the case for Jesus being a messianic figure (we know this is not true since the Book of Zechariah predates Christianity)? Or did Jesus really enter Jerusalem (not unlikely) riding the transport of his day – a donkey (not unlikely) – an event that the Gospel writers then described in the language of Old Testament scripture to show how Jesus' life was part of Old Testament prophecy being fulfilled? Taken further, the entry of the Quaker James Nayler into the English town of Bristol in 1656, riding on a donkey with women strewing fronds before him and singing 'Holy, Holy, Holy', obviously does not mean that Quakers concocted the Gospel story. Nayler was simply casting himself in the image of Christ as portrayed in scripture.[136] Similarly, some of the apparent anachronisms found in hadiths may simply be Muslims scripturalizing their own actions and history to dovetail with statements made by Muhammad.

Both Muslim and non-Muslim scholars of hadiths have agreed that there are many forged hadiths. In my opinion, explaining how this came about involves understanding the choices made by the Sunni scholarly tradition more than it does doubting the systematic effectiveness of their method of hadith criticism. In theory as well as practice, the Three-Tiered system of demanding a source, investigating its reliability and seeking out corroborating evidence is an effective way of determining the authenticity of a report. Modern reporters, after all, employ a similar method. Juynboll and Cook cited the practice of *tadlīs* as the loophole by which hadiths were attributed to major transmitters or equipped with additional *isnād*s. Juynboll states that *tadlīs* 'was hardly ever detected.'[137] But Muslim hadith scholars from the mid eighth century onward were obsessive about identifying which transmitters lapsed into *tadlīs* and when. Shu'ba (d. 160/776) said that '*tadlīs* is the brother of lying' and studied the transmissions of his teacher Qatāda b. Di'āma closely to know when he had heard a hadith directly from the person he was citing and when it was unclear if there was an unspecified intermediary. Yahyā b. Sa'īd al-Qattān (d. 198/813) made sure to identify *tadlīs* even when it was done by as revered a figure as Sufyān al-Thawrī. Later, master critics like 'Alī b. al-Madīnī (d. 234/849), al-Husayn al-Karābīsī (d. 245/859), and others wrote multivolume books identifying the names of those who committed *tadlīs* and the degree of their laxity.[138]

Juynboll states that the critical method of Muslim hadith scholars did not take into account the possibility that *isnād*s were fabricated wholesale. But the intensive focus on finding corroboration in order to evaluate a transmitter was aimed at isolating those individuals who cited *isnād*s not backed up by other students of the same teacher. If a transmitter was making up *isnād*s wholesale, he would be identified as someone who 'is not corroborated (*lā yutāba'u 'alayhi*)' or narrates 'unacceptable (*munkar*)' hadiths. As we discussed in Chapter 2, the number of hadiths transmitted by Ibn 'Abbās appears to increase incredulously only when we forget to distinguish between the relatively small number that Ibn 'Abbās actually heard from the Prophet and those in which he said 'the Prophet said …' leaving out the older Companion who had actually told him the hadith.

Clearly, Muslim scholars' rulings on the reliability of individual hadiths cannot be accepted without careful examination. But, as Motzki and others have shown, the classical Islamic method of filtering out forged hadiths was much more effective than earlier scholars like Goldziher and Juynboll have believed. However, Sunni scholars only chose to apply their critical methods *some of the time*. Masters of early Sunni hadith criticism such as Sufyān al-Thawrī, Ibn al-Mubārak, Ibn Hanbal, Ibn Ma'īn, and Ibn Abī Hātim al-Rāzī all stressed that they dealt stringently with the *isnād*s of hadiths dealing with law and dogma but were lax with material concerning history (*maghāzī*), the virtues of people or acts (*fadā'il*), pious preaching (*wa'z*), the end of days (*malāhim*), good manners, and the meaning of Quranic terms (*tafsīr*). As Abbott stated, this material easily passed through the hadith scholars' critical filters. These were the doors that Sunni scholars left open for forged material.

Al-Tirmidhī's collection offers a useful example, since he alone provided his own ratings for each hadith in his book. In chapters dealing with core legal topics, only a relatively small percentage of hadiths suffer from some lack or corroboration (*gharīb*): for the chapters on tithing (*zakāt*) and fasting (*sawm*), it is 17%. His chapter on inheritance (*farā'id*) has only 7%. Al-Tirmidhī's chapters on non-legal matters, however, have a much larger percentage of hadiths that the author himself acknowledges as problematic: apocalyptic strife (*fitan*) – 35%; the virtues of various early Muslims (*manāqib*) – 52%; pious invocations (*da'awāt*) – 50%; and manners (*ādāb*) – 27%. If corroboration was the keystone of Muslim hadith criticism, then al-Tirmidhī certainly dropped his critical guard in the non-legal chapters in comparison with legal ones. It is unfortunate that many of the areas that Western scholars consider the most important subjects of study – political history, apocalyptic visions, and Quranic exegesis – were simply not the priorities of Sunni hadith scholars. It is possible that it was prioritization of law over other areas that led to the inclusion of large numbers of unreliable hadiths in Sunni collections, not the failings of Sunni hadith-critical methods.

SUGGESTIONS FOR FURTHER READING

A great deal has been written about the Authenticity Question. Students interested in further reading would be best served by consulting the scholarly works cited in this chapter and its notes as the next step in examining the topic. In particular, Harald Motzki's digests of the various Western approaches to dating and evaluating hadiths in his article, 'Dating Muslim Traditions: a Survey,' *Arabica* 52, no. 2 (2005): 204–253, and his introduction to the edited volume on hadiths [*Ḥadīth: Origins and Development*, ed. Harald Motzki (Aldershot: Variorum, 2004), xiii–liii], are extremely useful surveys. A more recent survey of the field is Andreas Görke, Harald Motzki, and Gregor Schoeler, 'First Century Sources for the Life of Muḥammad? A Debate,' *Der Islam* 89, no. 1 (2012), pp. 2–59. The *Ḥadīth: Origins and Development* volume also includes influential pieces on the Authenticity Question from a number of scholars not mentioned in this chapter and translated from their original languages into English. Although it is slightly dated, the *Guide to Sira and Hadith Literature in Western Languages*, ed. Munawar Anees and Alia N. Athar (London: Mansell Publishing, 1986) is also useful. Myron Gilmore's *Humanists and Jurists* (Cambridge: Belknap Press, 1963), Edgar Krentz's *The Historical Critical Method* (Philadelphia: Fortress Press, 1975), Anthony Grafton's *Forgers and Critics* (Princeton: Princeton University Press, 1990), Owen Chadwick's marvelous *The Secularization of the European Mind in the 19th Century* (Cambridge: Cambridge University Press, 1975), Klaus Scholder's *The Birth of Modern Critical Theology*, trans. John Bowden (Philadelphia: Trinity Press, 1996), Hans Frei's *The Eclipse of Biblical Narrative* (New Haven: Yale University Press, 1974) and Ernst Troeltsch's essay 'Historical and Dogmatic Method in Theology' in *Religion in History*, trans. James A. Luther and Walter Bense (Minneapolis: Fortress Press, 1991) are very useful introductions to the Historical Critical Method. For more on European Orientalism and the study of Islam, see Ahmad Gunny, *The Prophet Muhammad in English and French Literature 1650 to the Present* (Islamic Foundation, 2010); Avril Powell, *Scottish Orientalists and India: The Muir Brothers, Religion, Education and Empire* (Boydell, 2010); and Suzanne Marchand, *German Orientalism in the Age of Empire* (Cambridge University Press, 2009).

ENDNOTES

1 Expanding on Marshall Hodgson, *The Venture of Islam*, vol. 1, p. 40.
2 Joseph Massad, *Islam in Liberalism*, pp. 65–73. See http://news.bbc.co.uk/2/hi/europe/7264903.stm.; http://blogs.reuters.com/faithworld/2008/03/07/turkey-explains-revision-of-hadith-project/ (last cited July 2016).
3 Al-ʿAjlūnī, *Kashf al-khafā*, vol. 1, p. 12; al-Makkī, *Qūt al-qulūb*, vol. 1, p. 177.
4 Lord Acton, *A Lecture on the Study of History*, pp. 40–42.
5 Leopold von Ranke, *Sämtliche Werke* (1868–90), vol. 33, pp. v–viii.
6 For example, twelfth-century paintings of Gospel scenes in the Swiss church of Zillis show characters dressed in medieval clothes; Rosalind and Christopher Brooke, *Popular Religion in the Middle Ages*, p. 137; Myron P. Gilmore, *Humanists and Jurists*, pp. 1–10.
7 Cicero, *The Nature of the Gods*, pp. I:60–62, 71–73; Petrarch, *The Secret*, pp. 68–69.

8 Eugene F. Rice, Jr. and Anthony Grafton, *The Foundations of Early Modern Europe*, p. 82.
9 This verse reads: 'And there are three that bear record in heaven, the Father, the Word and the Holy Ghost: and these three are one …' King James Bible 1 John 5:7–8. Only four Greek manuscripts mentioned this famous 'Johannan comma,' and all were historically late; Jerry Bentley, *Humanists and Holy Writ*, pp. 45, 152–153.
10 Klaus Scholder, *The Birth of Modern Critical Theology*, p. 67; Travis Frampton, *Spinoza and the Rise of Historical Criticism of the Bible*, pp. 208–216.
11 Peter Gay, ed., *Deism*, pp. 72–77.
12 Hans Frei, *The Eclipse of Biblical Narrative*, pp. 25–26.
13 Scholder, *Birth of Modern Critical Theology*, pp. 37–40.
14 Benedict Spinoza, *Theological-Political Treatise*, pp. 170–171.
15 See for a version of this, al-Khaṭīb al-Baghdādī, *Tārīkh Baghdād*, vol. 6, p. 115.
16 F. A. Wolf, *Prolegomena to Homer*, p. 233.
17 Voltaire, *Essai sur les Moeurs*, p. 1:288.
18 Frei, *Eclipse of Biblical Narrative*, pp. 56–57, 162; Robert Morgan and John Barton, *Biblical Interpretation*, p. 48. See also Pico's (d. 1494) *Oration on the Dignity of Man*.
19 Robert Morgan and John Barton, *Biblical Interpretation*, p. 47; Thomas Howard, *Religion and the Rise of Historicism*, p. 34.
20 Howard, *Religion and the Rise of Historicism*, pp. 2, 12–13.
21 Voltaire, *Essai sur les moeurs*, p. 1:288.
22 Mullā 'Alī al-Qārī, *al-Asrār al-marfū'a*, p. 407.
23 Edward Gibbon, *The Decline and Fall of the Roman Empire*, vol. 1, p. 186.
24 Polybius, *The Histories*, p. I:14.
25 John Herman Randall, *The School of Padua and the Emergence of Modern Science*, pp. 18, 46–47
26 Livy, *The Early History of Rome*, p. 3:1.
27 Herodotus, *The Histories*, p. II:120.
28 J. H. Brumfitt, *Voltaire, Historian*, p. 103.
29 Ernst Troeltsch, 'Historical and Dogmatic Method in Theology,' pp. 13–14; W. Von Leyden, 'Antiquity and Authority: A Paradox in the Renaissance Theory of History,' p. 488.
30 The scholar al-Kirmānī (d. 786/1384) said that it is an essential belief in Islam that there was no 'evil (*sharr*)' in the time of the Prophet; Ibn Hajar, *Fath*, vol. 13, p. 26.
31 Bart D. Ehrman, *The New Testament*, pp. 204–205; Arnaldo Momigliano, *Studies in Historiography*, p. 21.
32 Norman Perrin, *What Is Redaction Criticism?*, p. 16.
33 Voltaire, *La Philosophie de l'Histoire*, p. 121.
34 Suzanne Marchand, *German Orientalism in the Age of Empire*, pp. 157, 174, 183–184, 187; Nöldeke's *Geschichte des Qorans* has been translated as *The History of the Qur'ān*, trans. Wolfgang Behn (Leiden, Brill, 2013).
35 William Muir, *The Life of Mohamet*, p. xxxvii.
36 Ibid., pp. lxviii, lxxi.
37 Ibid., p. xlii.

38 Ignaz Goldziher, *Muslim Studies II*, pp. 19–22. Goldziher's German original, *Mohammedanische Studien*, was published in 1889–1890.
39 Goldziher, *Introduction to Islamic Theology and Law*, p. 40.
40 Goldziher, *Muslim Studies II*, pp. 22–23.
41 Ibid., p. 143.
42 Ibid., p. 40.
43 Ibid., pp. 44–45.
44 Ibid., p. 52.
45 Ibid., p. 44–47; Lecker, 'Biographical Notes on Ibn Shihāb al-Zuhrī.'
46 Goldziher, *Muslim Studies*, p. 75.
47 Ibid., pp. 38–40.
48 Ibid., p. 77.
49 Ibid., pp. 79–85.
50 Ibid., p. 99.
51 Ibid., p. 121.
52 Ibid., pp. 95–97; *Sunan Abī Dāwūd: kitāb al-fitan, bāb al-nahy 'an al-sa'ī fī al-fitna*.
53 Goldziher, *Muslim Studies*, p. 122.
54 Ibid., p. 108.
55 Ibid., pp. 113–114.
56 Ibid., pp. 123–124.
57 Ibid., p. 52.
58 Ibid. pp. 74–75.
59 Ibid., p. 18.
60 Ibid., pp. 55–56. Al-Bayhaqī and Ibn Khuzayma know of no one 'from the east to the west' who corroborates this report. A similar report, also considered unreliable, is in the *Musnad* of Ibn Hanbal, vol. 2, p. 367. See al-Suyūtī, *Miftāh al-janna fī al-ihtijāj bi'l-sunna* (Beirut: Dār al-Kutub al-'Ilmiyya, 1987), p. 39; Ibn Qudāma, *al-Muntakhab min al-'Ilal li'l-Khallāl* (Riyadh: Dār al-Rāya, 1998), p. 145.
61 Ibid., pp. 140–141.
62 Schacht, 'A Revaluation of Islamic Tradition,' pp. 146–147.
63 Ibid., p. 151.
64 Ibid., p. 149.
65 Ibid., p. 151.
66 Schacht, *The Origins of Muhammadan Jurisprudence*, p. 13.
67 Ibid., p. 22.
68 Ibid., p. 4.
69 Ibid., pp. 165–166.
70 Schacht, 'A Revaluation,' p. 151.
71 Schacht, *Origins of Muhammadan Jurisprudence*, p. 157.
72 Ibid., p. 157.
73 Ibid., pp. 4–5.
74 See Schacht, *Origins*, pp. 39, 165; idem, 'A Revaluation of Islamic Tradition,' p. 147.
75 Schacht, *Origins*, p. 175.
76 Ibid., p. 166.
77 Ibid., p. 156.

78 Juynboll, *Muslim Tradition: Studies in Chronology, Provenance and Authorship of Early Ḥadīth*, p. 71.
79 Juynboll, 'Some *isnād*-analytical methods illustrated on the basis of several women-demeaning sayings from Ḥadīth literature,' in *Studies on the Origins and Uses of Islamic Ḥadīth*, p. 352.
80 Ibid., p. 353.
81 Ibid., p. 353.
82 Juynboll, *Muslim Tradition*, p. 98.
83 Juynboll, 'Some *Isnād*-analytical methods,' p. 368.
84 Juynboll, 'Nāfi', the *mawlā* of Ibn 'Umar, and his position in Muslim *Ḥadīth* literature,' in *Studies on the Origins and Uses of Islamic Ḥadīth*, p. 215.
85 Juynboll, '(Re)Appraisal of some Hadith Technical Terms,' p. 318.
86 Juynboll, *Muslim Tradition*, pp. 52, 73, 75.
87 Ibid., pp. 5, 10.
88 Ibid., pp. 72–74.
89 Ibid., p. 30.
90 Juynboll, 'Nāfi', the *mawlā* of Ibn 'Umar,' pp. 219, 238–239.
91 Juynboll, *Muslim Tradition*, p. 98.
92 Christian Troll, *Sayyid Ahmad Khan: A Reinterpretation of Muslim Theology*, pp. 132–134.
93 Abbott, *Studies in Arabic Literary Papyri II: Qur'ānic Commentary and Tradition*, pp. 31–32.
94 Ibid., p. 29.
95 Ibid., pp. 21–22, 49–51.
96 Ibid., p. 71.
97 Ibid., pp. 66, 71–72.
98 Ibid., p. 74.
99 Ibid., p. 77.
100 Muhammad Azami, *Studies in Early Ḥadīth Literature*, p. 14.
101 Ibid., p. xvi.
102 Ibid., p. 218.
103 Ibid., p. 239.
104 Ibid.; for examples, see pp. 239–242.
105 Ibid., pp. 219–221.
106 Ibid., pp. 19, 246.
107 Patricia Crone, *Roman, Provincial and Islamic Law*, p. 33.
108 Ibid., p. 31.
109 Ibid., pp. 32–33.
110 Ibid., p. 33.
111 Crone, *Meccan Trade and the Rise of Islam*, pp. 109–110; 203–231; John Burton, *An Introduction to the Hadith*, p. 181.
112 Michael Cook, *Early Muslim Dogma: a Source-Critical Approach*, pp. 107–108.
113 Cook, *Early Muslim Dogma*, pp. 100, 110; idem, 'Eschatology and the Dating of Traditions,' pp. 23–47.
114 Fred Donner, 'From Believers to Muslims: Confessional Self-identity in the Early Islamic Community,' pp. 9–53; idem, *Muhammad and the Believers*.
115 Donner, *Narratives of Islamic Origins*, p. 27.
116 Motzki, 'Dating Muslim Traditions: a Survey,' p. 235.

117 David S. Powers, 'On Bequests in Early Islam,' pp. 199–200.

118 Ibid., p. 195.

119 See Motzki, '*Quo vadis, Ḥadīṯ*-Forschung?,' pp. 40–80. This has been translated as 'Whither Hadīth Studies?,' in Harald Motzki et al., *Analysing Muslim Traditions: Studies in Legal, Exegetical and Maghāzī Ḥadīth* (Leiden: Brill, 2010).

120 Motzki, 'The Murder of Ibn Abī Ḥuqayq,' pp. 231–232.

121 Ibid., p. 174.

122 Ibid., p. 182.

123 Ibid., p. 184.

124 Ibid., p. 187.

125 Motzki, 'The *Muṣannaf* of 'Abd al-Razzāq al-Ṣan'ānī as a Source of Authentic *Aḥādīth* of the First Century A.H,' pp. 8–9.

126 Ibid., pp. 4, 11.

127 Ibid., p. 11.

128 Ibid., p. 12.

129 See Motzki, 'Der Fiqh des Zuhrī: die Quellenproblematik.'

130 Al-Jawzaqānī, *Al-Abātīl*, pp. 114–115; al-Dhahabī, *Mīzān*, p. 3:277; Ibn 'Adī, *Al-Kāmil*, vol. 5, pp. 1744, 1751, 1756.

131 See the Caliph 'Umar b. 'Abd al-Azīz's (d. 101/720) letter on the subject, where he refers to them as those who hold '*al-qawl bi'l-qadar*'; Abū Nu'aym, *Hilyat al-awliyā'*, vol. 5, p. 351. Compare with Mālik b. Anas referring to them as the *qadariyya* in his *Muwatta'*: *kitāb al-qadar*, *bāb al-nahy 'an al-qawl bi'l-qadar*. The earliest appearance of the Qadarite hadiths is Dirār b. 'Amr (d. 200/815), *Kitāb al-Tahrīsh*, p. 99.

132 For the corresponding versions of these hadiths, see *Sunan Ibn Mājah*: introduction, *bāb fī al-qadar*; *Musnad Ibn Hanbal*, vol. 2, p. 125, etc.

133 Lecker, 'Biographical Notes on al-Zuhri,' p. 38.

134 Al-Humaydī, *Al-Musnad*, vol. 2, p. 330.

135 Al-Suyūtī, *Al-Jāmi' al-saghīr*, # 648.

136 *A True Narrative of the Examination, Tryall, and Sufferings of James Nayler* [London], n.p. 1657., p. 4–5.

137 Juynboll, *Muslim Tradition*, pp. 52, 73, 75.

138 Khatīb, *Al-Kifāya*, p. 2:371–378; idem, *Al-Jāmi'*, vol. 2, p. 312.

10

DEBATES OVER PROPHETIC TRADITIONS IN THE MODERN MUSLIM WORLD

INTRODUCTION: SETTING THE STAGE FOR MODERNITY AND ISLAM

In the eighteenth century, a network of interrelated economic, technological, social, and political changes began sweeping the world, beginning in England and Western Europe. Collectively known by scholars as Modernity, these forces ushered in a new phase of human history and raised inexorable questions about the nature of religion and its place in life. The challenges of Modernity have proven especially daunting for those peoples among whom it had not developed gradually before it was imposed through European colonization.

Perhaps nowhere has it been felt more sharply than among Muslims. Since their confrontation with the Modern West, Muslims have faced one daunting question: if Islam is God's true religion, and Muslims God's chosen community, why are they so powerless and subordinate before the Modern West? In attempts to answer and redress this question, Muslim discourse in the modern period has found discussing the role of hadiths in Islam unavoidable.

The stage for modern Muslim thought was set by two main forces: Western colonialism and indigenous Islamic movements of revival and reform. European arms quickly proved vastly superior to Muslim armies. The British East India Company had become the *de facto* government of several provinces of the Muslim Mughal Empire in India by 1764. In 1798 Napoleon occupied Egypt, and in 1882 the country was brought under British control.

More alarming for Muslim scholars, however, was the seeming superiority of European ideas to Islamic tradition. European scientists bent to their will technologies undreamt of in Muslim lands, and European society functioned with undeniably impressive organization. The rationalism and historicism of the European Enlightenment accompanied colonial administrations, and European Orientalists soon began turning their critical gaze on the Islamic religious tradition. Some Muslims immediately mistrusted Orientalism and sought to rebut it. Others were convinced by elements of European thought and swayed by Western scholars of Islam. Many Muslims were confused over what elements of Modernity they should embrace and what this entailed for their faith. Whether accepted or rejected, however, European thought and the civilization it represented became a central player in modern Islamic thought.

Interestingly, even before the impact of Modernity, Islamic civilization was shaken by entirely internal forces. In the mid 1700s, previously marginal parts of the Muslim world, such as West Africa, central Arabia, and India, brought forth unprecedented movements of Islamic revival and reform that would exercise tremendous influence on the whole Muslim world. These movements were driven by a sense that the Muslim community had lost its moorings in the legacy of the Prophet. It had been led astray by heretical accretions in theology and worship as well as by chauvinistic loyalty to the schools of law.

Although they did not abandon the classical Islamic tradition, these movements sought to revaluate it and revive Islam's primordial greatness by breaking with *taqlīd* (unquestioning loyalty to existing institutions and tradition) and embracing *ijtihād* (independent reasoning based on the original sources of Islam – the Quran and Sunna). Many of these revivalist scholars believed that they were just as capable as classical masters like al-Shāfiʿī and Abū Hanīfa of deriving laws directly from the Quran and the Prophet's teachings. As the great revivalist scholar Ibn al-Amīr al-Sanʿānī (d. 1768) wrote, '*that* gift of your Lord has not been made off-bounds, and the virtues that He has bestowed are not limited to those who have come before us.'[1]

Some of these movements were primarily scholarly, such as the reformist trend instigated in Yemen by al-Sanʿānī and in India by Shāh Walī Allāh (d. 1762). Others added a strong dimension of reforming Muslim society through force of arms, such as Osman dan Fodio's

(d. 1817) expansionist Sokoto Caliphate in modern-day Nigeria or Ibn ʿAbd al-Wahhāb's (d. 1792) militaristic *Muwahhid* movement (better known as Wahhābism) in central Arabia.

This common mission of bypassing the rigid institutions of the Late Sunni Tradition to revive the pure Islam of the Prophet's time and purge it of later cultural or intellectual impurities pushed the hadith tradition to the forefront. What better way to return to the source of Islam's original greatness than by renewing the study of the Sunna? Praising the Sunni devotees of hadith (*ahl al-hadīth*) in the early Islamic period, al-Sanʿānī recites:

> They quenched their thirst by drawing from the sea of Muhammad's knowledge,
> They did not have those schools of law for watering holes.[2]

Many revivalist scholars not only demonstrated a rejuvenated interest in hadith studies, they also believed that they were just as qualified as the great Sunni hadith critics of the classical period to rule on the authenticity of hadiths.

One of the interesting byproducts of the eighteenth-century movements of revival and reform was the shift of hadith studies from its medieval locus in Iran, Egypt, and Syria to the dynamic reformist regions of the Hejaz, Yemen, India, and eventually Morocco. Since the 1700s it has been Hejazi scholars like Muhammad Hayāt al-Sindī (d. 1750), Yemenis like Muhammad al-Shawkānī (d. 1834), Indians like Shāh Walī Allāh and ʿAbd al-Hayy al-Laknawī (d. 1886–7), and Moroccans like Muhammad b. Jaʿfar al-Kattānī (d. 1927) who have pioneered new creative ground in hadith studies.

Precisely why these similar but often unconnected movements arose at this time in distant corners of the Muslim world remains a mystery. Perhaps the Late Sunni Tradition, with its strict loyalty to schools of law, elaborate speculative theology, and Sufi brotherhoods had simply become too entrenched for Islam's inherent antipathy towards institutions of religious authority. When one considers that some late Sunni scholars like the Egyptian al-Sāwī (d. 1825) had asserted that anyone who did not follow one of the four Sunni schools of law was misguided, potentially an unbeliever, even if they followed clear indications from the Quran or Sunna, it seems easy to understand why some Muslims might conclude that reform was necessary.[3]

THE MODERN DEBATE OVER HADITHS: FOUR MAIN APPROACHES

In light of these forces, a thoughtful Muslim living in early twentieth-century Cairo, Istanbul, or Delhi might have pondered the following questions: Islam is clearly in a state of decline, whether in comparison to modern Europe or in relation to its own original greatness. But is this due to some inherent failing in the Islamic intellectual tradition or because Muslims have lost touch with Islam's true nature? If one seeks to recover Islam's true nature, does one take Modernity into account or ignore it completely? Ultimately, in the attempt to understand how to live as Muslims in the modern world, what components of Muslims' historical heritage (in Arabic, *turāth*) should they embrace, abandon, or alter, and how does one justify these choices in a way that is authentically 'Islamic'?

The hadith tradition in particular posed two major questions. In light of European historical criticism on the one hand and a revived commitment to the Prophet's authentic legacy on the other, 1) had the hadith tradition and its classical method of hadith evaluation produced a reliable representation of Muhammad's Sunna? and 2) what should be the overall place of hadiths and the Sunna in understanding Islam?

We can identify four broad approaches taken by Muslims to answering these questions: Islamic Modernism, Modernist Salafism, Traditionalist Salafism and Late Sunni Traditionalism. Although this four-fold division is useful, it is not watertight. Some thinkers sway between schools or change their positions depending on context. Also, some of these names are nomenclatures that I have chosen and have not actually been used by their adherents. Nonetheless, this division is helpful for understanding the complexity of Islamic thought in the modern period. Not surprisingly, Islamic responses to Modernity arose earliest in those areas earliest exposed to Europe, particularly India, Egypt, and Ottoman Istanbul.

ONE: ISLAMIC MODERNISTS AND THE 'QURAN ONLY' MOVEMENT

Beginning in the second half of the nineteenth century, some Muslim scholars began challenging core components of the pre-modern

Islamic tradition. Some concluded that the hadith tradition was not at all a reliable representation of Muhammad's message. A few of these thinkers went so far as to reject altogether the authoritativeness of the Prophet's precedent. We can label this overall trend as **Islamic Modernism**, which is characterized by a radical reconsideration of classical Islamic beliefs.

An early, well-known Modernist was Chirāgh 'Alī (d. 1895), an Indian who worked in the civil service of the local ruler of Hyderabad. 'Alī was a close associate of the pivotal Islamic thinker of South Asia in the modern period, Sir Sayyid Ahmad Khan (d. 1898), whom we will discuss shortly. 'Alī rejected all sources of Islamic law and dogma except the Quran, and called for a reinterpretation of Islamic law based on the ideals of humanism (such as rationalism, science, and non-religiously based ethics). Limiting the sources of Islamic law to the Quran was not a hindrance to the Shariah, he argued, since the Prophet had expected his community to revise their law occasionally in accordance with the needs of the times. Influenced by the revivalist movement of Shāh Walī Allāh, he embraced *ijtihād*. *Ijmā'* (consensus), he felt, had never been an acceptable source of law, since 'Alī argued that even Ibn Hanbal had been skeptical about the validity of claims of *ijmā'* (Ibn Hanbal is often quoted as denying any actual occurrence of *ijmā'*).[4]

'Alī accepted the criticism of hadiths published by Orientalists like Muir and Goldziher (see Chapter 9) and felt that the hadith corpus was unreliable. Interestingly, it was 'Alī's desire to defend Islam against Orientalists that led him to this stance. He was disturbed by Christian missionaries and European polemicists claiming that Islam was fossilized and replete with irrational beliefs, such as those found in hadiths.[5] Abandoning hadiths was necessary for saving the rest of Islam's message. Without the hadith corpus, 'Alī could offer unprecedented alternatives to beliefs that a modern mindset might consider backward. The *jinn*, a group of beings that the Quran mentions ambiguously as being composed of fire but that hadiths characterize as beings who inhabit earth in tandem with humans, he argued were actually another Semitic tribe.[6]

'Alī's thought was continued by what became known as the *Ahl-e Qur'ān* (The People of the Quran) movement in India. The *Ahl-e Qur'ān* saw hadiths as an embarrassing travesty in Islam and argued that Islamic dogma and law should be derived from the Quran alone. The movement was started by 'Abdallāh Chakrālawī (d. 1930) and Khwāja Ahmad Dīn Amritsari (d. 1936) between 1906 and 1917 and produced several journals devoted to elaborating its ideas. Amritsari had been a student at a missionary school, and his readings in hadiths led him to conclude that many hadiths were shockingly foul and patently false. He wrote a book on the Quran in which, among other things, he tried to demonstrate how Islamic inheritance law could be derived from the Quran without any reference to hadiths.[7]

The next generation of the *Ahl-e Qur'ān* was led by Muhammad Aslam Jayrapūrī (d. 1955), who mocked the traditional science of *isnād* criticism as senseless 'narration worship (*rivāyat parastī*).' Since whole *isnād*s were forged, he argued, it was impossible to distinguish truth from falsehood using *isnād* criticism.[8] His colleague, Mistrī Muhammad Ramadān (d. 1940) abandoned the idea of trying to extrapolate the labyrinthine details of Islamic law from the Quran. The holy book readily provided all the legal information Muslims needed, he argued, and anything omitted or left ambiguous was intentional – God had left humans free to use their reason in order to adapt to new times.[9] In recent decades, the 'Quran only' movement has flourished amongst the middle class and elite in Pakistan, particularly through the writings of Ghulam Ahmad Parwez (d. 1985) and his *Tulu-e Islam* (Islamic Dawn) foundation.

Although the 'Quran only' movement flourished in India and Pakistan, it flared only briefly in the Arab world. In a 1906 issue of the famous Islamic reformist journal *al-Manār* (The Lighthouse), the Egyptian physician Muhammad Tawfīq Sidqī (d. 1920) wrote an article entitled 'Islam is the Quran Alone (*al-Islām huwa al-Qur'ān wahdahu*)' in which he argued that Islam was never meant to be understood from anything other than the Quran. One key proof for this was that the Prophet did not explicitly order the recording of his Sunna, and indeed hadiths were not set down in any lasting or reliable form for over a century after Muhammad's death. How, Sidqī asked, could God ever allow His religion to depend on such a dubious source?[10] What has been understood as the 'Sunna' – the detailed precedent of the Prophet – was intended only to be binding on the first generation of Muslims; 'the Prophet gave the Sunna to the Arabs.'[11] After the Companions, Muslims were expected to adapt their law to circumstance according to the principles laid out in the Quran.[12] Like his Indian *Ahl-e Qur'ān* counterparts, Sidqī attempted to demonstrate how the details of Muslim prayer could be inferred from the Quran without hadiths.

Hadiths were patently unreliable in Sidqī's opinion, with the possible exception of those very few that could be considered *mutawātir*.[13] Hadith criticism had begun too late to catch many of the forged hadiths, and as a result many reports attributed to the Prophet were actually ***isrā'īliyyāt***, or stories from Jewish lore.[14] As a doctor, Sidqī devoted special attention to hadiths that he considered incompatible with the realities of modern medicine. He notes the controversial 'Hadith of the Fly' (found in *Sahīh al-Bukhārī* and other collections) in which the Prophet states that if a fly has landed in one's drink one should submerge it totally **'because on one wing is disease and on the other is the cure.'**[15] This was not only medically unsound, argued Sidqī, but it contradicted another command from the Prophet that if a mouse fell in liquid butter it should all be poured out.[16] Sidqī's writings caused such a furore in *al-Manār* and other publications that he quickly recanted his ideas, and they died out in the Arab world.[17]

Although they have not announced 'Quran only' positions as explicitly as Sidqī and the Indian *Ahl-e Qur'ān*, many Islamic Modernists have effectively adopted this stance. The influential modern Arab biography, 'The Life of Muhammad (*Hayāt Muhammad*),' by the Egyptian intellectual Muhammad Husayn Haykal (d. 1956) was based on the Quran with reference to only one hadith: the famous Mu'tazilite hadith urging Muslims to reject any hadith that contradicts the Quran![18] Haykal defended his 'Quran only' biography by saying he was using 'new critical methods' that were not allowed during classical times and writing his book 'in the modern scholarly manner.' Haykal echoed Orientalist criticisms that many hadiths were forged during the early period of sectarian and political strife and that many were fabricated merely to glorify Muhammad's miraculous powers. He therefore rejected any miracles attributed to the Prophet. Moreover, classical Muslim critics like al-Bukhārī and Ibn Hajar did not even agree on what was reliable or not.[19]

By far the most influential Modernist critique of the Sunni hadith tradition came from the Egyptian Mahmūd Abū Rayya (d. 1970). A disciple of the leading Syrian reformist Rashīd Ridā (see below), Abū Rayya wrote a scathing work entitled 'Lights on the Muhammadan Sunna (*Adwā' 'alā al-sunna al-muhammadiyya*)' (1958) in which he argued that only the Quran, reason, and unquestionably reliable *mutawātir* accounts of the Prophet's legacy were originally meant to be the basis of Islam. 'As for applying the term "Sunna" to what is subsumed by the hadith corpus [in general], that is a later convention.'[20]

Neither the Prophet nor his Companions had seen fit to record his every word, and the early jurists of Islam had followed in their footsteps by acting on the legal principles of the Sunna as opposed to random hadiths. Nothing in Islam required Muslims to read or believe the contents of hadith collections.[21]

Like earlier Modernists, Abū Rayya explained that early hadith critics had not paid attention to the contents of hadiths, and that outrageous reports such as 'The Devil flees, farting, when he hears the call to prayer' had been declared *sahīh*.[22] He also echoes the criticism about the long delay between the Prophet's death and the definitive recording of hadiths – a period in which myriad sectarian and political groups forged countless hadiths. The permissibility of 'narration of hadiths by general meaning (*riwāya bi'l-ma'nā*)' also led to the mutation and misunderstanding of many reports.

Notions that all the Companions were upstanding were patently absurd, Abū Rayya argued, since the Companions violently disagreed with one another. Although Abū Rayya built directly on the work of Ridā, his criticism of the Companions took him outside the fold of what his teacher and mainstream Sunni Islam could tolerate. Abū Rayya rejected exempting the Companions from hadith criticism, saying that 'people are people in every era, and humans have natures, appetites and agendas that do not change.'[23] This attitude closely resembles the Principle of Analogy used by Western scholars, and it is no coincidence that Abū Rayya referred his readers to the works of Goldziher and other Orientalists.[24]

Abū Rayya's most noteworthy contribution to Modernist criticisms of hadith was his multifaceted attack on the reliability of Abū Hurayra, the single most prolific transmitter of hadiths from among the Companions. Using reports from both Sunni and Shiite books of transmitter criticism, Abū Rayya produces evidence characterizing Abū Hurayra as a gluttonous and dishonest opportunist.[25] Noting how he joined the Muslim community only three years before the Prophet's death, Abū Rayya asks how Abū Hurayra could ever have heard the thousands of hadiths he claimed to transmit. Citing an early Hanafī criticism of Abū Hurayra, he argued that he was not learned in issues of ritual and law and therefore frequently mangled the meanings of hadiths he reported.[26] He added that Abū Hurayra was well known to be obsessed with *isrā'īliyyāt*, tales from Jewish lore about earlier prophets, and that he had no compunction about attributing such tales to the Prophet. Such reports included the unacceptably anthropomorphic hadith that **'God created Adam in His image'** and the dogmatically offensive report (both found in *Sahīh Muslim*) that Moses knocked out the eye of the angel of death when he came to take his soul.[27] Abū Rayya even considers the hadith urging Muslims to visit the Al-Aqsa Mosque in Jerusalem to be one of the forged *isrā'īliyyāt*.[28]

Isrā'īliyyāt proved constantly irksome to Modernists, and Abū Rayya wrote a separate 1946 article entitled 'Ka'b al-Ahbār: the First Zionist' on the early hadith transmitter and Muslim convert from Judaism, Ka'b al-Ahbār (d. *c.* 32/653).[29] Hadiths about the Messianic *mahdī* figure, Abū Rayya asserts, were similarly imported from Christian lore and falsely attributed to Muhammad by figures like the Companion Tamīm al-Dārī, who was a convert from Christianity.[30]

Abū Rayya's book proved extremely influential in the hadith debate, in part because of the author's broad erudition and in part because the book's style is less direct and caustic – and thus perhaps more convincing – than other Modernist works. It quickly prompted at least eight indignant book-length rebuttals from traditional Muslim scholars, the most famous of which was the Syrian Mustafā al-Sibā'ī's (d. 1964) *al-Sunna wa makānatuhā fī al-tashrī'al-islāmī* (The Sunna and its Place in Islamic Lawmaking) (1961).[31]

These rebuttals generally used orthodox Sunni arguments to respond to the criticisms of Abū Rayya as well as to those of Western scholars. Al-Sibā'ī, for example, deemphasizes the late writing down of hadiths by emphasizing the extraordinary memory of the early Arabs. Abū Hurayra's ability to transmit so many hadiths despite his relatively short exposure to the Prophet was due to his tremendous devotion to the Prophet's legacy, not any unscrupulousness. Finally, books of forged hadiths (*mawdū'āt*) showed that hadith critics did engage in content criticism (at least after the 1300s). Other defenses against 'Quran only' arguments relied solely on faith. The Pakistani Islamic political activist Abū al-'Alā' Mawdūdī (d. 1979) contended that the Sunna was intact because 'The God who preserved his last book also arranged for the preservation of the example and guidance of his last Prophet.'[32]

Islamic Modernism and its 'Quran only' trend have thrived among Western Muslim scholars. Although they have not always upheld explicit 'Quran only' positions, many have ignored hadiths in their discussions of Islamic law and dogma, as is the case with the American Amina Wudud's revaluation of the traditional Islamic view of gender, and Scott Siraj al-Haqq Kugle's argument for the permissibility of homosexual relationships in Islam.[33] The 'Quran only' movement has continued in Turkey, where the activist intellectual Edip Yuksel and his colleagues have published the *Reformist Quran*, an English translation and explanation of the holy book written without consulting hadiths.[34]

We should also note a Modernist who has proven extremely adept at navigating the tradition of Islamic hadith criticism in order to argue for radical reform. In her work *Women and Islam*, the French-educated Moroccan social scientist Fatema Mernissi (d. 2015) states her intent to 'disinter' the original message of Islam 'from the centuries of oblivion that have managed to obscure it.'[35] Her heroine is the Prophet's wife, Aisha, whose criticisms of other Companions' narrations from the Prophet Mernissi sees as epitomizing the critical spirit of Islam as well as the religion's original message of female empowerment. Mernissi argues that, with the exception of a minority of hadith critics, Muslim scholarship functioned as a tool of the social and political elite, indulging 'the desire of male politicians to manipulate the sacred.'[36]

In order to prove this, she examines two Companions known for transmitting hadiths that Mernissi considers misogynist and unbefitting her beloved Prophet: Abū Hurayra and Abū Bakra (not to be mistaken for Abū Bakr, the first caliph). The former transmitted *sahīh* hadiths such as the one that women, donkeys, and black dogs break a person's prayer if they pass in front of them, and the second narrated the hadith that **'The community that entrusts its affairs to a woman will not flourish'** (the first is found in *Sahīh Muslim*, the second in *Sahīh al-Bukhārī*).[37] Effectively engaging in historical psychoanalysis, Mernissi uses data from books of transmitter criticism to argue that Abū Hurayra harbored a deep personal resentment towards women and that Abū Bakra produced his hadith to secure his place with the caliph 'Alī after he had defeated Aisha at the Battle of the Camel in 656 CE.[38]

In a brilliant turn, Mernissi shows how Abū Bakra should be excluded as a hadith transmitter according to the Muslim hadith critics' own critical standards. Mālik is reported to have said that he would not accept hadiths from someone known to have lied about any matter, and Abū Bakra was once flogged for untruthfully accusing someone of committing adultery![39] Such misogynist figures as these transmitters, upon whom the most revered Sunni collections had relied, lead Mernissi to conclude that 'even the authentic Hadith must be vigilantly examined with a magnifying glass.'[40]

A unique Modernist vision for the proper treatment of hadiths came from the Pakistani intellectual and University of Chicago professor Fazlur Rahman (d. 1988). He acknowledged that the criticisms of Schacht and Goldziher were 'essentially correct' and that most hadiths were not actually spoken by the Prophet.[41] Where Orientalists saw deception, however, Rahman saw the creative implementation of the Islamic message. Though many of the details of the Sunna were fabricated, the *concept* of the Sunna was authentic. Muhammad's Sunna was not detailed case law, but rather an umbrella of behavioral norms and an interpretive process by which Muslims could adapt their law to changing circumstances.[42] This had been the practice of the Partisans of Reason (*ahl al-ra'y*), who had employed the legal reasoning learned from Muhammad, the original exemplar of Islam, to elaborate law in new situations. This was also why so many early hadiths were actually 'forgeries' – these early jurists had phrased the conclusions they reached using the interpretive process of the Sunna in the words of Muhammad. The Sunna was thus 'very largely the product of the Muslims themselves,' who acted organically on the principles inherited from the Prophet through the mental act of *ijtihād* in order to form new law. Consensus (*ijmā'*) was the acknowledgment of the community that a newly developed part of the Sunna was authoritative.[43]

For Rahman, the hadith tradition had been a creative process in which jurists had channeled the Prophet's authority to guide their community. Hadiths like those warning about the deterioration of Muslims' faith as time went on were designed to steer the community towards certain laudable goals.[44] Yes, the hadiths in al-Bukhārī's and Muslim's *Sahīhayn* that predict the future were clearly fabricated by Muslims after the death of Muhammad. But they were not sinister forgeries, and the hadith corpus was not a conspiratorial web of lies, since participants in the hadith tradition never saw themselves as engaged in a strict process of recording history.[45]

Unfortunately, Rahman continues, the formation of the hadith canon and the literal submission to hadiths introduced by al-Shāfi'ī turned the dynamic Sunna into a petrified and unchanging set of rules. Rahman states that hadiths need to be reexamined critically according to historical criticism in order to determine if they were really part of the original Sunna, 'whose very life blood was free and progressive interpretation.'[46] Once this is determined, modern Muslims can pick up with new interpretation where the jurists left off when the Sunna was frozen in the ninth century. Rahman acknowledges the value of *isnād* criticism in detecting forgeries. This method, however, can only tell us if a hadith *is* forged. It cannot ensure that it is *not* forged. For that we must employ modern historical criticism.[47]

One of the most dynamic Islamic modernist thinkers in South Asia since Rahman has been his fellow Pakistani Javed Ahmad Ghamidi. Trained as a youth in a Hanafī madrasa, Ghamidi later studied English literature and Islamic philosophy at university. He then became a disciple of Amin Ahsan Islahi (d. 1997), one of the most intellectually creative modern Muslim scholars of the Quran. Ghamidi has carried on and advanced Islahi's legacy, developing a novel method for reading the holy book that sees the Shariah as an eternal reality that must be clearly distinguished from Muslims' applications of its message in time and context – even its application by the Prophet. Certain aspects of Islamic law are thus, Ghamidi argues, meant to apply only in the Prophet's time, such as the death penalty for apostasy. Like Khan and other Islamic modernists (as well as Modernist Salafis, see below), Ghamidi enshrines the Quran as the primary source of Islamic law and dogma by reviving aspects of the classical Mu'tazilite and early Hanafī traditions. The Quran is thus unquestionably epistemologically and hermeneutically more powerful than the Prophet's Sunna, which Ghamidi trims down significantly. For him, the Sunna does not include the Prophet's optional acts of worship, his statements about science or nature, and it only pertains to 'religious,' not worldly, affairs. For Ghamidi, the Sunna is also qualitatively distinct from the hadith corpus, which he ranks as markedly lower in his epistemological and hermeneutic hierarchy. The Sunna can be known only through a combination of massively transmitted (*mutawātir*) hadiths and perpetual practice amongst the Muslim community. It cannot be known by isolated (*āhād*) hadiths, which should only be accepted if they concur with the Quran, the Sunna, reason and observed facts.[48]

TWO: MODERNIST SALAFĪS AND OPPOSING THE WEST

The **Salafī** movement was the name that many of the adherents of this school of thought derived from the *Salaf*, or the pious early generations of Muslims, from whose example these reformists hoped to reconstitute Islam's original purity. To a large extent, the eighteenth-century movements of revival and reform were all Salafī in their approach; for them the early Muslim community represented their hopes for the future. It was powerful, dynamic, and preceded what many reformists viewed as the superstitions, blind loyalty to tradition, and the havoc wreaked on medieval Islam by foreign cultural accretions such as Greek logic and Persian mysticism. In terms of their thought, by the mid 1800s these Salafī movements had split into two main branches, which we will call the Modernist and Traditionalist Salafī groups. These two branches interacted with and affected one another, for both shared a common vision of recapturing the early Islam of the *Salaf.* But they proposed different means and had opposing attitudes towards Modernity.

The Modernist Salafī trend has been the most influential and vigorous of the modern Muslim schools of thought. Nonetheless, it was essentially a response to Modernity. Its proponents looked back into history at the pure Arab Islam of the Prophet's time, but what they re-created by drawing unsystematically from the rich tradition of Islamic civilization was an Islam tailored to fit the modern world. Arguably the most influential Modernist Salafī was the Indian Sir Sayyid Ahmad Khan (d. 1898), whose thought ultimately aimed at the twin goals of the rationalization of Islamic dogma and 'the liberalization of Islamic law.'[49] An employee of both the British East India Company and the Mughal dynasty, after the Indian rebellion of 1857 Khan remained fiercely loyal to the British. He believed that only by reconciling with Modernity and Western rule could Islam survive. In 1868 he adopted a Western lifestyle, and in 1875 he successfully founded the Anglo-Muhammadan Oriental College at Aligarh in India, the most successful center of reformist Islamic education (today called Aligarh Muslim University).[50]

Khan authored numerous books, including a commentary on the Bible and a commentary on the Quran, and established an influential Urdu-language journal called *Tahdhīb al-akhlāq*. In general, Khan followed Shāh Walī Allāh's reformist rejection of *taqlīd* and innovations in Islamic belief and worship.[51] He also infused his works with distinctly modern notions, such as an acceptance of Darwinian evolution and the position that nothing in the Quran can be interpreted as contradicting the laws of nature. 'If the word [of the Quran] is not according to the work [the law of nature], then the word cannot be the word of God.'[52] Of course, he notes, humans have only begun to understand the laws of nature![53] He also rejected claims of *ijmā*ʿ as convincing proof in scholarly discourse.[54]

In the 1860s Khan encountered Muir's criticisms of hadiths, and he was immediately alarmed at this unsuspected attack on Islam from its external foes. In 1870 he began a refutation of Muir's book, although he also accepted many Orientalist criticisms.[55] He acknowledged, for example, that classical Muslim scholars had not performed proper content criticism of hadiths (he contends that they had intended this to be done by later scholars) and that the historical lag in writing down hadiths had resulted in copious forgeries, many concocted to sanctify and glorify Muhammad. He also noted that the permissibility of 'narration by general meaning' had led to the unintentional alteration of many hadiths.[56]

Khan struggled with the solution to the hadith problem throughout his life, but he consistently affirmed that the hadith corpus had to be reexamined according to a new method of content criticism that he drew partly from the Hanafī school of law and Muʿtazilism and partly from Western historical criticism. First of all, hadiths incompatible with modern reason, belittling to the Prophet, or contradicting the Quran must be rejected.[57] He embraced the Hanafī requirement that all the narrators of a hadith be competent legal scholars. Only *mutawātir* hadiths were immune from these critical standards, and these he defined as hadiths that have been accepted as reliable by Muslim scholars throughout history – only five of which he said exist. He added that hadiths should be screened to see if they describe miracles that could not be reasonably believed or historical events that could not have happened.[58]

Khan's critical method for hadith evaluation led him to revolutionary breaks with Islamic tradition. He believed that the Prophet's Sunna was only pertinent to matters of religion, not political or civil affairs.[59] He concluded that the Prophet's miraculous night voyage to Jerusalem was actually done in a dream (both Sunnism and Shiism generally held that he had been physically transported), and that the Prophet did not perform miracles. Like Chirāgh ʿAlī, he argued that the Quran's mentioning *jinn* did not really mean they existed as supernatural creatures. They could well be another Semitic tribe.[60]

Ultimately, defending Islam against infectious Western skepticism was Khan's real goal. Although he admitted many Orientalist criticisms of hadiths, he also understood that hadiths were essential for defending the basic Islamic worldview. When Muir suggested that part of the Quran might have been lost, Khan relied on hadiths to argue the contrary.[61] In proposing that the Quran be the standard against which the contents of hadiths be judged, Khan was seeking to find a critical litmus test that both Muslims and Western Orientalists could agree on (since Orientalists also believed that the Quran was the most historically reliable Islamic document).[62] Khan's concern for protecting religion from Modernity even led him to defend the Bible against European critics. Against claims that the global flood of Noah was impossible and not borne out in the historical record, Khan countered that the flood had really occurred but had been restricted to one locale.[63]

While Khan was writing in India, Egypt witnessed a simultaneous efflorescence of the Modernist Salafī movement. In fact, the most influential participants in Islamic thought in the late nineteenth- and twentieth-century Arab world were the Egyptian scholar Muhammad 'Abduh (d. 1905) and his Syrian student Rashīd Riḍā (d. 1935). 'Abduh was educated at the renowned al-Azhar University in Cairo but was exiled from Egypt in 1882 for several years due to involvement in an anti-British rebellion. He traveled to Lebanon and France and eventually returned to Egypt, where he became chief *muftī* (jurisconsult) under British rule.

Although 'Abduh never dealt with the issue of hadiths in a systematic way, he upheld the orthodox stance that the Sunna is the second major source of law and dogma in Islam. However, he accepted that the traditional methods of hadith criticism were insufficient and that the hadith corpus must be reexamined critically.[64] In theory, he states, disobeying what is known to have been the Sunna of the Prophet is anathema. This holds true, however, for 'a few only of the traditions.' In the case of non-*mutawātir* hadiths, whoever feels comfortable with them can believe them. But no one can be forced to believe in them or be declared an unbeliever for rejecting them. No hadith, for example, should be believed if it undermines God's total transcendence.[65] 'Abduh was also very skeptical about hadiths predicting the future, the end of the world or *isrā'īliyyāt*, and accepted very few such reports as authentic.[66] This notion of only requiring Muslims to believe in *mutawātir* hadiths would be a hallmark of both Modernism and Modernist Salafism. Decades later it would be elaborated in a formal religious ruling by the al-Azhar *Fatwā* Committee.[67]

'Abduh's senior student Rashīd Riḍā proved his chief acolyte, and his journal *al-Manār* was the main forum for reformist writings. Riḍā dealt with hadiths in much more detail than his teacher. Like 'Abduh, he argued that the Quran is the basis of Islam and that only *mutawātir* hadiths can truly be relied upon. After all, *āḥād* hadiths yielded no more than probable knowledge, while true certainty came only from *mutawātir* reports. He equated *mutawātir* hadiths with the 'practical', living Sunna that all Muslims know, such as prayer, pilgrimage rituals, and a few of the Prophet's sayings. The chapters of hadith books that list the obscure details of the Prophet's words and actions, such as chapters on manners (*adab*), all consist of *āḥād* hadiths and are not necessarily reliable.[68] Like Sir Sayyid Ahmad Khan, Riḍā believed that the permissibility of narrating the general meaning of hadiths had introduced many errors into the hadith corpus, since the narrators' opinions could be integrated accidentally into the hadith.

Accepting *isrā'īliyyāt* was another source of misguidance. Even though they had been used in some of the canonical hadith collections, Riḍā dismissed Ka'b al-Aḥbār and another early transmitter, Wahb b. Munabbih, as unreliable because of their lax transmission of *isrā'īliyyāt*. Interestingly, Riḍā argued that modern scholars were justified in overturning earlier approval of these two transmitters because, unlike classical Muslim critics, they could compare *isrā'īliyyāt* reports to the actual Jewish scriptures. Riḍā thus dismisses Ka'b and Wahb as unreliable because their descriptions of the Torah were factually inaccurate (note: as the ninth-century scholar al-Jāḥiẓ observed, by 'Torah' Ka'b and other early Muslims meant the Hebrew scriptures writ large).[69] Like other reformists, Riḍā called for *āḥād* hadiths to be resubmitted to content criticism, a process that was originally part of the critical method of Muslim jurists but had been neglected. At one point, Riḍā even states that the content criticism of classical Muslim scholars was the forerunner of modern historical 'analytical criticism.'[70]

Riḍā devoted numerous articles in *al-Manār* to addressing problematic hadiths. He sometimes declared hadiths that had traditionally been considered authentic to be unreliable because their contents were unacceptable according to him. Using his in-depth knowledge of *isnād* criticism, however, Riḍā could attribute this to a problem in the chain of transmission.[71] The famous story of God ordering the moon to be split miraculously in half as proof of Muhammad's message to his opponents in Mecca had been a required belief in Sunni

Islam (it is mentioned ambiguously in the Quran). Riḍā, however, said that the various hadiths describing this event were so at variance with one another that one could not base one's faith on them.[72] Another controversial hadith, found in *Ṣaḥīḥ al-Bukhārī*, that the sun passes under the earth and prostrates itself before the throne of God when it sets he declared false because it flatly contradicted modern science.[73] The position of only requiring belief in *mutawātir* hadiths allowed Riḍā ample leeway for some controversial hadiths. The Hadith of the Fly, for example, could be false or it could be true, since scientists used the flesh of a snake to help prepare antidotes to its poison.[74] Since it was *āḥād*, Muslims are not required to believe in the hadith either way.

Riḍā's and 'Abduh's approach to hadiths won many adherents among Muslim reformists. The Egyptian Modernist Salafī Maḥmūd Shaltūt (d. 1963) was at first persecuted by conservative ulema for his reformist ideas but was eventually appointed as the head of al-Azhar by the Egyptian government (which had a reformist agenda). He held that Muslims cannot be declared unbelievers for rejecting any article of faith that is derived from *āḥād* hadiths.[75] Breaking with an essential tenet of faith in classical Sunni Islam, Shaltūt followed his reasoning to its logical but controversial conclusion: Muslims could not be repudiated for rejecting the long-held tenet of Jesus' return at the end of time or the belief in an Antichrist.[76] Furthermore, he argued that one could not use consensus as proof for these issues of faith because even the consensus of the Muslim community means nothing on questions known only to God.[77]

'Abduh's and Riḍā's school of thought was continued by Shaltūt's most famous pupil, the Azhar scholar Muhammad al-Ghazālī (d. 1996), in his prolific and extremely popular series of books on reviving Islam in the modern world. Like Shaltūt, al-Ghazālī reminds his readers of the classical legal theory stance that *āḥād* hadiths are 'merely probable in their reliability and merely probable in their indication' and thus not suitable for essential beliefs.[78] Similarly, he affirms the predominance of the Quran, saying, 'We believe that the Quran is the basis, and the Sunna is built on it.'[79]

Al-Ghazālī's overriding concern throughout his works is the looming presence of the West. Although he reiterates his profound respect for classical hadith scholars like al-Bukhārī, he admits that he will reject a hadith from the canonical collections 'if it touches upon the most intimate part of our religion, or opens frightening borders through which our enemies could pour.'[80] When a student asks him about the *sahīh* hadith of Moses knocking out the angel of death's eye, he replies that its contents show that it is false, since God's prophet could not try to avoid his fate. Muslims, however, should worry about more important matters such as 'the fact that the enemies of Islam are encircling us.'[81]

THREE: TRADITIONALIST SALAFĪS AND THE ELEVATION OF HADITHS

What we have termed Traditionalist Salafism emerged directly from the early modern movements of revival and reform. The most persistent and most politically active Traditionalist Salafī movement was founded by Muhammad b. 'Abd al-Wahhāb in the mid eighteenth century in central Arabia, expanding through its alliance with the Saud family and eventually becoming the predominant religious movement on the Arabian peninsula. A second Salafī school appeared in the Yemeni city of Sanaa with the iconoclastic hadith scholars al-San'ānī (d. 1768) and al-Shawkānī (d. 1834). A third school developed in Damascus in the second half of the nineteenth century around revivalist hadith scholars Jamāl al-Dīn al-Qāsimī (d. 1914) and Tāhir al-Jazā'irī (d. 1920). At this same time an influential Salafī school also formed in Baghdad through the Hanbalī revival led by the famous Ālūsī family.[82] In India, some of the devotees of Shāh Walī Allāh's revivalist scholarship formed their own strict Traditionalist Salafī school, dubbed the *Ahl-e Hadīth* (The People of Hadith), whose most famous representative was Siddīq Hasan Khān (d. 1890). Other heirs to Shāh Walī Allāh's legacy combined his hadith-based revivalism with India's longstanding adherence to the Hanafī school of law. This movement resulted in the founding of the influential school at Deoband in India.

The most illustrative example of Traditionalist Salafīs is Muhammad Nāsir al-Dīn al-Albānī (d. 1999), an Albanian whose family immigrated to Syria. Growing up in Damascus, al-Albānī was deeply affected by Ridā's *al-Manār* articles on the extent to which unreliable hadiths had been used to justify Sufi practices.[83] He began to speak out against what he saw as heretical innovations in every area of Syrian religious life and penned many works attempting to reorient social and religious practices to the pure Sunna of Muhammad as communicated by hadiths.

Like the other reform movements, Traditionalist Salafīs have aimed at reviving Islam's original purity and greatness by clearing away the dross of later cultural accretions. Unlike Modernist Salafīs, who drew eclectically on Hanafī legal theory, Mu'tazilism, and modern rationalism, they have struggled literally to revive the Prophet's Sunna through a narrow focus on hadiths. Like their Modernist Salafī counterparts, Traditionalist Salafīs identify the causes of the Muslim community straying from the Sunna as excessive loyalty to the schools of law instead of a reverence for their sources, indulgence in speculative theology, and popular Sufi practices such as visiting the graves of saints.

To cure these ills, Traditionalist Salafīs have not merely engaged in the study of hadiths, they have tried to cultivate its most critically rigorous spirit. They reject the use of weak hadiths in any matter, breaking with the practice of the classical Muslim scholars (see Chapter 3). Al-Albānī asks rhetorically: if we do not dismiss hadiths once we have determined that they are unreliable, what is the point of the science of hadith criticism?[84] Al-Albānī thus published numerous books dividing the hadiths contained in classical works such as the Four Sunans of Abū Dāwūd, al-Nasā'ī, al-Tirmidhī, and Ibn Mājah, the *Jāmi' al-saghīr* of al-Suyūtī, and the *al-Targhīb wa al-tarhīb* of al-Mundhirī into sound and unreliable. The Saudi hadith scholar 'Abdallāh al-Sa'd rejects the Late Sunni Tradition's method of bolstering evidence for a hadith's authenticity by using other dubious narrations (see Chapter 3).[85] The Indian hadith scholar Shibli Numani (d. 1916), a traditionalist associate of Ahmad Khan, compiled a new biography of Muhammad that purged it of reports transmitted by early Muslim historians that hadith critics had considered unreliable.

Like Modernist Salafīs, Traditionalists were willing to cast aside the institutions of classical Islam, relying on hadiths as the ultimate source for interpreting the faith. The Sunna was preserved in the authentic hadiths, which are accessible to any Muslim. Like Modernists, Traditionalist Salafīs have been skeptical of claims of consensus, which served as the primary defense for employing weak hadiths as evidence and the legitimacy of many Sufi practices. They do not doubt the theoretical proof value of consensus, but the large number of dissenting scholarly opinions in Islamic history means that it was actually achieved only rarely.

Unlike Modernists, however, Traditionalist Salafīs avow the same intense trust in hadiths found among the early *ahl al-hadīth*. They do not concur with the Modernist reemphasis on the Quran as the ultimate arbiter in matters of faith and law. Like the early *ahl al-hadīth*, al-Albānī asserts that in both law and dogma 'we cannot distinguish between God and His Prophet.'[86] It is thus perfectly acceptable to derive articles of faith from *āhād* hadiths, which Muslims must accept. Did the Prophet not send single individuals as ambassadors to newly converted communities in order to teach them fundamental Islamic beliefs?[87] Although Traditionalist Salafīs are willing to criticize a hadith for content reasons, like the early *ahl al-hadīth* they explain such faults by finding a flaw in the *isnād*. 'Abdallāh al-Sa'd thus declares, 'It is impossible for a hadith to have an untrue meaning without there being a flaw in the *isnād*.'[88] Unlike their Modernist and Modernist Salafī counterparts, these Traditionalists do not approve of Aisha's criticisms of other Companions for narrating hadiths that seemed to contradict the Quran. Since these hadiths are well established by multiple *sahīh isnād*s, such apparent contradictions only mean that she did not interpret the Prophet's words correctly.[89]

Traditionalist Salafīs preserve the spirit of *ijtihād*. For them, hadith criticism did not end with the formation of the hadith canon in the classical period. It continues to this day, and modern scholars can achieve just as high a level of critical mastery as great classical scholars such as al-Dāraqutnī or Ibn Hajar. Tāhir al-Jazā'irī defends the right of modern scholars to criticize the meanings of hadiths in the *Sahīhayn*, rejecting the argument of those who warn that allowing criticism of the meaning of hadiths will open the door to the 'people with heretical agendas.' He disagrees, saying that proper criticism is a worthy practice.[90] When asked about his controversial criticism of a famous classical hadith transmitter, al-Albānī replied that the science of hadith criticism 'is not simply consigned to books,' it is a dynamic process of critical review.[91] Al-Albānī explained that one of the principles of Islamic scholarship is that 'religious knowledge cannot fall into rigidity.'[92]

This spirit of picking up the classical hadith tradition at its most critical point and applying it today has led to substantial achievements by Traditionalist Salafī scholars. Al-Albānī completed two voluminous series, 'The Series of Weak Hadiths and their Negative Effect on the Muslim Community' and 'The Series of Authentic Hadiths,' in which he revaluates thousands of hadiths. Many that he authenticates had previously been declared unreliable, and many hadiths that he criticizes had earlier won the approval of great classical critics like al-Bukhārī and Muslim. One of al-Albānī's students, the Yemeni Muqbil al-Wādiʿī (d. 2001) similarly compiled a large work entitled 'The Compendium of *Sahīh* Hadiths Not Found in the Two *Sahīh*s of al-Bukhārī and Muslim.'

Traditionalist Salafīs have also revived the genre on the technical terminology and rules of hadith criticism (*mustalah al-hadīth*). The two most famous modern contributions are Jamāl al Dīn al-Qāsimī's *Qawāʿid al-tahdīth min funūn mustalah al-hadīth* (The Principles of Regeneration from the Technical Science of Hadith Study) and Tāhir al-Jazā'irī's *Tawjīh al-nazar ilā usūl al-athar* (Examining the Principles of Transmitted Reports). These works are continuations of the classical *mustalah* books, such as that of Ibn al-Salāh, but are imbued with Salafī themes. Tāhir al-Jazā'irī, for example, lambasts the excessive traditionalism of the Sunni schools of law: 'The jurists interpret away any hadith that disagrees with their school, or oppose it with another hadith even if it is not well-known, even if that [first] hadith is found in the *Sahīhayn*.'[93]

Because the Salafī approach to Islamic scholarship centers on bypassing centuries of consensus-building among scholars and instead approaches the Quran and hadiths anew, it can produce divergent results. A set of Moroccan brothers who have proven the most adept hadith scholars of our time, Ahmad b. al-Siddīq al-Ghumārī (d. 1960) and his younger siblings 'Abdallāh (d. 1993) and 'Abd al-Hayy (d. 1995), followed the Traditionalist Salafī methodology. They felt entitled to reverse centuries-old rulings on the authenticity of specific hadiths and arrived at legal rulings that broke with all four Sunni schools of law. 'Abd al-Hayy argued conclusively that none of the founders of the four Sunni schools of law had access to all the necessary hadiths and that it was thus entirely acceptable to reject their rulings on the basis of hadith evidence. 'Abdallāh al-Ghumārī repeatedly wrote that '*taqlīd* never comes to any good.'[94] Ahmad al-Ghumārī concluded that the famous hadith in which the Prophet explained that the **'Greatest Jihad'** was **'the struggle against one's own soul'** was authentic, while classical critics had considered it weak or forged.[95]

Despite this similarity in approach to Traditionalist Salafīs like al-Albānī, the Ghumārī brothers emerged with polar opposite positions. Salafīs, both Modernist and Traditionalist, have consistently been deeply opposed to Sufism and intolerant of the Shiite veneration of ʿAlī. The Ghumārīs' analysis of the Quran, hadiths, and scholarly tradition, however, has led them to embrace ʿAlī as the best and most knowledgeable of all the Companions (and in Ahmad's case, to declare Muʿāwiya an unbeliever) as well as to defend vehemently Sufi practices such as visiting graves and engaging in group liturgies not practiced during the time of the Prophet.[96] ʿAbdallāh al-Ghumārī repeatedly accused al-Albānī of unmitigated heresy, and at least one Wahhābī hadith scholar called ʿAbdallāh al-Ghumārī an unbeliever.

Unlike Modernists and Modernist Salafīs, Traditionalist Salafīs have no concern for the pressures of Modernity. They believe that if Muslims return to the authentic Sunna of the Prophet as preserved in the hadith corpus, the Muslim world will once again enjoy God's favor regardless of any perceived superiority boasted by the West today. Traditionalist Salafīs consider the other schools of thought discussed so far in this chapter to be misguided by Western influence. Al-Albānī thus calls both Abū Rayya and Muhammad al-Ghazālī 'Occidentalists (*mustaghribūn*)' and 'imitators of the Orientalists.'[97]

The most furious conflict among schools of Sunni thought in modern times has surged between the Traditionalist Salafīs and the Late Sunni Traditionalists (see below). Because Salafīs allow a scholar to break with the established rulings of the Sunni schools of law and perform *ijtihād*, Late Sunni Traditionalists accuse this movement of arrogantly claiming to be the equal of the great scholars of yesteryear. Muhammad Zāhid al-Kawtharī (d. 1952), a high religious official in the moribund Ottoman Empire, wrote that it was pure error and misguidance to believe that, today, 'at the end of time,' one could correct the great early scholars of Islam.[98] Moreover, adherents of the schools of law accuse Traditionalist Salafīs of total ignorance of legal theory and thus of ignorantly following random hadiths instead of understanding how those hadiths fit into the process of deriving law. These factors combine to create, in the eyes of Late Sunni Traditionalists, interpretive chaos. Muhammad al-Ghazālī, for example, admits that he dislikes chauvinism towards one particular school of law. But it is 'less harmful than the childish *ijtihād*' of Salafī movements like Wahhābism, which he calls simplistic 'Bedouin legal thought.'[99] Contrary to such polemical claims, Traditionalist Salafī scholars do advocate the study of basic books of legal theory (al-Albānī, for example, cites advanced legal principles such as 'Evidence that breaks with analogy cannot be used as the basis for another analogy').[100] However, the Traditionalist Salafīs' egalitarian argument that any scholar can break with an established ruling if he feels it has not taken certain hadith evidence into account has undeniably led to a proliferation of erratic rulings.

FOUR: LATE SUNNI TRADITIONALISTS

All the approaches to understanding Islam in the modern period that we have discussed so far have advocated the rejection of significant components of Sunni Islam as it existed in the medieval world through the 1600s. Conversely, what we can call Late Sunni Traditionalism argues that it is precisely these institutions that are essential for properly living as a Muslim today. In other words, closely following one of the accepted Sunni schools of law, believing in the traditional Ashʿarī school of theology, and participating in a Sufi brotherhood provides modern Muslims with all the legal, spiritual, and theological tools they need to succeed. Properly understood and correctly combined, these classical institutions allow Muslims to answer all the challenges of Modernity. Advocates of Late Sunni Traditionalism generally refer to their school of thought as 'Traditional Islam' or 'Sunnism in its authentic form (*ahl al-sunna ʿalā al-mashrib al-aṣīl*).' Prominent representatives of this school include Muhammad Zāhid al-Kawtharī, Muhammad al-Ghazālī,[i] the late Syrian scholar Muhammad Saʿīd al-Būṭī (d. 2013) and the former Grand Mufti of Egypt, ʿAlī Jumʿa.

Late Sunni Traditionalism mitigates the stipulations of Islamic law that seem incompatible with Modernity by drawing on the collective diversity of the four Sunni legal schools and the rich intellectual heritage of Sunni legal theory. Although engaging in interest-bearing commercial transactions is generally prohibited in Islamic law, a minority opinion in the Hanafī school allows Muslims to take and pay interest if living in a non-Muslim country.[101] A principle of Late Sunni legal theory, 'Let he who is afflicted with some need take the permissive ruling,' permits a Muslim to act on this minority

[i] Earlier in this chapter we referred to Muhammad al-Ghazālī as a Modernist Salafī. In terms of the structure of his thought, this is correct. But al-Ghazālī's environment, Egypt in the 1970s, 1980s and 1990s, was much more religiously conservative than that of ʿAbduh or Shaltūt. As a result, in his language and positions al-Ghazālī fits into the Late Sunni Traditionalist category.

ruling. As Muhammad al-Ghazālī states, 'when I am defending Islam ... I must move between the opinions of all the imams and benefit from the full range of understandings.'[102] As a result of this methodology, Late Sunni Traditionalism produces a manfestation of Islam that adapts to many of the stringencies of the modern world while remaining grounded in 'authentic' Islamic tradition.

This school of thought also uses the relationship between law and ethics to circumvent seemingly harsh elements of Islamic law. Islamic marriage law, for example, seems to clash with modern sentiments with its legalistic requirements that a woman meet her husband's sexual needs and that a husband bear the full financial responsibilities of a family. Late Sunni Traditionalists, however, argue that the Shariah only addresses people's strict legal rights, and that a husband and wife should turn to the Sufi tradition in order to learn how to treat one another with love and compassion.

Just as Traditionalist Salafīs have resurrected the approach of the *ahl al-hadīth*, Late Sunni Traditionalists have revived the methods of the *ahl al-ra'y* jurists. Late Sunni Traditionalists subordinate hadiths to the interpretive traditions of the Sunni schools of law and Sunni legal theory. Late Sunni Traditionalists affirm their total confidence in the classical method of hadith criticism; as al-Ghazālī says, 'I do not know its equal in the history of human culture in terms of establishing principles for verification.'[103] They also, however, entrust jurists, not hadith scholars, with the ultimate authority in determining the authenticity and implication of a hadith. Al-Kawtharī explains that hadith scholars and jurists had divided up the duties of hadith criticism, with the latter responsible for content criticism.[104] In an analogy similar to the doctors versus pharmacists comparison mentioned in Chapter 5, al-Ghazālī states:

> The jurists have been, throughout our intellectual history, the leaders of the Muslim community... and the scholars of hadiths have been content to provide them with the reports they transmit just as raw building materials are given to the engineer who builds a structure.[105]

Al-Ghazālī adds that the classical criteria for a *sahīh* hadith require that it does not include any hidden flaw ('*illa*) or contradict more reliable evidence. Although hadith scholars can criticize *isnād*s, it is the jurists who are properly trained to spot such errors in the text of a hadith and issue the definitive ruling on its reliability. Al-Ghazālī thus declares that a hadith that al-Albānī authenticated[ii] saying that **'In the meat of a cow is disease'** is false because the Quran notes the blessings of beef. The hadith is thus untrue 'whatever its *isnād* may be.'[106]

Late Sunni Traditionalists also circumvent hadiths that appear to be problematic in the modern world by relying on the classical juristic concept of communal practice or interpretation. Just as Mālik had ignored hadiths he acknowledged as authentic because the Muslim community had never acted on them in law, today's Late Sunni Traditionalists use the collective rulings of Muslim jurists to overrule hadiths. 'Alī Jum'a admits that numerous authentic hadiths exist that command Muslims to kill apostates, such as **'Whoever changes their religion [from Islam], kill them.'**[107] The fact that neither the Prophet nor the early caliphs actually implemented these rulings when individuals left Islam means that these hadiths addressed the issue of treason to the Muslim community and not a person's individual choice of belief.[108] Another influential modern scholar, the Egyptian Yūsuf al-Dijwī (d. 1946), emphasized how classical Muslim scholarship had always employed reason, scriptural interpretation and the observation of nature to avoid the literal or superficial understanding of hadiths so mocked by Modernist critics. In a long-running dispute with Riḍā, al-Dijwī argued that there was no need to reject the hadith of the sun prostrating because pre-modern Muslim scholars had always interpreted it figuratively and acknowledged that the sun is always shining on some parts of the earth and not visible elsewhere.[109]

THE CONTINUITY BETWEEN CLASSICAL AND MODERN DEBATES ON HADITHS

It is worthy of note that debates over hadiths in the modern Muslim world have echoed or recast debates that occurred in the formative period of Islamic thought. Sidqī and other 'Quran only' advocates rehash the debate between early Muslim rationalists and Sunnis such

[ii] Although al-Albānī rules that this hadith is authentic, he also notes that it cannot be interpreted literally since we know that the Prophet ate beef; al-Albānī, *Silsilat al-ahādīth al-sahīha*, p. 4:46.

as al-Shāfi'ī in the eighth century. Like al-Shāfi'ī's opponents in this debate, Sidqī argued that the Quran described itself as 'elucidating everything (*tibyān li-kull shay'*)' (Quran 16:89). So how can one argue that Muslims need hadiths to understand their faith as well? The principal argument used by conservative Sunnis like al-Sibā'ī against the writings of 'Quran only' scholars is drawn directly from al-Shāfi'ī's rebuttal of that point: if you reject the Prophet's Sunna, how do you know how to pray or fast?[110]

The raging debate between Traditionalist Salafīs and Late Sunni Traditionalists parallels the eighth-century dispute between the *ahl al-hadīth* and the *ahl al-ra'y*. The principle invoked by Islamic Modernists and Modernist Salafīs that the hadith corpus should be submitted to content criticism revives the long-dormant debate between the Mu'tazilites and the early Sunnis, as does the specific call to use the Quran as the criterion of judgment. The hadith that Haykal cited as his evidence for the determinative role of the Quran – **'There will come to you many different hadiths from me, so what agrees with the Book of God, accept it, and what disagrees with it, reject it'** – was used as evidence by early Mu'tazilites like al-Jāhiz. Sunni scholars, of course, universally deemed the hadith a forgery. Even the reliability and piety of Abū Hurayra was a major item of contention between the Mu'tazilites and the early Sunnis in the eighth century. In an audience before the Abbasid caliph Hārūn al-Rashīd, the early Sunni Umar b. Habīb (d. 204/819-20) responded to Mu'tazilite and *ahl al-ra'y* arguments that Abū Hurayra was unreliable by claiming that if one opened the door to criticizing the Companions of the Prophet, Muslims would lose the whole Shariah.[111] Even before modern medicine, the Hadith of the Fly was raising skeptical eyebrows and prompting Sunni defensiveness as early as the writings of Ibn Qutayba (d. 276/889).[112]

Of course, modern Muslim scholars have utilized this classical heritage in unprecedented ways. Mahmūd Shaltūt used the distinction between the different levels of certainty yielded by *āhād* and *mutawātir* hadiths – a purely academic distinction in classical Islamic thought – to excuse modern Muslims from believing in 'backwards' or 'irrational' beliefs. Before Mernissi, no classical Muslim scholar had used historical reports about Abū Hurayra or Abū Bakra to claim a misogynist conspiracy at the root of Islamic law.

SUGGESTIONS FOR FURTHER READING

For the best introductions to the revolution of modernity, see the Conclusion of Keith Thomas' *Religion and the Decline of Magic* (New York: Oxford University Press, 1971) and Marshall Hodgson, *The Venture of Islam* (University of Chicago Press, 1974) vol. 3, pp. 163–248. The most useful books on debates over hadiths in the modern Muslim world are Daniel Brown's superb *Rethinking Tradition in Modern Islamic Thought* (Cambridge: Cambridge University Press, 1996) and G.H.A. Juynboll's *The Authenticity of the Tradition Literature* (Leiden: Brill, 1969). For more general discussions of modern Islamic thought, see Albert Hourani's *Arab Thought in the Liberal Age* (Cambridge: Cambridge University Press, 1983) and Aziz Ahmad's *Islamic Modernism in India and Pakistan* (London: Oxford University Press, 1967). The two best resources on Salafism are Henri Lauzière, *The Making of Salafism* (Columbia University Press, 2016) and Roel Meijer, ed., *Global Salafism* (Columbia University Press, 2009). A recent study on the Quran-only movement is Ali Usman Qasmi, *Questioning the Authority of the Past: The Ahl al-Qur'an Movement in the Punjab* (Oxford University Press, 2011). For more on the eighteenth-century movements of revival and reform, see John Voll, 'Foundations of Renewal and Reform: Islamic Movements in the Eighteenth and Nineteenth Centuries,' in *The Oxford History of Islam*, ed. John Esposito, pp. 509–548 (Oxford: Oxford University Press, 1999) and the initial chapters of Barbara Metcalf's *Islamic Revivalism in British India: Deoband 1860–1900* (Princeton: Princeton University Press, 1982).

A difficult-to-find translation of Abū Rayya's *al-Adwā' ʿalā al-sunna al-muhammadiyya* has been published as *Lights on the Muhammadan Sunna*, trans. Hasan Najafi (Qum: Ansariyan Publications, 1999). Muhammad Husayn Haykal's biography of the Prophet, translated by Ismail al-Faruqi, has been published in several editions as *The Life of Muhammad.* Yūsuf al-Qaradāwī's influential *Kayfa nataʿāmalu maʿa al-sunna al-nabawiyya* has been translated as *Approaching the Sunna: Comprehension and Controversy*, trans. Jamil Qureshi (Washington DC: International Institute of Islamic Thought, 2007). Sir Sayyid Ahmad Khan's response to William Muir's critique of the *sīra* has been published as *A Series of Essays on the Life of Muhammad* (Lahore: Premier Book House, 1968), and Shibli Numani's biography of the Prophet has been published as

Sirat-un-Nabi: The Life of the Prophet, 2 vols. (Delhi: Idarat Adabiyat Deli, 1979).

ENDNOTES

1 Al-San'ānī, *Irshād al-nuqqād ilā taysīr al-ijtihād*, p. 58.
2 Al-San'ānī, *Dīwān al-Amīr al-San'ānī*, p. 168.
3 'Abdallāh al-Ghumārī, *Al-Khawātir al-dīniyya*, vol. 1, p. 123; Ahmad b. Muhammad al-Sāwī, *Hāshiyat al-Sāwī 'alā Tafsīr al-Jalālayn*, vol. 3, p. 9.
4 Aziz Ahmad, *Islamic Modernism in India and Pakistan*, pp. 60–61. Ibn Hanbal does show extreme skepticism towards claims of consensus; 'Abdallāh b. Ahmad, *Masā'il al-imām Ahmad*, p. 439.
5 Aziz Ahmad, *Islamic Modernism in India and Pakistan*, p. 63.
6 Ibid., p. 59.
7 Daniel Brown, *Rethinking Tradition in Modern Islamic Thought*, pp. 38–39.
8 Ibid., p. 98.
9 Ibid., pp. 46–47.
10 Muhammad Tawfīq Sidqī, 'al-Islām huwa al-Qur'ān wahdahu,' pp. 516–517; idem, 'al-Islām huwa al-Qur'ān wahdahu: radd li-radd,' p. 912 (found in Ridā, ed., *al-Manār* 9, n. 7 and 12).
11 Sidqī, 'al-Islām huwa al-Qur'ān wahdahu: radd li-radd,' p. 910.
12 Sidqī, 'al-Islām huwa al-Qur'ān wahdahu,' p. 524.
13 Sidqī, 'al-Islām huwa al-Qur'ān wahdahu: radd li-radd,' p. 911.
14 Juynboll, *The Authenticity of the Tradition Literature: Discussions in Modern Egypt*, pp. 28–30; Brown, *Rethinking Tradition*, p. 89.
15 *Sunan Abī Dāwūd: kitāb al-at'ima, bāb fī al-dhubāb yaqa'u fī al-ta'ām*; *Sahīh al-Bukhārī: kitāb al-tibb, bāb idhā waqa'a al-dhubāb fī al-inā'*.
16 Juynboll, *Authenticity*, p. 141.
17 Brown, *Rethinking Tradition*, p. 47.
18 Muhammad Husayn Haykal, *Hayāt Muhammad*, p. 67.
19 Ibid., pp. 64–66.
20 Abū Rayya, *Adwā' 'alā al-sunna al-muhammadiyya*, pp. 350–351.
21 Ibid., pp. 252 ff., 278.
22 Juynboll, *Authenticity*, pp. 41–43; see *Sahīh al-Bukhārī: kitāb al-adhān, bāb fadl al-ta'dhīn*. Ibn Hajar notes that this should not be understood literally; Ibn Hajar, *Fath al-bārī*, vol. 2, pp. 108–109.
23 Abū Rayya, *Adwā'*, p. 233.
24 Ibid., p. 148.
25 Ibid., pp. 151 ff.
26 Ibid., p. 169.
27 Juynboll, *Authenticity*, pp. 88, 133.
28 Abū Rayya, *Adwā'*, p. 169.
29 Abū Rayya, 'Ka'b al-Ahbār huwa al-sahyūnī al-awwal,' *al-Risāla wa'l-riwāya* 665 (1946), pp. 360–62.
30 Abū Rayya, *Adwā'*, pp. 140 ff.

31 Juynboll, *Authenticity*, pp. 30–40.
32 Brown, *Rethinking Tradition*, p. 57. Al-Albānī also argues that the Prophet's speech is part of the revelation God promises to protect in the Quran; al-Albānī, *Adab al-zaffāf*, p. 168–9.
33 Wadud does not deal with hadiths in her discussion, while Kugle avoids discussing hadiths that command the death penalty for those 'committing the sin of the people of Lot' because they are not in the *Sahīhayn* (they are found in the Four *Sunan*). See Amina Wadud, *The Quran and Woman* (New York: Oxford University Press, 1999) and Scott Kugle, 'Sexuality, Diversity and Ethics in the Agenda of Progressive Muslims,' in *Progressive Muslims*, ed. Omid Safi (Oxford: Oneworld, 2003), pp. 220–221.
34 See http://www.yuksel.org/e/books/rtq.htm (last accessed 11/1/07).
35 Fatema Mernissi, *Women and Islam: An Historical and Theological Enquiry*, p. 77.
36 Ibid., p. 43.
37 *Sahīh Muslim*: *kitāb al-salāt, bāb al-iʿtirād bayn yaday al-musallī*; *Sahih al-Bukhārī*: *kitāb al-fitan, bāb* 18.
38 Mernissi, pp. 56 ff., 71–72.
39 Ibid., p. 60.
40 Ibid., p. 76.
41 Fazlur Rahman, *Islamic Methodology in History*, pp. 6, 33.
42 Ibid. p. 6, 12.
43 Ibid., pp. 15–16, 19.
44 Ibid., p. 56.
45 Ibid., pp. 72–73.
46 Ibid., p. 40.
47 Ibid., p. 72.
48 Javed Ahmad Ghamidi, *Islam: A Comprehensive Introduction*, pp. 61–69.
49 Ahmad, *Islamic Modernism*, p. 53.
50 Ibid., p. 31.
51 Ibid., p. 41.
52 Aziz Ahmad and G.E. von Grunebaum, eds., *Muslim Self-Statement in India and Pakistan 1857–1968*, p. 34; Ahmad, *Islamic Modernism*, pp. 43, 46.
53 Ahmad and von Grunebaum, p. 30.
54 Ahmad, *Islamic Modernism*, p. 54.
55 Christian W. Troll, *Sayyid Ahmad Khan: A Reinterpretation of Muslim Theology*, p. 113.
56 Ibid., pp. 134, 139–140.
57 Ahmad, *Islamic Modernism*, pp. 49 ff.
58 Troll, pp. 137–139.
59 Brown, *Rethinking Tradition*, p. 64.
60 Ahmad, *Islamic Modernism*, pp. 47–48.
61 Troll, p. 129.
62 Ibid., p. 141.
63 Ibid., p. 111.
64 Juynboll, *Authenticity*, p. 15.
65 Muhammad ʿAbduh, *The Theology of Unity*, pp. 155–156.
66 Ridā, *Al-Manār*, 21, no.1, p. 67.
67 Muhammad al-Ghazālī, *Turāthunā al-fikrī*, p. 176.

68 Ridā, *Al-Manār*, 27, no. 8, p. 616.
69 Ridā, *Al-Manār*, 27, no. 7, pp. 539 ff., 615; ibid., 28, no. 1, p. 67. See al-Jāhiz, *al-Hayawān*, ed. 'Abd al-Salām Hārūn (Beirut: Dār al-Jīl, 1996), vol. 4, pp. 202–3.
70 Ridā, *Al-Manār*, 27, no. 8, p. 615; ibid., p. 3:620.
71 Ridā, *Al-Manār*, 19, no. 2, p. 100.
72 Juynboll, *Authenticity,* pp. 145–146; 'Abd al-Majīd Mahmūd, *Abū Ja'far al-Tahāwī wa atharuhu fī al-hadīth*, p. 117.
73 Ridā, *Al-Manār*, 27, no. 8, p. 615; *Sahīh al-Bukhārī: kitāb bad' al-khalq, bāb sifat al-shams wa al-qamar*.
74 Juynboll, *Authenticity*, p. 143.
75 Mahmūd Shaltūt, *Al-Fatāwā*, p. 52.
76 Ibid., pp. 61 ff., 82.
77 Ibid., p. 79.
78 Al-Ghazālī, *Turāthunā al-fikrī*, p. 169.
79 Ibid., p. 181.
80 Al-Ghazālī, *al-Sunna al-nabawiyya*, p. 190.
81 Ibid., pp. 35–36.
82 Brown, *The Canonization of al-Bukhārī and Muslim*, pp. 309–310.
83 Al-Albānī, '*Tarjamat al-shaykh al-Albānī – Nash'at al-Shaykh fī Dimashq*.'
84 Al-Albānī, *Sahīh al-Targhīb wa al-tarhīb*, p. 1:60.
85 'Abdallāh al-Sa'd, '*Sharh al-Mūqiza* 3.'
86 Al-Albānī, '*Tafsīr* 1.'
87 Al-Albānī, '*Tafsīr* 2.'
88 'Abdallāh al-Sa'd, '*Sharh Kitāb al-Tamyīz* 3.'
89 Al-Albānī, *Tafsīr* 3.'
90 Tāhir al-Jazā'irī, *Tawjīh al-nazar ilā usūl al-athar*, vol. 1, pp. 331–332.
91 Al-Albānī, '*Silsilat as'ilat Abī Ishāq al-Huwaynī li'l-shaykh Muhammad Nāsir al-Dīn al-Albānī*.'
92 Al-Albānī, *Sahīh al-Targhīb wa al-tarhīb*, vol. 1, p. 4.
93 Al-Jazā'irī, *Tawjīh al-nazar ilā usūl al-athar*, p. 1:320.
94 'Abdallāh al-Ghumārī, *Tawjīh al-'ināya li-ta'rīf 'ilm al-hadīth riwāya wa dirāya*, p. 15.
95 Ahmad al-Ghumārī, *Dar' al-da'f 'an hadīth man 'ashiqa fa-'aff*, p. 121.
96 'Abdallāh al-Ghumārī, *Itqān al-san'a fī tahqīq ma'nā al-bid'a*, p. 41; Ahmad al-Ghumārī, *Ju'nat al-attār*, vol. 2, p. 154.
97 Al-Albānī, *Mukhtasar Sahīh al-Bukhārī*, vol. 2, pp. 8–9.
98 Al-Kawtharī, *Maqālāt*, p. 225.
99 Al-Ghazālī, *al-Sunna al-nabawiyya*, pp. 14–15.
100 '*Mā kāna 'alā khilāf al-qiyās fa-'alayhi ghayruhu lā yuqās*,' al-Albānī, '*al-Zawāj*.'
101 'Alī Jum'a, *al-Bayān li-mā yushghalu bihi al-adhhān*, pp. 99 ff.
102 Al-Ghazālī, *Turāthunā al-fikrī*, p. 153. Jum'a, *al-Bayān*, pp. 103–4.
103 Al-Ghazālī, *al-Sunna al-nabawiyya*, p. 19.
104 Al-Kawtharī, *Maqālāt*, p. 55.
105 Al-Ghazālī, *al-Sunna al-nabawiyya*, p. 32.
106 Ibid., pp. 19–20.
107 *Sahīh al-Bukhārī: kitāb al-jihād, bāb* 149.

108 Jumʿa, *al-Bayān*, pp. 78–81.
109 J. Brown, 'The Rules of *Matn* Criticism: There are No Rules,' pp. 389–91.
110 Al-Shāfiʿī, *al-Risāla*, p. 177.
111 Al-Khatīb, *Tārīkh Baghdād*, vol. 11, pp. 197–198.
112 Ibn Qutayba, *Ta'wīl mukhtalif al-hadīth*, p. 228.

11

CONCLUSION

We must possess a grasp of the hadith tradition and its many functions in order to understand the past and present of the Islamic world. This grasp is indispensable for comprehending Muslim debates over the future as well. When we look behind the headlines today, we see that much of the time hadiths are at the vortex of the most salient debates in Islamic thought. On controversial issues from jihad and martyrdom to women's rights under Islamic law, hadiths always provide key and often determinative evidence. As we have seen, even those Muslims who reject heeding hadiths at all in such debates face the challenge of justifying this position with evidence from the classical hadith tradition.

Even if we understand the importance of hadiths in parsing complex problematics such as 'Islam and the West' or 'Islam and Women,' we must always keep history in mind. History gave birth to the complexities of the present and holds the keys to unraveling them. Debates over the necessity of hadiths, their place in articulating Islamic law and dogma, and how Muslims should know true claims about revelation from the false have been of perennial importance throughout Islamic history.

Let us retrace some of the main thematic steps in the reasoning of Muslim scholars throughout Islamic history, specifically those regarding hadiths. If the Quran is God's manifest revelation to mankind, do we need any other source for understanding His religion? If not, then how do we know how to perform (or, perhaps, how do we justify the fact that we perform) our five daily prayers and fast during Ramadan? – these practices are not explained in the holy book. If we *do* need another source, then does our sense of reason alone suffice?

The answer seems to be 'no,' as reason on its own cannot provide the basis or specifics for Muslim prayer and fasting, which can only be known through some form of tradition handed down from Muhammad and the early Muslim community. If we must rely to some extent on this tradition, then how do we balance it with the Quran and reason? What happens when revelation, reason, and tradition seem to conflict? Does tradition trump reason and our *prima facie* understanding of the Quran, or vice versa? If we are to subordinate some elements of our rational thought and understanding of the Quran to tradition, how do we know when tradition is authentic or inauthentic? How is tradition transmitted or preserved? If tradition overrules the Quran and reason, then can the principles of the Quran or reason be used to authenticate tradition? These are some of the questions that have driven Islamic intellectual history in its various streams and embodiments.

In this book, we have proposed thinking about hadiths in terms of their two essential functions in Islamic civilization. First, the hadith as a text (*matn*) – authoritative statements by the Prophet that shape Islamic law, dogma, and worldview. Second, the hadith as a chain of transmission (*isnād*) – a medium of connection to the Prophet and a paradigm of constructing a relationship between the Muslim present and the Muslim past. Interestingly, in both these cases, the functions of hadiths and the questions surrounding them are common to faith traditions other than Islam.

In an *interpretive* tradition, namely one in which meaning is developed by turning (back) towards and interpreting an authoritative source such as a revealed text or constitution, the interpreter of the source is effectively more powerful than the source itself. Using the analogy of a king or ruler, the king's interpreter is more powerful than the king himself, since the interpreter controls and shapes the king's message. Similarly, it is the lens through which we view an object that controls our perception of that object, not the object itself.

Early in Islamic history, both Sunni and Shiite Muslims decided that the Quran was a source that had to be interpreted through specific lenses. It could not speak on its own ('Quran only' advocates today have challenged this). The Prophet was the first interpreter, and his Sunna was what the Muslim scholar 'Alī Jum'a has called 'an infallible application of the Book of God.'[1] But who, in turn, would interpret the Prophet's Sunna? Who would provide the second interpretive layer that would translate the Sunna and apply it among the coming Muslim generations in new Muslim lands? Sunnis chose the Muslim community as a whole, represented by the ulema, as the authoritative interpreter, while Shiite Muslims selected the family of the Prophet and the scholars who followed in the footsteps of the imams.

But how should the Sunna be communicated and preserved? Some Sunnis believed that the Sunna was preserved mainly in the form of communal practice (like the Mālikī school of law), others in the form of the methods of problem-solving inherited from the Prophet through his Companions and their Successors (like the Partisans of Reason). The Quran is a written text, but these approaches treated the Sunna as a living and unwritten entity. Ultimately, Sunnis accepted that the Sunna must take a written form as well, that of hadiths. Although Sunni scholars continue to debate the proper relationship between practice, interpretive method, and the text of hadiths to this day, Muslim scholars generally recognize that hadiths are a powerful, even if not the ultimate, vehicle for the Sunna.

This process is common to Islam, Judaism, and Christianity. In all these traditions, a written scripture is interpreted through an oral lens that is eventually also consigned to written form. Classical rabbinic Judaism is based on the idea that Moses received two Torahs on Mount Sinai, the written revelation of the scriptures, designated collectively as the Written Torah, and an oral Torah, which transmitted the authoritative interpretations of these books. This oral tradition was inherited from Moses by subsequent leaders of the Jewish people through the biblical period and on through the time of the rabbis. Eventually, in the early third century CE it was set down in written form in the Mishna.

Among Christians, a Greek translation of the Old Testament served as the community's revealed scripture during the first two centuries CE. Christians read and understood the significance of the Old Testament through the orally transmitted teachings of Jesus and the elucidations of the Christian church fathers – the stories of the Old Testament and pronouncements of Hebrew prophets like Isaiah were interpreted as referring allegorically or literally to Christ. At the same time as the Jews were setting down their oral Torah in written form, the Christians adopted as their written interpretive lens a selection of written accounts of Jesus' life and mission in the form of the New Testament Gospels.[2]

In Islam more than in the other Abrahamic traditions, however, there arose a particular interpretive problem. From the time of the Prophet and the revelation of the Quran itself, Muslims have been self-consciously obsessed with *textual authenticity*. The Quran explains that previous communities had corrupted or altered the revealed books of God. Muslim scholars therefore proclaimed an enduring devotion to assuring the authenticity of their religion's teachings and its textual sources. This is most obvious in the text of the Quran itself. From the time of Muhammad's Companions, Muslim scholars have obsessively safeguarded the textual integrity of the Quran, meticulously recording any variations in wording or pronunciation.

The hadith corpus, however, was not set down in writing at such an early date, so the authenticity of this interpretive lens quickly became a major matter of contention. Early Sunni Muslims developed their methods of *isnād* criticism in an effort to assure the textual authenticity of the Sunna without relying on the same flawed rational faculties that had led earlier nations astray. However, the tension between surrendering to the *isnād* and its power to authenticate versus the role of reason as a criterion for evaluating truth remains unresolved among Muslim scholars.

When Sunni legal theory matured fully in the tenth and eleventh centuries CE, scholars grappled with a more philosophical problem: how can you interpret a source whose historical reliability is certain (the Quran) through a lens of questionable historical reliability (hadiths)? Classical Sunni legal theorists employed the concepts of consensus (*ijmā*ʿ) and the certainty produced by massive transmission (*tawātur*) to reach a solution to this problem, but it continues to drive the debate between Islamic modernists and traditionalists today.

Interestingly, there are remarkable similarities between the Islamic tradition of hadith criticism and a genre of books in Chinese Zen Buddhism known as *Ching Lu*, which flourished among Chinese Buddhist scholars in the period just before and during the Tang dynasty (618–907 CE). *Ching Lu* books were catalogs devoted to distinguishing between writings that were thought to be authentic records of the Buddha's teachings as transmitted to China from India and books that were written by Chinese scholars and thus did not originate in the Buddhist homeland of India. With an attitude very similar to Muslim hadith critics, the authors of *Ching Lu* books saw themselves as sorting the 'rubies from pebbles' in a struggle to preserve the authentic teachings of the Buddha from the accretions of Chinese philosophy and superstition. Unlike Muslim hadith critics, however, *Ching Lu* authors depended primarily on searching for anomalous contents in the books they critiqued – teachings that resembled Chinese lore, for example, were red flags for forgery. Although identifying the authors or translators of books of Buddhist teachings served as part of the *Ching Lu* critical arsenal, the absence of an elaborate *isnād* tradition and the many anonymously written texts made such transmission criticism much less common than in the Islamic hadith tradition.[3]

The second function of hadiths, that of a medium of connection to the Prophet and a framework for imagining historical relationships through the *isnād*, is only partially concerned with authenticity. It is more than anything the foundation of a religious worldview. Although the *isnād* was developed as a tool for authenticating hadiths, it reflected and eventually became the embodiment of a more general conception of the transmission of authority. The *isnād* was the key to distinguishing between reliable and unreliable hadiths for Muslim scholars, but it was also a language for expressing connections with teachers, saints, and the Prophet himself.

As a criterion for textual reliability, the strength and historical accuracy of an *isnād* was essential. As a medium for connection, the *isnād* took on a meaning far beyond and indeed in spite of its historicity. Even if only as a formality, possessing some sort of *isnād* back to the Prophet was the essential mark of a Muslim scholar. Short *isnād*s for hadiths became a means of close connection to the Prophet's blessings. Bizarre *isnād*s were collected like rare coins – it was the rarity and supposed shortness of an *isnād* that made it valuable, not the authenticity of the hadith it communicated. In Sufism, the *isnād* was the chain of transmission for the Prophet's blessings (*baraka*), ethical instruction, and esoteric knowledge. The cloak (*khirqa*) served as the outward manifestation of this chain, literally a means of investiture into the socially expansive class of Sufi devotees.

Even in its abstract sense of a connection to the first and most authoritative interpreter of God's revelation, the Prophet, however, the *isnād* had practical groundings. Arabic texts, whether individual hadiths or entire treatises, were written in a script that left many vowels unwritten and that could easily be misread. Reading a book or a hadith properly thus required the presence of a teacher who had heard that text read aloud. Transmission from teacher to student, however, involved more than just this practical utility. Muslim scholars believe that this living relationship passed on the light of sacred learning and the 'living word of knowledge,' as Plato (d. 347 BCE) called it, from one generation to the next.[4] Transmission creates and passes on authority.

Muslims have often touted this connective function of the *isnād* as unique to Islamic thought. Indeed, neither Christianity nor Judaism developed a tradition as intricate or ubiquitous as the *isnād*. But the concept of transmission creating and controlling interpretive authority is also a common theme in other traditions.[5] When the Christian philosopher and maverick theologian Peter Abelard (d. 1142 CE) dared to offer a class in which he provided his own commentary on biblical scripture, students were aghast. To innovate one's own commentary on the scriptures without having the collective commentaries of generations of church scholars painstakingly explained by a teacher, one's link to this interpretive chain, was unthinkable.[6] In medieval Judaism the concept of a chain of transmission that passed on an understanding of the revealed scriptures and bequeathed authority in the process was known as 'the chain of tradition (*shalshelet hakabbalah*).'[7]

The commonalities that the Islamic hadith tradition shares with other faith traditions remind us of the supreme importance of context at the close of this study. The grand tradition of Muslim hadith criticism emphasizes the paramount place of *authenticity* in the Islamic religious worldview. When the great hadith scholar al-Khatīb al-Baghdādī died in 1071 CE, crowds carrying his casket through the streets of Baghdad shouted 'Make way! Make way for him who fended off lies from the Messenger of God!'[8]

But discussing the words attributed to Muhammad, debating their authenticity and potential meaning, has never been a discourse that has taken place in objective or neutral isolation. Always there are great consequences. Discussions of the proper place of the Prophet's Sunna began among Muslims in the shadow of unspoken assumptions about the true nature of God's message to Muhammad. Ever looming over these debates have been weighty implications for how that religion would take shape on earth. If we cannot trust a body of hadiths, Muslims have asked, or if we lose the hadith corpus to modern historical criticism, how do we know God's will and sacred law? As al-Shāfiʿī asked, how do we know how to pray?[9] Torn between a commitment to critical rigor and the duty to provide answers for the masses, Muslim hadith critics have always had to balance the scholarly integrity of rigorous historians with the needs and expectations of the Muslim community as a whole.

In no matter have consequences been more intimidating than in that of protecting the purity of the Prophet's message from alien influences. The study and criticism of hadiths among Muslims began as a means to protect the Muslim community from competing claims to truth, such as Greek philosophy, Christian thought, or purely rational approaches to law and worship. The Partisans of Hadith, who later formed the core of Sunni Islam, and the *isnād* itself arose as a conservative reaction to fears of the foreign influence that other Near Eastern faiths and philosophies might have upon the still maturing Muslim community. Later, debates over the *isnād*s of Sufism centered on doubts over and defenses of the Islamic authenticity of Sufi beliefs and practices. Concerns over the influence of Greek philosophy or Christianity have faded into history. But today questioning whether or not Muslims can trust the historical reliability of hadiths conjures the twin specters of Western control over defining Islam and Muslims' anxieties about how to reconcile their faith with the hegemonic power of Western science. Always there are consequences for Muslims' sense of Islamic authenticity.

Difficult as it has been to achieve in reality, Muslim scholars have always clung to the ideal of freeing the historical criticism of words attributed to Muhammad from the grasp of consequence and the hopes and multiform fears that always surround us. Yet the modern world is perilous and unrelenting in its temptations and terrors. After our discussion of Muslim and Western perspectives on the hadith tradition and Islamic history, we are left with a great quandary for both Muslim and non-Muslim scholars: what forces should determine our interactions with the past? Plato's Socratic voice, a voice long heeded in Islamic civilization as intently as it has been in the West, echoes across the aeons: 'I have heard a report of the ancients, whether it is true or not only they know; although if we had found the truth ourselves, do you think that we should care much about the opinions of men?'[10]

Wa Allāhu aʿlam (And God knows best).

ENDNOTES

1 ʿAlī Jumʿa, personal communication.

2 James A. Sanders, *Canon and Community*, p. 14.

3 Kyoko Tokuno, 'The Evaluation of Indigenous Scriptures in Chinese Buddhist Bibliographical Catalogues,' pp. 31–59.
4 Plato, *Phaedrus*, p. 276a.
5 Al-Nawawī, *Sharh Sahīh Muslim*, vol. 1, p. 119.
6 Peter Abelard, 'Historia Calimatatum,' p. 63.
7 See *Pirkei Avot*, 1.1; Martin Jaffe, *Torah in the Mouth* (Oxford University Press, 2001), pp. 30, 56–61.
8 Al-Dhahabī, *Tadhkirat al-huffāz*, vol. 3, p. 226.
9 Al-Shāfi'ī, *al-Risāla*, p. 177.
10 Plato, *Phaedrus*, p. 274c.

GLOSSARY

'Adl: literally, 'justice' or 'just'; half of the qualification for being a reliable hadith transmitter (along with *dabt*). In the early period of hadith criticism, being *'adl* simply meant generally being an honest and truthful person. In the later period of hadith criticism, *'adl* meant being 'Muslim, of age, of sound mind, free of the paths of sin and flaws in honor.' This later definition included not being an extremist or proselytizing member of a non-Sunni group.

Āḥād: literally 'individuals'; a category of hadiths transmitted by individuals as opposed to being massively transmitted (*mutawātir*). *Āḥād* hadiths were any hadiths that did not meet the requirements for massive transmission (*tawātur*). This categorization was introduced into Muslim hadith scholarship in the tenth and eleventh centuries CE by legal theorists.

Ahl-e Quran: a twentieth-century Muslim school of thought particularly prominent in India and later Pakistan, which advocated the rejection of hadiths and a reliance on the Quran alone (see pp. 280–286).

Akhbār: 'reports'; transmitted stories about historical events. *Akhbār* as a category includes hadiths, but *akhbār* often do not involve the life of the Prophet or feature *isnād*s. Muslim scholars such as Ibn Ishāq (d. 150/767) and al-Madā'inī (d. 228/843), who collected and compiled *akhbār* (*Akhbāriyūn*), are closer to 'historians' than 'hadith scholars.'

'Ālī: 'elevated'; a transmission of a hadith with a relatively short *isnād* (see pp. 48–51).

Amālī: hadith dictation sessions, often occurring in major mosques, in which a scholar read out a selection of hadiths with full *isnāds* back to the Prophet before an audience.

Ansāb: 'genealogies'; an early genre of Arab-Islamic historical writing that traced and recorded the genealogies of tribes along with stories and historical information about individuals.

Ash'arī: one of the three main schools of Sunni theology, named after Abū al-Hasan al-Ash'arī (d. 324/935–6), which began as a defense of Sunni literalist theology using rationalist methods but later incorporated many rationalist beliefs into Sunni Islam as well.

Baraka: 'blessings'; the spiritual benefit that one receives from proximity to God, the Prophet, or pious individuals.

Bid'a: literally 'innovation'; although it is generally understood as heretical innovation in religious matters.

Companions (Arabic, **Sahāba**): the founding generation of Muslims who knew and lived with the Prophet. In Sunni Islam, anyone who saw the Prophet and died as a Muslim is considered a Companion (see pp. 89–91).

Dabt: literally 'accuracy'; or the requirement that a hadith transmitter generally be corroborated in his or her transmissions. Along with *'adāla* (see *'adl*), *dabt* was one of the two components necessary to make a transmitter 'reliable (*thiqa*)' – although *dabt* was the more important of the two.

Da'īf: 'weak'; a complex term that generally denoted an unreliable hadith (see pp. 102–106).

Gharīb: 'strange'; denoting a hadith with limited corroboration but not necessarily meaning that it contradicted more reliable hadiths or was unreliable (see p. 98). In the later period of hadith criticism it was used to describe a hadith that was *sahīh* but was only known through one chain of transmission.

Hasan: 'fair'; a term describing a hadith that, while not meeting the *isnād* requirements to be *sahīh*, either did not have flaws serious enough to be considered weak or enjoyed some form of bolstering corroboration. *Hasan* hadiths were admissible as proofs in law but not theology (see p. 105).

Idrāj: the phenomenon of the words of a hadith transmitter being mistaken for part of the hadith itself (see *mudraj*).

Ihsān: the highest level of faith for Muslims, namely acting as if you could physically sense God watching over you (see p. 198).

Ijāza: the permission to transmit a hadith or book. *Ijāza*s could take three forms: 1) *ijāzat al-riwāya* (the permission of transmission), which simply gave a student the right to transmit a hadith from a scholar; 2) *ijāzat al-dirāya* (the permission of knowledge), which meant that a teacher had acknowledged that a student had mastered the contents of a book and was thus qualified to teach it to others; 3) *ijāzat al-tazkiya* (the permission of purification), which meant that a student had spent sufficient time around a scholar to absorb that scholar's ethics and good behavior, with that chain of learning going back to the Prophet (see pp. 44–46).

Ijtihād: independent interpretation; the action of a scholar returning to the Quran, Sunna, and interpretive methods of Muslim scholars to revaluate a legal ruling or find an answer to an unanswered question.

'Ilal: plural of *'illa*, or 'flaw'; flaws in the *isnād* of a hadith that only become evident when that *isnād* is compared with other chains of transmission for that hadith (see pp. 98–99).

Imam: in Sunni Islam, either the person leading the prayer or an exceptionally prominent scholar; in Shiite Islam, one of the descendants of the Prophet who inherited his interpretive authority.

Isnād: the chain of transmission of a hadith.

Isrā'īliyyāt: stories from Jewish lore, usually about biblical prophets, included in the Islamic tradition.

Jinn: creatures mentioned in the Quran and hadiths who are composed of fire or hot wind and live unseen alongside human beings.

Kashf: 'unveiling'; direct inspiration from God granted to a pious Muslim (see pp. 114–115).

Khirqa: the shawl or cloak with which a Sufi initiate was invested when joining a Sufi order or receiving the blessings of a Sufi saint (see pp. 202–204).

Late Sunni Tradition: the version of Sunni orthodoxy that emerged in the 1300s and has characterized Islamic civilization in the Middle East and South Asia until the modern period. It consists of an institutional combination of the four Sunni schools of law, the Ash'arī or Māturīdī schools of speculative theology, and Sufi brotherhoods.

Madhhab: a Muslim school of law.

Maghāzī: literally 'campaigns'; early collections of reports about the Prophet's battles and the early Muslim conquests.

Mahdī: 'the guided one'; an apocalyptical figure descended from the Prophet whom both Sunnis and Shiites believe will return at the end of time to bring justice to the earth.

Mashhūr: in the early period of hadith criticism, *mashhūr* meant a hadith that was well known, widely corroborated, and held to be an authentic representation of the Prophet's Sunna. With the influence of legal theorists in the tenth and eleventh centuries, it took on the meaning of a hadith that, while not reaching the technical requirements for the certainty provided by massive transmission (*tawātur*), had been verified by communal consensus and was thus reliable enough to inform dogma and restrict the meaning of Quranic verses.

Matn: the text of a hadith.

Mudraj: adjective describing a hadith in which *idrāj* (see above) has occurred.

Mu'jam: a hadith collection in which a scholar organized hadiths around a certain theme.

Munkar: 'unacceptable' or merely 'unfamiliar'; in the early period of hadith criticism it meant a hadith that was either uncorroborated or broke with other similar narrations either in its *isnād* or its meaning. In the later period, it came to mean a hadith that had only one chain of transmission without that *isnād* being strong enough to justify accepting it.

Munqati': 'broken'; an *isnād* in which some transmitter, usually not in the early part of the *isnād*, cites a source whom he never actually met.

Mursal: literally 'cast'; in the early period of hadith criticism it meant a hadith in which a transmitter cited someone or the Prophet without actually having met him. The term later came to mean a hadith in which a Successor quotes the Prophet without naming the intermediating Companion (see pp. 94–95).

Mustakhraj: a genre of hadith collections in which a scholar used his own hadith corpus to replicate an existing hadith collection (see pp. 52–54).

Mutāba'a: 'parallelism'; a narration that corroborated that a certain person had heard a hadith from a certain teacher by serving as evidence that a different student had heard the same hadith from that teacher (see pp. 95–98).

Mutawātir: 'massively transmitted'; a term imported into hadith criticism from legal theory to describe a hadith that is so widely transmitted that there can be no possibility of it being forged (see p. 107).

Mu'tazila: a school of Muslim rationalists that died out in Sunni Islam in the fourteenth century CE but survived in Imami and Zaydi Shiism.

Muttasil: 'contiguous'; describing an *isnād* whose components all met and studied with one another and thus includes no breaks.

Naskh: the abrogation of Quranic verses either by other verses or the Sunna. Also, it can be the abrogation of one hadith by another hadith.

Nāzil: a relatively long *isnād* for a hadith; the opposite of *'ālī*.

Qudsī: adjective for hadiths in which the Prophet quotes God speaking (see p. 63–64).

Sahīh: 'sound' or 'authentic'; the highest level of strength for an *isnād* (see pp. 104–107).

Salafī: a complex and multifaceted term that came into use in the early twentieth century to describe the return to the methods and beliefs of the *Salaf*, 'the Righteous Forebears,' usually understood to mean the first three generations of Muslims.

Sariqat al-hadīth: 'stealing a hadith,' or fitting an existing hadith with a new *isnād*.

Shādhdh: 'anomalous'; although influential hadith critics like al-Hākim al-Naysābūrī (d. 405/1014) used the term *shādhdh* to mean a hadith that had only one narration, al-Shāfi'ī (d. 204/820) and the vast majority of scholars used it to mean a hadith that contradicted more reliable narrations or the Quran.

Shāhid: a 'witness' narration or attestation, usually meaning a hadith narrated from a totally different *isnād* but containing the same meaning as the hadith in question and thus bolstering its reliability.

Sharh: a commentary that a scholar composes about an existing book, such as a hadith collection or book of law.

Sīra: literally 'biography'; generally referring to the biography of the Prophet. *Sīra* is distinct from hadith collections because it follows a chronological or narrative structure and often includes material without complete *isnād*s.

Successors: the generation of Muslims who followed and learned from the Companions.

Tadlīs: obfuscation in transmission; either intentionally or unintentionally narrating a hadith in a manner that obscures or omits transmitters in the *isnād*.

Tafsīr: Quranic exegesis; during the first two centuries Hijrī *tafsīr* mainly consisted of glosses, or explanations of Quranic words. It soon developed into a genre of more expansive Quranic commentary on the linguistic contents, historical circumstances and meanings of verses.

Takhrīj: 'indexing'; finding all the appearances of a hadith in various books and hadith collections.

Taqlīd: 'imitation'; a term with both positive and pejorative connotations. Supporters of *taqlīd* define it as a non-scholar or non-specialist following the opinion of a qualified scholar. Those who reject *taqlīd*, especially adherents of the Salafī tradition, would translate it as 'blind imitation,' namely following scholars without any concern for proof.

Taraf*/*Atrāf: the first part of the text of a hadith or its most well-known part.

Ulema: the Arabic word for Muslim scholars.

Sunna: the normative precedent of the Prophet. In the early Islamic period, Sunna meant the normative precedent of the early Islamic community (namely the Companions and the Successors) as a whole.

Zawā'id: a genre of hadith books that listed all the hadiths found in books outside the hadith canon as well as any narrations of hadiths from the canonical collections found in the non-canonical works.

BIBLIOGRAPHY

PRIMARY SOURCES

'Abdallāh b. Ahmad b. Hanbal. *Kitāb al-sunna*, ed. Muhammad al-Qahtānī. Dammam, Dār Ibn al-Qayyim, 1986

—— *Masā'il al-imām Ahmad Ibn Hanbal riwāyat ibnihi*, ed. Zuhayr al-Shāwīsh. Beirut, al-Maktab al-Islāmī, 1981

'Abduh, Muhammad. *The Theology of Unity*, trans. Ishaq Musa'ad and Kenneth Cragg. London, George Allen & Unwin, 1966

Abelard, Peter. 'Historia Calimatatum,' in *The Letters of Abelard and Heloise*. Trans. Betty Radice. London, Penguin Books, 1974

Abū Ghudda, 'Abd al-Fattāh (ed.). *Arba' rasā'il fī 'ulūm al-hadīth*, 6th ed. Beirut, Maktab al-Matbū'āt al-Islāmiyya, 1999

Abū Khaythama Zuhayr b. Harb. *Kitāb al-'ilm*, ed. Muhammad Nāsir al-Dīn al-Albānī. Beirut, al-Maktab al-Islāmī, 1983

Abū Rayya, Mahmūd. *Adwā' 'alā al-sunna al-muhammadiyya*. Cairo, Dār al-Ta'līf, 1958

Acton, John Lord, *A Lecture on the Study of History*. London, MacMillan & Co., 1905

Al-Ahdal, 'Abd al-Rahmān b. Sulaymān. *Al-Nafas al-yamānī*. Sanaa, Markaz al-Dirāsāt wa al-Abhāth al-Yamaniyya, 1979

Al-'Ajlūnī, Ismā'īl b. Ahmad. *Kashf al-khafā'*, ed. Ahmad al-Qalāsh. Cairo, Dār al-Turāth, [n.d.]

Al-'Alā'ī, Salāh al-Dīn. *Jāmi' al-tahsīl fī ahkām al-marāsīl*, ed. Hamdī 'Abd al-Majīd. Beirut, 'Ālam al-Kutub, 2005

Al-Albānī, Muhammad Nāsir al-Dīn. *Mukhtasar Sahīh al-Bukhārī*. Riyadh, Maktabat al-Ma'ārif, 2002

—— *Adab al-zaffāf*. Beirut, al-Maktab al-Islāmī, 1989

—— *Da'īf Sunan Ibn Mājah*. Riyadh, Maktabat al-Ma'ārif, 1998

—— *Sahīh al-Jāmi' al-saghīr*, ed. Zuhayr al-Shāwīsh. 3rd ed. Beirut, al-Maktab al-Islāmī, 1988

—— *Sahīh al-Targhīb wa al-tarhīb*. Riyadh, Maktabat al-Ma'ārif, 2000

—— *Silsilat al-ahādīth al-da'īfa wa al-mawdū'a*, 2nd ed. Riyadh, Maktabat al-Ma'ārif, 2000

—— *Silsilat al-ahādīth al-sahīha*, new ed. Riyadh, Maktabat al-Ma'ārif, 1995

—— '*Silsilat as'ilat Abī Ishāq al-Huwaynī li'l-shaykh Muhammad Nāsir al-Dīn al-Albānī*,' lecture from www.islamway.com, last accessed 6/3/2004

—— '*Tafsīr*,' lecture from www.islamway.com, last accessed 6/3/2004

—— '*Tarjamat al-shaykh al-Albānī – Nash'at al-Shaykh fī Dimashq*,' lecture from www.islamway.com, last accessed 6/3/2004

—— '*al-Zawāj*,' lecture from www.islamway.com, last accessed 6/3/2004

Al-Ash'arī, Abū al-Hasan. *Maqālāt al-islāmiyyīn,* ed. Helmut Ritter. Istanbul, Dar al-Funūn, [1928]

Al-'Askarī, Abū Hilāl. *Kitab al-awā'il*, ed. Walīd Qassāb. Riyadh, Dār al-'Ulūm, 1981

Al-Baghawī, al-Husayn b. Mas'ūd. *Masābīh al-sunna*. Beirut, Dār al-Qalam, [197–]

Al-Barbahārī, Abū Muhammad. *Sharh al-sunna*, ed. Khālid al-Raddādī. Beirut, Dār al-Sumay'ī, 2000

Al-Bayjūrī, Burhān al-Dīn Ibrāhīm. *Hāshiyat al-imām al-Bayjūrī 'alā Jawharat al-tawhīd*, ed. 'Alī Jum'a. Cairo, Dār al-Salām, 2006

Al-Buhūtī, Mansūr. *Al-Rawd al-murbi'*, ed. Bashīr Muhammad 'Uyūn. Damascus, Maktabat Dār al-Bayān, 1999

Al-Bukhārī, Muhammad b. Ismā'īl. *Kitāb al-du'afā' al-saghīr*, ed. Muhammad Zāyid. Beirut, Dār al-Ma'rifa, 1986

—— *Sahīh al-Bukhārī*. Cited by chapter, subchapter system

—— *Al-Tārīkh al-awsat*, ed. Muhammad al-Luhaydān. Riyadh, Dār al-Sumay'ī, 1998

Cicero, Marcus. *The Nature of the Gods* (*De Natura Deorum*), trans. Horace McGregor. New York, Penguin, 1967

Al-Dārimī, 'Abdallāh b. 'Abd al-Rahmān. *Al-Sunan*. Cited according to chapter, subchapter system

Al-Dhahabī, Shams al-Dīn. *Mīzān al-i'tidāl fī naqd al-rijāl*, ed. 'Alī Muhammad al-Bijāwī. [Beirut], Dār Ihyā' al-Kutub al-'Arabiyya, n.d. Reprint of the Cairo edition published by 'Īsā al-Bābī al-Halabī, 1963–4

—— *Siyar a'lām al-nubalā'*, ed. Shu'ayb al-Arnā'ūt et al. Beirut, Mu'assasat al-Risāla, 1992–1998

—— *Tadhkirat al-huffāz*, ed. Zakariyyā 'Umayrāt. Beirut, Dār al-Kutub al-'Ilmiyya, 1998

Al-Dimashqī, Abū Zur'a. *Tārīkh Abī Zur'a al-Dimashqī*, ed. Khālid Mansūr. Beirut, Dār al-Kutub al-'Ilmiyya, 1996

Al-Fadlī, 'Abd al-Hādī and al-Shahīd al-Thānī. *Introduction to Hadīth, including Dirāyat al-Hadīth*, trans. Nazmina Virjee. London, Islamic College for Advanced Studies, 2002

Al-Fārisī, 'Abd al-Ghāfir. *Tārīkh Naysābūr*, ed. Muhammad Kāzim al-Hamūdī. Qum, Jamā'at al-Mudarrisīn, 1983

Al-Ghazālī, Abū Hāmid. *Ihyā' 'ulūm al-dīn*, ed. Muhammad Wahbī Sulaymān and Usāma 'Ammūra, 5 vols. Damascus, Dār al-Fikr, 2006

—— *Al-Iqtisād fī al-i'tiqād*. Cairo, Mustafā al-Bābī al-Halabī, n.d.

—— *Al-Mankhūl min ta'līqāt al-usūl*, ed. Muhammad Hasan Hītū. [Damascus], n.p., [1970]

Al-Ghazālī, Muhammad. *Al-Sunna al-nabawiyya bayn ahl al-fiqh wa ahl al-hadīth*, 13th ed. Cairo, Dār al-Shurūq, 2005

—— *Turāthunā al-fikrī*, 8th ed. Cairo, Dār al-Shurūq, 2003

Al-Ghumārī, 'Abdallāh. *Itqān al-san'a fī tahqīq ma'nā al-bid'a*, ed. 'Abdallāh al-Minshāwī. Cairo, Maktabat al-Qāhira, 2005

—— *Al-Khawātir al-dīniyya*. Cairo, Maktabat al-Qāhira, 2004

——*Tawjīh al-'ināya li-ta'rīf 'ilm al-hadīth riwāya wa dirāya*, ed. Safwat Jawda Ahmad. Cairo, Maktabat al-Qāhira, 2002

Al-Ghumārī, Ahmad. *Al-Burhān al-jalī fī tahqīq intisāb al-sūfiyya ilā 'Alī*, ed. Ahmad Mursī. Cairo, Maktabat al-Qāhira, [n.d.]

—— *Dar' al-da'f 'an hadīth man 'ashiqa fa-'aff*, ed. 'Iyād al-Ghawj. Cairo, Dār al-Imām al-Tirmidhī, 1996

—— *Ibrāz al-wahm al-maknūn min kalām Ibn Khaldūn*. Damascus, Maktabat al-Taraqqī, 1928

—— *Ju'nat al-attār fī taraf al-fawā'id wa nawādir al-akhbār* (n.p., n.d.)

—— *Al-Mudāwī li-'ilal al-Jāmi' al-saghīr wa sharhayy al-Munāwī*. Egypt, Dār al-Kutub, 1996

Gibbon, Edward. *The Decline and Fall of the Roman Empire*. New York, The Modern Library, n.d.

Hammām b. Munabbih. *Sahīfat Hammām b. Munabbih*, ed. Rif'at Fawzī 'Abd al-Muttalib. Cairo, Maktabat al-Khānjī, 1985

Al-Hārūnī, Ahmad b. al-Husayn. *Al-Amālī al-sughrā*, ed. 'Abd al-Salām al-Wajīh. Sa'da, Yemen, Dār al-Turāth al-Islāmī, 1993

Haykal, Muhammad Husayn. *Hayāt Muhammad*, 10th ed. Cairo, Dār al-Ma'ārif, 1969

Herodotus. *The Histories*, trans. Aubrey De Sélincourt. London, Penguin Books, 1996

Hujvīrī, 'Alī. *Kashf al-mahjūb*. Tehran, Ketābkhāne-ye Tūrī, 1979

Al-Humaydī, Abdallāh b. al-Zubayr. *Al-Musnad*, ed. Habīb al-Rahmān al-A'zamī. Karachi, al-Majlis al-'Ilmī, 1963

Ibn 'Abd al-Barr, Yūsuf. *Jāmi' bayān al-'ilm wa fadlihi*, ed. 'Abd al-Rahmān Muhammad 'Uthmān. Medina, al-Maktaba al-Salafiyya, [1968]

—— *Kitāb al-Tamhīd*, ed. Mustafā al-'Alawī and Muhammad al-Bakrī. [Rabat], Wizārat 'Umūm al-Awqāf, 1982

Ibn Abī al-ʿIzz al-Hanafī, Muhammad. *Sharh al-ʿAqīda al-Tahāwiyya*, ed. Muhammad Nāsir al-Dīn al-Albānī. Amman, al-Dār al-Islāmī, 1998

Ibn Abī Yaʿlā al-Hanbalī. *Tabaqāt al-hanābila*, ed. ʿAlī Muhammad ʿUmar. Cairo, Maktabat al-Thaqāfa al-Dīniyya, 1998

Ibn ʿAdī, ʿAbdallāh. *Al-Kāmil fī duʿafāʾ al-rijāl*. Beirut, Dār al-Fikr, 1985

Ibn ʿAqīl, Muhammad. *Al-ʿAtb al-jamīl ʿalā ahl al-jarh wa al-taʿdīl*, ed. Hasan al-Saqqāf. Amman, Dār al-Imām al-Nawawī, 2004

Ibn ʿAsākir, ʿAlī b. Hasan. *Tārīkh madīnat Dimashq*, ed. ʿUmar al-ʿAmrawī. Beirut, Dār al-Fikr, 1995–1997

Ibn Bābawayh, Muhammad b. ʿAlī. *Amālī al-Sadūq*, ed. Muhammad Mahdi al-Musawī. Najaf, al-Matbaʿa al-Haydariyya, 1970

—— *Man lā yahduruhu al-faqīh*, ed. Muhammad Jaʿfar Shams al-Din. Beirut, Dar al-Taʿāruf li'l-Matbūʿāt, 1994

Ibn Battāl, ʿAlī b. Khalaf. *Sharh Sahīh al-Bukhārī*, ed. Ibrāhīm Yāsir Ibrāhīm. Riyadh, Maktabat al-Rushd, 2003

Ibn al-Farrā, Abū Yaʿlā. *Al-ʿUdda fī usūl al-fiqh*, ed. Ahmad Sīr al-Mubārak. Beirut, Mu'assasat al-Risāla, 1980

Ibn Hajar al-ʿAsqalānī. *Fath al-bārī sharh Sahīh al-Bukhārī*, ed. ʿAbd al-ʿAzīz b. Bāz and Ayman Fu'ād ʿAbd al-Bāqī. Beirut, Dār al-Kutub al-ʿIlmiyya, 1997

—— *Huda al-sārī*, ed. Ayman Fu'ād ʿAbd al-Bāqī and ʿAbd al-ʿAzīz b. Bāz. Beirut, Dār al-Kutub al-ʿIlmiyya, 1997

—— *Hidāyat al-ruwāt ilā takhrīj ahādīth al-Misbāh wa'l-Mishkāt*, ed. Muhammad Nāsir al-Dīn al-Albānī. Dammam, Dar Ibn al-Qayyim, 2001

—— *Al-Matālib al-ʿāliya fī zawāʾid al-masānīd al-thamāniya*, ed. Habīb al-Rahmān al-Aʿzamī. Kuwait, Wizārat al-Awqāf, 1973

—— *Al-Nukat ʿalā kitāb Ibn al-Salāh*, ed. Masʿūd al-ʿAdanī and Muhammad Fāris. Beirut, Dār al-Kutub al-ʿIlmiyya, 1994

—— *Talkhīs al-habīr*. Cairo, Sharikat al-Tibāʿat al-Fanniyya, 1964

Ibn Hajar al-Haytamī, Ahmad b. Muhammad. *Al-Fatāwā al-hadīthiyya*, ed. Muhammad al-Marʿashlī. Beirut, Dār Ihyā' al-Turāth al-ʿArabī, 1998

Ibn Hanbal, Ahmad. *Kitāb fadāʾil al-sahāba*, ed. Wasī Allāh Muhammad ʿAbbās. Beirut, Mu'assasat al-Risāla, 1983

—— *Al-Musnad*. Citations are to the standard Maymaniyya print of the book

Ibn Hibbān al-Bustī. *Sahīh Ibn Hibbān*, ed. Shuʿayb al-Arnāʾūt and Husayn Asad. Beirut, Mu'assasat al-Risāla, 1984

Ibn al-Jawzī, ʿAbd al-Rahmān. *Kitāb al-qussās wa al-mudhakkirīn*, ed. Merlin S. Swartz. Beirut: Dar El-Machreq, 1986

—— *Kitāb al-mawdūʿāt*, ed. ʿAbd al-Rahmān ʿUthmān. Medina, al-Maktaba al-Salafiyya, 1966–1968

—— *Mashyakhat Ibn al-Jawzī*, ed. Muhammad Mahfūz. Beirut, Dār al-Gharb al-Islāmī, 2006

—— *Talbīs Iblīs*. Cairo, Matba'at Nahda, 1928

Ibn Khaldūn, 'Abd al-Rahmān. *The Muqaddimah: An Introduction to History*. Trans. Franz Rosenthal. Ed. N.J. Dawood. Princeton, Princeton University Press, 1967

Ibn Khuzayma, Muhammad b. Ishāq. *Sahīh Ibn Khuzayma*, ed. Muhammad Mustafā al-A'zamī. Beirut, al-Maktab al-Islāmī, [1970]

Ibn Ma'īn, Yahyā. *Kitāb al-'ilal wa ma'rifat al-rijāl*, ed. Muhammad al-Jazā'irī. Beirut, Dār Ibn Hazm, 2004

Ibn Mājah, Muhammad b. Yazīd. *Sunan*. Cited according to chapter, subchapter system

Ibn Manda, Muhammad b. Ishāq. *Shurūt al-a'imma*, ed. 'Abd al-Rahmān al-Farīwā'ī. Riyadh, Dār al-Muslim, 1995

Ibn al-Mubrad, Yūsuf. *Tahdhīb al-nafs li'l-'ilm bi'l-'ilm*, ed. Adīb al-Kamdānī. [Damascus], [n.p.], 1995

Ibn al-Murtadā, Ahmad b. Yahyā. *Tabaqāt al-mu'tazila*, ed. Suzanna Diwald-Wilzer. Beirut, Dār Maktabat al-Hayāt, [1980]

Ibn al-Nadīm. *The Fihrist*, ed. and trans. Bayard Dodge. New York, Columbia University Press, 1970; Chicago, Kazi Publications, 1998

Ibn Nuqta, Muhammad b. 'Abd al-Ghanī. *Kitab al-Taqyīd li-ma'rifat ruwāt al-sunan wa al-masānīd*, ed. Kamāl Yūsuf al-Hūt. Beirut, Dār al-Kutub al-'Ilmiyya, 1988

Ibn Qayyim al-Jawziyya. *I'lām al-muwaqqi'īn*, ed. Tāhā 'Abd al-Ra'ūf Sa'd. Beirut, Dār al-Jīl, 1973

—— *Kitāb al-rūh*, ed. 'Ārif al-Hājj. Beirut, Dār Ihyā' al-'Ulūm, 1988

Ibn Qutayba al-Dīnawarī. *Ta'wīl mukhtalif al-hadīth*, ed. Muhammad Zuhrī al-Najjār. Beirut, Dār al-Jīl, 1973

Ibn Sa'd, Muhammad. *Al-Tabaqāt al-kubrā*. Beirut, Dār Sādir, [1968]

Ibn al-Salāh, Abu 'Amr 'Uthmān. *Muqaddimat Ibn al-Salāh*, ed. 'Ā'isha 'Abd al-Rahmān. Cairo, Dār al-Ma'ārif, 1990

Ibn Taymiyya, Taqī al-Dīn. *Majmū'at al-fatāwā*, ed. Sayyid Husayn al-'Affānī and Khayrī Sa'īd. Cairo, al-Maktaba al-Tawfīqiyya, [n.d.]

Ibn al-Wazīr, Muhammad. *Kitāb tanqīh al-anzār fī ma'rifat 'ulūm al-āthār*, ed. Muhammad Subhī Hallāq. Beirut, Dār Ibn Hazm, 1999

Al-'Irāqī, Zayn al-Dīn 'Abd al-Rahīm. *Al-Bā'ith 'alā al-khalās min hawādith al-qussās*, ed. Muhammad Lutfī al-Sabbāgh. Damascus, Dār al-Warrāq, 2001

—— *Al-Taqyīd wa al-īdāh*, ed. Muhammad 'Abbās Shāhīn. Beirut, Dār al-Kutub al-'Ilmiyya, 1999

Al-Isbahānī, Abū Nu'aym. *Dhikr akhbār Isbahān*, ed. Sayyid Khusrawī Hasan. Beirut, Dār al-Kutub al-'Ilmiyya, 1990

—— *Hilyat al-awliyā' wa tabaqāt al-asfiyā'*. Beirut, Dār al-Fikr, 2006

Al-Ishbīlī, Muhammad b. Khayr. *Fahrasat mā rawāhu ʿan shuyūkhihi min al-dawāwīn al-musannafa fī durūb al-ʿilm wa anwāʿ al-maʿārif.* Beirut, al-Maktab al-Tijārī, 1963

Al-Jāhiz, Abū ʿUthmān. *Rasāʾil al-Jāhiz*, ed. ʿAbd al-Salām Muhammad Hārūn. Cairo, Maktabat al-Khānjī, 1964

Al-Jassās, Abū Bakr. *Ahkām al-Qurʾān,* ed. Muhammad Qamhāwī. 5 vols. Beirut, Dār Ihyāʾ al-Turāth al-ʿArabī, 1985

—— *Usūl al-Jassās*, ed. Muhammad Tāhir. Beirut, Dār al-Kutub al-ʿIlmiyya, 2000

Al-Jawzaqānī, al-Husayn b. Ibrāhīm. *Al-Abātīl wa al-manākīr wa al-sihāh wa al-mashāhīr*, ed. Muhammad Hasan Muhammad. Beirut, Dār al-Kutub al-ʿIlmiyya, 2001

Al-Jazāʾirī, Tāhir. *Tawjīh al-nazar ilā usūl al-athar*, ed. ʿAbd al-Fattāh Abū Ghudda. Aleppo, Maktabat al-Matbūʿāt al-Islāmiyya, 1995

Jumʿa, ʿAlī. *Al-Bayān li-mā yushghalu bihi al-adhhān.* Cairo, Muqattam, 2005

Al-Juwaynī, Imām al-Haramayn. *Ghiyāth al-umam fī tiyāth al-zulam.* Ed. Mustafā Hilmī and Fuʾād ʿAbd al-Munʿim. Alexandria, Dār al-Daʿwa, 1400/1980

Al-Kawtharī, Muhammad Zāhid. *Maqālāt al-Kawtharī.* Cairo, al-Maktaba al-Azhariyya, 1994

Al-Khalīlī, al-Khalīl b. ʿAbdallāh. *Al-Irshād fī maʿrifat ʿulamāʾ al-hadīth*, ed. ʿĀmir Ahmad Haydar. Mecca, Dār al-Fikr, 1993

Al-Khatīb al-Baghdādī. *Jāmiʿ akhlāq al-rāwī wa ādāb al-sāmiʿ*, ed. Muhammad Saʿīd. Mansoura, Egypt, Dār al-Wafāʾ, 2002

—— *Al-Kifaya fī maʿrifat usūl ʿilm al-riwāya,* ed. Abū Ishāq Ibrāhīm al-Dimyātī. Cairo, Dār al-Hudā, 2003

—— ʿNasīhat li-ahl al-hadīth.ʾ In *Majmūʿat al-rasāʾil fī ʿulūm al-hadīth*, ed. Nasr Abū ʿAtāyā, pp. 111–126. Mansoura, Egypt; Dār al-Khānī, 1994

—— *Taqyīd al-ʿilm*, ed. Yūsuf al-ʿIshsh. Aleppo, Dār al-Waʿī, [n.d.]

—— *Tārīkh Baghdād*, ed. Mustafā ʿAbd al-Qādir ʿAtā. Beirut, Dār al-Kutub al-ʿIlmiyya, 1997

Al-Khattābī, Hamd. *Maʿālim al-sunan*, 2nd ed. Beirut, al-Maktaba al-ʿIlmiyya, 1981

Al-Kulaynī, Muhammad b. Yaʿqūb. *Al-Kāfī*, trans. Muhammad Hasan al-Rizvani. Karachi, Islamic Research Center, 1995

—— *Al-Usūl al-kāfī*, ed. Muhammad Jaʿfar Shams al-Dīn. Beirut, Dār al-Taʿāruf liʾl-Matbūʿāt, 1998

Livy, Titus. *The Early History of Rome*. London, Penguin Books, 1960

Mālik b. Anas. *Muwattaʾ*. Cited according to the chapter, subchapter system

Al-Maqdisī, Ibn Qudāma. *Al-Mughnī*, ed. ʿAbd al-Fattāh al-Hulw and ʿAbdallāh al-Turkī. Cairo, Hujr, 1986–1990

Al-Miswarī, Ahmad b. Sa'd al-Dīn. *Al-Risāla al-munqidha min al-ghiwāya fī turuq al-riwāya*, ed. Hamūd al-Ahnūmī. Sana'a, Maktabat Badr, 1997

Al-Munāwī, 'Abd al-Ra'ūf. *Fayd al-qadīr sharh al-Jāmi' al-saghīr*. Mecca: Maktabat Nizār Mustafā al-Bāz, 1998

—— *Al-Jāmi' al-azhar min hadīth al-nabī al-anwar*. Cairo, al-Markaz al-'Arabī li'l-Bahth wa al-Nashr, 1980

Al-Mundhirī, 'Abd al-'Azīm. *Jawāb al-hāfiz Abī Muhammad 'Abd al-'Azīm al-Mundhirī 'an asi'la fī al-jarh wa'l-ta'dīl*, ed. 'Abd al-Fattāh Abū Ghudda. Beirut, Maktabat al-Matbū'āt al-Islāmiyya, 1990

Muslim b. al-Hajjāj. *Kitāb al-tamyīz*, ed. Muhammad al-A'zamī. Riyadh, Matba'at Jāmi'at Riyād, [1975]

—— *Sahīh Muslim*. Cited according to the chapter, subchapter system

Al-Najāshī, Ahmad b. 'Alī. *Rijāl al-Najāshī*, ed. Muhammad Jawād al-Nā'īnī. Beirut, Dār al-Adwā', 1988

Al-Nasā'ī, Ahmad b. Shu'ayb. *Sunan*. Cited according to the chapter, subchapter system

Al-Nawawī, Muhyī al-Dīn. *Al-Adhkār al-muntakhab min sayyid al-abrār*. Cairo, Dār al-Manār, 1999

—— *Sharh Sahīh Muslim*. Beirut, Dār al-Qalam, 1987

Al-Naysābūrī, al-Hākim. *Kitāb al-madkhal ilā ma'rifat kitāb al-iklīl*, ed. Ahmad b. Fāris al-Sulūm. Beirut, Dār Ibn Hazm, 2003

—— *Al-Mustadrak*. Hyderabad, Dā'irat al-Ma'ārif al-'Uthmāniyya, 1917–1925

Petrarch, Francesco. *The Secret*, trans. William H. Draper. London: Chatto & Windus, 1911

Polybius. *The Histories*, trans. Mortimer Chambers. New York, Washington Square Press, 1966

Al-Qābisī, 'Alī b. Muhammad. *Muwatta' al-imām Mālik*, ed. Muhammad b. 'Alawī al-Mālikī. Abu Dhabi, al-Majma' al-Thaqāfī, 2004

Al-Qādī 'Iyād b. Mūsā. *Kitāb al-shifā bi-ta'rīf huqūq al-mustafā*. Beirut, Dār Ibn Hazm, 2002

Al-Qaradāwī, Yūsuf. *Kayfa nata'āmalu ma'a al-sunna al-nabawiyya*. Herdon, VA, International Institute for Islamic Thought, 1990

Qārī, Mullā 'Alī. *Al-Asrār al-marfū'a fī al-akhbār al-mawdū'a*, ed. Muhammad Lutfī Sabbāgh. Beirut, al-Maktab al-Islāmī, 1986

—— *Al-Masnū' fī ma'rifat al-hadīth al-mawdū'*, ed. 'Abd al-Fattāh Abū Ghudda. Beirut, Dār al-Bashā'ir al-Islāmiyya, 2005

Qazvīnī, Nāsir al-Dīn. *Ketāb-e naqd-e ma'refat beh ba'd-e mathāleb al-navāseb fī naqd ba'd fadā'eh al-ravāfed*, ed. Jalāl al-Dīn Hosaynī Ormavī. [Tehran], Chāp-khāne-ye Sepehr, [1952]

Al-Qurtubī, Muhammad b. Ahmad. *Al-Jāmi' li-ahkām al-Qur'ān,* ed. Muhammad Ibrāhīm al-Hifnāwī and Mahmūd Hāmid 'Uthmān. 20 vols in 10. Cairo, Dār al-Hadīth, 1994

Al-Rāfi'ī, Muhammad b. 'Abd al-Karīm. *Al-Tadwīn fī akhbār Qazwīn*, ed. 'Azīz Allāh al-'Utāridī. Beirut, Dār al-Kutub al-'Ilmiyya, 1987

Al-Rāzī, Abū Zur'a. *Abū Zur'a al-Rāzī wa juhūduhu fī al-sunna al-nabawiyya ma'a tahqīq kitābihi al-Du'afā' wa ajwibatihi 'alā as'ilat al-Bardha'ī*, ed. Sa'dī al-Hāshimī. Medina, Cairo, Dār al-Wafā' and Maktabat Ibn al-Qayyim, 1989

Al-Rāzī, Ibn Abī Hātim. *'Ilal al-hadīth*. Beirut, Dār al-Ma'rifa, 1985

—— *Al-Jarh wa al-ta'dīl*. Hyderabad, Dā'irat al-Ma'ārif al-'Uthmāniyya, 1952–1953

—— *Al-Taqdima*. Hyderabad, Dā'irat al-Ma'ārif al-'Uthmāniyya, 1952

Ridā, Muhammad Rashīd. *Al-Manār* (journal)

Al-Sa'd, 'Abdallāh. '*Sharh Kitāb al-Tamyīz*,' lecture from www.islamway.com, last accessed 6/3/2004

—— '*Sharh al-Mūqiza*,' lecture from www.islamway.com, last accessed 6/3/2004

Al-Sakhāwī, Shams al-Dīn. *Fath al-mughīth*, ed. 'Alī Husayn 'Alī. Cairo, Maktabat al-Sunna, 2003

—— *Al-Maqāsid al-hasana*, ed. Muhammad Khisht. Beirut: Dār al-Kitāb al-'Arabī, 2004

Al-Sam'ānī, Abū Sa'd. *Adab al-imlā' wa al-istimlā'*. Beirut, Dār al-Kutub al-'Ilmiyya, 1981

Al-San'ānī, 'Abd al-Razzāq. *Musannaf*, ed. Habīb al-Rahmān al-A'zamī. Beirut, al-Maktab al-Islāmī, 1983

Al-San'ānī, Muhammad b. Ismā'īl. *Dīwān al-Amīr al-San'ānī*. Beirut, Manshūrāt al-Madīna, 1986

—— *Irshad al-nuqqād ilā taysīr al-ijtihād*, ed. Muhammad Subhī Hasan. Beirut, Mu'assasat al-Rayyān, 1992

—— *[Question and Answer]*, Ms. Majāmī' 1, Dār al-Awqāf, Sana'a

Al-Sarakhsī, Muhammad b. Ahmad. *Usūl al-Sarakhsī*, ed. Abū al-Wafā' al-Afghānī. Beirut, Dār al-Kutub al-'Ilmiyya, 1993

Al-Sarraj, Abū Nasr. *The Kitáb al-Luma' fi'l-Taṣawwuf*, ed. Reynold Nicholson. London, Luzac & Co., 1963

Sāwī, Ahmad b. Muhammad. *Hāshiyat al-Sāwī 'alā Tafsīr al-Jalālayn*, ed. 'Alī Muhammad al-Dabbā'. Bombay, Surtis Sons, [1981]

Al-Shāfi'ī, Muhammad b. Idrīs. *Al-Risāla*, ed. Ahmad Shākir. Beirut, al-Maktaba al-'Ilmiyya, [n.d.]

—— *Al-Umm*. Cairo, Dār al-Sha'b, 1968

Shaltūt, Mahmūd. *Al-Fatāwā*. Cairo, Dār al-Shurūq, 1983

Al-Sha'rānī, 'Abd al-Wahhāb. *Al-Mīzān al-kubrā*. Cairo, Maktabat Zahrān, [n.d.]

—— *Al-Tabaqāt al-kubrā / Lawāmih al-anwār fī tabaqāt al-akhyār*, ed. Sulaymān al-Sālih. Beirut, Dār al-Ma'rifa, 2005

Al-Sijistānī, Abū Dāwūd. 'Risālat al-imām Abī Dāwūd al-Sijistānī ilā ahl

Makka fī wasf Sunanihi.' In *Thalāth rasā'il fī 'ilm mustalah al-hadīth*, ed. 'Abd al-Fattāh Abū Ghudda, pp. 27–54. Aleppo, Maktab al-Matbū'āt al-Islāmiyya, 1997

—— *Al-Sunan*. Cited according to chapter, subchapter system

Spinoza, Benedict. *Theological-Political Treatise*, trans. Michael Silverthorne and Jonathan Israel. Cambridge: Cambridge University Press, 2007

Al-Subkī, Tāj al-Dīn. *Tabaqāt al-shāfi'iyya al-kubrā*, ed. Mahmūd Muhammad al-Tanāhī and 'Abd al-Fattāh Muhammad al-Hulw. [Cairo], 'Īsā al-Bābī al-Halabī, 1964

—— *Al-Sayf al-saqīl fī al-radd 'alā ibn al-Zafīl*, eds. Muhammad Zāhid al-Kawtharī and 'Abd al-Hafīz 'Atiyya. [Cairo], Matba'at al-Sa'āda, 1937

Al-Suhrawardī, 'Umar b. Muhammad. *'Awārif al-ma'ārif*, ed. Adīb al-Kamdānī and Muhammad al-Mustafā. Mecca, al-Maktaba al-Makkiyya, 2001

Al-Sulamī, Abū 'Abd al-Rahmān. *Kitāb al-arba'īn fī al-tasawwuf*. Hyderabad, Dā'irat al-Ma'ārif al-'Uthmāniyya, 1950

—— *Tabaqāt al-sūfiyya*, ed. Nūr al-Dīn Shurayba. Cairo, Maktabat al-Khānjī, 1997

Al-Suyūtī, Jalāl al-Dīn. *Al-Azhār al-mutanāthira fī al-ahādīth al-mutawātira*, ed. 'Abd al-'Azīz al-Ghumārī. Cairo, Dār al-Ta'līf, [n.d.]

—— *Al-Hāwī li'l-fatāwī*, 2nd ed. Beirut, Dār al-Kutub al-'Ilmiyya, 1975

—— *Jam' al-jawāmi' al-ma'rūf bi'l-Jāmi' al-kabīr*. [Cairo], Majma' al-Buhūth al-Islāmiyya, 1970

—— *Al-Jāmi' al-saghīr*. Beirut, Dār al-Kutub al-'Ilmiyya, 2004

—— *Al-La'ālī'al-masnū'afī al-ahādīth al-mawdū'a*, ed. Sālih b. Muhammad b. 'Uwayda. Beirut, Dār al-Kutub al-'Ilmiyya, 1996

—— *Al-Khasā'is al-kubrā*. Beirut, Dār al-Kitāb al-'Arabī, n.d.

—— 'al-Ta'zīm wa al-manna fī anna abawayh rasūl Allāh fī al-janna.' In *Silsilat matbū'āt Dā'irat al-Ma'ārif al-'Uthmāniyya,* 50, 1915, pp. 1–46

—— *Nazm al-'iqyān fī a'yān al-a'yān*, ed. Philip Hitti. Beirut, al-Maktaba al-'Ilmiyya, 1927

Al-Tabarānī, Abū al-Qāsim. *Al-Mu'jam al-saghīr*, ed. 'Abd al-Rahmān Muhammad 'Uthmān. Beirut, Dār al-Fikr, 1981

Al-Tabrīzī, Muhammad al-Khatīb. *Miskhat al-Masabih*, trans. James Robson. Lahore, Sh. Muhammad Ashraf, 1963

Al-Tirmidhī, Muhammad b. 'Īsā. *Al-Jāmi'*. Cited according to the chapter, subchapter system

Al-Tūfī, Najm al-Dīn. *Risāla fī ri'āyat al-maslaha*, ed. Ahmad 'Abd al-Rahīm al-Sāyih. Cairo, al-Dār al-Misriyya al-Lubnāniyya, 1993

Al-'Uqaylī, Abū Ja'far. *Kitāb al-du'afā' al-kabīr*, ed. 'Abd al-Mu'tī Qal'ajī. Beirut, Dār al-Kutub al-'Ilmiyya, 1984

Voltaire. *La Philosophie de l'Histoire*. Utrecht, n.p., 1765

Al-Wādi'ī, Muqbil bin Hādī. *Majmū' fatāwā al-Wādi'ī*, ed. Sādiq al-Baydānī. n.p., 2005

—— *Al-Makhraj min al-fitna*, 3rd ed. Sa'da, Maktabat San'ā' al-Athariyya, 2002

Al-Wā'ilī, Abū Nasr. *Risālat al-Sijzī ilā ahl Zabīd fī al-radd 'alā man ankara al-harf wa al-sawt*, ed. Muhammad b. Karīm b. 'Abdallāh. Riyadh, Dār al-Rāya, 1994

Al-Wāsitī, Aslam b. Sahl Bahshal. *Tārīkh Wāsit,* ed. Kūrkīs 'Awwād. Baghdad, Matba'at al-Ma'ārif, 1967

Al-Wazīrī, Sārim al-Dīn Ibrāhīm. *Al-Falak al-dawwār fī 'ulūm al-hadīth wa al-fiqh wa al-āthār*, ed. Muhamad Yahyā 'Azzān. Sa'da, Dār al-Turāth al-Yamanī, 1994

Wolf, Friedrich August. *Prolegomena to Homer*, ed. and trans. Anthony Grafton, Glenn W. Most and James E.G. Zetzel. Princeton, Princeton University Press, 1985

Al-Zarkashī, Badr al-Dīn Muhammad. *Al-Bahr al-muhīt fī usūl al-fiqh*, ed. Muhammad Muhammad Tāmir. Beirut, Dār al-Kutub al-'Ilmiyya, 2007

—— *Al-Tadhkira fī al-ahādīth al-mushtahira*, ed. Mustafā 'Abd al-Qādir 'Atā. Beirut, Dār al-Kutub al-'Ilmiyya, 1406/1986

Zayd b. 'Alī. *Musnad Zayd b. 'Alī*. Beirut, Dār Maktabat al-Hayāt, 1966

Al-Zayla'ī, Jamāl al-Dīn. *Nasb al-rāya li-ahādīth al-Hidāya*, ed. Muhammad 'Awwāma. Jeddah, Mu'assasat al-Rayyān, 1997

SECONDARY SOURCES

Abbott, Nabia. *Studies in Arabic Literary Papyri II: Qur'ānic Commentary and Tradition*. Chicago, University of Chicago Press, 1967

Abd al-Rauf, Muhammad. '*Ḥadīth* Literature – I: The Development of the Science of *Ḥadīth*,' in *The Cambridge History of Arabic Literature: Arabic Literature until the End of the Umayyad Period*, eds. A.F.L. Beeston *et al.*, pp. 271–288. London, Cambridge University Press, 1983

Abū Zahra, Muhammad. *Abū Hanīfa*. Cairo, Dār al-Fikr al-'Arabī, 1965

—— *Ibn Hanbal*. Cairo, Dār al-Fikr al-'Arabī, [1965]

—— *Ibn Taymiyya*. Cairo, Dār al-Fikr al-'Arabī, 1964

—— *Mālik*. Cairo, Dār al-Fikr al-'Arabī, 2002

—— *Al-Shāfi'ī*. Cairo, Dār al-Fikr al-'Arabī, 1996

Ahmad, Aziz. *Islamic Modernism in India and Pakistan*. London, Oxford University Press, 1967

—— and G.E. von Grunebaum, eds. *Muslim Self-Statement in India and Pakistan 1857–1968*. Wiesbaden, Otto Harrassovitz, 1970

Amir-Moezzi, Mohammed Ali. *The Divine Guide in Early Shi'ism*. Trans. David Streight. Albany, SUNY Press, 1994

Anjum, Ovamir. *Politics, Law, and Community in Islamic Thought*. Cambridge, Cambridge University Press, 2012

Al-'Awd, Sahl. *Al-Mu'īn 'alā ma'rifat kutub al-arba'īn*. Beirut, 'Ālam al-Kutub, 2005

'Awwāma, Muhammad. *Athar al-hadīth al-sharīf fī ikhtilāf al-a'imma al-fuqahā'*, 2nd ed. Cairo, Dār al-Salām, 1987

Azami, Muhammad. *Studies in Early Ḥadīth Literature*. Kuala Lumpur, Islamic Book Trust, 2000

Al-'Azzān, Muhammad Yahyā. *Al-Sahāba 'ind al-zaydiyya*. Sana'a, Markaz al-Turāth, 2004

Benjaminson, Peter and David Anderson. *Investigative Reporting*, 2nd ed. Ames, Iowa, Iowa State University Press, 1990

Bentley, Jerry. *Humanists and Holy Writ*. Princeton, Princeton University Press, 1983

Brooke, Rosalind and Christopher. *Popular Religion in the Middle Ages: Western Europe 1000–1300*. New York, Barnes and Noble, 1984

Brown, Daniel. *Rethinking Tradition in Modern Islamic Thought*. Cambridge, Cambridge University Press, 1996

Brown, Jonathan A.C. *The Canonization of al-Bukhārī and Muslim*. Leiden, Brill, 2007

—— 'Critical Rigor versus Juridical Pragmatism: How Legal Theorists and Ḥadīth Scholars Approached the Backgrowth of *Isnād*s in the Genre of *'Ilal al-Ḥadīth*,' *Islamic Law and Society* 14, no. 1, 2007, pp. 1–41

—— 'A Man for All Seasons: Ibn 'Uqda and Crossing Sectarian Boundaries in the Fourth/Tenth Century,' *Al-'Usul al-Wusta* 24, 2016, pp. 139–144

—— 'How We Know Early Ḥadīth Critics Did *Matn* Criticism and Why It's So Hard to Find.' *Islamic Law and Society* 15, 2008, pp. 143–184

—— 'The Last Days of al-Ghazzālī and the Tripartite Division of the Sufi World,' *The Muslim World* 96, 2006, pp. 89–113

—— 'The Rules of Matn Criticism: There Are No Rules.' *Islamic Law and Society* 19, 2012, pp. 356–396

Brumfitt, J.H. *Voltaire, Historian*. Oxford, Oxford U. Press, 1958

Buckley, Ron. 'On the Origins of Shī'i Hadīth.' *Muslim World,* 88, no. 2, 1998, pp. 165–184

Burton, John. *An Introduction to the Hadith*. Edinburgh, Edinburgh University Press, 1994

Buzpinar, Tufan. 'Opposition to the Ottoman Caliphate in the Early Years of Abdülhamid II: 1877–1882,' *Die Welt des Islams*, 36, no. 1, 1996, pp. 59–89

Chittick, William. *Imaginal Worlds: Ibn 'Arabī and the Problem of Religious Diversity*. Albany, SUNY Press, 1994

—— *The Sufi Path of Knowledge*. Albany, SUNY Press, 1989

Cook, Michael. *Early Muslim Dogma: a Source-Critical Approach*. Cambridge, Cambridge University Press, 1981

—— 'Eschatology and the Dating of Traditions,' *Princeton Papers in Near Eastern Studies* 1, 1992, pp. 23–47

Crone, Patricia. *Meccan Trade and the Rise of Islam*. Princeton, Princeton University Press, 1987

—— *Roman, Provincial and Islamic Law*. Cambridge, Cambridge University Press, 1987

Donner, Fred. 'From Believers to Muslims: Confessional Self-identity in the Early Islamic Community,' *al-Abḥāth,* 50–51, 2002–3, pp. 9–53

—— *Muhammad and the Believers*. Cambridge, MA, Belknap Press, 2010

—— *Narratives of Islamic Origins*. Princeton, Darwin Press, 1998

Ehrman, Bart D. *The New Testament*, 2nd ed. New York, Oxford University Press, 2000

Federspiel, Howard M. *Sultans, Shamans and Saints*. Honolulu, University of Hawai'i Press, 2007

Frampton, Travis. *Spinoza and the Rise of Historical Criticism of the Bible*. New York, T&T Clark, 2006

Frei, Hans. *The Eclipse of Biblical Narrative*. New Haven, Yale University Press, 1974

Gay, Peter, ed. *Deism: An Anthology*. Princeton, D. van Nostrand Co., 1968

Ghamidi, Javed Ahmad. *Islam: A Comprehensive Introduction*. Trans. Shehzad Saleem Lahore, Al Mawrid, 2014

Gilmore, Myron P. *Humanists and Jurists*. Cambridge, MA, Belknap Press, 1963

Gleave, Robert. 'Between *Hadīth* and *Fiqh*: The "Canonical" Imāmī Collections of Akhbār.' *Islamic Law and Society* 8, no. 3, 2001, pp. 350–382

Goldziher, Ignaz. *Introduction to Islamic Theology and Law*, trans. Andras and Ruth Hamori. Princeton, Princeton University Press, 1981

—— *Muslim Studies II*, trans. and ed. S.M. Stern and G.R. Barber. Chicago, Aldine Atherton, 1971

Hallaq, Wael. 'On the Authoritativeness of Sunni Consensus,' *International Journal of Middle East Studies,* 18, no. 4, 1986, pp. 427–454

Halm, Heinz. *Shi'ism*, trans. Janet Watson and Marian Hill. 2nd ed. New York, Columbia University Press, 2004

Hanioğlu, M. Şükrü. *A Brief History of the Late Ottoman Empire*. Princeton, Princeton University Press, 2008

Hassan, Mona. *Longing for the Lost Caliphate*. Princeton, Princeton University Press, 2016

Hodgson, Marshall. *The Venture of Islam*. Chicago, University of Chicago Press, 1974

Howard, Thomas A. *Religion and the Rise of Historicism*. Cambridge, Cambridge University Press, 2000

Ishaq, Muhammad. *India's Contribution to Hadith Literature*. Dhaka, University of Dacca, 1955

Al-'Izzī, 'Abdallāh Hamūd. *'Ilm al-hadith 'ind al-zaydiyya wa al-muhaddithīn*. Sana'a, Mu'assasat al-Imām Zayd b. 'Alī, 2001

Jum'a, 'Alī. *Qawl al-sahābī 'ind al-usūliyyīn*. Cairo, Dār al-Risāla, 2004

Juynboll, G.H.A. *The Authenticity of the Tradition Literature: Discussions in Modern Egypt*. Leiden, Brill, 1969

—— *Muslim Tradition: Studies in Chronology, Provenance and Authorship of Early Ḥadīth*. London, Cambridge University Press, 1983

—— '(Re)Appraisal of some Hadith Technical Terms,' *Islamic Law and Society,* 8, no. 3, 2001, pp. 303–349

—— *Studies on the Origins and Uses of Islamic Ḥadīth*. Aldershot, Variorum, 1996

Karateke, Hakan and Maurus Reinkowski, eds. *Legitimizing the Order: The Ottoman Rhetoric of State Power*. Leiden, Brill, 2005

Kohlberg, Etan. *A Medieval Muslim Scholar at Work*. Leiden, Brill, 1992

—— 'Shī'ī Hadīth,' in *The Cambridge History of Arabic Literature: Arabic Literature until the End of the Umayyad Period*, eds Beeston, A.F.L. *et al*. London, Cambridge University Press, 1983, pp. 299–307

—— 'Al-Usūl al-Arba'umi'a,' *Jerusalem Studies in Arabic and Islam,* 10, 1987, pp. 128–166

Kramer, Martin. *Islam Assembled: The Advent of the Muslim Congresses*. New York, Columbia University Press, 1986

Krentz, Edgar. *The Historical Critical Method*. Philadelphia, Fortress Press, 1975

Al-Lahhām, Badī' al-Sayyid. *Al-Imām al-ḥāfiz Jalāl al-Dīn al-Suyūtī wa juhūduhu fī al-hadīth wa 'ulūmihi*. Damascus, Dār Qutayba, 1994

Lecker, Michael. 'Biographical Notes on Ibn Shihāb al-Zuhrī,' *Journal of Semitic Studies,* 41, 1996, pp. 21–63

Levtzion, Nehemia, ed. *Conversion to Islam*. New York, Holmes & Meier, 1979

Von Leyden, W. 'Antiquity and Authority: A Paradox in the Renaissance Theory of History,' *Journal of the History of Ideas* 19, no. 4, 1958, pp. 473–92

Lings, Martin. *What is Sufism?* Berkeley, University of California Press, 1975

Lucas, Scott. *Constructive Critics: Ḥadīth Literature and the Articulation of Sunnī Islam*. Leiden, Brill, 2004

Mahmūd, 'Abd al-Majīd. *Abū Ja'far al-Tahāwī wa atharuhu fī al-hadīth.* Cairo, al-Maktaba al-'Arabiyya, 1975

Marchand, Suzanne L. *German Orientalism in the Age of Empire.* Cambridge, Cambridge University Press, 2009

Massad, Joseph A. *Islam in Liberalism.* Chicago, University of Chicago Press, 2015

Melchert, Christopher. 'The *Musnad* of Aḥmad Ibn Ḥanbal: How It Was Composed and What Distinguishes It from the Six Books.' *Der Islam,* 82, 2005, pp. 32–51

Mernissi, Fatema. *Women and Islam: An Historical and Theological Enquiry,* trans. Mary Joe Lakeland. Oxford, Basil Blackwell, 1987

Modaressi, Hossein. *Tradition and Survival: A Bibliographical Survey of Early Shī'ite Literature, Vol. 1.* Oxford, Oneworld, 2003

Momigliano, Arnaldo. *Studies in Historiography.* London, Weidenfeld & Nicolson, 1966

Morgan, Robert and John Barton. *Biblical Interpretation.* Oxford, Oxford University Press, 1988

Motzki, Harald. 'Dating Muslim Traditions: a Survey,' *Arabica,* 52, no. 2, 2005, pp. 204–253

—— 'Der Fiqh des Zuhrī: die Quellenproblematik,' *Der Islam,* 68, 1991, pp. 1–44

—— 'The Murder of Ibn Abī Ḥuqayq.' In *The Biography of Muḥammad,* ed. Harald Motzki, pp. 170–239. Leiden, Brill, 2000

—— 'The *Muṣannaf* of 'Abd al-Razzāq al-Ṣan'ānī as a Source of Authentic *Aḥādīth* of the First Century A.H.,' *Journal of Near Eastern Studies,* 50, 1991, pp. 1–21

—— '*Quo vadis, Ḥadīṯ*-Forschung? Eine kritische Untersuchung von G.H.A. Juynboll: "Nāfi' the *mawlā* of Ibn 'Umar, and his position in Muslim *Ḥadīṯ* Literature," ' *Der Islam,* 73, no. 1, 1996, pp. 40–80

Muir, William. *The Life of Moḥammad.* Edinburgh, John Grant, 1923

Nakissa, Aria. 'The Fiqh of Revolution and the Arab Spring: Secondary Segmentation as a Trend in Islamic Legal Doctrine,' *Muslim World,* 105, 2015, pp. 398–421

Nurbakhsh, Javad. *Traditions of the Prophet.* New York, Khaniqahi-Nimatullahi Publications, 1981

Perrin, Norman. *What Is Redaction Criticism?* Philadelphia, Fortress Press, 1969

Powers, David S. 'On Bequests in Early Islam,' *Journal of Near Eastern Studies,* 48, no. 3, 1989, pp. 185–200

Rahman, Fazlur. *Islamic Methodology in History.* Karachi, Central Institute for Islamic Research, 1965

Randall, John Herman Jr. *The School of Padua and the Emergence of Modern Science.* Padua, Editrice Antenore, 1961

Reichmuth, Stefan. 'Murtaḍā al-Zabīdī (d. 1791) in Biographical and Autobiographical Accounts: Glimpses of Islamic Scholarship in the 18th Century,' *Die Welt des Islams,* 39, no. 1, 1999, pp. 64–102

Rice, Eugene F. Jr. and Anthony Grafton. *The Foundations of Early Modern Europe, 1460–1559*. 2nd ed. New York, W.W. Norton, 1994

Rodenbeck, Max. *Cairo: the City Victorious*. Cairo, American University in Cairo Press, 1998

Safi, Omid, ed. *Progressive Muslims*. Oxford, Oneworld, 2003

Sanders, James A. *Canon and Community*. Philadelphia, Fortress Press, 1984

Sayeed, Asma. *Women and the Transmission of Religious Knowledge in Islam*. Cambridge, Cambridge University Press, 2015

Sayoud, Halim. 'Author discrimination between the Holy Quran and the Prophet's statements,' *Literary and Linguistic Computing* 27, no. 4, 2012, pp. 427–444

Schacht, Joseph. *The Origins of Muhammadan Jurisprudence*. Oxford, Clarendon Press, 1975

—— 'A Revaluation of Islamic Tradition,' *Journal of the Royal Asiatic Society,* 1949, pp. 143–154

Scholder, Klaus. *The Birth of Modern Critical Theology*, trans. John Bowden. Philadelphia, Trinity Press, 1996

Sezgin, Fuat. *Geschichte des arabischen Schrifttums*. Leiden, Brill, 1967–2000

Stewart, Devin. 'The Genesis of the Akhbārī Revival.' In *Safavid Iran and Her Neighbors*, ed. Michel Mazzaoui, pp. 169–189. Salt Lake City, University of Utah Press, 2003

Al-Tahāwī, Abū Ja'far. *The Creed of Imam al-Tahāwī*, trans. Hamza Yusuf. N.p., Zaytuna Institute, 2007

Tokuno, Kyoko. 'The Evaluation of Indigenous Scriptures in Chinese Buddhist Bibliographical Catalogues.' In *Chinese Buddhist Apocrypha*, ed. Robert Buswell, Jr., pp. 31–59. Honolulu, University of Hawaii Press, 1990

Trimingham, J. Spencer. *The Sufi Orders in Islam*. New York, Oxford University Press, 1971

Troeltsch, Ernst. 'Historical and Dogmatic Method in Theology.' In *Religion in History*, ed. and trans. James A. Luther and Walter Bense. Minneapolis, Fortress Press, 1991

Troll, Christian W. *Sayyid Ahmad Khan: A Reinterpretation of Muslim Theology*. New Delhi, Vikas Press, 1978

Voll, John. 'Two Biographies of Ahmad Ibn Idris al-Fasi (1760–1837),' *International Journal of African Historical Studies*, 6, no. 3, 1973, pp. 633–645

Wadud, Amina. *The Quran and Woman*. New York, Oxford University Press, 1999

Wen Fong. 'The Problem of Forgery in Chinese Painting: Part One,' *Artibus Asiae,* 25, no. 2/3, 1962, pp. 95–110

Woods, John. *The Aqquyunlu*. Salt Lake City, University of Utah Press, 1999

INDEX

The definite article in Arabic (al-) is omitted from the beginning of index entries, but is included in other parts of entries. Hence, 'al-Shāfi'ī, Muhammad' is listed under 'Shāfi'ī, Muhammad'. Names of individuals include death dates as per the conventions set out in the Conventions section (xii ff.).

A

Abān b. Taghlib (d. 140/757) 153
'Abbāsid Dynasty 212–4, policy towards hadiths 241–2
Abbott, Nabia (d. 1981) 252–4
'Abd al-Ghanī b. Sa'īd (d. 409/1019) 66
'Abd al-Hamīd II, Sultan (r. 1876–1909) 214
'Abd al-Rahmān b. Mahdī (d. 198/814) 25, 81, 83, 85
'Abd al-Rahmān b. Sālih (d. 235/849–50) 86, 153
'Abd al-Razzāq al-San'ānī (d. 211/827) 25–7, 118, 151
  use of his *Musannaf* by Western scholars 262–6
'Abdallāh b. Ahmad b. Hanbal (d. 290/903) 37
'Abdallāh b. al-Zubayr (d. 73/692) 7, 241
'Abdallāh b. 'Amr b. al-'Ās (d. 65/684) 19
'Abdallāh b. Sālih (d. 223/837) 97
'Abdallāh b. 'Umar (d. 73/692) 20
'Abduh, Muhammad (d. 1905) 291–3
Abelard, Peter (d. 1142) 313
abrogation/*naskh* 165, 166, 174–7, 320
Abū al-Zinād (d. 131/748–9) 179
Abū al-Zubayr al-Makkī (d. 126/743–4) 21, 23, 119, 122
Abū Bakr (d. 12/634) 20, 212
Abū Bakra 286, 302
Abū Dāwūd al-Sijistānī (d. 275/889) 7, 25, 40–1, 176
  commentary on his *Sunan* 54
  four essential hadiths of 182, 197
  Sunan of 34–5, 53, 221, 295
Abū Dharr al-Harawī (d. 430/1038) 43, 66
Abū Hanīfa (d. 150/767) 17–18, 29–30, 75–6, 220; *see also* Hanafi school of law
  in eyes of Partisans of Hadith 186
  on *mursal* hadiths 94, 169
  on power of hadiths 166
  on rebellion 220
  hadiths of 43, 55
  support for Alid causes 150
Abū Hātim al-Rāzī, Muhammad b. Idrīs (d. 277/890) 25, 81, 83, 89, 97
Abū Hudhayl (d. 200/815) 167
Abū Hurayra (d. 58/678) 7, 19, 21, 22, 154–5, 201
  criticism/defense of 73, 253, 284–5, 302

number of hadiths 17, 20, 73
and women 73, 286
Abū Ishāq al-Sabīʿī (d. 127/745) 25, 264–5
Abu Nuʿaym al-Isbahānī (d. 430/1038) 38, 43, 47, 53, 56–7, 62, 90, 152
Abū Rayya, Mahmūd (d. 1970) 283–5, 298
Abū Yaʿlā al-Mawsilī (d. 307/919) 31, 60, 110, 204
Abū Zurʿa al-Rāzī, ʿUbaydallāh (d. 264/878) 25, 39, 81, 83, 86, 90, 112
Acton, John Lord (d. 1902) 229
ʿāda 181
ʿadāla 85–7, 109, 148
Adam 14, 188, 230–1, 285
ʿadhāb al-qabr/Punishment of the Grave 187, 190–1
ʿAdī b. Thābit (d. 116/764) 86, 153
āhād hadiths 107–9, 317
certainty yielded by 165–6, 181
in modern Islamic thought 288, 292–3, 296, 302
in Shiite Islam 143
in theology 185 ff., 191–3
ahkām al-hadīth, books 62–3
Ahl al-hadīth, *see* Partisans of Hadith
Ahl al-kalām 164
Ahl al-Ra'y, *see* Partisans of Legal Reasoning
Ahl-e Hadīth 294
Ahl-e Qur'ān, *see* Quran Only movement
Aisha (d. 58/678) 9, 32, 164, 175
criticism of hadiths by 73, 91, 286, 296
in modern Islamic thought 286, 296
number of hadiths 20–1
ʿAjlūnī, Ismāʿīl b. Ahmad (d. 1748–9) 116
Akbar the Great (d. 1605 CE) 214
akhbār/reports 13, 317
akhbaranā (he transmitted to us) 92–3
Albānī, Muhammad Nāsir al-Dīn (d. 1999) 123–7, 129–30, 221, 301
as leading Traditionalist Salafi 294–9
ʿālī/elevated *isnād*s, *see Isnād*
ʿAlī al-Naqī (d. 868 CE) 136
ʿAlī al-Ridā (d. 203/818) 8, 136, 141, 146, 203
ʿAlī b. Abī Tālib (d. 40/660) 8, 37, 72, 147, 149–50
esoteric knowledge of 2, 112, 201
hadiths/books praising 37–8, 86, 140, 144, 151–3, 243, 297–8
number of hadiths 21
role in Shiism 37, 135–8, 155–7
role in Sufi *isnād*s 202–4
sahīfa of 19
strictness in hadiths 73
ʿAlī b. al-Madīnī (d. 234/849) 25, 81, 83, 88, 90
ʿIlal book of 99
on *tadlīs* 270
ʿAlī b. Hamshādh (d. 388/950) 42
ʿAlī Zayn al-ʿĀbidīn (d. 94/712) 136, 140, 155, 203
ʿAlqama b. Qays (d. 62/681) 17
amālī/dictations 43, 47, 144, 151, 158, 316–7
Aʿmash, Sulaymān b. Mihrān (d. 148/765) 7, 25, 81
ʿĀmilī, Muhammad b. al-Hasan (d. 1104/1693) 144
ʿAmr b. Dīnār (d. 126/744) 25
ʿAmr b. ʿUbayd (d. 144/761) 77, 79
Amritsari, Ahmad Dīn (d. 1936) 282
ʿan/according to 92–3
anachronism 231–4, 236, 240, 243, 245, 267–9
Anas b. Mālik (d. 93/711) 7, 20, 22, 26, 49, 73
ansāb/genealogy 13, 317
anthropomorphism 38, 103, 158, 193, 285
Antichrist/*Dajjāl* 187–8, 191, 293
apostasy 288
Arab Spring/Winter 216, 221
Arabic, deficiencies of alphabet 23, 312
Aristotle 235
Asamm, Abū al-ʿAbbās (d. 346/957) 42–3

Asbāb wurūd al-hadīth 175
Ash'arī school of theology 58, 108–9, 166, 190 ff., 299, 317
Ash'arī, Abū al-Hasan (d. 324/935–6) 108, 190–4
asl, as basis for hadith 96, 102, 106, 111–2
as Shiite hadith collection 140
'Atā' b. Muslim al-Khaffāf 24
'Atā' b. Abī Rabāh (d. 114/732) 27, 265–6
Athram, Abū Bakr Ahmad (d. 261/875) 174
atrāf/indices 61–2
Augustine, Saint (d. 430) 230
authenticity, concern over 32–3, 38, 48–9, 56, 182, 190, 199, 296
Awzā'ī, 'Abd al-Rahmān (d. 157/773–4) 18, 25, 81, 93, 127
'Aynī, Badr al-Dīn (d. 855/1451) 88
Ayyūb al-Sakhtayānī (d. 131/749) 163
Azami, Muhammad 254 ff.
Azhar Mosque 1, 180, 291–3

B

Baghawī, Abū al-Qāsim (d. 317/929–30) 51
Baghawī, al-Husayn b. Mas'ūd (d. 516/1122) 59
Baghdad 11, 56, 143, 185, 200, 211–3, 294, 313
Baghdadi, Abu Bakr (d. 2017) 211
Bahshal, Aslam b. Sahl (d. 292/905) 56
Balkhī, Abū al-Qāsim al-Ka'bī (d. 319/931) 100
Baqī b. Makhlad (d. 276/889) 31
Bāqillānī, Abū Bakr (d. 403/1013) 190
baraka/blessing 48, 50, 153, 201–2, 204, 312, 317
Barbahārī, al-Hasan b. 'Alī (d. 329/941) 37
Basā'ir al-darajāt 141
Bastāmī, Bayazid (d. 261/874) 192, 195
bay'a/oath of allegiance 210
Bayhaqī, Abū Bakr Ahmad (d. 458/1066) 36, 38, 40
declaration about the end of hadith collection 43
Sunan al-kubrā of 42, 170
Bazdawī, Fakhr al-Islām (d. 482/1089) 179
Bazzār, Abū Bakr (d. 292/904–5) 31, 60, 62
Bible 201, 233, 252, 271
historical criticism of 231–8
bid'a/heretical innovation 37, 101, 186, 199, 278, 294, 317
Buddhism, critical tradition of 311–2
Buhūtī, Mansūr (d. 1051/1641) 170–1
Bukhārī, Muhammad b. Ismā'īl (d. 256/870) 7, 14, 25, 85, 186
Adab al-mufrad of 36, 64
Sahīh of 32–5, 39–42
commentaries on his *Sahīh* 54
criticism/evaluation of his *Sahīh* 39, 239, 247, 283, 287
definition of Companion 90
digest of his *Sahīh* 58–9
as hadith critic 81, 83, 85, 87
index of his *Sahīh* 62
legal theory of 107
matn criticism by 100
pro-'Alid hadiths of 150
transmitter criticism books of 87–8
Burton, John 258
Būsīrī, Ahmad (d. 840/1436) 60, 62, 120, 123

C

caliph & caliphate in Islam 211–216
Calvin, John (d. 1564) 232
Chakrālawī, 'Abdallāh (d. 1930) 281
Ching Lu books 311–2
Chirāgh 'Alī (d. 1895) 281, 290
Cicero (d. 43 BCE) 200, 230, 235
coitus interruptus 10
commentaries, *see sharh*s
Common Link 246 ff., 258–63, 266–7
Companions/*Sahāba* 6–7, 14, 156–7
books on virtues of 37–8
definitions of 6, 89–90
standing in Sunni Islam 90–1, 236

hadith collection and criticism by 19–22, 31, 73
Modernist criticisms of 244, 284–6
numbers of 90
opinions as source of law 11, 14, 26–8, 163, 169, 173, 176
consensus/*ijmā‘* 40, 85, 100, 112, 135, 163, 311
hadiths justifying 180–1
in modern Islamic thought 281, 287, 290–5
skepticism towards 281, 293, 295
Constitution of Medina 257
content criticism 70–1, 108–9, 147–9, 189, 240 ff., 250, 269, 312
by early Sunni hadith critics 99–104
and modern Muslim scholars 284, 290–6, 300, 302
conversion to Islam 211
Cook, Michael 256–8, 260, 269
corroboration 70, 80, 84, 95–9, 105, 110, 270–1
Crone, Patricia (d. 2015) 256–8, 260–1

D

Dabbāgh, ‘Abd al-‘Azīz (d. 1719) 115
dabt/accuracy 84, 86, 317
da‘īf, *see* weak
Dalā’il al-nubuwwa/Proofs of Prophecy 38, 262
Dānī, ‘Uthmān b. Sa‘īd (d. 444/1053) 62
Dāraqutnī, Abū al-Hasan ‘Alī (d. 385/995) 37, 43, 79, 81, 83, 98–9, 152, 154, 207
criticism of Muslim’s *Sahīh* 98, 221
Sunan of 40, 60, 171
Dārimī, ‘Abdallāh b. ‘Abd al-Rahmān (d. 255/869) 32, 60, 73
Day of Judgment 7, 10, 37, 75, 98, 100, 186–9, 190, 193, 211
Daylamī, Shahrudār b. Shīrawayh (d. 558/1163) 42, 50, 112
Deism 232
Deoband School 294
Dhahabī, Shams al-Dīn (d. 748/1348) xi, 44, 83–4, 92, 153, 267
on al-Hākim’s accuracy 110
love for ‘Alī b. Abī Tālib 150
Mīzān al-i‘tidāl of 88
on content criticism 103
Dhuhlī, Muhammad b. Yahyā (d. 258/873) 25, 32
Didū, Muhammad Hasan 221
Dimashqī, Abū Mas‘ūd Ibrāhīm (d. 401/1010–11) 62
Donner, Fred xii, 259
Dreams, authentication of hadiths by 113–15

E

e silentio, argument 246, 249, 254, 257, 261
Erasmus, Desiderius (d. 1536) 231, 233

F

fahrist 51–2
Fāsī, Abū al-‘Alā’ (d. 1770–1) 61, 88
Fātima 135, 150–2
Fātima al-Jūzdāniyya (d. 514/1120) 49–50
Fatimid Dynasty 212
fitna/civil strife 216–9, 221
Hadiths on 44, 216–9, 242
Fly, Hadith of 283, 293, 302
Forgery
of hadiths 30, 56, 71 ff., 110–4, 124, 136, 145, 192
in Western Historical Critical Method 240 ff.
as identified by modern Muslim scholars 282 ff.
Form Criticism 236–7
Forty Hadith collections 57–8
Fūshanjī, Abū al-Hasan (d. 348/959) 200

G

Gabriel, Angel 6, 64, 197–8
Ghadīr Khumm, Hadith of 151, 155, 158, 243
Ghamidi, Javed Ahmad 288
gharīb/isolated 98, 271, 317

Ghazālī, Abū Hāmid (d. 505/1111) 108, 199
on anthropomorphic hadiths 193
hadiths in his *Ihyā' 'ulūm al-dīn* 116
on *mutawātir* hadiths 191–93
on need for *isnād*s 45
proofs for consensus 181
on nature of the caliphate 213
Ghazālī, Muhammad (d. 1996) 293–4, 298–300
on relationship between hadiths and law 300
on women as rulers 175
Ghiyāth b. Ibrāhīm 141, 244
Ghumārī, 'Abd al-Hayy (d. 1995) 297
Ghumārī, 'Abdallāh (d. 1993) 50, 103, 113, 297–8
Ghumārī, Ahmad (d. 1960) 47, 111, 130, 204, 297–8
Gibbon, Edward (d. 1794) 243–5
Goldziher, Ignaz (d. 1921) 239 ff., 250–2, 254, 262–8
governance
in the Quran 210, 217
rebellion, legitimacy of 216–22

H

haddathanā/he transmitted to us 92–3
hadith canon 32–5, 39–42, 52–3
indexes of 61–2
number of hadiths in 41
Shiite hadith canon 141–3
Shiite transmitters in Sunni canon 153
hadith criticism, *see also* forgery of hadiths
books of Sunni transmitters criticism 87–8
books of Shiite transmitter criticism 146–7
by Companions 73
dreams as means of authentication 113–15
on heretics 85
list of hadith critics 81, 83
periodization of 71
Sunni method of 79 ff.
Sunni acceptance of Shiite leanings 85, 153
technical terms of 84–7
hadiths 3–4; *see also* traditions vs. narrations; *see also* hadith criticism
definition of hadith literature 13–4
adjusting the Quran 165–7
debates over writing down 21–4
explanations for conflicts between 171–8
forms of hadiths in Shiism 136–8
hadith forgery, *see* forgery of hadiths
multiplication of 253, 258
number of 41
pinnacle and end of collection of 42–4
Qudsī 63–4
scripturalization of 269
women as transmitters of 50–1
Hajjāwī, Mūsā (d. 958/1560) 170
Hākim al-Naysābūrī (d. 405/1014) 38, 56, 81, 83, 151, 192
approval of pro-'Alid hadiths 151–2
on *ijāza* 45–6
as lax critic 110
Mustadrak of 43, 60, 88
Hallāj, Mansūr (d. 309/922) 205
Hammād b. Salama (d. 167/784) 25, 81
Hammād b. Zayd (d. 179/795) 81
Hammām b. Munabbih (d. 130/747) 22, 66
Hanafi school of law; *see also* Abū Hanīfa
in modern Islamic thought 284, 288, 290, 295
on *mursal* hadiths 168–9
interpretation of hadiths in law 167, 174, 176–7, 179
on hadiths and theology 191
stance on hadiths 41, 107–8, 163–7
hadith collections & scholarship 31, 40, 43, 54–5, 88, 115, 178
on rebellion against rulers 220
Hanbali school of law; *see also* Ibn Hanbal
origins of 41, 170–1

hadith collections of 59, 63
sources of law 163
and legal theory 166
use of hadiths 18, 31, 33, 176
on *mursal* hadiths 169
revival of 294
Hārith b. Abī Usāma (d. 282/896) 31, 60
Hārūnī, Ahmad b. al-Husayn (d. 421/1030) 8, 158
hasan/fair 59, 111–2, 120, 124, 148
definition of 105–7, 317
in law 165
Hasan al-ʻAskarī (d. 260/874) 136, 138, 139, 141
Hasan al-Basrī (d. 110/728) 21–2, 26–7
letter to Umayyad caliph 245–6
mursal hadiths of 94–5
on narration by general meaning 24
role in Sufi *isnād*s 201–4
sahīfa of 22, 253
Hasan b. ʻAlī 136
Hasan b. Yahyā b. Zayd 156
Haykal, Muhammad Husayn (d. 1956) 283, 302
Haythamī, Nūr al-Dīn (d. 807/1405) 56 60
Hāzimī, Abū Bakr Muhammad (d. 584/1188–9) 174
headscarf/*hijāb* 3, 180
Heaven and Hell 12, 44, 64, 111–3, 188–9
Heretics, narration of hadiths from 85–6
Herodotus (d. *circa* 420 BCE) 236
Hidden Imam 136, 138–9, 145, 156
Hidden Jewel/Treasure, Hadith of 206–7
Hillī, ʻAllāma Muhammad b. Idrīs (d. 726/1325) 148
Historical Critical Method 229 ff., 239, 267, 288
Holmes, Sherlock 237
Hudhayfa b. Yamān 201, 218
Humayd b. Zanjawayh (d. 251/855–6) 36
Humaydī, ʻAbdallāh b. al-Zubayr (d. 219/834) 31, 40, 60
Humaydī, Muhammad b. Futūh (d. 488/1095) 58
Husayn b. ʻAlī (d. 61/680) 136
Hushaym b. Bashīr 25, 81

I

Ibn Abān, ʻĪsā (d. 221/836) 108–9
Ibn ʻAbbās, ʻAbdallāh (d. 67/686–7) 20–1, 124, 174, 192, 206, 251, 258
Ibn ʻAbd al-Barr, ʻUmar (d. 463/1070) 54, 93, 102, 168
Ibn ʻAbd al-Wahhāb, Muhammad (d. 1792) 279, 294
Ibn Abī al-Dunyā (d. 281/894) 36
Ibn Abī ʻĀsim (d. 287/900) 37–8, 127–9
Ibn Abī Hātim al-Rāzī (d. 327/938) 81, 83, 87, 110, 270
ʻIlal of 99
isnād through the imams of 153
on *mursal* hadiths 95
Ibn Abī Huqayq 263
Ibn Abī Shayba, Abū Bakr (d. 235/849) 25, 28, 48, 60, 81, 121
Ibn ʻAdī, ʻAbdallāh (d. 365/975–6) 81, 83–4, 87, 89, 97, 101, 100, 154
Ibn al ʻArabī, Qādī Abū Bakr (d. 543/1148) 54
Ibn al-Athīr, Majd al-Dīn (d. 606/1210) 59
Ibn al-Hājj, Muhammad (d. 737/1336) 228–9
Ibn al-Jabbāb (d. 322/934) 43
Ibn al-Jārūd (d. 307/919–20) 34, 60
Ibn al-Jawzī, ʻAbd al-Rahmān (d. 597/1201) 43, 59
ʻIlal of 99
on forged hadiths and *Kitāb al-mawdūʻāt* of 102–3, 124, 130
on popular hadiths 116
on Sufism 200–1, 203
Ibn al-Kalbī, Hishām (d. 204/819) 13
Ibn al-Mubārak, ʻAbdallāh (d. 181/797) 25, 35, 57, 80–1, 97, 105, 189
Ibn al-Mubrad (d. 909/1502) 202–3
Ibn al-Mudhhib, al-Hasan (d. 444/1052–3) 45

Ibn al-Mulaqqin, ʿUmar (d. 804/1401) 88, 115
Ibn al-Qaddāh (d. *c.*180/796–7) 141
Ibn al-Qattān al-Fāsī (d. 628/1231) 99, 119
Ibn Qayyim al-Jawziyya (d. 751/1350) 103, 113, 199
Ibn al-Salāh al-Shahrazūrī (d. 643/1245) 104, 109, 111–2, 148, 297
  on the Sufi cloak (*khirqa*) 203–4
Ibn al-Sunnī, Ahmad (d. 364/975) 36
Ibn al-Waddāh, Muhammad (d. 286/899) 37
Ibn ʿArabī, Muhyī al-Dīn (d. 638/1240) 57, 64, 114–5, 205 ff.
Ibn ʿAsākir (d. 571/1176) 56–7, 62, 83
Ibn Bābawayh (d. 381/991) 8, 139, 141–2, 152
  dictation sessions of 143, 151
  as hadith critic 145
  use of Sunni hadiths by 154
Ibn Daqīq al-ʿĪd (d. 702/1302) 63
Ibn Daybaʿ, ʿAbd al-Rahmān (d. 944/1537) 5, 64
Ibn Fūrak, Abū Bakr (d. 406/1015) 166, 190
Ibn Hajar al-ʿAsqalānī, Ahmad (d. 852/1449) 84, 104, 110–12, 123
  atrāf book of 62
  books of transmitter criticism 88–90
  Bulūgh al-marām of 63
  criticism by Juynboll 250
  Fath al-bārī of 54
  on the Sufi cloak (*khirqa*) 203
  on *tadlīs* 94
  takhrīj books of 115–16
  zawāʾid book of 60
Ibn Hajar al-Haytamī (d. 974/1566) 58
Ibn Hanbal, Ahmad (d. 241/855) 25, 35, 37, 40, 81, 83, 99, 163, 197, 216
  commitment to Sunna 11, 19
  library of 253
  Musnad of 31, 44–5, 55, 59–60, 62, 88, 221, 253
  opinions of 170–1, 177
  use of weak hadiths in law 34, 104–6, 228
  Shiite perspective on 147
  skepticism towards consensus 65n. 2, 281
  unreliable hadiths of 32
  on use of hadiths in theology 189, 190
  on virtues of ʿAlī 38, 151
Ibn Hibbān al-Bustī (d. 354/965) 34, 60, 83, 85, 87, 96, 109
Ibn Ishāq, Muhammad (d. 150/767) 13, 14, 25, 76, 88–9, 91, 94, 257
Ibn Jurayj, ʿAbd al-Malik (d. 150/767) 25–8, 81, 127, 257, 261, 265–6
Ibn Kathīr, Ismāʿīl (d. 774/1373) 62, 116
Ibn Khaldūn, ʿAbd al-Rahmān (d. 808/1406) 216
Ibn Khayr al-Ishbīlī, Muhammad (d. 575/1179) 46, 52
Ibn Khuwayz Mindād (d. 390/1000) 220
Ibn Khuzayma, Muhammad (d. 311/923) 34, 38, 40, 53, 60, 88, 104, 151
Ibn Maʿīn, Yahyā (d. 233/848) 24–5, 81, 83, 86, 89, 112, 270
Ibn Mājah, Muhammad (d. 273/887) 34, 40, 54, 64, 121–2, 168, 295
Ibn Manda, Muhammad b. Ishāq (d. 395/1004–5) 40
Ibn Masʿūd, ʿAbdallāh (d. 32/652–3) 7, 17, 21, 73, 182, 202
Ibn Nuqta, Abū Bakr Muhammad (d. 629/1231) 88
Ibn Qāniʿ, ʿAbd al-Bāqī (d. 351/962) 90
Ibn Qudāma, Muwaffaq al-Dīn (d. 620/1223) 170–1
Ibn Qutayba, ʿAbdallāh (d. 276/889) 101, 178, 302
Ibn Rāhawayh, Ishāq (d. 238/853) 25, 60, 81, 177
Ibn Rajab al-Hanbalī (d. 795/1392) 58, 183
Ibn Rīdha (d. 440/1049) 49

Ibn Sa'd, Muhammad (d. 230/845) 86–7, 118, 251
Ibn Shāhīn, 'Umar (d. 385/996) 174
Ibn Shahrāshūb, Muhammad b. 'Alī (d. 588/1192) 144
Ibn Sīrīn, Muhammad (d. 110/728) 24, 80, 95–6, 118
Ibn Tāwūs, Jamāl al-Dīn (d. 673/1274) 148
Ibn Tāwūs, Radī al-Dīn (d. 664/1266) 154
Ibn Taymiyya, Majd al-Dīn (d. 653/1255) 63
Ibn Taymiyya, Taqī al-Dīn Ahmad (d. 728/1328) 63, 150, 180
  on forged hadiths 116
  on judgments of early hadith critics 111
  on reasons for disagreement over law 172–3
  on sins of Companions 90
  on Sufism 200, 203, 207
  on theology 193
  on weak hadiths 102, 104–5
Ibn 'Uqda, Ahmad (d. 332/944) 92, 141, 146, 154, 159
Ibn Wahb, 'Abdallāh (d. 197/812) 29
Ibrāhīm al-Nakha'ī (d. 95/714) 17, 118, 167
ihsān/perfection 198, 201, 318
ijāza/permission to transmit 45–6, 49–50, 92, 318
'Ijlī, Ahmad b. 'Abdallāh (d. 261/875) 87
ijmā', *see* consensus
ijtihād 278, 281, 287, 296, 298, 318
ikhtilāf al-hadīth 171–8
'ilal/flaws 31, 98–9
'ilm/knowledge 18, 82, 107, 202, 215
ilzāmāt books 43
Imam/Imams 135 ff., 217–8, 219, 300, 310
  as from Quraysh, Hadith 211, 215–6
'Imrān b. Husayn 101, 162
'Irāqī, Zayn al-Dīn 'Abd al-Rahīm (d. 806/1404) 47, 116, 123
Isfarā'īnī, Abū Ishāq (d. 418/1027) 190–1
ISIS/Daesh 211
Islamic Modernism 280 ff.
Ismā'īl b. 'Ulayya (d. 193/809) 86, 201
Ismā'īlī, Abū Bakr (d. 371/981–2) 51, 89
isnād/chain of transmission 4–6, 14, 16, 21, 28–34, 36, 43–56
  backgrowth of 247 ff.
  as bolstered by local practice 113, 168–9
  of books 44–6
  as connection to the Prophet and medium of blessing 16, 58, 196 ff.
  cum matn analysis 263–6
  elevated ones 48–51
  forgery of 77–9
  as guarantor of hadiths and religion 4, 80–2, 99
  last books to include 47–8
  in Shiism 136–7, 147–8
  in Sufism 199 ff.
isrā'īliyyāt 283–5, 291–2, 318
i'tibār/consideration 84, 95–7

J

Jābir b. 'Abdallāh 10, 19, 21, 24, 119, 122, 151
Ja'far al-Sādiq (d. 148/765) 135–7, 150, 157, 159, 203
  on hadith criticism 146
  on *matn* criticism 149
Jāhiz (d. 255/869) 189, 292, 302
jāmi', in Shiism 141
Jarh wa ta'dīl 82, 87
Jassās, Abū Bakr (d. 370/981) 191, 220
Jawzaqānī, al-Husayn (d. 543/1148–9) 103, 109
Jayrapūrī, Muhammad Aslam (d. 1955) 282
Jazā'irī, Tāhir (d. 1920) 294, 296–7
Jesus 75, 77, 187, 231, 233, 237, 269, 293, 310; see also Messiah/*Mahdī*
Jihad, Hadiths of the Greatest 216, 297
jinn 50, 67n. 61, 206, 281, 290, 318
Jubbā'ī, Abū 'Alī (d. 303/915) 100

Jum'a, 'Alī 1–3, 216–7, 299, 301, 309
Junayd, Abū al-Qāsim (d. 298/910) 200–3
Juwaynī, Imām al-Haramayn (d. 478/1085) 45, 57, 108, 191, 213, 215
Juynboll, G.H.A. 248 ff.
Jūzajānī, Ibrāhīm b. Ya'qūb (d. 259/873) 81, 87, 89

K

Ka'b al-Ahbār (d. *c.*32/653) 158, 285, 292
Kalābādhī, Abū Bakr (d. 384/994) 55
Kāndahlawī, Muhammad Zakariyyā (d. 1982) 55
Kanz al-'ummāl 61
Karābīsī, Husayn (d. 245/859) 270
Karbala 74
Karīma al-Marwaziyya (d. 473/1071) 50
Kāshānī, Mullā Muhsin Fayd (d. 1091/1680) 144
kashf/unveiling 114–5, 206–7
Kashshī, Muhammad b. 'Umar (d. *c.*340/951) 146–7
Kattānī, 'Abd al-Hayy (d. 1963) 52
Kattānī, Muhammad b. Ja'far (d. 1927) 279
Kawtharī, Muhammad Zāhid (d. 1952) 298–300
Khalaf al-Wāsitī (d. 400/1010) 62
Khalīlī, Abū Ya'lā (d. 446/1054) 98
Khallāl, Abū Bakr b. (d. 311/923–4) 170
Khān, Siddīq Hasan (d. 1890) 294
Khan, Sir Sayyid Ahmad (d. 1898) 252, 281, 288–92, 295, 303
Khatīb al-Baghdādī, Ahmad (d. 463/1071) 50, 83, 87, 93, 313
  History of Baghdad of 56
  on *matn* criticism 109
  on *mutawātir* hadiths 108–9, 191–2
  on *tadlīs* 94
Khattābī, Hamd (d. 388/998) 54, 105
Khidr (Khadir) 115
Khiraqī, Abū al-Qāsim (d. 334/945–6) 170–1
khirqa/cloak 202 ff., 312, 318
Khwāje Abdallāh al-Ansārī (d. 481/1089) 37, 193
Kitāb al-fitan 36
Kitāb al-saqīfa 140
Kufa 18
Kulaynī, Muhammad b. Ya'qūb (d. 329/939) 141–3, 145, 149, 154, 158

L

Laknawī, Abd al-Hayy (d. 1886–7) 102, 279
Late Sunni Tradition 58, 109–15, 279–80, 295, 298–301
Layth b. Sa'd (d. 175/791) 25, 32, 81, 82, 97, 119, 246
legal theory 85, 107 ff., 162 ff.; *see also* consensus; *see also maslaha*
liar/*kadhdhāb* 87
Lu Shih-hua (d. 1779) xi
Lucretius (d. *circa* 55 BCE) 235

M

Madā'inī, 'Alī b. Muhammad (d. 228/843) 72, 254, 316
maghāzī/campaigns 13–14, 106, 270, 319
Mahāmilī, al-Husayn (d. 330/942) 43
Mahdī/Messiah 57, 136–9, 187, 192, 214, 269, 285, 319; *see also* Hidden Imam
majhūl/unknown 84
Majlisī, Muhammad Bāqir (d. 1110/1700) 144–5
Majority school of theology, *see* Ash'arī school
malāhim/End of Days 106, 270
Mālik b. Anas (d. 179/796) 4, 17–18, 25–6, 81–2, 141; *see also Muwatta'*
  feud with Ibn Ishāq 88–9
  first known use of terms 80, 83
  gharīb hadith of 98, 110
  on liars 286
  mistake by 246, 251, 254
  mursal hadiths of 94, 169

not knowing some hadiths 28–30, 172
on sources of law and practice of Medina 17–18, 28 163
stance on hadiths vs. Medinan custom 167, 174
use of weak transmitters 91
Māliki school of law 41, 163, 166–7, 169
Ma'mar b. Rāshid (d. 153/770) 25–8, 257, 264–6
Mamluk Dynasty 213
Manār journal 282–3, 292, 294
Maqdisī, 'Abd al-Ghanī (d. 600/12031) 63, 87
Maqdisī, Diyā' al-Dīn (d. 643/1245) 47
Maqdisī, Muhammad b. Tāhir (d. 507/1113) 40, 102
Marghīnānī, Abū al-Hasan 'Alī (d. 593/1196–7) 115
Marwazī, Abū Bakr (d. 292/904–5) 31
Marwazī, Muhammad b. Nasr (d. 294/906) 37
Masābīh al-Sunna 59
Māsarjisī, al-Hasan (d. 365/976) 42
mashhūr/well-known 104, 107–8, 166–7, 191, 319
maslaha/public interest 182
matn/text of hadith 4, 6, 45, 319
matn criticism, *see* content criticism
Māturīdī school of theology 58, 190, 319
mawdū'/mawdū'āt, *see* forgery of hadiths
Mawdūdī, Abū al-'Alā'(d. 1979) 285
Mawsilī, 'Umar b. Badr (d. 622/1225) 103
Māzarī, Muhammad b. 'Alī (d. 536/1131) 54
Mernissi, Fatima (d. 2015) 286–7
Messiah, *see* Jesus; *Mahdī*
miracles, scriptural criticism of 115, 233, 236, 283, 290–2
Mishkāt al-masābīh 59
Mishna 310
Mizzī, Jamāl al-Dīn (d. 742/1341) 44, 62, 88, 262
Modernist Salafism 280, 288 ff.
Modernity 277–8
Mongols 213
moon, splitting of 292
Morocco, as center for hadiths 279, 297
Moses 72, 75, 107, 188, 285, 294, 310
Motzki, Harald 260 ff.
Mu'āwiya (d. 60/680) 72, 157–8, 212, 215, 267
Mubārakpūrī, Muhammad 'Abd al-Rahmān (d. 1935) 55
mubawwab 141
mudraj 78, 317, 319
muftī 1–2, 4, 5, 216, 255, 291, 299
Mughal Empire of India 213
Muhammad al-Bāqir (d. 114/732) 136, 152
Muhammad al-Taqī 136
Muhammad b. Bashshār al-Bundār (d. 252/866) 25
Muhammad, the Prophet
nature of his authority 9–11, 71–2
style of speech 12–13
appearance in dream 60, 113–5, 229
books on virtues of 37–8
miracles of 283, 290
as 'Perfect Man' 205
obligation to obey 210
Muir, William (d. 1905) 239, 240, 252
mu'jam 42, 49, 51–2, 319
Mullā 'Alī Qārī (d. 1014/1606) 55, 59, 153, 220
book of forged hadiths 102–4
on *matn* criticism 234
on Sufi hadiths 207
use of weak hadiths 112
munāwala/handing over 92
Munāwī, 'Abd al-Ra'ūf (d. 1621 CE) 61, 64, 130
Mundhirī, 'Abd al-'Azīm (d. 656/1258) 36, 115, 295
munkar/unacceptable 78, 97–8, 102, 104, 107, 270, 319
munqati'/cut 92, 319
mursal hadiths 91, 94–5, 152, 169, 207, 247, 319

Murtadā Muhammad b. Yahyā 156
Mūsā al-Kāzim (d. 183/799) 136–7, 139–40, 151, 203
Mūsā b. 'Uqba (d. 141/758) 13
Musaddad (d. 228/843) 31, 60
musalsalāt hadiths 47
musannaf 25–9, 32
Musayyab b. Rāfi' (d. 105/723–4) 180
Muslim b. al-Hajjāj al-Naysābūrī (d. 261/875) 25, 110, 114, 153
  commentaries and digests of his *Sahīh* 53–4,58–60
  evaluations of his *Sahīh* 98, 154, 285
  as hadith critic 81, 83, 95, 93
  matn criticism by 100
  pro-'Alid hadith of 153
  Sahīh of 32–5, 38–42
  Shiite transmitters in his *Sahīh* 151
musnad 14, 25, 29–32, 38, 40, 42–4, 55, 60, 82
Musnad al-Firdaws 42, 50, 112
Musnad al-Shihāb 50, 112
mustafīd 108, 191, 215
mustakhraj 52–4, 320
mustalah al-hadīth 69, 297
mutaba'a/parallelism 95–6, 249, 320
mutawātir hadiths 107–9, 157, 215, 320
  books on 112
  criticism by Juynboll of 251–2
  in modern Islamic thought 283, 288, 290–3, 302
  requirements of 107, 191–2
  in theology 191–2
Mu'tazilites/Rationalists 38, 77, 79, 123, 190, 302
  advocacy of *matn* criticism 100–2
  approach to hadiths 107–9, 165, 167, 189, 190–3
  in modern Islamic thought 283, 288, 290, 295
  in Shiism 142, 145, 148, 156–7
  sources of law 167
Muttaqī al-Hindī, 'Alī (d. 975/1567) 61
muttasil/contiguous 92, 320
muwaththaq/verified 148
Muwatta' of Mālik 4, 26–8, 44, 54–5, 60, 62, 169, 247, 254, 267
Muzanī, Ismā'īl (d. 264/878) 179

N

Nāfi', the client of Ibn 'Umar (d. 117/735) 27, 127, 251, 253
Nahj al-balāgha 144, 158
Najāshī, Abū al-'Abbās Ahmad (d. 450/1058) 147
Naqvi, Asad xiii
narration by general meaning/*riwāya bi'l-ma'nā* 24, 284, 290, 292
narration, vs. tradition 7, 215–6, 221, 251, 253, 258
Nasā'ī, Ahmad b. Shu'ayb (d. 303/915–16) 25, 34, 36–7, 40, 54, 81, 83
  on the family of the Prophet 158
naskh, *see* abrogation
Nabhānī, Yūsuf (d. 1932) 219
Nawawī, Muhyī al-Dīn (d. 676/1277) 23, 110–12
  Adhkār and *Riyād* of 36
  commentary on Muslim's *Sahīh* 54
  Forty hadith collection of 58
  on the importance of the *isnād* 47
  opinion on hadith canon 41
  on nature of the caliphate 213
  on rebellion against the ruler 219, 221
Nawbakhtī, Hasan b. Mūsā (d. *c.*300–10/912–22) 138–9
Noah, flood of 75, 231, 291
Nöldeke, Theodor (d. 1930) 238
Nu'aym b. Hammād (d. 228/842) 36
Numani, Shibli (d. 1916) 295

O

Obeying the Ruler, Hadiths of 217–22
orality 23–4, 45–50, 310–3
Osman dan Fodio (d. 1817) 278
Ottoman Empire 213–6

P

paper, effect of discovery on hadiths 19
papyrus 19, 252–3

Partisans of Hadith 18–19, 100, 314
see also Ahl-e Hadīth and Salafism
according to Goldziher 242–3
development into Hanbalī and Shāfi'ī schools 41
legal theory of 30, 32, 101–5, 165–6
in modern Islamic thought 279, 296, 300, 302
on relation between the Quran and hadiths 107, 162–4
on theology 186–9, 190, 192–4
use of weak hadiths 32–3, 39, 77–9, 102, 165, 168–9
response to the *Sahīhayn* 39–40
Partisans of Legal Reason 18–19, 310
according to Goldziher 242
on the interaction of the Quran and Sunna 165–7
early Sunni view on 37, 39, 101
in modern Islamic thought 287, 300, 302
stance on hadiths and law 166–7
criticism of hadiths 79–80
Pascal, Blaise (d. 1662) 235
Perizonius, Jakob (d. 1715) 236
Petrarch, Francesco (d. 1374) 230, 234
Peyrère, Isaac de la (d. 1676) 231
Plato 312, 314
politics, *see* governance
Polybius (d. 118 BCE) 234
positivism 237
Powers, David 260–1
Principle of Analogy 236, 240, 284
Principle of Dissimilarity 236, 240, 257
Prophet, *see* Muhammad, the Prophet

Q

qadar/free will 85, 123 ff., 189, 240, 267–8, 276n. 131
Qādī 'Abd al-Jabbār (d. 415/1025) 108
Qādī 'Iyād b. Mūsā (d. 544/1149) 10n., 38, 52
Qaradāwī, Yūsuf 303
qasas al-anbiyā'/stories of the prophets 13
Qāsim b. Muhammad b. Abī Bakr (d. 108/726–7) 17
Qāsimī, Jamāl al-Dīn (d. 1914) 294, 297
Qatāda b. Di'āma (d. 117/735) 25, 93, 121
Qazvīnī, Abū al-Husayn (d. *c.*560/1165) 155
qiyās/analogy 166, 181, 298
Quakers 232, 269
Qudā'ī, Muhammad b. Salama (d. 454/1062) 50, 112
Qudsī, see hadiths
Qummī, 'Abbās (d. 1936) 145
Qummī, Muhammad al-Saffār (d. 290/903) 141
Qummī, Sa'b b. 'Abdallāh (wr. 292/905) 139
Quran 3; *see also* legal theory
abrogated by hadiths 164–5
criticism of speculation by 186–9
designating Muhammad as teacher 9–10
elucidating all things 302
hadiths as exegesis of 258
on nature of God 193
creation of 75
preeminence in modern Islamic thought 283, 288, 292–3, 296
as source of law 162–5, 171–2, 180–2
as test for hadiths 100, 157, 290–1, 296
on governance 210, 217, 219
as valid in all times 135, 232
Quran-Only movement 280–3, 303, 316
Quraysh, as caliphate requirement 211–216
Qurtubī, Muhammad b. Ahmad (d. 671/1273) 218
Qushayrī, Abū al-Qāsim (d. 465/1072) 47, 201
Qutayba b. Sa'īd (d. 240/854) 25, 32, 97

R

Ra'y 18, 180; *see also* Partisans of Legal Reason

Rāfiʿī, ʿAbd al-Karīm (d. 623/1226) 40, 44, 116
Rahman, Fazlur (d. 1988) 287–8
Ramadān, Mistri Muhammad (d. 1940) 282
von Ranke, Leopold (d. 1886) 229
Rāshidūn/Rightly Guided caliphs 214
Rāzī, Fakhr al-Dīn (d. 606/1210) 178
reason/*ʿaql* 18–9, 37, 39, 79, 100–4, 108, 163, 228, 308–9; *see also Ra'y*
 Hadith of 79, 206–7
 in Shiism 142, 148, 157
 in theology 186, 189, 190–4
 in Western HCM 231–5
 in modern Islamic thought 283, 288, 290
rebellion, *see* governance
Reimarus, Hermann (d. 1768) 233
Revisionist History 239, 255 ff.
revival and reform, movements of 277–9
Ridā, Rashīd (d. 1935) 283–4, 291–4
rihla fi talab al-ʿilm/voyage in search of hadiths 32
riwāya bi 'l-maʿnā, *see* narration by general meaning
Ruler as God's shadow, Hadith of 211
Rūmī, Jalāl al-Dīn (d. 672/1273) 205
Rūyānī, Abū Bakr (d. 307/919–20) 31, 60

S

Saʿd, ʿAbdallāh 295–6
sadūq/sincere 87, 89
Saghānī, al-Hasan b. Muhammad (d. 650/1252) 40
sahīfa/notebook 19–24, 66n. 9, 74, 119, 140, 153, 253
sahīh/authentic; *see also* hadith canon; Bukhārī, Muhammad; Muslim b. al-Hajjāj
 hadith collections 32–5, 39–42
 as technical term 16, 32, 98, 104–7, 111, 165, 167, 185, 194, 300, 320
sahīh gharīb/authentic but uncorroborated 98
sahīh li-ghayrihi/authentic due to corroborations 111
Sahīhayn, *see* Bukhārī, Muhammad; Muslim b. al-Hajjāj
Saʿīd b. al-Musayyab (d. 94/713) 17, 94, 169
Saʿīd b. al-Sakan (d. 353/964) 34, 40
Saʿīd b. Mansūr (d. 227/842) 32
Said, Edward (d. 2003) 227
Sakhāwī, Shams al-Dīn (d. 902/1497) 116, 203, 207
Salafism 280; *see also* Modernist Salafism; Traditional Salafism
 as school of theology 193–94
 use of *ahkām al-hadīth* books 63
sālih/good 87
samāʿ/audition 44–5, 48
Samʿānī, Abū Saʿd (d. 562/1166) 51
Sanʿānī, Muhammad b. al-Amīr (d. 1768) 63, 85, 278–9
Saraqustī, Ibn Razīn (d. 524/1129) 40, 59
sariqat al-hadīth/stealing hadiths 77–8, 320
Sāwī, Ahmad b. Muhammad (d. 1825) 279
Schacht, Joseph (d. 1969) 245 ff., 254–7, 260–3, 265–6
Sextus Empiricus (d. *circa* 210 CE) 235
Shaʿbī al-Himyarī (d. 103–10/721–8) 241
Shādhakūnī, Sulaymān (d. 234/848–9) 86
shādhdh/anomalous 105, 320
Shāfiʿī, Muhammad b. Idrīs (d. 204/820) 75, 81, 89, 90, 107, 313
 advocacy of hadiths 30, 41, 163–4
 explanations for conflicting hadiths 143, 164–6, 174–8
 hadiths in his *Umm* 42–3, 169
 Musnad of 42–3, 55, 60, 88
 on hadiths needed for law 172
 on the *isnād* 80
 in modern Islamic thought 287, 302
 on *mursal* hadiths 94, 169
 Schacht's evaluation of 246–7, 254–5

on Shiism 85, 150
on using weak hadiths 169, 247
Shāfiʿī school of law 34, 41–2, 169–70
Shāh ʿAbd al-ʿAzīz al-Dihlawī (d. 1824) 65
Shah Jahan (d. 1666 CE) 214
Shāh Walī Allāh al-Dihlawī (d. 1762) 278–9, 281, 289, 294
Shahīd al-Thānī (d. 965/1558) 148
shāhid/witness report 95–6, 321
Shaltūt, Mahmūd (d. 1963) 293, 302
shamāʾil 37–8, 65
Sharaf al-Dīn, Imam (d. 965/1557–8) 157
Shaʿrānī, ʿAbd al-Wahhāb (d. 973/1565) 48
sharh/commentaries 54–5, 59, 60, 63, 321
Sharīf al-Murtadā (d. 436/1044) 148
Sharīf al-Radī (d. 406/1015) 144, 158
Shawkānī, Muhammad b. ʿAlī (d. 1834) 63, 102, 279, 294
Shaybānī, Muhammad b. al-Hasan (d. 189/805) 182
Shaykh al-Mufīd (d. 413/1022) 142–6
Shiblī, Abū Bakr (d. 334/945–6) 196, 201, 203
Shiism 72, 135–41; *see also* Zaydism
attitude of Sunni hadith critics towards 85, 89, 92, 150
different schools of Imāmī 144–5, 149
major hadith collections of Imāmī 141–3
narration from Sunnis 144, 148, 153–4, 157.
relation between Sunni and Shiite hadiths 149 ff.
Shīrāzī, Abū Ishāq (d. 476/1083) 115
Shuʿba b. al-Hajjāj (d. 160/776) 25, 80–4, 88, 91, 173
knowledge of hadiths vs. Sunna 163
on *tadlīs* 93–4, 270
Shuhda al-Kātiba (d. 574/1178–9) 51
Sibāʿī, Mustafā (d. 1964) 285, 302
Sidqī, Muhammad Tawfīq (d. 1920) 282–3, 302
Silafī, Abū Tāhir (d. 576/1180) 41, 52, 57
Sindī, Abū al-Hasan (d. 1728) 55
Sindī, Muhammad Hayāt (d. 1750) 279
sīra/biography of Muhammad 13–14, 257, 321
Six Books, *see* hadith canon
Slave Girl (*jāriya*), Hadith of the 193–4
Songhay Empire of Mali 213
Spinoza, Benedict (d. 1677) 232–3
Storytellers (*qussās*) 75–6, 116
Strauss, David Friedrich (d. 1874) 233
Subkī, Tāj al-Dīn (d. 771/1370) 154
Successors (*tābiʿūn*) 21–3, 25
Sufism 196 ff., 312, 314
*isnād*s in 196 ff.
in modern Islamic thought 298–300
theosophical 204–7
criticism of 294–7
manuals on 47, 116, 152
Sufyān al-Thawrī (d. 161/778) 25, 27, 81, 82, 91, 120, 122, 163, 270
Sufyān b. ʿUyayna (d. 196/811) 25, 81, 82, 94, 172, 189
Suhrawardī, Abū Hafs (d. 632/1234) 47, 178
Sulamī, Abū ʿAbd al-Rahmān (d. 412/1021) 116, 197
Sulaym b. Qays al-ʿĀmirī (d. *c.*85/705) 140
Suleiman the Magnificent (d. 1566 CE) 214
Sunan collections 25, 32–35, 38–43, 54, 60–3, 141; *see also* hadith canon
Sunna/Prophet's precedent 3–4, 10, 12, 31, 103
books of 36–8
interaction with Quran in law 164–5
questioning in the modern period 278–9, 282–8
as source of law 162–9
role in theology 81, 186–9
vs. hadiths 41, 163
as test for authenticating hadiths 103, 108, 142, 149

Suyūtī, Jalāl al-Dīn (d. 911/1505) 124, 130, 152, 174, 295
attempts to compile whole Sunna 60–1
on circumstances of hadiths 175
on *mutawātir* hadiths 112
shamā'il of 38
on Sufi *isnād*s 203–4
on forged hadiths 102–3, 111, 113
commentaries by 54–5

T

Tabarānī, Abū al-Qāsim (d. 360/971) 8, 42, 51, 60, 62, 126–7
example of elevated *isnād*s 49–50, 79
using dream to verify hadith 114
Tabarī, Muhammad b. Jarīr (d. 310/923) 25, 34, 158
Tabarī, Muhibb al-Dīn (d. 694/1295) 220
Tabligh-i Jamā'at 36
Tabrīzī, Muhammad al-Khatīb (d. *c.*737/1337) 59
Tacitus (d. *circa* 117 CE) 234
tadlīs/obfuscation 93–4, 119, 250, 257–8, 270, 321
tafsīr/exegesis 14, 106, 141, 270, 321
Tahāwī, Abū Ja'far (d. 321/933) 55, 60, 88, 93, 178
Tahdhīb al-ahkām 141–2
takhrīj 115–6, 321
takhsīs/specification 166
taqlīd 142, 278, 289, 297, 321
targhīb wa al-tarhīb 36, 254, 295
tārīkh 13, 106
Tayālisī, Abū Dāwūd (d 204/818) 31, 60, 82
thabat 51–2
thabt/reliable 87
Thaqalayn, Hadith of 151
theology, role of hadiths in 185 ff.
thiqa/reliable 83, 87, 91, 96, 98, 104, 147
Tirmidhī, Muhammad b. 'Īsā (d. 279/892) 5, 102, 174
approval of pro-'Alid hadith 151
commentary & *mustakhraj* on his *Jāmi'* 53–5
conflicting hadiths in 172–6
on corroboration 98
inclusion of weak vs. strong hadiths in his *Jāmi'* 98, 168, 271
introduction of term *hasan* 105
Jāmi' of 34–5, 40–1, 59
Shamā'il of 38
on use of hadiths in theology 189
Toland, John (d. 1722) 232
Torah 75, 292, 310
tradition vs. narration 7, 253
Traditional Islam 285, 299
Traditionalist Salafism 280, 289, 294–9
transmitters of hadiths, *see* hadiths
Tūfī, Najm al-Dīn (d. 716/1316) 182
Turāth/heritage 2–4, 280
Turayfī, 'Abd al-'Azīz 221
Turkish government hadith project 227
Tūsī, Muhammad b. al-Hasan (d. 460/1067) 143, 146–7

U

ulema 1, 76, 135, 158, 178, 293, 310, 321
'Umar b. 'Abd al-'Azīz (d. 720/101) 24, 253
'Umar b. al-Khattāb 17, 20, 73, 182
Umayyad Dynasty and hadiths 24, 72, 74, 150, 157, 212, 219
rebellion against 155, 217, 220
Western theories on hadith fabrication 241–5, 253–4, 259, 268
'umūm al-balwā 166
University of Chicago 252, 287
'Uqaylī, Abū Ja'far (d. 323/934) 81, 124, 127, 207
usūl al-fiqh, *see* legal theory
usūl, as Shiite hadith collection 140

V

Valla, Lorenzo (d. 1457) 230–1, 240
Voltaire (d. 1778) 233–7

W

Wā'ilī, Abū Nasr (d. 444/1052) 194
Wādi'ī, Muqbil b. Hādī (d. 2001) 60, 221, 259
Wahb b. Munabbih (d 114/732) 12, 297
wahdat al-wujūd 199
Wahhābī movement 194, 279, 294. 298
Wakī' b. al-Jarrāh (d. 197/812) 25, 35, 81, 122
Walīd b. 'Uqba 90, 157
Wansbrough, John 258
Wāqifiyya sect of Shiism 139, 148
Wāqidī, Muhammad b. 'Umar (d. 207/822) 89, 253
Wāsil b. 'Atā' (d. 131/750) 167
Wazīrī, Sārim al-Dīn (d. 914/1508) 158–9
weak hadiths 84, 102–6, 317
  as bolstered by practice 168–9
  in legal theory 178 ff.
  rejection of by Salafism 295–7
  in Shiite hadith criticism 147
  use of 111–3, 163, 165, 295
Weber, Max (d. 1920) 234
Wellhausen, Julius (d. 1918) 238
women, hadiths on 165, 175, 286
Wudud, Amina 285

Y

Yahyā b. Abī Kathīr (d. 129/747) 25, 118, 162
Yahyā b. Ādam 25
Yahyā b. Sa'īd al-Qattān (d. 198/813) 25, 76, 81, 83
  on *tadlīs* 270
  on *mursal* hadiths 95
  use of term *munkar* 102
Yuksel, Edip 286

Z

Zabid 4
Zabīdī, Murtadā (d. 1791) 50
zann/probability 107, 165, 185, 191
Zarkashī, Muhammad b. Bahādur (d. 794/1392) 116
zawā'id books 59–60
Zayd b. 'Alī (d. 122/740) 155–6, 158
Zayd b. Wahb (d. 96/714–15) 140
Zaydism, 217, hadith tradition of 155 ff.
Zayla'ī, Jamāl al-Dīn (d. 762/1361) 110, 115
zuhd 35–6, 39, 105, 207
Zuhrī, Muhammad b. Shihāb (d. 124/742) 24–5, 80–1, 91, 98
  collections of hadiths by 252
  as generally reliable 261, 266
  library of 253
  mursal hadiths of 94
  as Umayyad official 241, 253
  on writing down hadiths 24